MEDIEVAL SENSIBILITIES

In memory of Jacques Le Goff

MEDIEVAL SENSIBILITIES

A History of Emotions in the Middle Ages

Damien Boquet and Piroska Nagy

Translated by Robert Shaw

polity

First published in French as *Sensible Moyen Âge: Une histoire des émotions dans l'Occident médiéval*
© Éditions du Seuil, 2015

This English edition © Polity Press, 2018
Foreword © Barbara H. Rosenwein, 2018

FRENCH VOICES

This work received the French Voices Award for excellence in publication and translation. French Voices is a program created and funded by the French Embassy in the United States and FACE (French American Cultural Exchange).

Polity Press
65 Bridge Street
Cambridge CB2 1UR, UK

Polity Press
101 Station Landing
Suite 300
Medford, MA 02155, USA

ISBN-13: 978-1-5095-1465-6
ISBN-13: 978-1-5095-1466-3 (pb)

A catalogue record for this book is available from the British Library.

Library of Congress Cataloging-in-Publication Data
Names: Boquet, Damien, author. | Nagy, Piroska (College teacher) author.
Title: Medieval sensibilities : a history of emotions in the middle ages / Damien Boquet, Piroska Nagy.
Description: Medford, MA : Polity Press, [2018] | Includes bibliographical references and index.
Identifiers: LCCN 2017052168 (print) | LCCN 2017054820 (ebook) | ISBN 9781509514694 (Epub) | ISBN 9781509514656 (hardback) | ISBN 9781509514663 (pbk.)
Subjects: LCSH: Emotions–History.
Classification: LCC BF531 (ebook) | LCC BF531 .B66 2018 (print) | DDC 152.409/02–dc23
LC record available at https://lccn.loc.gov/2017052168

Typeset in 10 on 11.5 pt Sabon by Toppan Best-set Premedia Limited
Printed and bound in Great Britain by CPI Group (UK) Ltd, Croydon

For further information on Polity, visit our website: politybooks.com

CONTENTS

FOREWORD

Barbara H. Rosenwein

What were the emotional consequences of the Christianization of Europe? In *Medieval Sensibilities*, Damien Boquet and Piroska Nagy bring to the English-speaking audience the fruits of their long reflection on this question. They show how, far from being a stagnant 'Middle Age' standing between the learned ancient world and discontented modernity, the period was in constant affective ferment. Social and economic changes in themselves brought new sensibilities and needs. These new milieus, drawing on and filtering, but also adding to, the many intellectual traditions increasingly available to an expanding clerical elite, transformed their thoughts about Christ's Passion. In turn, these new understandings, taught in the schools, proclaimed in the churches, preached on the streets, and acted out by rulers, transformed the feelings and behaviours of Europeans in general.

Theologies of the Passion were thus put into practice. As Boquet and Nagy show, the emotions implied by new understandings of Christ's human nature and passion came to shape the very ways in which medieval people lived their lives. Initially, this was not the case; the affective implications of the Christian God were at first largely the monopoly of one man (Augustine). But they soon became the focus of an ever-expanding religious elite, taken up first by men and women in hermitages and monasteries and then, eventually, becoming the concern of people in every walk of life.

This book is itself the fruit of a different sort of progressive inclusion. The authors began their careers working separately. Boquet's dissertation, which became his first book, was on the affective life and thought of Aelred of Rievaulx, a twelfth-century monk and abbot who wrote extensively on the meaning of love and friendship. Nagy's early work was on the 'gift of tears': she unravelled the tangled threads involved in the idea that crying could have salvific meaning. When they began to work together, they founded a website, emma.hypotheses.org, dedicated to 'the study of medieval emotions in tandem with the scholarship of the humanities and social sciences'. They organized conferences to which they invited speakers to consider medieval sensibilities from every point of view. Together the two scholars edited and published the results of these conferences in books ranging in topic from the political uses and meanings of emotions to the role of the body to intellectual history.

Medieval Sensibilities reflects that prior work – and goes beyond it. Its emphasis on the suffering Christ as the starting point for medieval sensibilities draws on the authors' interest in the role of the body in experience and expression. In taking up theologians like Augustine, Anselm of Canterbury, and Thomas Aquinas, they distil the fruits of long rumination on medieval theories of the passions. When considering the 'politics of princely emotions', they exploit their own and others' work on performativity. Above all they weave together these and other topics in a coherent narrative covering the entire medieval period.

The story really gets underway with the missionizing work of the Irish monk Columbanus. Charismatic and fiercely determined, he brought the monastic ideals of affective restraint first to the Frankish royal court and thence to the elites. A still more thorough diffusion of Christian values occurred under Charlemagne (d. 814) and his early successors, as churchmen incorporated Christianized notions of the passions into masses for monks and books for the laity. Learned clerics turned the idea of Christian love, *caritas*, into an ideal of worldly love as well, as if the Christian community could come together through the bonds of charity.

Secular society did not live up to these expectations, except in its cultivation of vernacular literature, which expressed the ideals of measure and restraint, put emphasis on joy, and celebrated longing. But in the monastery the accent on love became something of an obsession. Eleventh- and twelfth-century monks were in their era what neuroscientists are in our own: recognized experts on emotions. Above all, the monks considered themselves – and were seen as – the go-to authorities on love. Hermits, ascetics, Cistercians, even some secular clerics parsed the various forms of love, explored their causes and effects, elaborated ways to show affection, tenderness, and compassion, and taught themselves and others how to practise the right – that is, Christianized – emotions. They elaborated on new forms of meditation, dwelling on and participating in the life, feelings, and travails of Christ. Just as significantly, they unabashedly celebrated love among friends, so that what had hitherto been seen as the 'secular' institution of friendship became as holy as love of God and neighbour.

Once worldly love was valorised, the question of sex was not far behind. In a brilliant chapter, Boquet and Nagy illustrate the tensions that came in the wake of this development: between clerical models of chaste love and the sexualized intimacies praised by the troubadours; between sexual consummation regardless of matrimony and sex within marriages alone; between heterosexual love and same-sex love. Churchmen harnessed the energies behind these tensions, turning marriage into a sacrament: an efficacious conduit of God's grace.

For all its emphasis on love, however, *Medieval Sensibilities* is in many ways a history of pain. Unlike today, when most of us anaesthetize ourselves to avoid even the slightest agony, medieval Christians increasingly sought to experience suffering. The age of martyrdom was long over, and gradually the age of ascetic monasticism came to an end as well. But physical torment based on the model of Christ's torments was ever more valued. St Francis suffered the stigmata, the very wounds of the crucified God; Henry Suso carved the initials of Jesus on his chest over his heart; flagellants walked the streets of medieval towns, beating themselves until their blood ran. Mental pains were also privileged, as penitence – along with the sad, fearful, embarrassed feelings that accompanied it – was ever more stressed in the course of the Middle Ages. These phenomena were connected with the growth of medieval mystical movements, so often associated with women. But, as Boquet and Nagy point out, the narratives of female mystics were generally written by men, who controlled the evidence for their own purposes.

The Middle Ages of *Medieval Sensibilities* is complex, nuanced, and in constant flux. It is a period in which ancient ideas are endlessly transformed and new ones tirelessly elaborated as men and women grapple with the legacy of a passionate and afflicted God. Boquet and Nagy are learned and eloquent guides to the many ways in which Christ's model was both imitated and pushed to limits never before imagined.

xi

ACKNOWLEDGEMENTS

From conception to completion, this book is the result of many years' work, following in the footsteps of our EMMA research programme ('Emotions in the Middle Ages', emma.hypotheses.org). The latter's success has astonished us, delighted us, and strengthened our desire to give emotion and the affective life their due place within historical study, and to do so in the spirit of the Annales school, which Jacques Le Goff, to whom we dedicate these pages, so thoroughly embodied. We take this opportunity to thank once again the dozens of researchers from France and further afield who have participated in the EMMA programme. The fruits of their research have nourished us. The unknown territories they explored have expanded our horizons.

Writing in tandem was an adventure in itself! Our shared voyage has lasted over ten years or thereabouts. Sometimes we have sailed side by side, but more often than not, we have had to defy the seas and the continents that separate us. Throughout this journey, there are few emotions present in this book that we have not felt, imagined, or dissected. In short, we have sailed with and towards the emotions, both our own and those of our historical subjects. This book of emotions and history can be seen as our logbook.

At various stages of the writing process, many friends and colleagues have read or annotated chapters, or even the entire book, asked us useful questions, or responded to our anxious queries. The following all deserve our heartfelt and sincere thanks. Their names are arranged in alphabetical order for convenience: Emmanuel Bain, Jacques Dalarun, Jeroen Deploige, Julien Dubouloz, Margot Farthouat, Cédric Giraud, Martin Gravel, Patrick Henriet, Pierre Levron, Serge Lusignan, Laurence Moulinier, Monique Paulmier, Jean Pichette, Sylvain Piron, Martin Roch, Barbara H. Rosenwein, Laurent Smagghe, Clément Vauchelles, and Laure Verdon. Elyse Dupras was kind enough to help us with the Old French translations. Thanks are also due to Dionysios Stathakopoulos for researching an image and to Xavier Biron-Ouellet for some final checks. Finally, Lucie Obermeyer provided significant assistance by compiling the general bibliography and improving the chapter structure.

Last but not least, we are very grateful to Robert Shaw for his meticulous work in translating our book for this English edition.

INTRODUCTION

The history of the emotions: that great silence![1]

What remains of the joys and pains of the men and women of the Middle Ages? Their laughter, their moans, and their cries built no monuments, and yet their echoes live on within them. Reading texts and studying images from across the long thousand years of the Middle Ages, a historian would have to possess a heart of stone not to be moved by the life behind them. That life was not solely one of hierarchies, means of production, and taxes. It was also full of desires, tensions, sudden gasps, and endless sighs.

It is impossible to understand any human society without exploring its emotional rhythms, from the most dramatic to the most subtle. For too long, historians have ignored this simple truth. At times, they have perhaps been myopic; but above all, they have been too tied to their own times. The discipline of history that took root in the nineteenth century had trouble taking emotions seriously, and even more in admitting that they were not merely intimate expressions, but also an essential part of cultural and social systems.[2] Yet in the Middle Ages, emotions were everywhere. They could be found not only deep within the heart but far beyond it: they were present in the churches, in the palaces, in the shacks, in the markets, and on the battlefields. Saint Louis (d. 1270), on return from Egypt in 1254, was inconsolable at the loss of the crusade: 'Fixing his eyes to the earth with a profound sadness and sighing deeply, he lingered on his captivity and the general confusion of Christianity wrought through it.'[3] The princes grieved for the misfortunes of their realms and were loved for doing so. Yet they did not hesitate to unleash their wrath, the terrible *ira regis*, which struck rebels like divine lightning. While Louis the Pious (d. 840) was known for his wisdom, he still

1

blinded his own nephew, Bernard of Italy (d. 818), king of the Lombards, for daring to defy his authority.

All manner of emotions – hate, laughter, jealousy, and so on – could serve to enliven the theatre of politics and engender social harmony. Through them one negotiated, through them one governed. In the celebrated fresco painted in 1337 by Ambrogio Lorenzetti (d. 1348) that adorns the walls of the Palazzo Pubblico of Siena, a winged figure personifying 'Security', who protects the gates of the city, assures that 'without fear, let every man may walk safely'.[4] She seems to add that, while the inhabitants should not fear chaos, they should still tremble before justice – in her hand she brandishes a gibbet, from which a corpse hangs. The fear brought to life in this image was encouraged by others elsewhere, such as the innumerable depictions of the Last Judgement that adorned church walls by the end of the Middle Ages. Here, it was no longer the marks of good and bad government that were portrayed, but rather those of a virtuous life and one abandoned to sin. In the mid-thirteenth century, the Dominican Humbert of Romans (d. 1277), author of a preaching manual, *On the Gift of Fear*, encouraged priests to go ever further in reminding their congregations of the horrible demonic figures who visited every sort of torture on the damned. The faithful were to fear the torturers of hell on account of their ceaseless cruelty. They were to tremble before the anger of God – for if he was roused by the people of Israel, he would surely be merciless with inveterate sinners at the moment of judgement. Already horrified at the thought of demons, they would only be more aghast when they learned that the anger of God would 'be so great that it will attack them like a furious madman'.[5] Worse still, God would compound their pain with humiliation, heightening the suffering of the damned by mocking them: 'I also will laugh in your destruction, and will mock when that shall come to you which you feared' (Prov 1: 26).[6]

In societies where the imperatives of honour were profoundly important, shame was often even more dreaded than physical suffering. One can thus understand the way in which the Church came to challenge the faithful: it maintained that there was nothing better for delivering man from sin than shame, a shame which had to be deeply felt, and at times even acted out in public. By the eleventh century, a time when honour was defined less by material wealth or office than by a collection of values and sentiments synonymous with good repute (*bona fama*), the reparation of faults was no longer enough to complete the penitential journey: one was also expected to make a sincere, moving expression of moral suffering and repentance. Emotions went to the very heart of man's social and symbolic bonds: there was nothing secondary or incidental about them.

2

Difficult though it is to believe, for the last twenty years the history of the emotions has been seen as essential.[7] Without doubt, that is a testament to the tenacity of a certain set of historians, both in France and further afield. Their work nevertheless stands on the shoulders of some notable pioneers: Johan Huizinga, Lucien Febvre, Robert Mandrou, Georges Duby, and Jacques Le Goff. This recent development is a sign of the times and especially of changing attitudes towards the emotions within Western societies. Prior to the mid-twentieth century, emotion had a bad reputation, mistrusted at best, especially when it appeared outside of the cathartic enclosure of the arts or the private sphere. Today, however, it appears to be a central component of social life. This new emphasis can be attributed to various factors. For one, the collapse of globalist ideologies and the crisis of liberal democracy has brought the individual and the inner life to the fore.[8] Other factors include the rise of many new disciplines (neuroscience, cognitive psychology) that have highlighted the rationality of emotions;[9] the reaction against an all-powerful economy that has rendered man an object of management;[10] and the multifaceted achievements of therapeutic culture.[11] The effects of this transformation are palpable. They have challenged the dichotomy of reason and emotion, which for so long had structured the Western conception of man, and in turn revealed its strangeness.[12] Integrating emotion into how we understand society – as it is today and as it was in days gone by – has consequently become essential. Past and present here go hand in hand.[13]

In 1941, Lucien Febvre published an article in *Annales* that would become the manifesto for a history of the emotions.[14] Here, he called for a 'vast collective study of the fundamental sentiments of humanity and their forms'. The project was prompted by one conviction: emotions, contagious by nature, reveal the most profound cultural phenomena, which language and social codes are unable to embrace. At the same time, and like his contemporaries, Febvre saw them as irrational and spontaneous, an expression of unconscious trends. How then are historians to understand the medieval period, a period characterized by exactly this sort of emotional enthusiasm? The Dutch historian Johan Huizinga made this question the foundation of his masterwork, *The Autumn of the Middle Ages*. First published in 1919 and translated into English in 1924, this book has fascinated generations of historians. For Huizinga, affectivity, aesthetics, and the life of the senses were at the heart of the mindset of medieval civilization. He stressed the 'extravagance and emotivity' of the men and women of the Middle Ages: they seemed to pass in a split-second from laughter to tears, from sweetness to cruelty. Incapable of controlling the emotions that overpowered them, medieval people were 'like giants with the heads of children'. Behind the flamboyant

3

scene that Huizinga painted lay a grand historical narrative founded on the emotions: the Middle Ages heralded the Modern Age, characterized by self-mastery and reflective distance. The vitality of the Middle Ages resided in its raw and violent emotional dynamism. Its decline resulted from an exhaustion that led to formalism. Incapable of regeneration, medieval civilization fell into a kind of *fin de siècle* depression according to Huizinga: 'Here above all, if men were not to fall into crude barbarism, there was a need to frame emotions within fixed forms.'[15]

Michelet had already said something similar when he compared the Middle Ages to a tormented child that had to die 'in heartfelt anguish' so that modernity and its triumphant herald, the rational spirit, could arrive.[16] Historians have long sought to trace the development of this civilizing march of reason. They thus enthusiastically took up the idea of 'the civilizing process', a model first elaborated by Norbert Elias in 1939, but which only became widely influential in the 1970s.[17] Elias established a truly bold parallel between the advent of monarchical states and the developmental psychology of individuals: he bound the two together under a governing principle of rationality. As orderly political regimes expanded in Europe, individuals became better able to master their emotions and to transcend them within the social theatre. The power of Elias' model came from its capacity to theoretically unify the individual and society, the political and the unconscious. But this grand theory – influenced by Freud as much as Huizinga – only perpetuated the view that the Middle Ages had an infantile character: 'Because emotions were here expressed in a manner that in our own world is generally observed only in children, we call these expressions and forms of behaviour "childish".'[18]

Today we see just how distorting such conceptions can be: the emotions of the Middle Ages were no less codified and rational than our own.[19] But in the 1930s, for humanist intellectuals witnessing the collapse of Enlightenment civilization, the cradle of their education, the matter was existential. How could they understand this historic defeat of reason and respond to the perceived decline of the West, if the past was not also interrogated in a new way? At that very moment, Marc Bloch took aim at the present and came up with a similar diagnosis:

> Quite deliberately – as one can see by reading *Mein Kampf* or the records of Rauschning's conversations – Hitler kept the truth from his servile masses. Instead of intellectual persuasion he gave them emotional suggestion. For us there is but one set of alternatives. Either, like the Germans, we must turn our people into a keyboard on which a few leaders can play at will (but who are those leaders? The playing of those at present on the stage is curiously lacking in resonance); or we can so train them that they

4

may be able to collaborate to the full with the representatives in whose hands they have placed the reins of government. At the present stage of civilization this dilemma admits of no middle term ... The masses no longer obey. They follow, either because they have been hypnotized or because they know.[20]

The urgency was palpable. Despite these expectations, however, the appeal for a history of the emotional life was barely followed up in the postwar decades.[21] The history of mentalities and sensibilities that took off in the 1970s certainly made space for what was 'felt', sometimes even placing one emotion or another at the heart of a study. But it did so without truly questioning the historicity of the emotions and, above all, without reconsidering how enduring their definitions were.[22] The real goal is not simply to recognize that the emotions have a role within history, but to acknowledge that they themselves have a history, a history as complex and diverse as the social and cultural environments in which they are expressed.

Studying medieval emotions and grasping their capacity to shape a vision of humanity and its world enables us to better understand our own social outlooks and customs by way of a historical 'detour'. We can understand more clearly how we apprehend and shape our emotional lives, and why we sometimes no longer know how or no longer dare to cultivate this aspect of our humanity.[23] Conversely, this critique of emotional modernity allows us to take stock of the biases through which we consider the past and which feed our complacency: in our transitory position of superiority, we must not become drunk on hindsight. To make the emotional culture of the Middle Ages the object of study is thus to dispute the validity of the 'civilizing process' thesis inherited from Norbert Elias, which is also a history of Western rationalization. An infantilized vision of the men and women of the Middle Ages has wormed its way into our imaginations, a result of how emotions were publicly and often very demonstratively expressed. Mobs yelled out their hatred in public places. Princes failed to temper their anger or, worse still, their sobbing. The devout wailed their love for Christ in the churches. Surely, such displays could only derive from a culture of immature people still on the path towards civilization ...

It is this dialogue – the epistemological foundations of which have evolved significantly from the 1930s – that we continue here. Since the 1980s, numerous researchers across Europe and North America have begun to explore the history of emotions, responding to what some have already christened the 'emotional turn'.[24] The success of this new field has fostered a flourishing body of research. It has presented new tools of investigation and inquiry, many of them referenced in this work:

notions of 'emotional community' (Barbara H. Rosenwein),[25] of 'emotional regimes', 'emotives', and 'emotional navigation' (William M. Reddy),[26] and of 'ennobling love' (Stephen Jaeger).[27] Such approaches help us to conceive and guide a truly mature history of the emotions, disentangled from theories concerning the historical progress of reason.

Today's historians face a two-pronged challenge. Firstly, to propose an alternative to the grand theory of the 'civilizing process' without eschewing a long-term history of the emotions. Secondly, to write that history in a manner true to its strict cultural context in an age where thought on affectivity seems more than ever to be dominated by scientists.[28] Building on their epistemological and institutional foundations, the human and life sciences each propose their own definition of emotion, distinguish it meticulously from feeling, mood, and affect, and define some emotions as positive, others as negative. How can historians find their feet in this environment, especially when discussing an era where emotional anthropology and terminology were so radically different from our own?[29] To follow a discrete, closed definition of emotion, to pay blind faith to the scientific categories of our times, themselves rather confused, would not only be a purely practical illusion, but the mark of a ruinous 'scientism' projected onto a malleable human reality.[30]

Neither universal nor timeless, emotions are whatever the men and women of each era, of each society, of each group make of them. How do they conceive of the nebula of affections and the mysteries of feeling, and what role do they accord to them? As historians tackle these issues, they must, by necessity, cast their nets wide. If the focus needs to tighten, the frameworks should not be those of psychology or neuroscience, but the outlooks of medieval men and women themselves. They too named, considered, and experienced 'affective matters', and did so according to their own codes, motivations, and aims. The use of the term 'emotion' to terminologically encompass the various affective categories also merits explanation.[31] It is absent from medieval vocabulary: it first appeared in French during the fifteenth century within descriptions of uprisings and popular revolts.[32] The most obvious justification stems from the very emergence of the historiographical current which focuses on it: in the last twenty years, this terminology has become increasingly common in almost every Western language, paralleling the rise of the 'sciences of emotion'.

Departing from this consensus, we prefer to speak of what, in French, we call the *sensible* – a term dear to Lucien Febvre and the Annalist historians[33] – when approaching this vast field. The meaning intended here is neither that of 'sensoriality', nor of 'sensitivity', but of 'sensibility': the title of this English translation indeed derives from the latter. We speak often of feelings, of passions, of affects, and of impulses. But

6

affectivity also includes more stable aspects: atmospheres, moods, and lasting dispositions. Wherever we have found emotions, we have tried to draw together the sparse traces of emotional feeling – pleasures, pains, joys, and sorrows – as much as possible. As historians, we seek to analyse norms, rhetoric, games of interaction and of power, and cultural products and performances: we thus try to avoid any distinction between felt emotion and expressed emotion, any frontier between the authentic and the uncertain. The emotions that were voiced, expressed by an action, or displayed by the body possessed their own cultural and social efficacies. They are, in any case, the only emotions to which we have access. As Marcel Mauss understood so well, the ritualization of an emotion and its expression in a pre-defined scenario do not necessarily mean that it is not sincerely felt.[34]

This book proposes a cultural history of affectivity for the medieval West. It aims to prove the essential importance of emotions in history – and *a fortiori* in the Middle Ages – and also to offer an emotional journey through this thousand-year epoch. This history is a cultural history, since emotion was expressed in images and texts, the works of medieval culture. Our approach takes account of the Christian religious dynamic of the Passion and the passions, a dynamic which had so much structural importance on an anthropological as well as an institutional level. In fact, this is truly our thesis: we are convinced that emotion was at the heart of the anthropology of the Western Middle Ages. Thus, our aim has been to produce a history of medieval sensibilities, albeit not the only one that could be written or that demands to be studied. This history, tied to other cognitive processes (imagination, memory, reasoning, etc.), is founded on a history of experience – that total psychological fact – but also pertains to social history. To take an interest in the history of the emotions is in no way to promote an atomized history, one centred on the individual and microscopic level. Rather it is an anthropological history: a history of humankind, of the human being as a whole, and of shared singularities.

We have of course made choices, followed some paths, and departed from others. Christian anthropology was founded on the centrality of the emotions, above all love and suffering (Chapter 1): God sent his Son who suffered, through love, in order to save humanity. Augustine (d. 430) made the sensitivity of the soul a consequence of original sin. From then on, humanity was passionate and life on earth was anything but impassive. Nevertheless, the emotions could be turned towards God or away from him, since they pertained to the system of vices and virtues. The education of monks, that elite of an ideal Christian society, was founded on this idea: it was present even within the earliest desert monasticism. To 'convert' the soul towards God meant to turn the emotions towards salvation by adopting a way of life and an interior disposition that promoted this spiritual movement (Chapter 2).

Rooted in the experiences of the Desert Fathers and the doctrinal formulas of the Church Fathers, medieval sensibilities were continuously evolving. During the early Middle Ages (fifth to tenth centuries), normative and moral texts written by monks and clerics charted a course for the conversion of the emotions. These were initially intended for monastic circles, but soon turned their gaze on lay society (Chapter 3). In the age of Charlemagne and again, with fresh force, during the Gregorian reforms of the eleventh and twelfth centuries, a new project for society took shape atop that key pedestal of Christian social relationships: the love present in charity and true friendship.

Within this Christian context, a slew of new processes began to direct the emotional culture of societies from the eleventh century onwards. Reformed monasticism nurtured the possibility of direct contact with God, attainable through the sincere expression of emotions (Chapter 4). Courtly literature, written in the vernacular, displayed a complex and refined emotional culture, an expression of the values and tensions that cut across aristocratic and bourgeois settings. It was directly related to the religious re-purposing of desire and the clerical offensive to spiritualize conjugal love and supervise the interior life; at the same time, it also frequently came into conflict with them (Chapter 5). From the end of the eleventh century, in the learned circles of the monasteries and urban schools, the rise of a naturalistic spirit led to the integration of the emotions within human nature (Chapter 6). Such varied discussions spurred and spread a positive re-evaluation of the emotions at the end of the Middle Ages: their religious and social uses became richer and more diverse than ever before. This can be sensed in political theory and the practices of princely government, which gave star-billing to the emotions (Chapter 7). On another level, the extraordinary promotion of the Incarnation and Passion of Christ from the high Middle Ages onwards further reinforced the religious efficacy of the emotions. They became the foundations of affective mysticism in the thirteenth and fourteenth centuries, a current which enjoyed an ambiguous relationship with the institutional Church (Chapter 8). Finally, the more numerous and diverse sources from the last centuries of the Middle Ages open a window onto the emotions of those who were previously anonymous, especially in the towns. They demonstrate not only the diversity of emotional cultures that existed at that time, but above all the importance of emotional levers within social relationships (Chapter 9).

— 1 —

THE CHRISTIANIZATION OF EMOTION (THIRD TO FIFTH CENTURIES)

A large part of the Western medieval conception of emotions and of the affective life was established between the third and fifth centuries. This period in the development of Christian thought exerted a considerable influence on culture – and learned culture most of all – throughout the remaining centuries of the Middle Ages. This was in part because this period witnessed the general adoption of the Vulgate, the Latin version of the Bible translated by St Jerome (d. 420), which was read and ruminated on for the next thousand years, but it was also a result of the position of authority enjoyed by the earliest generations of Christian theologians and philosophers. Yet the authors to be discussed here were not understood or read by medieval people as they are understood and read today. Notably, their works were transmitted by multiple paths, both direct and indirect, at times encumbered by erroneous attributions or in incomplete or corrupted states. Over the course of the Western Middle Ages, the thought of the Church Fathers, always invoked as an inviolable authority, was constantly reinterpreted, adapted, even distorted by the contemporary inspirations of the authors who claimed to represent them. This book will follow the evolution of Christian thought on the emotions, which innovated only while hiding behind the prestige of the past. Here it will be shown how the Latin masters who espoused the Christian faith in this formative period developed, both from the Bible and their inherited philosophical culture, a conception of humanity, and especially of the emotions, that was profoundly new.

The theology of emotion

An emotional God

The Bible is rich in emotions of every sort and every intensity.[1] From the most violent to the most subtle, from the most noble to the most vile, they abound in its historical and prophetic books and saturate those of poetry and wisdom (the Psalms, the Song of Songs, the Wisdom of Sirach). These latter texts were given pride of place in the meditations of medieval intellectuals, especially those in religious orders. The emotions described in the Scriptures are not solely those of humans, but also those of God. The God of the Bible was neither unemotional nor impassive – especially in his often tumultuous relations with his people. The Old Testament overflows with situations where the wrath of God is palpable: 'Therefore the Lord heard, and was angry; a fire was kindled against Jacob, and wrath came up against Israel' (Ps 77: 21).[2] In return, this irascible God could also show mercy and let himself be moved: 'But he is merciful, and will forgive their sins: and will not destroy them. And many a time did he turn away his anger: and did not kindle all his wrath. And he remembered that they are flesh: a wind that goeth and returneth not' (Ps 77: 38–9). The image here is of a wrathful God rendered suddenly tender, almost hesitant, by the fragility of his creation.

In the New Testament, divine wrath is likewise present. The advent of God made man in the person of Jesus changed everything, however.[3] More than his Father, Jesus overflowed with emotions that he sought neither to hide nor to neutralize, since they were signs of his own humanity. Christ, God made flesh, thus experienced compassion, fear, love, and pity. He felt no jealousy, envy, or hate. Rather his emotions were virtuous, contributing to salvation but also to just wrath. On the Mount of Olives on the eve of his death, Jesus' anguish and pain were so intense that an angel came to comfort him (Luke 22: 42–3). He wept for the fate of Jerusalem before bringing his full wrath to bear against the merchants of the Temple, whom he ruthlessly expelled (Luke 19: 41). By contrast, the canonical Gospels are less inclined to evoke Christ's emotions during the Passion, beyond his famous cry of anguish: 'My God, my God, why have you forsaken me?' (Mark 15: 34; Matt. 27: 46). How did Jesus experience the outrages and humiliations he suffered? Did he feel shame or indignation when faced with the jibes and spitting of the crowd? Did he suffer in spirit over and above the physical pain that he had to endure during his ordeal? In paradise, did he continue to suffer as a man for the sins of humanity? The authors of the Middle Ages posed all of these questions. They were especially crucial in so far as they determined the very nature of God, and the writers developed specific responses to them. During his corporeal life, Jesus was able to feel all of the virtuous emotions as a man, from the sweetest to the most painful. On the other hand, if the resurrected Jesus continued to feel emotions, these were experienced in a non-carnal – and thus non-human – manner. He could thus no longer shed tears, however great his pain.[4]

The first and foremost commandment of the Gospels is the commandment of love: 'Thou shalt love the Lord thy God with thy whole heart, and with thy whole soul, and with thy whole mind' (Matt. 22: 37); 'This is my commandment, that you love one another, as I have loved you' (John 15: 12); 'Love your enemies: do good to them that hate you: and pray for them that persecute and calumniate you' (Matt. 5: 44). To love God, to love oneself, to love one's neighbour, to love one's enemies: such is the order of love – both in the sense of injunction and of hierarchy – which ought to preside over the social life of man and his ties to God. When Western Christians received the message of the Gospel, they identified this commandment with a specific form of love: 'charity'. Jerome used *caritas* to translate the Greek *agapè*, a term which described a measured and impartial attachment that engaged every aspect of one's being, including both reason and the will. This love could be distinguished from *amor – erôs* in Greek – without necessarily being opposed to it. The latter term implied longing, a drive to possess something, whether spiritual or material, that was often irrepressible.[5] Described as an encompassing and inclusive embrace, the love found in charity was meant to expand outwards, without excess or passion: it called for the care of one's neighbour as well as oneself. The love described by *amor*, however, was an intense state of feeling which picked its target and plunged towards it, like a hunter's spear towards its prey. It was a hazardous, exclusive, and violent experience. As such, it galvanized mystics, pulling them wholly towards God and creating an inseparable bond, while blinding the greedy, who remained ensnared in worldly desires.

The theologians of these first Christian centuries also used the word *dilectio* to describe the love that emanated from the spirit and the soul. Its meaning was very close to *caritas*, but more personal: the term was related to *electio*, choice.[6] If the term *caritas* was not unheard of in pagan Latin – Cicero includes it within the family of virtues upon which social life was founded – this *dilectio* was absent. The duty of Christian love proved a fitting substitute for the Roman ethical value of *fides*, i.e. trust in one's word and in the law. 'Trust' configured as 'faith' developed into 'love'. For Paul, this 'commandment of love' – a neat expression of this new alliance – subsumed the Mosaic Law: 'Love [*dilectio*] is the fulfilment of the Law' (Rom. 13: 10). St John completed this emotional revolution. He bound the Law and God himself together to form a conclusion that contained the quintessence of Christianity in the medieval West: 'God is charity: and he that abideth in charity, abideth in God, and God in him.' God was not only endowed with emotions: he was himself the emotional force of love.

11

God's wrath: a proof of his existence

For the most part, the Latin theologians of these first Christian centuries were educated in the schools of the Empire. From Tertullian (d. *c.* 220) through to Augustine, all the Latin Fathers – a list that includes Lactantius (d. *c.* 320), Ambrose of Milan (d. 397), Arnobius (d. early fourth century), and Jerome – had a solid formation in classical culture.[7] Some, like Lactantius and Augustine, had even been masters of rhetoric and philosophy before devoting their life and their quills to their new faith. Christian theology did not emerge by spontaneous generation: it was deeply anchored in the Scriptures but also nourished by pagan culture, especially the immense Greco-Roman philosophical heritage. This was a great accumulation of thought, beginning with Socratic philosophy and continuing through to the Neo-Platonic thought of Plotinus, the Peripatetic school, and the Stoicism of the late Empire.[8] For these philosophical schools, however, the mere mention of a God capable of wrath was nonsensical. Wrath was a passion, and as such, a deviation from reason. God, the prime mover, was by nature *apathès*, and thus devoid of all passion. This doctrine of divine *apatheia*, an impassivity which the Latins sometimes called *tranquilitas*, the tranquillity of the soul, was essential. Nevertheless, impassivity, the absence of passions, did not necessarily mean insensibility, the incapacity to feel emotions or an indifference towards them. How rigid these philosophical conceptions were depended on the school. The disciples of Aristotle were less dismissive of such possibilities than the Stoics, for whom God was a being of pure reason: for them, certain palpable emotions, such as measured joy, could be considered compatible with *apatheia*.

Greek theologians, greatly influenced by Stoicism, did not seek to break from philosophical tradition on this point. They professed a belief in divine impassivity, whilst holding that *agapè*, charitable love, was the very expression of the total freedom enjoyed by the Logos. They thus stood for a 'sensitive *apatheia*'.[9] Yet the question over the wrath of God remained: how could a God without passions display fits of anger? Origen (d. *c.* 253) disposed of the contradiction quite rapidly by invoking the spiritual sense of the Scriptures. Passages which spoke of the wrath of God were not to be understood literally. Rather, it was necessary 'to understand them in a way worthy of God'.[10] The function of such 'stories' was to reinforce the faith of mankind by promoting a healthy fear of God. Nevertheless, was the paradox actually removed? In a significant break from Eastern perspectives on the matter, the response of Latin Christianity suggested that it was not.

The theologians of the West were less receptive than their Eastern peers to the philosophical theory of divine *apatheia*. Using Latin as a scriptural language rather than Greek, the 'maternal' language of philosophy, they lacked a certain legitimacy within this field: it seems that they sought to resolve this by more clearly distinguishing themselves from the philosophers and increasing the separation. In the fertile culture of these first Christian centuries, there were of course Latin authors who proclaimed the impassivity of God: this was the case with Marcion (d. *c.* 160), and later with Arnobius. In fact, it was in the context of his dispute with Marcion that Tertullian came to refute this doctrine. For Tertullian, divine wrath was not a disorder, but an expression of the power and justice of God. He thus shifted the debate's centre of gravity from the territory of philosophical anthropology (whether wrath was a passion or not) towards that of morality (whether wrath was good or bad). The wrath of God was an expression of God's goodness. Seen from a certain aspect, it was in fact the twin of charity. Charity upheld man in the justice of the Law, while wrath brought him back to it when he strayed: 'For if God is angry, it stems from no vice in Him. Rather, He is angry for our benefit.'[11]

This split from philosophical tradition was significant. Moving beyond the apologetic enterprise of legitimizing the divine wrath found in the Bible, a radical critique of the disruptive nature of passion had begun. Against this background, the entire ancient anthropology of the emotions was being reshaped.[12] Lactantius likewise followed suit. More than just a theologian, Lactantius should be read as a Christian philosopher.[13] He is a perfect example of the Christian acculturation that affected part of the elite educated in the schools of the Empire from the end of the third century. As such, his profile is characteristic of the new learned culture within Latin Christianity. Lactantius was a professor of Latin rhetoric, which he taught to the emperor Diocletian (d. 305) at Nicomedia in Bithynia. It was probably during his stay at the imperial court that he was converted to Christianity and came into contact with the future Emperor Constantine (d. 324), whom he is said to have tutored. Following the great persecutions in the latter part of Diocletian's reign, he began writing his masterpiece, the *Divine Institutes*. This vast work, divided into seven books, represents the first Latin synthesis of Christian doctrine. In parallel, Lactantius also composed a number of other works: uniquely within the literature of late antiquity, one of these was dedicated to *The Wrath of God*.[14] In this text, Lactantius immediately engaged the philosophers in debate over divine impassivity, a question he saw as vital for the new Christian faith. For beyond the question of wrath itself, the very nature of God was at stake. If the philosophers were correct when they affirmed that anger was always a failure of judgement, then it would follow that the God of the Bible was a weak God. To counter such an accusation, Lactantius reprised Tertullian's argument: the wrath of God

13

was not of the same nature as the wicked anger that man was capable of, but rather a product of his omnipotent goodness and justice. It was proof of God's mercy.

But Lactantius went further still when he refuted wholesale the theories of the Epicureans and the Stoics on divine impassivity. The reasoning was simple but powerful. For Epicurus to be correct, it was necessary to conceive of an immovable and indifferent God who existed in a state of perpetual rest. But would such a God – unmoved by the worship of his followers, unable to exercise his providence, and disinclined to perform any other activity – not lack divine character altogether? Meanwhile, to those Stoics who believed in a God who was solely benign and never succumbed to anger, Lactantius asked: how can one love the good without hating the bad? For loving what was good derived from hating what was bad. In order to be provident and show his omnipotence, God had to be moved by these two emotions: 'he is not God if he is not moved (*movetur*)'.[15] As shown by this construction, which consciously identified impassivity with immobility, the debate had shifted significantly. What began as an attempt to legitimize the biblical anomaly of a God who was both good and prone to anger had ultimately resulted in a doctrine which made God's power – and thus his existence – conditional on his emotivity. This original position on divine emotion, which was further developed by Lactantius through philosophical argument, became the standard position of the Catholic Church from the fifth century onwards.

God is love

The argument over divine wrath was only one of the avenues that led to the proclamation of a God who was sensitive to emotion. That debate had primarily been a matter of justifying Christian doctrine, founded on the Scriptures, from an apologetic perspective in the face of a philosophical consensus. From an early stage, however, the ontological value that was assigned to love was more of an intrinsic construction.[16] For Augustine, love shown towards God was much more than simply an expression of a just piety. Rather it gave meaning to man's relationship with himself and with his neighbour, to the entirety of creation, and even to the mystery of the Trinity, in which three persons were bound together by love. Across his sizeable oeuvre, the Bishop of Hippo delivered this message in numerous guises. This analysis will look at just one of these descriptions, drawn from his early writings.

In his treatise *The Happy Life*, written just after his conversion in 386, Augustine took as his point of departure the existential observation made by the pagan philosophers, most notably Cicero: all men want to be happy.[17] From this perspective, man was a being of desire and joy, always reaching towards aims and objects which he hoped might provide him with that state of complete contentment. Augustine related this desirous nature to the statement of Genesis that man was made 'in the image and likeness' of God. For Augustine, and for the Church Fathers more broadly, these notions of the 'image' and of the 'likeness' were critical in illuminating the relationship between man and God. The 'image' expressed the essential bond between the creature and his creator, while the notion of 'likeness' conveyed that man played a part in realizing his true nature, thus signifying a conscious attraction towards his ultimate origin.

Since man was created in the 'image' and the 'likeness' of God, he felt a fundamental absence, and an overriding need to be joined to his source, his origin. In its purest sense, love expressed the singular and desirous force which bound subject and object together:

> Now love is of someone who loves, and something is loved with love. So then there are three: the lover, the beloved, and the love. What else is love, therefore, except a kind of life which binds or seeks to bind some two together, namely, the lover and the beloved?[18]

This was also the case for the most carnal matters. But that sort of love was doomed to exhaustion. For the desire for joy, and thus for contentment, would never be satisfied by ignoring the real nature of what was missing. The origin of the lack that created desire, and thus placed love at the centre of human life, was clearly God. This is why the love of God held importance beyond any moral injunction (i.e. it is good to love God for your well-being): it was the sole path that led man towards beatitude. This also meant that, by loving God 'with all of his heart and all of his soul', man was simply fulfilling his destiny by working towards his divine likeness. In experiencing absence, Augustinian man came to participate in the profound purpose of his existence, the return to his origin.[19] Similarly, according to Augustine, love was the ultimate political bond on which human community was built.[20] This conception, influenced by the Neo-Platonic idea of 'the One', was one of the sources of medieval love mysticism in the Middle Ages, which exalted love and made it the *ratio ultima* of creation. Such a Christian metaphysical doctrine of love, bound together with the supporting dynamics of the 'image' and of the return to 'the One', would spread through the monasteries of the West, especially from the end of the eleventh century; it profoundly shaped Christian spirituality.[21] This spirituality found another equally ancient path (second half of the fifth century) by which God could be identified with love in the Eastern works of Pseudo-Dionysius the Areopagite, the anonymous Syrian monk who assumed his name in homage to a convert of

15

St Paul. He elaborated a theology founded on the gradual return of the created back into God, a deification of man that occurred by the process of 'unition' (*henosis* or *unitio*). This signified a union between the creature and the Creator which went beyond all human understanding and intellectual grasp. In *The Divine Names*, Pseudo-Dionysius identified God with the name of 'Love' when describing the power of attraction – which applied to both God and man – that allowed for the ultimate unification:

> This is why the great Paul, swept along by his yearning for God and seized by its ecstatic power, had this inspired word to say: 'It is no longer I who live, but Christ who lives in me' (Gal. 2: 20). Paul was truly a lover and, as he says, he was beside himself for God, possessing not his own life but the life of the One for whom he yearned, as exceptionally beloved.[22]

The Dionysian theology of a union with God gained through an emotional grasp quickly proved seductive for those in the West. It gained a foothold in the early Carolingian court and subsequently reached a larger learned audience from the twelfth century onward. The spiritual writers of the late Middle Ages tended to lean on either Augustine or Pseudo-Dionysius for support; at times, they even attempted to synthesize these two great sources of 'Neo-Platonic Christianity'.[23]

Passion incarnate

If God was Love, Jesus was Passion. The authors of the final centuries of the Middle Ages took up this banner: the suffering of Jesus on the cross, proof of both his immeasurable love for man and his total obedience to his father, was necessary to redeem the sins of humanity. To follow Christ meant first of all to follow the cross, and thus to participate in the sufferings (sadness, pain, humiliation) of his Passion, just as the apostle Peter had described: 'But if you partake of the sufferings of Christ (*Christi passionibus*), rejoice that, when his glory shall be revealed, you may also be glad with exceeding joy.' (1 Pet. 4: 13). Nevertheless, the path which directly linked redemption to the suffering of the Passion was not the only one imaginable. In both the Jewish and early Christian traditions, messianic revelation did not emphasize the suffering of the Passion. To make that leap, two prerequisite assumptions were in fact required. The first was theological in nature: it was necessary to accept that the divine humanity of Jesus encompassed all aspects of human affectivity, including physical suffering and susceptibility to spontaneous emotions (those which might arise unwillingly). The second ran counter to this logic: it required the belief that the suffering of the Passion was

16

no simple consequence of Christ's humanity. If that were the case, it would have no value that distinguished it from the other emotions felt during his human life. Rather the fact that he had suffered on the cross as a man was the indispensable proof of his humanity.

The first condition posed a problem for certain Christians who believed that Jesus could not have suffered physically on the cross. For instance, Docetism, an early Christian current of thought, did not deny the humanity of Christ but nevertheless refuted the need for any physical suffering during his crucifixion. Jesus certainly had the appearance of a man but he could not be humbled by his flesh, as implied by the Gospel of Peter, a second-century apocryphal text often associated with this doctrine: 'And they brought two malefactors, and crucified the Lord between them. But he held his peace, as (if) he felt no pain.'[24] The Docetists took up a Judeo-Christian line of thought which viewed the Messiah as an angelic being. Against this, another equally ancient line of thought insisted on the reality of Jesus' suffering, taken as confirmation that his humanity was full and complete. This relationship between the redemption and sufferings of the Messiah drew strength from the Old Testament: 'Despised, and the most abject of men, a man of sorrows, and acquainted with infirmity: and his look was as it were hidden and despised, whereupon we esteemed him not. Surely he hath borne our infirmities and carried our sorrows' (Isa. 53: 3–4). The Passion of the Messiah was as necessary for his glory as it was for the salvation of humanity. Apocryphal Christian writings often emphasize Jesus' Passion as the key event of his life, at the same time as making suffering the ultimate proof of his humanity. The Acts of John, written in the second century and influenced by Gnostic circles, provide a strong example:

> For you could not at all have comprehended what you suffer if I had not been sent to you as the Word by the Father. When you saw what I suffer, you have seen me as one suffering; and seeing that, you have not stood firm but were wholly moved. Moved to become wise, you have me for a support. Rest upon me![25]

This mystical theme of resting on the bed of the cross would be reprised time and again at the end of the Middle Ages.

Thus both the East and the West witnessed the very early development of the idea that Jesus could not have fully been man without the reality of suffering, and thus without passion. Tertullian stated the matter pithily: 'the sufferings proved there was the flesh of man'.[26] The logical displacement described above was complete. It was less the Incarnation which rendered Jesus capable of emotions than the inverse: the emotions he felt and displayed proved his humanity in the eyes of the world, just as, for

17

Lactantius, the wrath of the Father proved God's providence. Jesus had to be human so that he could suffer on the cross and, by the sacrifice of his suffering – the ultimate act of love – save humanity. The capacity to suffer was not merely an element like any other within the life of Christ, but rather *the* condition on which his humanity was founded and which made redemption possible.[27] An original capacity, which Origen called the 'passion of charity' (*caritatis passio*),[28] thus completed the circle of love and suffering. The love of charity that defined God's essence was presented as an emotional mould that prefigured and heralded the suffering humanity of Jesus. It was because God was Love that he chose to suffer authentically as a man; conversely, his Passion was the very expression of his boundless love for humanity.

The anthropology of emotion

What about the emotions of mankind more broadly? There was no question of natural *apatheia* here. On the contrary, the philosophers of antiquity were clear that the 'affects' occupied a place at least as important as that of 'thoughts' in the lives of men: they were indeed rather worried about the former disturbing the latter. As for the early Latin theologians, those Church Fathers who would be read and reread by the learned and who shaped generations of thought, they approached the question of human sensibility from two related but distinct angles. Firstly, they wanted to understand the physical and bodily 'machinery' behind human affects. How did man feel? What were the respective places of the body and the soul in the life of the emotions. Was it necessary to differentiate between instinctive urges, emotions, and feelings? Were the affects allied with reason or a menace to it? Alongside this, a major question arose: were the affects good for mankind or a frailty of nature that one ought to neutralize? They wanted thence to determine the role that the emotions played in the quest for salvation on earth: did the affects hinder spiritual ascent and the quest for divine likeness?

The Christian passions

In the age when the Latin Fathers constructed Christian anthropology, between the second and fifth centuries, academic debates concerning affectivity were framed by the problematic of the passions of the soul, most often expressed in Stoic terms. Christian theologians were naturally also influenced by other heritages: the Platonic and Aristotelian *corpora*, even Epicureanism, and of course the Hebrew anthropology they could read throughout the Bible. But the Stoic doctrine of the passions remained the basis and point of departure for these debates. This familiarity – which did not always prevent radical departures – was due to a number of factors. The Christian authors of late antiquity were steeped in the works of those classical masters influenced by Stoicism: Cicero, Seneca, and Quintilian. It was especially from these that Christian theologians drew their vocabulary of the emotional life and, in doing so, the categories that organized it.

As a result, they very rarely employed the word *passio* – drawn from the Greek *pathos* – when speaking of the passions. They did not ignore it and could even return to it on occasion when discussing the role of the passions within the soul. When they did employ it, however, it was usually in the sense of suffering, naturally linked to the Passion of Jesus, or that of an illness of the soul. Here, the Christian authors followed in the footsteps of classical Latin writers. Cicero had in fact laboured to give a unique translation of the Greek *pathos*. He proposed many terms: *perturbatio, commotio, affectio*. Seneca, meanwhile, translated *pathos* as *affectus* and stuck to it. The rhetorician Quintilian followed suit. Without entirely dispensing with the other terms, Christian authors in turn principally employed *affectus* when speaking of the passions; in a much broader sense, the term also described the entire emotional register. *Passio* would only come to rival it in scholastic and medical usage from the thirteenth century.[29]

In approaching the Latin Christian reading of the passions, it is instructive to begin again with Lactantius.[30] Firstly, because he wrote the first account of the Christian conception of the passions, found in the sixth book of his *Divine Institutes*. Secondly, because like many other writers of late antiquity and many more in the early Middle Ages, Lactantius does not seem to have read directly the Greek philosophers and scholars (Plato, Aristotle, Chrysippus, Posidonius, Galen, or Zeno of Citium). Rather, the knowledge he had of their positions on the matter of the passions was filtered by the Latin classical authors who spoke of them, especially Cicero and Seneca. The question here is thus less of knowing if his opinion on the philosophers was in keeping or not with their original doctrines, than of grasping what the commentaries and critiques he produced reveal of his own conceptions of affectivity. Lactantius took aim at two principal doctrines on the emotions (*affectus*): that of the Stoics who wanted to eradicate them, and that of the disciples of Aristotle, the Peripatetics, who called for their moderation.[31] The most harshly criticized were the Stoics, who turned emotions (desire, joy, fear, sadness) into illnesses of the soul that exposed errors of judgement. No matter that Seneca had in fact made a distinction between primary emotion – what he called the 'first movement' of the soul – from which nothing could be subtracted, and passion, which required the voluntary acceptance of emotional momentum. In the eyes of Lactantius, the Stoic doctrine aimed at a total suppression of the emotions, reducing them to agents that disturbed reason. Yet, for Lactantius, such an outlook was not merely arrogant but also entirely absurd, since it attempted to cut man off from a profound part of his nature. In a most revealing metaphor, Lactantius declared that to attempt to subtract the emotions was to 'castrate a man' (*castrare hominem*).[32] To remove them from a man was 'to extract something from [his] body, which is to want to change the nature of the animal'.[33] Lactantius here drew from the medical approaches of his age which placed the origin of emotions within organs: anger within the heart, and joy in the spleen. The emotions were thus the 'natural richness of souls',[34] placed by God within the nature of Adam when he was created. For the Christian Lactantius, God could not have created a man marred by a defect: thus man's capacity to feel emotions was a blessing to him. Yet this did not mean that all emotions were beneficial. On the contrary, this capacity to be moved, which God had placed in man, was like an empty field where vices and virtues could be cultivated.

The scale of the shift in perspective brought about by the Christian philosopher bears consideration. Emotional disturbance was no longer conceived of as a source of poor cognitive reasoning. Rather, it was placed on another plane, that of morality: a badly directed emotion could lead to vice. Above all, he stood for the neutrality of emotions: their moral ambivalence was rooted in this. No emotion was good or bad in and of itself. Its value depended entirely on the causes which motivated it and the ends to which it led. In this way, desire, fear, and even anger, which had been given to man by God, could be useful and lead to virtue: desire (*libido*) allowed mankind to continue from generation to generation, fear of God was the beginning of wisdom, and anger could have educative qualities that were preferable to excessive indulgence. Nevertheless, it was not a matter of 'giving free reign' to the emotions, as Lactantius often emphasized.[35] On this point he drew from the Platonic metaphor of the chariot of the soul: 'If that chariot of life, which is drawn by the passions as though by pernicious horses, holds to the right road, it will perform its function.'[36] Behind this suspicion lay the lingering influence of philosophical tradition: although naturally good, the emotions nevertheless seemed marked by a no less natural propensity for excess. It is why Lactantius labelled certain affects as 'Furies'.[37] Emotions led by wisdom were sources of virtue; conversely, if they exceeded the boundaries set by God's will, they promoted vice. The risk was all the greater since the emotions were often dominated by sensory pleasures, which were themselves condemned in their entirety by Lactantius due to their strictly corporal origin. Only sexual pleasure escaped this condemnation, since it was naturally tied to reproduction and thus constituted the sole carnal pleasure common to all animal species. For Lactantius, the risk of vice was not inherent within the emotions, but derived from the external factors which aroused them: it was thus these external causes which required moderation. If Lactantius was not entirely consistent in this line, he conserved its essence. He applied it, for example, to sexual desire, which could be 'vehement (*vehemens*)' and yet 'still free from fault' if restricted to the marital bed.[38]

The Christian humanism of Lactantius would come to seduce the men of the Renaissance. By replacing the ancient philosophers' principle of nature with a God of kindness, the author of a good creation, he had imbued man with an immense individual liberty. This encompassed man's emotions, that most impetuous part of himself: they were no longer considered to be agents of disturbance but companions of reason. The man he depicted was not defined solely by his reason; and reason, in turn, did not have to be guarded within an interior fortress as the Stoics had wanted. He was a whole being, who might find wisdom through employing his emotions as much as his reason. In this rejection of *apatheia*, Lactantius even went as far as to justify the existence of vice, deeming it necessary for the demonstration of virtue: 'Where there are no vices, there is not even place for virtue.'[39] This benevolent position towards the emotional life bears a Christian stamp, in the sense that it derived from the essential goodness of a nature created by God. It thus helps to clarify the specificity of Christian emotional culture in the Middle Ages. The principle of the original goodness of human affectivity and the conviction that certain emotions carried man towards virtue, even in their most demonstrative occurrences, was perpetuated in medieval clerical thought. Nevertheless, in the century which followed the death of Lactantius, Christian theologians came to cast doubt on his optimistic vision.

Augustine: father of medieval affectivity

In the space of just fifty years, between 380 and 430, Western Christian thought found a new standing, moving beyond apologetics towards a true theology. The actors in this transformation were Ambrose of Milan, Jerome, and, above all, Augustine of Hippo. Augustine was born in 354 at Thagaste, in North Africa.[40] His father was a local notable and his mother Monica came from a Christian family. Despite this, Augustine responded only belatedly to the appeals of the Christian faith. The young Augustine, who received a classical education, began a career as a professor of rhetoric, first at Carthage, then in Milan. He had been seduced by Manichaeism, a philosophy of Eastern origin which had been superficially coloured by Christianity in the preceding centuries. But his favourite intellectual authority remained Cicero, whose philosophical eclecticism appealed to him. In Milan, during the 380s, Augustine frequented – and became fascinated by – a Christian intellectual circle, well-versed in classical culture, which gravitated around the bishop of the city, Ambrose, a patrician from a high aristocratic Roman background and the former governor of Liguria-Emilia. There, he discovered a Christian thought influenced by the Neo-Platonism of Plotinus, the depth of which impressed him much more than anything he had read or heard among the clergy of North Africa. Following a rather tortured interior progression, Augustine converted in 386 and was baptized the following year.

Augustine wrote no treatise on the passions,[41] but he addressed the subject on many occasions, particularly in books IX and XIV of *The City of God*, written in the years that followed the sack of Rome by the Visigoth – and Arian Christian – Alaric (d. 410) in August 410. Although the Empire had been officially Christian for nearly a century, Augustine recognized that he was witnessing its political death-throes. Rome was in decline. The city of God, which alone heralded the eternal kingdom, had to take its place. Up to a point, Augustine approached the matter of the emotions from the same sources as Lactantius. Again, any reflection on the Christian passions had to be clear on its relationship to philosophical tradition, dominated as ever by the Stoics and the Peripatetics:

> There are two opinions among the philosophers as to those motions of the mind which the Greeks call *pathe*. Some of our writers, such as Cicero, call them disturbances (*perturbationes*), others call them affections (*affectiones*) or affects (*affectus*) and others again, like Apuleius, call them passions (*passiones*), which expresses the Greek word more closely.[42]

Nevertheless, for the Latin thinkers of the early fourth century, it seemed that the very terminology of the passions had become somewhat loose, something which was not unproblematic when they attempted to clarify the nature of their debate with the philosophers. More neutral terms for the emotional movements, such as *affectus* and *affectio*, coexisted with words such as *perturbatio* and *passio*, which in and of themselves seemed to suggest the trouble and disorder produced in the soul by emotional impetus: this did not facilitate dialogue. A distance was about to form between the new Christian anthropology of the emotions and the philosophical tradition.

More explicitly than Lactantius, Augustine refused to distinguish between what the philosophers had called 'prepassions' (*propatheiai*)

– the first movements of feeling – and the passions.[43] For the ancients, the prepassions designated the first pang of emotion felt when confronted with an unexpected situation: for instance, the shock of a surprise, sudden pallor in the face of danger, or even the rising of anger in response to injury. For the Stoics especially, these first emotions were involuntary and irrepressible. For that very reason, they could not be considered passions, since these latter involved a willingness to entertain a state of emotional feeling. While it was characteristic of passion to override reason when it was not resisted, thus rendering the soul *passive* to its control, this could only begin if there was, at one moment or another within the progression, a form of assent. Yet the Latin Fathers were very reticent in distinguishing the natures of prepassion and passion. For them, the power of the emotions was indivisible, and the affects were thus felt as part of a singular process. An affective continuum thus joined the first pang of emotion and the eventual establishment of the powerful sentiment of passion.

Augustine explained this clearly, drawing from an anecdote recounted by Aulus Gellius in the *Attic Nights*.[44] While the writer was at sea in the company of a celebrated Stoic philosopher, a terrible storm put the whole crew in peril. Amid this danger, the passengers noticed that even the philosopher, who claimed to be untouched by passionate disturbances, had grown pale in fear. Once the storm had passed, the philosopher did not escape the mockery of some of his companions on the voyage: as wise as he claimed to be, he nevertheless reacted like any other man, when confronted with the danger of death. The philosopher responded that the first pang of emotion, from which in fact no man could escape, was in no way the same as passion, which required consent. He had thus not truly feared death, since in the eyes of a Stoic, such fear was indeed a passion. Rather he had been shaken by a sort of emotional reflex, provoked by a sudden external impetus: the storm. It was natural that a wise man would then succeed in stopping this emotional reflex from embedding itself within his soul and turning into fear. For Augustine, such quibbles only sought to mask the attachment of man to life and to the integrity of his body. The first pang of emotion was perhaps involuntary, in the sense that it escaped the control of those who experienced it. Nevertheless, it was the first sign of a passion.

What was at stake here was the moral responsibility of man for his emotions. It is why it was important to know whether the first movement which shook the soul was a precursory phase to passion, thus arriving before it, or whether it was in fact the first symptom. The distinction might seem trivial, and yet it was crucial. What would happen if the impulse of prepassion contained an orientation towards sin, as was the case, for example, with adulterous desire? Should the person who felt it consider himself free from all responsibility, provided that he refused not only to act on it, but also to take pleasure in the thought? Or must he admit that he was already, from the time of that first impulse, sliding towards sin? The response of the Fathers was not very reassuring, as seen in Jerome's statement: 'There is a difference between *pathos* and *propatheia*, that is to say, between passion and prepassion. Passion is regarded as a vice, while prepassion (though it may have blame in its commencement) is not reputed as a sin.'[45] In Jerome's definition, prepassion thus seems entirely exempt from sin, unless the will consented to it; but how should the words 'though it may have blame in its commencement' be understood? Did they mean that desirous temptation was related to the sinful nature of man, as if an outgrowth of the original sin that he carried within him; or rather, more prosaically, that prepassion, despite still not being a sin, was indeed what induced it? Augustine's response to the same question was no less ambiguous: if the soul which felt this initial pleasure (which was linked to the desire) did not consent to it, there was still fault, but it was 'so light that it is almost nothing'.[46]

This matter aside, the debate over the moral responsibility of the Christian for his emotions said much about the very nature of the emotional process that the Fathers conceived. The theologians of these first centuries of Christianity were hostile to any division of affectivity. It is thus understandable why they preferred the term 'affect' (*affectus*) to that of 'passion' (*passio*). The first was better able to marry all the stages of the affective process, from the initial emotional shock to the lasting implantation of a sentiment, while the second could only describe the final state of embedded emotion and also had connotations of disturbance, which likewise posed a problem. It is why the dialogue between theologians and philosophers was not always easy, since, using the same term *affectus*, they sometimes spoke of different emotional realities. We must remember that from the fifth century, the term *affectus*, the most commonly used to describe emotion, was capable, according to the context in which it was used, of describing emotional states that were very varied in their nature and their manner of expression. This semantic fluidity did not so much express the vagaries of vocabulary as signal the newfound unity of affectivity within a referential context that was now moral above all else: the value of emotions was to be judged by the yardstick of vice and virtue.

Augustine in turn rejected the Stoic theory that the affects were *a priori* disturbances of the rational soul. Here, Augustine drew an example from the teachings of Paul – 'The citizens of the City of God are delighted to behold him with the eyes of Faith. They behold him rejoicing with those who rejoice, and crying with those who cry' – and concluded: 'If these emotions and affections, coming from the love of the good and from holy charity, are to be called vices, then let us allow that real vices should be called virtues.'[47] It is thus unsurprising that Augustine swept away the Stoic ideal of apathy: it was an ineptitude which could also be seen as enormously unjust, since it would stop man from feeling the salutary fear of God and deprive spiritual love and charity of their blessedness. The capacity to feel emotions was good since it was the condition which God chose for man. Emotions were to be envisaged as movements of the will: 'And universally, as a man's will is attracted or repelled by a variety of things which are pursued or avoided, so it changes and turns into emotions (*affectus*) of one kind or the other.'[48] Who would want to tear man away from his will? The philosophers had misunderstood the debate. The question was not one of welcoming or rejecting emotions, but rather of knowing how and to what end to use them: 'Within our discipline, then, we do not so much ask whether a pious soul is angry, as why he is angry; not whether he is sad, but whence comes his sadness; not whether he is afraid, but what he fears.'[49]

Such a position was entirely in line with what Lactantius had already pronounced. While relying on the ancient terminology of the emotions, the theologians built a new paradigm, one where primacy was given to the examination of conscience and to questioning oneself on the arrival of every new emotional feeling. Whenever an emotion arose, the wise Christian would not seek to moderate it, still less to get rid of it. Rather, he would analyse it. What motivated the fear he experienced? Why did he feel moved by desire? What was the object of his disgust? Emotion called for enquiry and introspection. It was thus recognized as a cognitive aptitude: through emotion, man would understand the world, evaluate his human and material environment, and above all determine the place he wished to take in it. Certainly, earlier ancient philosophers had also espoused the rational dimension of the passions. But for them it was largely a matter of a negative, anti-cognitive rationality, in the sense that the passions obscured the correct functioning of judgement. Furthermore, the passions had an irrational origin in the prepassions. In the process of including all emotions within the will, Augustine also seemed to restore them to rationality.

Sin and punishment

This re-evaluation of the emotions was perhaps not quite as spectacular as first appearances suggest. For something else came to disturb this reconciliation between man and his emotional nature: original sin. It was indeed during the fourth and fifth centuries that the doctrine of original sin first formed within Western theology. Augustine played a decisive role in its construction. He interpreted the disobedience of Eve, 'the weaker

25

of the human couple',[50] and then that of Adam as being more than a transgression: it was a rebellion. Adam and Eve had believed they could place their own wills on the same plane as the will of God. In reality, by this ill-considered act, they had passed sentence upon themselves. The man who believed for one mad moment in the absolute judgement of his will found himself condemned to lose control over it: 'For what else is man's misery but his own disobedience to himself?'[51] The tearing of the will would be man's gravest penalty for sin. The punishment inflicted on Adam and Eve became a frailty of nature for humanity thereafter:

> How happy, then, were our first parents, neither troubled by any distur-
> bance of mind nor pained by any disorder of the body! And the whole
> universal fellowship of mankind would have been just as happy, had our
> first parents not committed that evil deed whose effect was to be transmit-
> ted to their posterity, and if none of their stock had sown in wickedness
> what they must reap in damnation.[52]

What was this damaged will, which wrested man from himself? It was a veritable interior schism. This disorder of the will, which became the lasting weakness of humanity after the Fall, Augustine named the 'carnal will' (voluntas carnalis). The carnal will did not only represent the desires of the flesh, the sexual lust provoked by bodily excitement. That would be too simple. Rather, the carnal will was the source of concupiscence, encompassing all the impetuses of the soul which had their source in the flesh. Yet, according to the reading provided by the apostle Paul, which Augustine followed scrupulously here, the flesh was not the body, nor even simply bodily matter; it was anything that distanced man from God and from the spirit. In this way, Augustine constructed a duality right at the core of man's will: the carnal will was set against the spiritual will. Augustine's Manichaean past can be sensed here: in his youth, he believed in a natural dualism of the body and the soul. In order to escape this sort of accusation, Augustine stressed that the body was not the origin of sin, and that the desires which riddled it indeed came from the soul. Moved by the will, it was the soul that was responsible for sin, and not the body. The duality of the will, torn between the flesh and the spirit, constituted a terrible punishment for the sons of Adam. Mortifying the body would never suffice to liberate man from sin and temptation, since the origin of evil was within the soul itself.

Man's curse thus became a rift in his nature, felt in the very depths of the soul, indeed within the will itself. The body was only a vessel which supported and amplified the impulses of the carnal will. What of the emotions within this confusion? Set at the heart of the will, they too were caught up in this storm. In this way, and despite several detours,

Augustine came to concur with the Stoics that the emotions had the power to disturb. For Augustine, however, it was not emotion in and of itself that was the problem, but any emotion which arose from the carnal will. The Bishop of Hippo called any form of desire and any impulse of the soul directed towards the flesh 'concupiscence'. Yet since emotions often arose within the core of the will, since they were intimately joined to the body and its humours, and finally, since they depended on exterior temptations, they were in a way the weak point of man's will. Emotions were the soul in its most fragile form.

This reversal might seem dramatic. Doubtless it was presaged by the many centuries of philosophical heritage which identified the emotions with the passions and the passions with a disorder of the soul: this could not be so easily erased. If Augustinian concupiscence, understood as a disturbance of the will, was the slave of the flesh and of matter, was it not simply a metamorphosis of ancient passion, adapted to the doctrinal context of Christianity? For the Christian theologians, man could not have been marred by such a frailty of nature at creation. Rather he became that way, incurring a self-inflicted punishment by an act of disobedience whose consequences he did not understand.

The Christian man of the Middle Ages was born with and lived with this legacy of the Fall. Hardened by the ancient suspicion towards emotions, the temptation for clerics to judge them by the yardstick of the menace of sin would be great. Even if emotions were of a morally neutral nature, the curse which weighed upon them seemed to incline them more naturally towards the carnal will than the spiritual, since they were related to the body and initial impulses. Thus it was right to submit the passions to the mind, 'so that they may be moderated and bridled and turned to righteous use', as Augustine wrote.[53] It should not be forgotten, however, that original sin now conditioned man's entire nature: it had an effect as much on his thoughts as his feelings.

A new order of humanity

In order to better understand the meaning of the new emotional ambivalence created by Latin Christianity, and above all to measure how far the emotions defined the contours of a new anthropology, it is instructive to focus on the moment when the primordial couple, Adam and Eve, were chased from paradise and assumed their new moral and emotional condition. Given his lasting and considerable influence over medieval religious culture, Augustine again serves well as a guide. Indeed, he devoted over half of Book XIV of *The City of God*, the very place where the passions were discussed, to the emotions of Adam and Eve. Did they feel passions in paradise prior to the Fall? How did their sin engender disorder among the emotions? And above all, how could a new humanity be redefined after this sin?

Medieval preachers incessantly reminded their audiences of original sin's dramatic consequences for humanity. For the theologians who considered this new state of man, it should not be forgotten that there was a corollary question that was even more crucial than that of his punishment: how, after the Fall, should salvation be sought? To respond to this essential question, one had first to establish the diagnosis (what had man lost in being chased from paradise?) before envisaging a cure (how could it be restored?). As seen, for Augustine an important part of the punishment (which he placed on the same level as mortality) took the form of concupiscence, a generalized disorder of the will which was particularly apparent in the lusts of the flesh. But Augustine did not forget that, in the story of Genesis, an emotion accompanied this disturbance: shame, which he called *pudor*, modesty, or *verecundia*, reserve.[54] This simultaneous emergence of lust and shame was crucial. For shame, despite its painful character, was not part of the penalty but rather one of the conditions of redemption. If Adam and Eve felt ashamed of their nudity after the Fall, it was because they received the capacity to discern good from evil at the same time as suffering the punishment of concupiscence. It was by an emotion that they became aware of the gravity of their act and its consequences (see Figure 1).

The shame that came with taking stock of the Fall was clearly painful, but it was also an extraordinary gift from God. For the fallen man, this gift of shame was the sign that God had not abandoned him. The mantle of shame now counterbalanced the loss of the mantle of grace. The equivalence between the two was not self-evident, since nothing could efface the catastrophe of the Fall: nevertheless it allowed for a sense of continuity within human nature. Without the shame he felt over his indecency, Adam could not even have understood what he had done. The consequences of this would have been appalling, since he would have been a slave to his desires without ever knowing it, and lacked hope of redemption as result.

Shame was thus the first emotion felt by man alongside his concupiscence: it was through them that he entered into this new humanity, that of the terrestrial city. Feeling shame was at once humanity's last line of defence (he who had no shame had lost his humanity entirely) and the first moment of entry into it (it was through shame that the entire journey of redemption began). A similar idea had coloured Greek thought since Plato. Shame was an assistant of sorts to reason, as can be seen, for instance, in Galen: 'But you must be ashamed of yourself and pay special heed to him who says: "Of all things, be most ashamed of yourself".'[55]

28

Augustine explicitly gave shame and modesty the same function in relation to concupiscence: in the face of anger, man could always rely on his
will, but against concupiscence, his first weapons were shame and
modesty, the latter being the fear of shame.

Medieval societies were deeply marked by a culture of honour. Within
them, the Christian acculturation of shame would remain a central value
in the fight against sin, whether in the guise of the remorse required for
penitence and thus for the redemption of faults, or the preventative forms
of reserve and modesty, which were supposed to prevent vice through
fear of embarrassment.[56] It should not be forgotten that Augustine,
having set human emotions in a spin, immediately turned to an emotion
to give new hope to the fallen creature – even if, at this stage of history,
the emotion chosen had to be one of sorrow. This was no chance coin-
cidence. At the very moment when he placed the rift of the Fall at the
heart of man's most spontaneous emotions – which struck so rapidly that
they inclined the will towards the flesh – he cited another emotion,
shame, as defining the first phase of man's attempt to reconquer himself.
After the Fall, the emotional part of man was enfeebled by the weight
of concupiscence, just as he was made frail in every faculty by the stain
of sin. Nevertheless, that same emotional part conserved its cognitive
and moral function, and its ambivalence. Centuries later, Bernard of
Clairvaux (d. 1153) would still reference these Augustinian terms: after
his sin, Adam had lost the *posse non turbari*, the capacity to remain
untroubled by the sting of evil passions.[57] Nevertheless, through the
combined force of grace and his free will, he conserved intact the *posse
non peccare*, his capacity not to sin. Whether it be in judgement, introspection, or prayer, emotions were called upon to play a decisive role in
individual destinies.

The Bible, especially the New Testament, gave too much weight
to the emotions for the encounter between pagan cultural heritage and
the Scriptures to have passed without friction. Judging them from the
derogatory perspective of 'passion' alone, the philosophers saw the emotions as shackling the calm use of reason, the mother of wisdom. Yet
conversely, the Gospels placed emotions at the foundations of the new
Christian religion, love most of all, but also compassion for Christ's suffering on the cross. During late antiquity, these Gospel accounts became
the basis of theology. From then on, the name of God himself was Love.
By the power of a sentiment, humanity was saved. Nevertheless, Christian intellectuals did not break with philosophical tradition: rather they
inflected and adapted Greek heritage. They not only critiqued it, but
integrated it into a new vision of man, where 'passions' became 'affects'
and had a clear role to play at the very heart of the rational soul: they

were placed in close contact with the intellect. Even if the disruptive whirlwind that followed in the wake of original sin obscured hopes for a total reconciliation of emotion and reason, Christianity had defined new anthropological and religious contours in which emotional power was the centre of gravity for each man's destiny, between heaven and earth, spirit and matter, virtue and vice. The Christian man of the Middle Ages would be emotional, or he would be nothing at all!

— 2 —

THE CITY OF DESIRE: THE
MONASTIC LABORATORY

The first Christian centuries laid the foundations for a new philosophy of affectivity. At first in the East, and then, from the fifth century, in the West, it was the monks who questioned, experienced, adapted, and felt the contradictions of the Christian emotional universe. As part of their spiritual quest, ascetics drew Christian affective and ethical thought together through constant introspection. In the context of both the individual bond with God and the relationships between monks, the exploration of affectivity possessed a dimension at once spiritual and psychological within monastic communities. At a time when the emotional soul came to be seen as the true nature of man – or at least its essential component – his relationship with the body found new expressions.

The desert: from the care of the body to the care of the soul

The Christian ascetic adventure began in the first century, in the deserted plains and valleys of Egypt and Syria. It was there, between the end of the third and the fifth century, that those models of monastic life that would so greatly influence both Eastern and Western monasticism were elaborated. It was there too that the first mythical and historical heroes of monasticism lived: St Anthony (d. *c.* 356), who spearheaded the movement of withdrawal to the desert, as well as secondary figures such as Pacomius (d. 346), Poemen (d. *c.* 450), and the great thinker of monastic anthropology, Evagrius of Pontus (d. 399).

To grasp the radical ethos of these first monks, we must immerse ourselves in the sights and sounds of this austere and fascinating world. At first sight, desert monasticism appears organized around very down-to-earth preoccupations, far removed from any emotional sophistication.

31

In an age where all of Egypt beyond the fertile Nile valley region was threatened by famine, the late antique ascetics who retired to the desert – most often peasants – decided to pursue their heroic combat in the most hostile regions: it was an almost inhuman world.[1] Reading the *Apophthegmata*, the *Lausiac History*, or the *History of the Monks in Egypt*, those origin stories which served as a mirror for Western monasticism throughout the Middle Ages, their recommendations concerning the emotions appear rather paradoxical. The 'teachings of the ancients', which form the core of the Desert Fathers' corpus, consist of short exemplary stories: most often organized under the names of their protagonists, they recount the virtues and actions of the most famous monks. In this context, the fantasies brought about by the demons that haunted them are related to the needs of the body, and above all to earthly nourishment, all the more of an obsession given the extreme aridity of these regions.

The *History of the Monks in Egypt* often shows much more interest in the pilfering of vegetables and the miraculous increase of food than with reflections on the affective and spiritual life. The renunciation of the world represented a rejection of social constraints that was bound up with a battle against bodily needs: that battle could only be won with the help of an appropriate lifestyle, the ascetic life. A monk of the *Lausiac History* expressed this most strikingly when asked how his aged body could cope with the heat of the desert: 'It kills me, I kill it.'[2] Killing the body – its needs being the most pressing – was the major concern.

This was the origin of the spiritual and affective practice of mourning, which would define the monastic atmosphere for many centuries to come. This meditation on death was called *pénthos* in Greek monasticism, and signified both mourning and tears. Rendered in Latin as *luctus*, the term conserved all of this ambivalence. Numerous vignettes show monks in mourning; one was expected 'to mortify all the desires of the flesh', according to the injunction of St Paul (Col. 3: 5, Eph. 2: 3).[3] Mourning became the ideal state for the soul of an ascetic, to the point where the life of a monk represented a life of mourning.[4] Some constructed tombs close to their cells, where they could grieve for their sins[5] and constantly remind themselves of death. The monastic path of conversion thus found its form and its force amid an emotional fervour. The retreat from worldly concerns was accompanied by very harsh corporal penances, which led to the opening of the soul to the spiritual world: in the monks' desire to lead 'lives pleasing to God', they vigorously 'subjected their own bodies'.[6] To be a perfect monk was to be pure spirit, and to hope for deliverance from bodily torture through this transformation. In later centuries, the medieval monks of the West still cited an adage attributed to Jerome: a monk was 'he who mourned', *is qui luget.*

The monk mourned for mankind, condemned to mortality as a consequence of sin; he mourned for Christ, the Saviour of humanity, tortured on the cross; and at the same time, he mourned the delights and riches of the world he had left behind. The horizons of this penitential progression stretched far beyond the individual: by mourning his past faults, the ascetic grieved for the sins of humanity as a whole.

The emotional anthropology of the desert placed the soul a great distance above the body. It was riddled with seemingly uncompromising currents that incited monks to either subdue the body or to punish it discerningly. The dualism of this conception was moderated by the idea of a reciprocal influence between the body and soul. If the monk had to work on his spirit above all else, he could only do so within the limits of his body. For some, this work implied a moderation that was even more emotional than it was dietary. Their prescriptions directly linked corporal regimes with spiritual and emotional states. In good health, the monk was to abstain from superfluity. If he was sick or sad, he could supplement his regime, and use food as a remedy, albeit still avoiding all 'things harmful where the soul is concerned – things such as anger, envy, vainglory, torpor, backbiting, and unreasonable suspicion'.[7]

When the emotions appear in these texts, they are thus integrated within the spiritual regime of the monks and defined as good or evil, as pertaining to the life of salvation or to perdition. When confronted by emotions that they deemed harmful, they looked to 'the fruits of those who direct their lives with reason and knowledge': 'charity, joy, peace, patience, benignity, goodness, and longanimity'.[8] The list of vices and virtues, which would become the beacons of inner life and Christian society, began to take shape. In his daily combat against himself, the monk could be pulled between thoughts and emotional desires that were either salutary or carnal. If he was primarily a solitary, he had to constantly examine what it was within him that drew him towards virtue and pushed him towards vice. All attachment to the world, whether real or merely a matter of intent, had to be limited, and perhaps even banned or demonized. This was especially the case when it came to women, who were seen as instigators of 'bad thoughts' or demonic incarnations.[9] On the other hand, in communities that were still largely informal, the relationships between brothers were both marked by emotional concerns and little codified. The harmonious community directed towards salvation replaced a corrupt society riddled with tensions. Disciples and spiritual masters often lived apart and saw each other rarely; some journeyed great distances to consult a highly respected master. Effusive scenes could then be witnessed. Upon receiving their visitors, the elders became overjoyed: they embraced them and washed their feet, a memento of Christ washing the feet of his apostles. The affectionate relationship between the elder and his disciple was exempt from any suspicion of emotional distraction. The elder, solidly grounded in a life of virtue, was the spiritual guide of the more novice monk in his battle against sin. While mourning and affliction reigned in their day-to-day solitude, their meetings were bathed in an atmosphere of emotional communion, physical proximity, trust, and confidence.

The bad thoughts of Evagrius of Pontus

Evagrius of Pontus was an atypical figure in this desert world.[10] An intellectual among the peasant monks of the Kellia (the 'Cells'), he structured the spiritual and affective teachings of the earliest age of monasticism.[11] Strongly influenced by Stoicism, his reflections on the passions were rooted in the Platonic anthropology of renunciation, tending towards *apatheia* and detachment. Imported into the West by John Cassian (d. *c.* 435), his doctrine became a counterpoint to the more moderate theory of affectivity promoted by Augustine.[12]

For Evagrius, the monk had to reach towards God through *apatheia*, a detachment from the passions. He thus became a gnostic, a man who sought spiritual knowledge and could climb the rungs of contemplation to reach a purity of prayer and the sight of divine light.[13] Likewise, the monk who sought virtue had first to defeat his body through practice (*praktike*), to fight off the demons who attacked him in the passionate part of his soul, and allow only the rational portion – which could also be attacked – to be stimulated.[14] At the end of this battle, the intellectual part of the human soul – the direct extension of his originally created spirit – could unite with God through knowledge.[15] In order to reach God, whose nature was incorporeal and immaterial, the monk had to purify himself and rid his spirit of any images and preconceptions: Evagrius spoke of a 'meditation on death and a flight from the body', aimed at 'separating soul from body'.[16]

This vision of mourning lent a deep meaning to monastic practice. Emotions and passions had to be left behind. This was the object of the three ascetic tracts of Evagrius – *Exhortations to Monks*, the *Treatise on Practical Life*, and the *Gnostikos*. In these, the author studied the strategies and tactics of demons, whose weapons were 'bad thoughts', the first stirrings of passion: when consented to, they led to vices. For Evagrius, passion appears first and foremost as a negative thought. The 'bad thoughts' were eight in number, and the vices derived from them appear to be demons personified: gluttony, fornication, greed, sorrow, anger, sloth, vainglory, and pride, presented always in that order. Thoughts and demons attacked specific parts of the soul: gluttony and fornication the concupiscible part, sorrow and anger the irascible part.

Sloth, the monastic evil *par excellence*, stood out: this disgust for God and oneself was inspired by the 'noontide demon', itself an invention of Evagrius, and attacked the entire soul. The origins of the 'deadly sins' can be found here. Later fixed to seven in number by Gregory the Great (d. 604), they were a subject that medieval literature would greatly expand upon.[17]

According to Evagrius, bad thoughts were only the roots of these passions, and the monk could prevail against them: 'Whether or not all these thoughts trouble the soul is not within our power; but it is for us to decide if they are to linger within us or not and whether or not they stir up the passions.'[18] It was thus consent that created vice or the passion identified with it. Evagrius took account both of the relationship between thoughts, representations, and passions and of the relationship between what was sensed/felt and man's affective and spiritual interior.[19] In doing so, he posed some fundamental questions that would flow through monastic psychology for centuries thereafter. For instance, was 'it the representation that set the passions in motion, or the passions that set the representation in motion'?[20]

> Sadness sometimes occurs through the frustration of one's desires, or sometimes it follows closely upon anger. When it is through the frustration of one's desires, it occurs in this way. When certain thoughts gain the advantage, they bring the soul to remember home and parents and one's former life. And when they observe that the soul does not resist but rather follows right along and disperses itself among thoughts of pleasures, then with a hold on it they plunge it into sadness with the realization that former things are no more and cannot be again because of the present way of life. And the miserable soul, the more it allowed itself to be dispersed among the former thoughts, the more it has now become hemmed in and humiliated by these latter ones.[21]

The question and its response illustrate the richness of Evagrius' reflections. This passage suggests a vision of the soul that was both material and personified, and which could delight in pleasure, follow thought-demons, and expose itself to exterior influence. This description of 'bad' sorrow – which was opposed, in the Christian world, to the 'sorrow that is according to God' that St Paul (2 Cor. 7: 10) had defined – brings together a range of affective states and emotions: desire, pleasure, frustration, dejection, and the feeling of humiliation. The analysis of anger, in the subsequent chapter of the work, fleshes out these emotional mechanisms:

> Anger is a passion that arises very quickly. Indeed, it is referred to as a boiling over of the irascible part and a movement directed against one who

has done injury or is thought to have done so. It renders the soul furious all day long, but especially during prayers it seizes the mind and represents to it the face of the one who has hurt it. Sometimes when this goes on for a while and turns into resentment, it provokes disturbances at night accompanied by wasting and pallor of the body, as well as the attacks of venomous wild beasts. One could find these four signs that follow upon resentment accompanying numerous thoughts.[22]

Attentive to its signs and bodily effects, Evagrius described anger as both a thought and a passion. Far from being opposed, thought and emotion are here indistinct, as if fused in the dynamism of the soul. He likewise analysed the action of anger on the soul (the irascible part was affected), its bodily effects (troubled sleep, pallor), its interior manifestations (a boiling feeling, demonic assaults), and its transformation over time (into resentment). Further on, he explained that anger brought on the thought of fornication, which in turn impeached the purity of prayer and gave birth to sloth, the most pernicious of vices.[23]

Without being exhaustive, Evagrius' 'treatise on the passions' was coherent and outlined a true regime of emotional medicine. At this founding moment, when monasticism began to systematically reflect on the emotions, the 'natural' line between emotions and thoughts promoted by ancient thinkers was maintained, but also moralized within a Christian framework. The remedies to the eight bad thoughts could only be found in practice, above all in the daily routines of the monastic life. Evagrius aligned these works with the three parts of the soul drawn from Platonism: 'When the mind wanders, reading, vigils, and prayer bring it to a standstill. When desire bursts into flame, hunger, toil, and anachoresis extinguish it. When the irascible part becomes agitated, psalmody, patience, and mercy calm it.'[24] Elsewhere, he prescribed emotional remedies: 'Anger and hatred increase irascibility, but compassion and gentleness diminish even that which is present.'[25] The virtues, defined as spiritual works and presented in a chain, could also be reinforced through bodily and affective works:

> The fear of God, my child, strengthens faith, and abstinence in turn strengthens fear of God, and perseverance and hope render abstinence unwavering, and from these is born impassibility of which love is the offspring; love is the door to natural knowledge, which is followed by theology and ultimate blessedness.[26]

Evagrius thus offered a clear theory of asceticism – harsh yet optimistic – in which emotional labour went hand-in-hand with physical, intellectual, and spiritual exercises. Distanced from some of the material concerns of existence, the monk had to train the passionate parts of his soul to gain the tranquillity of *gnosis*. Even if the ascetic regime was almost unbearably harsh, victory was possible. Freed from passions, he could devote himself to the most rational part of his soul, the intellect, before finally uniting with God.

Cassian and the foundations of community: from charity to virtuous friendship

It was John Cassian who armed nascent Western monasticism with its spiritual weapons at the start of the fifth century. He compiled his *Institutes* (*c.* 420–4), then his *Conferences* (*c.* 426–8) after having spent time in the Egyptian desert at the end of the fourth century, most notably at Kellia, where he was part of Evagrius' circle. When he arrived at Marseille around 415, he already benefited from significant prestige and quickly became a person of the greatest importance in the Provençal church. His texts, written in Latin from the outset, disseminated the Egyptian ascetic programme. *The Institutes* are divided into two major parts: the first focuses on the regulation of the daily life of the monk (habit, offices, behaviour); the second develops the teaching of Evagrius on the eight thoughts. Cassian conserved their order, but the 'thoughts' became 'vices': indeed, they were now the principal vices, *principalia vitia*. They no longer preceded sin, but were its very essence. He dedicated a book to each: gluttony, fornication, greed, anger, sorrow, sloth, vainglory, and pride.

The sins were thus directly linked to emotion, in a manner that would smooth the monastic encounter with Augustinian anthropology that would eventually occur.[27] In his *Conferences*, Cassian often returned to the eight principal sins – they are in fact the subject of the fifth Conference – and to the difficulties of the spiritual life. Monastic virtues were the remedy, and charity above all. For Cassian, bodily and spiritual conversion was also a conversion of the emotions: the three elements (corporeal, spiritual, and affective) were inextricably linked. In *The Institutes*, he described joining a monastery as becoming dead to the world, a spiritual crucifixion which called for progressive renunciation. First came disregard for the exterior world, then for oneself and for the vices, and finally for all elements of the visible world.[28] The author classified the vices by whether they required the body (i.e. gluttony and luxury) or not (pride and vainglory); and also by whether their origin was internal (sorrow, sloth/idleness) or external (greed, anger).[29]

Cassian reflected equally on the mobility of thoughts, on the distractions which stopped the soul from maintaining a steady focus on God during prayer and reading.[30] When he discussed concupiscence and nocturnal pollutions, he appears concerned over the mastery of the body, sexuality, and, most especially, intra-communal affection between men. He described monastic renunciation as a painful but healing process, after which affectivity would be given over to spirituality and could play a greater role on the path towards salvation.[31] Cassian likewise proposed a severe version of asceticism. But he was also optimistic regarding the monk's capacity to achieve affective conversion. Once unmoved by the exterior world, he who attained spiritual perfection would be filled with a new sensitivity of divine origin, expressed by the gift of tears.[32] At the end of the journey, the soul would be steeped in love, in divine charity.[33] This conversion of the heart was not an outpouring, but a heroic feat. The ascetic was an athlete: well-disciplined emotional strength was one of his weapons on the road to victory.

Cassian was in complete accord with Evagrian tradition when he stated that charity was also key to social relationships. In the Conference dedicated to friendship,[34] he discussed a theme seemingly distant from his usual preoccupation with the 'spirituality of combat'.[35] In a text not only directed at monks but also at a wider audience, Cassian gave friendship an essential role in consolidating, and even founding, the monastic estate.[36] He distinguished three types of friendship. The varieties derived from kinship and self-interest were rejected as illusory due to their amorality (they drew no distinction between the good and the wicked) and above all their instability. True friendship, the only stable kind, was found where the individual learned to persevere in virtue with the aid of another.[37] Monks and converts were encouraged to lean on friends, who would help them progress in their fight against the passions. To describe how virtuous friendship operated, Cassian referenced the two levels of monastic life defined by Evagrius.[38] The first level corresponded to the ascetic journey, the second to the state of perfection attained by those who had gained steady virtue and a steady will. These latter were steadfast in their work of renunciation, that condition of stability so dear to Cassian. This stability was not a state of ecstatic inactivity but of ascetic discovery, of constant introspection.

Cassian returned to the first objective of the ascetic: the extirpation of the soul's disorderly tendencies, the crushing of all sensual appetites – in other words, the quest for *apatheia*.[39] Whether in the monastic context or otherwise, friendship thus served that fundamental objective of Stoic inspiration, the weight of which was so well known in the Eastern tradition:

> Just as nothing is to be preferred to love, nothing is to be esteemed less than anger. For everything, however beneficial and necessary it may appear, should nonetheless be put aside in order to avoid the disturbance of anger, and everything that may seem inimical should be put up with and tolerated

in order to maintain unharmed the tranquillity of love and peace, for it must be believed that nothing is more destructive than anger and annoyance and nothing more beneficial than love.[40]

According to Cassian, one could not even set aside the first interior pangs of emotion: 'the interior man may not be disturbed even silently within itself at the blow dealt the exterior man'.[41] In order to seek a perfect self-mastery, 'it is not merely the thing itself which is done but also the character of the mind and the intention of the doer that must be looked at'.[42] In the face of this challenge, monastic friendship played the role of a tutor throughout the journey. From the disciplinary and normative dimension, it was necessary for peace and cloistral harmony, but also for the tranquillity of the soul. Thus, even if eremitic solitude remained the ultimate spiritual horizon, friendship became the conduit of its own perfection.

This horizontal relationship, which one might call natural friendship, took part in the vertical strategy, individual and collective, of the quest for salvation. It was a crucible that functioned similarly to the cloister: within it, the tranquillity of the soul and the spirit of charity could be maintained and expanded in the expectation of ultimate spiritual perfection. Cassian gave a name to the fruit of this virtuous, peaceful, and charitable practice of friendship which perfected the ascetic path: it was *diathesis* – *affectio* in Latin. We translate this here as affection, but it carried the same meaning as *affectus*. In the context of this reflection, he related *agapè/caritas* with *diathesis/affectio*, the latter specifically conceived of here as the enjoyment of virtuous friendship:

> It is possible for this love, then, which is called *agapè*, to be shown to all. The blessed Apostle says about it: 'Therefore, while we still have time, let us do good to all, but especially to the household of the faith' (Gal. 6: 10). So much is it the case that it must be shown to all in general that we are commanded by the Lord to bestow it even on our enemies. For he says: 'Love your enemies' (Matt. 5: 44). But *diathesis*, or affection, is shown to very few, to those who are linked by a similarity of behaviour and by the fellowship of virtue.[43]

Moreover, the affection of friendship displayed the quintessence of charity, drawing from it the force of desire and attachment that went beyond any moral imperative. For Cassian, this purified affection explained the attachment of Jacob to his son Joseph, of Jesus to his favourite disciple John, and even of bride to bridegroom in the Song of Songs.[44] Cassian drew from that biblical poem to advance the semantic ties between *affectio*, *amicitia*, and *caritas*:

39

It is singled out as something sublime inasmuch as it is set apart not by an odious comparison but by the overflowing favour of a most abundant love. Such is also what we read in the Song of Songs in the person of the bride, when she says: 'Set in order love in me' (Song 2: 4). For this is a properly ordered love which, while hating no one, loves certain persons more by reason of their good qualities. Although it loves everyone in a general way, nonetheless it makes an exception for itself of those whom it should embrace with a particular affection. And, again, among those who are highest and chiefest in this love it chooses for itself some who are set apart from the others by an extraordinary affection.[45]

The identification of friendship with a charity ordered by affection was thus the outcome of this Conference, which concluded by inverting its guiding principles. The ascetic phase of amicable practice in fact served to tame the danger such sensitivity posed to the tranquillity of the soul and the peace of the monastery. With this tranquillity acquired, the stability that was so longed for could be maintained at both an individual and communal level by another form of energized sensitivity, which itself became an ordering power: pacified affection was in turn rendered a support to peace. Thus, in the teaching of Cassian, which bridged the monastic cultures of East and West, the mutual model of virtuous friendship became a strategy for spiritual perfection. It was relevant to the Church as a whole, but monastic life constituted its privileged setting. His thought was distinct from Augustine, for whom virtuous apathy was an illusion. For this reason, Cassian's cautious approach to friendship – a friendship that was the province of the wise alone – remained a minority viewpoint for a long time to come. It would only find success from the twelfth century onward, when a synthesis between the two conceptions would arise.

Affective conversion in Western monasticism

Monastic norms for converting the emotions

The monasticism that arose from the desert was the province of small, isolated ascetic groups and of semi-anchorites. Both the harshness of the solitary life, found in retreat from society or even revolt against it,[46] and the sparseness of their interactions, often reduced to weekly liturgical celebrations, allowed for strong emotional expressions. It was a fitting accompaniment to the burning intensity of their spiritual lives. The hermits of the desert were entirely consumed by their personal, material, emotional, and spiritual lives, far more than by their relationships

with others. These characteristics were again visible during the formative era of Western monasticism – the fourth and fifth centuries – a
period for which the sources are rare. There, the monastic experience
seems defined by charismatic figures who often appear unsettled and
transient. This impression is even stronger given that the 'renouncers',
as they were called, were perceived by surrounding society, especially
in the towns, as bizarre and subversive individuals who rejected the
social order.[47]

Since ascetics caused concern to bishops or even menaced the authority
of the Church, it was through the instigation and initiative of bishops
that monastic legislation began to take shape, first in the East, then in
the West.[48] Among the first original texts of this sort written in Latin
was a rule of instructions written by Augustine – his *Praeceptum* (*c.*
395–400) – which went on to enjoy enormous influence.[49] A series of
further rules, mostly short and largely composed in Gaul and Italy
between the end of the fourth and the seventh centuries, document the
formation of a cenobitic monasticism still strongly influenced by Eastern
Christian asceticism.[50] An aristocratic phenomenon in the era of St
Martin (d. 397), monasticism expanded rapidly; it was popularized in
the fifth century and even more so in the sixth. Communal institutions
became unavoidable; each monastery put regulations in place, combining
both old and new material. Rules thus proliferated in the fifth and sixth
centuries. It was in this context that Benedict of Nursia (d. *c.* 547),
fashioning a synthesis from preceding monastic traditions, wrote a rule
for his new monastic foundation at Monte Cassino.

Above all else, these Western rules relate to the organization of material and liturgical life: the conditions of entry into the community, discipline, clothing, and food occupy a fundamental place within them,
alongside the daily routine of the monks. The explicit regulation of
affectivity found little place within them, unless it was a matter of some
or other practical consideration concerning daily life. Emotions appear
in the passages which discuss vices and virtues, and again in those concerning the mastery of the body. Monasticism indeed had very much
higher ambitions in these domains than most social norms. From the
emotional point of view, the separation for the monk from his earlier life
was the fundamental element: becoming a monk meant a change of
affective community. Contacts with their family were reduced to a
minimum, and those with women totally banned. In his *Precept*, Augustine devoted long passages to the possibility of brothers and women
exchanging gazes, and sanctioned this severely. The gaze, perceived as a
conveyor of sensuality, became an object of grave suspicion, since it was
thought to reveal carnal and emotional leanings and act as a vehicle for
the 'exchange of hearts':

41

Even if your gaze chances to fall on a woman, you should not stare at her. There is no rule forbidding you to see women when you go out, but to attract or encourage their attention is wrong (Matt. 5: 28). Nor is it only by touch and strong feelings that desire (*concupiscentia*) for women is aroused but also by the way of looking. You cannot claim to have pure minds if you have impure eyes, for an impure eye is the messenger of an impure heart. When impure hearts exchange messages by their glances, even though the tongue remains silent, and when through wrong desire they take pleasure in each other's ardour, then chastity takes flight from their behaviour even though there has been no despoiling of the body.[51]

The idea that the gaze was the gateway of the soul was likewise cited in the *Rule of Virgins* of Caesarius of Arles (d. 543), who was Abbot of Lérins before becoming a bishop in 503.[52] It endured throughout the Middle Ages. For Augustine, the warning aimed to hold back the emotional and moral danger found outside the community. The only passage in the *Praeceptum* concerning brothers in interaction with each other which explicitly describes potentially dangerous relationships underlines that 'you are to love one another with a spiritual rather than an earthly love'.[53] The converts had to turn themselves entirely towards God. This injunction called for a grave soul, in line with the spirit of mourning fostered by the desert monks. The *Rule of the Master*, and that of Benedict, likewise prescribe a tearful seriousness for their monks.[54]

In the monastic context, joy could only be directed towards God. Monks were solitaries who lived in a community: they were thus not to distract each other. Idle chatter, joking, and laughing, all of which were noisy, betrayed an impure heart and carnal weakness. From this period onward, such displays would be considered as contrary to the spirit of the Scriptures.[55] By the era of Benedict, monastic rules had already subjected them to increasingly explicit revile. Under the heading of banned habits came any affectionate act that might allow the monks to form bonds with each other, whether of friendship or of love. Many rules stated that holding hands or sleeping on the same mattress were bad behaviour. According to the Rule of Benedict, each monk had to have his own bed, and the young were placed in the dormitory among the oldest and most veteran in monastic life, who were thought to be the most incorruptible.[56] The affection of monks was directed towards heaven; personal relationships between brothers were subordinated firstly to their devotion, and then to the interests of the community, which commanded that all monks receive equal treatment. In his *Rule of Nuns*, Caesarius of Arles likewise made clear that the election of the superior could not be influenced by the affection that one might have for them, but only by their capacity to lead. The sisters also had to avoid becoming godmothers so that they would not be obliged to care for children.[57] From this point on, the vertical reorientation of affectivity would always play a part in conversion, in breaking away from the world, and in devotion. Monastic affectivity was encompassed by a relationship with God that was built through prayer and penitence, even if the way this was expressed would vary: while visible and obvious in the *Rule of the Master*, for Benedict it was silent and contemplated in prayer.

In these monastic rules, the spiritual relationship between the individual and God became the very condition of the horizontal bond between brothers that was subordinated to it. 'Sorrow that is according to God' and spiritual mourning, made physical through tears, were required in the monastery to avoid impudent laughter, useless chatter, and the other little pleasures of daily life. Joy, spiritual by definition, could have no other cause or purpose than God, whether it resounded in the individual soul or spread throughout the monastery, reflected on the face of every monk. Emotional acts were defined as corresponding to the ethical divide between vices and virtues, as has already been seen with Evagrius and Cassian. Anger could not last: forgiveness had to follow before nightfall at the latest, since 'no one should dare go to bed in anger'.[58] Gluttony, mud-slinging, or – worse still – hatred had no place in the monastery, which was perceived as an ideal community bonded by charity, humility, patience, and respect for others. Reflecting this ideal, a certain gentleness of tone predominated in the rules of Gaul and Italy and presaged the success of the Rule of Benedict. The love joining the monk to God was placed to the fore, personified in the abbot who was to be at once charitable, tender, and severe, the father of the community and the representative of God in the monastery.[59] Charitable love was here presented as the cement of the community.[60]

The two rules of the celebrated Irish monk Columbanus (d. 615), which had a strong influence in Gaul from the end of the sixth century up to the Carolingian reform, reflect a much more austere climate. Columbanus landed in Gaul around 591 and quickly became well known in Merovingian courts for prescribing a monastic life which simulated martyrdom.[61] His two rules, which hardly discuss the affective life of the monks, extol a very strict penitential asceticism. The fact of desiring a woman already amounted to a betrayal of God in one's heart.[62] In *The Rule of Monks*, the dichotomy of good (that which remained in an unchanged state from creation) and evil (that which had been corrupted by the devil) separates the virtues from the vices: among the latter one finds anger placed in opposition to joy.[63] The only emotions which retained a modicum of interest for Columbanus were those which enlivened the monk before God: fear and perpetual love were monastic perfections which resulted from commitment to poverty, the purging of vices, and forsaking worldly things.[64] Monks had to present themselves as zealous and joyous in their obedience to God.[65] His correspondence shows that Columbanus could be affectionate towards his monks. Only fear, however, whose model was the dread of God, was a truly positive emotion in his eyes.[66] The last chapter of the Rule perfectly encapsulates the general tone:

> Let him not do as he wishes, let him eat what he is bidden, [...] be subject to whom he does not like. Let him come weary to his bed and sleep walking, and let him be forced to rise while his sleep is not yet finished. Let him keep silence when he has suffered wrong, let him fear the superior of his community as a lord, love him as a father, believe that whatever he commands is healthful for himself.[67]

The other 'rule' of Columbanus, entitled the *Regula coenobialis* or the *Conventual Rule*, is really a penitential, a collection of provisions codifying the punishments for various sins that one could commit in the monastery. For the most part, the latter were punished by corporal penalties, fitting with the penitential spirit of Irish monasticism and justified by the fact that 'confession and penance free man from death'.[68]

In sum, the monastic humanism which developed primarily in Italy and Provence and emphasized an emotional approach to God found an opposing force in Columbanus: an austere penitential monasticism drawn from Ireland, which essentially aimed to discipline the body and showed less concern for the emotional and spiritual lives of the monks. Despite the latter's immediate success in Merovingian Gaul, the monasticism that won out in the long term was much more gentle and supple, and above all more attentive to the inner and affective life. At the beginning of the ninth century, Carolingian reform elevated the Rule of St Benedict to the rank of the sole rule in usage in the Empire; little by little, it eclipsed the other traditions. The precocious 'little' rules survived only where the Rule of Benedict cited them or occasionally showed their influence, or in later collections, such as the *codices regularum* or the *concordia regularum* of Benedict of Aniane (d. 821).[69]

Gregory the Great and sacrificial emotion

Gregory the Great was born to an aristocratic family in Rome. He had been a monk and a preacher before being elected Bishop of Rome, head of the Christian community as well as a member of the Roman elite. His writings number as some of the most widely read among the monks of the medieval West, alongside those of Augustine and Cassian. Gregory in fact proposed a sort of a synthesis between the two, adding a sacrificial and sacramental dimension of his own.

As seen, Cassian showed a profound suspicion towards emotion, which he related to the passions that distanced man from God. The affective conversion of the monk took the route of *apatheia*, of 'dispassion'. This path was not always that of an unfeeling soul. Charity, which contained an emotional aspect, was certainly compatible for him with the ideal of a total liberation from violent passions. If such emotional passions were bad, positive emotions also existed. Augustine, on the other hand, placing emphasis on the will and its frailties, saw a moral ambiguity at the very heart of emotive power. Emotions were good when they were well led, but could be bad if poorly directed. Just like Cassian, Gregory insisted upon the ascetic mastery of the emotions above all else; but at the same time, like Augustine, he extolled the necessity of their correct orientation for salvation.[70] Gregory viewed the emotions as an insidious evil which attacked man; lacking the power to eradicate them, it was necessary to control them. He took account of Cassian's list of vices, reducing them to seven thoughts (*cogitationes*). These became the seven capital sins that are encountered across the entire Middle Ages: vainglory, envy, wrath, sorrow, avarice, gluttony, and luxury. All of them were rooted in pride, *superbia*, according to Gregory.

The ascetic thought of Gregory was also tied to a pastoral perspective which impregnated his vision of man. This combination was brought to life in his *Moralia in Job*, a figure who embodied the human condition in his eyes.[71] The sufferings which were the lot of the worldly life would only find recompense in salvation. For Gregory, the duality of man, composed of a body and a soul, was in and of itself a paradox. The body, or the flesh, represented the unstable, corruptible, animal side of man. Only the soul, his spiritual part, could reach towards perfection, and only if it was governed by reason. That these two opposing realities were perfectly united in man in an interdependent and complementary relationship was a miracle of God. It left man in an ambivalent and dynamic position: the union of the soul and the body tended sometimes towards harmony, sometimes towards conflict. For Gregory, man himself became the field of unceasing battle between good and evil, the heavenly and the worldly.[72] The essential role of the ascetic process was to put an end to this psychomachia and bring peace (see Figure 2). In his role as pastor, Gregory also projected this division, unique to man, into the realm of community. From one aspect, the men of God, saints and preachers, hauled Christians up towards salvation; from another, ordinary men were drawn towards the depths by the weight of the Fall. For Gregory, the emotional dynamic he cited thus found its echo in a social dynamic conducive to salvation, with the figure of Christ at its centre. It was indeed the Incarnation and the Passion which completed this joining of the opposites: the unity of the flesh and the spirit, of the visible and the invisible. This unity, furthermore, could only come through tears, suffering, and sacrifice.

The inescapable figure of Christ the Saviour was thus placed at the centre of the temporal and symbolic architecture of the world. Man had to submit his bodily actions to reason and spiritual ends and to present his works as sacrifices to God so as to complete the unity of the carnal and the spiritual in his terrestrial life. It was possible for man to unite with God in charity through sacrifices made in his present life: the Eucharistic sacrifice of the mass, the sacrifice of good works for the good of others, and the personal, bloodless sacrifices made by Christians.[73] Like the rejection of the carnal life and the evisceration of sins, sacrifice allowed man to be purified so that he could unite with God in love. Individual acts of conversion, obedience, continence, prayer, and virtuous deeds could heal mankind through the sacrifice of Christ. They became acts of love and, more specifically, of charity.[74] Saints and men of God could thus save others by their deeds and pastoral efforts. The union of the highest and the lowest was made possible by imitating Christ, the saviour of men: the force of divine passion descended into human charity, an inclusive process Gregory described as 'the condescension of passion' (*condescensio passionis*). A celebrated reflection of his, encountered many times in his works, encapsulates these two ways of joining with God. Here, Gregory commented on a passage from the Old Testament, the description of the blessing of Achsa by her father Caleb:[75]

Achsa, the daughter of Caleb, sighed as she sat on her beast of burden. And Caleb asked her. 'What is troubling you?' She answered, 'Give me an additional gift! Since you have assigned to me land in the Negeb, give me also pools of water.' So he gave her the upper and the lower pools.

We say that Achsa sat on an ass because her soul presided over the irrational movements of her flesh. Just as she begged her father with a sigh for pools of water, so must we with deep groans obtain from our Creator the grace of tears. There are some who have received the gift of speaking out openly for justice, of defending the oppressed, of sharing their possessions with the needy, of professing their faith ardently, who still do not have the grace of tears. These we may say received 'land in the Negeb', that is, 'southern and dry land', but are completely lacking in 'pools of water'. It is of utmost importance, however, that those who are zealous for good works and devote much time to performing them should also weep over their past sins, either through fear of eternal punishment or through longing for God's kingdom.

Caleb gave Achsa the upper and lower pools. These correspond to the two kinds of compunction. The soul receives the upper pools when it weeps because of its longing for heaven; it receives the lower pools when the fear of hell causes it to break forth in tears. Actually, the lower pools are given first; then, only, the upper. Yet, since the compunction of love is greater in dignity, the upper pools were necessarily mentioned first and then the lower.[76]

The first Latin passage to mention the *gift* or *grace of tears*, this commentary shows the conjunction of the two emotional movements that joined one to God: the movement of fear, which distanced one from the world, and the movement of love, born of desire for God. The practice and theory of the spiritual path drawn from Evagrius and Cassian are present, but in an adapted form. By this clear blueprint and image, which could be seen as the origin of the notion of compunction, Gregory – to whom tradition bequeathed the title, 'doctor of compunction' – in turn placed emotion at the heart of salvation. The painful sting of sins committed allowed one to progress from the terror of judgement towards the love of God, weeping penitential tears that would wash the sin away. Converts navigated through the stages of a veritable emotional progression.[77] Emotivity found a salvifying power in the anthropology of Gregory. Emotions were still very much related to bad thoughts, but thanks to the transformative power of sacrifice, they could be sweetened and directed towards charity, towards the love of God. A new perspective here began to unfold. It made the sacrificial vision of life, and monastic life above all, the bedrock of the Gregorian image of affectivity.[78]

In establishing itself as a social practice, monasticism put in place a programme of conversion which embraced all aspects of daily life, including emotional and spiritual transformation. The conversion of the emotions fell into two anthropological and soteriological templates. On the one hand, there was the total detachment from worldly things, following the Eastern tradition. In the West, on the other hand, the mastery of the body and the emotions was emphasized, and placed within a hierarchical template where the soul was elevated far above the body.

At work in the age of the first desert ascetics, and adapted in the West during the great age of monastic legislation at the end of antiquity (fifth and sixth centuries), affective conversion was omnipresent at the beginning of the Middle Ages, even if its role varied across different texts. Over the course of the centuries discussed here, monasticism gradually found its place within society, as well as a form of life that became durable. In this form of life, a new emotional *praxis* that placed the body on the frontline played a fundamental role. The grand structures for converting the emotions were perpetuated, summarized, and developed in tools that might seem rudimentary, but which were well-known and widely disseminated by the compilations found at the end of this period.

47

Yet in order to ensure the conditions required by the members of a community for their highly elevated ethical and spiritual goal, monasticism paradoxically needed very strong grounding in society and the support of authorities. Placed in tension, this paradox animated monastic communities as much as the individuals that composed them. They fought against vice to attain virtue, and against worldly passions to come towards the love of God and charity towards their brothers: such battles shaped the daily life of the monk in this city of desire. Texts that are almost unheard of even today, such as the highly original treatises composed in the first person by Valerio of Bierzo, a seventh-century hermit from Northern Spain heavily influenced by the desert ethos, likewise bear witness to the dissemination and creative adaptation of an emotional model – born in the East and refined by the Western rules – which placed psychomachia at its core.[79]

Until the Carolingian Renaissance, monasteries often relied on a 'mixed rule', just as St Eligius advised for his monastery of Solignac. This is indeed how the rule of St Benedict came to be known in Northern Gaul.[80] Yet the monastic rules of the early Middle Ages remained tied to a tradition of regulation focused on practice and daily life, as the austere rule of St Columbanus or that of Isidore of Seville (d. 636) make clear. While there was reflection on the affective life in this age, it was more a process of reinforcement than of re-imagining; in the seventh and eighth centuries this only intensified further. These two centuries witnessed the assimilation of the Fathers' legacy, even though monasticism was implanted and disseminated in societies that were in the throes of Christianization and often prone to violence. It was with Carolingian reform that Western monasticism reached its mature state. Established over the course of four centuries, it had acquired its principal characteristics. From that point on, moreover, it began to play its part in a wider programme of reform which embraced all of society in an effort towards moral and affective conversion. A new wave of exploration and bold re-imagining of the affective and inner life thus took shape with the Carolingian Renaissance.

— 3 —

EMOTIONS FOR A CHRISTIAN SOCIETY: THE FRANKISH WORLD (FIFTH TO TENTH CENTURIES)

The early Middle Ages: a fragmented age?

When we think of emotions in the Merovingian kingdom of the Franks, the images which flash before our eyes are not far from those so masterfully painted by J. Huizinga in the *Autumn of the Middle Ages*. Theatrical emotions seem to animate its actors: they can be seen, for instance, in the well-known tale of the vase of Soissons or in the courtly intrigues which tore the Merovingian elite asunder in the sixth and seventh centuries. We are left with a fluid image, that of a society in rapid transformation, with informal powers and poorly defined frontiers, where the construction of identity was governed by Christianization and incessant internecine wars. This picture is not only fluid, but also fragmented, as much the result of the very incomplete survival of sources as the instability of polities.[1] It is doubtless one of the reasons why Barbara H. Rosenwein, author of the first work dedicated to the emotions in the Merovingian age,[2] chose the concept of 'emotional community' to help describe this world. It is a conception which allows the peculiarities of each community within a multicultural and evolving context to be taken into account and for their diversity to be thought of in terms of emotional practices, without straitjacketing this world into a grand, unitary thesis that might efface its principal traits.

What were the emotional experiences of men and women in the early Middle Ages made of? The sources most pertinent to this question are less numerous than for late antiquity or for later periods. Almost without exception, the writings of these centuries derive from clerics and monks, and were addressed to their own colleagues or members of the lay elite. Whether these very varied texts served to describe the upheavals of political life, prescribe the punishment of sinners, or transmit the norms of

49

affective conversion to the laity, their horizons and their values were already Christian. This did not prevent a great diversity in the value attributed to the emotions and the forms of communication they employed. To say that Roman, German, and Christian cultures met and combined to create a new synthesis in this era does not suffice: it is necessary to understand how far the points of reference and practice varied from one social group to another, from one generation to another, and from one region, or even one locality, to another. Rather than attempting to paint such a nuanced picture of barbarian Europe in its entirety, impossible within a single chapter, we focus here on the Frankish kingdoms.

Emotional bonds

The men and women of the early Middle Ages were *bound*: to their family and their relatives first and foremost, but also to their community or a larger social group, to their followers or to a lord, and of course to the Lord. In the *extra muros* Merovingian cemeteries of Trèves in Austrasia, 100 funeral inscriptions from the fourth to seventh centuries bear witness to familial affection and help us to reconstruct it. The dead man or woman – father, mother, son, husband, or wife – is described as *carissimus* (*-a*) or *dulcissimus* (*-a*), dearest or sweetest, and the term *charity*, that most Christian term for love, is often used.[3] Nevertheless, the use of vocabulary attesting to a Christianization of values affected different communities and regions to different degrees. At Vienne, a key Burgundian Catholic stronghold even in the age of Arianism, situated in a highly Romanized region that received Christianity early, the emotions portrayed in the epitaphs directly expressed Christian teaching on death: it was transformed into a happy episode on the road towards salvation.[4]

In this world where ties of blood and alliance mattered as much as hierarchies, emotion became the very fabric of social relationships, and even their means of expression. It was far from an interior and individual matter. Rhetorical and ethical in its expressions, emotion expressed one's place in society, or at least referred to it. Emotion confirmed and renegotiated status; it could signal both its loss and indeed the fight against that loss. Affectivity even pertained to hierarchical relationships: political loyalty and friendship had an emotional component. Passionate love was thus owed to one's king or lord; in return, the latter was to display his love for his people publicly.[5] By taking account of this entirely different positioning of affectivity, we can grasp the meaning and importance of the principal emotions which the aristocratic elite 'performed' on the social stage and which we can witness in contemporary chronicles, from that of Gregory of Tours (d. 594) through to that of Fredegar (seventh century). Men and women expressed relationships of kinship, friendship, and enmity, of submission and domination, and of alliance and rivalry by gestures of honour and shame, by demonstrations of vehement love and explosions of virulent hate, and by sardonic laughter, resounding with jealousy and anger. To understand what was at stake in these often exuberant emotions and their performance, the status of the men and women must be treated as comparable. Whether the latter were queens, concubines, or mothers, theirs was a world in which they often possessed a political role and remarkable economic autonomy, and where the public and private spheres were barely distinguishable.[6]

Amicitia/inimicitia

The obligations of familial solidarity, which found a variety of expressions in barbarian laws, shaped the contours of the most fundamental emotional relationships. To leave one's kin, it was necessary to obtain authorization from a court; conversely, this bond protected all within it, especially when affronted.[7] For example, a Frankish murderer who was unable to pay the settlement fine defined by Salic law could transfer the obligation of payment to his closest relatives by an ancient practice, the *chrenecruda*, in which he threw the ashes of his hearth onto his closest relative.[8] While this practice – and likewise the obligation it created – gradually disappeared, it nonetheless served to underline the firmness of kinship bonds, in which the maternal and paternal lines played an equal role.

Beyond this, relationships with one's closest relatives set the tone for emotional expression. Love was central. On the one hand, there was the maternal variety, sometimes judged excessive by those sons who fled from it, not to mention by the Church when it was too expressive. On the other, the deferential love owed to a father was fundamental: 'Now I must do my best to guide you in how you should fear, love, and be faithful to your lord and father, Bernard, in all things, both when you are with him and when you are apart from him', wrote Dhuoda (d. after 843), an aristocratic lady married to Bernard of Septimania (d. 844), to her eldest son William.[9]

Of course, father-son relationships were equally ambivalent. As seen in Gregory of Tours and the history of the Carolingian dynasty, they could be full of love, but also allow for rivalry. It was doubtless to minimize this major social risk that filial bonds intersected and overlapped with those of brotherhood, fealty, and friendship in so many lasting emotional relationships: all consolidated solidarity amongst men. Fealty – at once freely willed and hierarchical – was part and parcel of filial relationships but went far beyond them: it could encompass spiritual kinship (patronage) and the artificial variety (adoptions). Entrance into a relationship of fealty, essential among the Franks, was ritualized through the surrender of arms or adoption by arms. That moment set in stone a bond between equals and a filiation, founded on dependence and love, between adult men, as well as sealing a mutual alliance and peace.[10] Fraternity united siblings through horizontal bonds: it could be expanded to encompass the most distant cousins, adopted sons and companions, thus creating those groups of young men studied by Georges Duby in the feudal period.[11]

Amicitia, a freely chosen and egalitarian relationship of reciprocal support, could encompass one's favoured relatives as well as individuals beyond one's kin: it was the keystone of the Frankish socio-affective edifice. Often, it reinforced the natural and more practical bonds of *familiaritas* and *propinquitas* (familiarity and proximity): the reality of being together nurtured benevolence.[12] Friendship helped to cement the personal links begun and experienced in proximity. Aimed at stabilizing and providing a framework for a fluid society, it engaged entire families, including those on the path towards war. Contracted voluntarily by free men, the bond of friendship indeed presupposed that one could be called upon for military aid. The entire clan or kin group had to form a bloc in the event of division, enmity, or *faide* (feud), just as when celebrating a marriage. Friendship thus had both collective implications and a strong political and military tenor; these traits explain the importance of displays – accompanied by affectionate words – of giving or abandoning oneself and of peaceful intent. All these gestures underlined the honour which such a bond brought to the person who undertook it. It was confirmed at special occasions, such as banquets, where gifts of friendship were exchanged, as well as consultations, where the lord addressed himself to and relied upon his *familia*.[13] Political engagement and public demonstration together built the social and affective bond of friendship: it reinforced kinship and political alliance in a concrete manner – daily, material, and emotional – without requiring the subordinating bond of fealty.[14] This did not stop the passionate and tender language of friendship from being twisted for the purposes of flattery and sarcasm.

Bonds of local solidarity further enriched a social fabric which, by its very principles, superimposed numerous structures of peace and alliance and created many occasions for division and competition. Filiation, fraternity, friendship, and all their associated practices sketched the contours of aristocratic honour in Frankish society. These values were not only specified and recognized. They also had to be expressed publicly at feasts and rituals that brought together members of an alliance through words and gestures overflowing with emotion. To embrace one's friend, to drink, to eat, or to sleep with him was to express the symbolic gift of oneself, one's body, and one's soul in a much more profound way than through the exchange of trinkets: the intention of peace was fulfilled carnally, so to speak, before the eyes of all.

Reading the texts which recount these ostentatious gestures, one could ask what real emotional content lay within these public, political, rhetorical, and ritualized relationships. To answer this question, we must put aside the baggage of our own culture, where rituals are so often devoid of meaning, where 'ritual' might even seem to signify 'devoid of meaning'. By contrast, in the oral culture of early medieval societies, where the knowledge and production of writing was the preserve of a narrow elite and employed only within very limited fields, the entirety of social life (or close to it) was conducted through gestures and rituals. Friendships were sometimes even understood as a form of contract, of political alliance,[15] where the affectionate language used by friends played a solely rhetorical role. At first sight, sentiment, the inner life, and heartfelt engagement seem to hold a secondary place within such friendships. In the early Middle Ages, friendships spread through capillary action as the direct result of alliance treaties: they ran from kings and great men, who became 'friends' to their followers or *leudes*, all the way down to the people.[16] They served to maintain peace in a time of political instability.[17] While the friendships that are known to us were not always entirely political, the available sources greatly privilege such bonds, and not without reason: they focus almost exclusively on elite society.

Whether written to his patrons, to kings and their familiars, to his aristocratic friends or clerics, the poems of Venantius Fortunatus (d. *c.* 600/609) employ a language of fervent friendship that sometimes contains erotic accents. For instance, he compared his soul, shaken by the absence of his friend, to a sea stirred up by the wind.

> Just like the rough sea when the Eurus blows,
> without you, dear friend, my soul does not rest.
> A charming storm stirs in the bright spells of my heart
> And, moving this way and that, draws closer to you.[18]

When he addressed nuns – such as Radegund (d. 587), widow of Clothar I (d. 561), or Agnes, a young lady whom Radegund raised then installed as abbess in her convent – the poetic language of affection understandably takes on a rather pious and chaste tone:[19]

> Mother to me by honour, and delightful sister by friendship,
> whom I cherish for piety, faith, affection, and heart,
> through heavenly feeling, rather than bodily fault:
> In you I love not what the flesh desires, but the spirit.[20]

Thus, beneath those bonds that were strictly political, friendship also had an important role in the construction of networks that defined a person's social identity. It was not by chance that the rhetoric of friendship drew from the language of affection which characterized familial bonds. In letters, the vocabulary of intimacy and affection and the addresses to one's 'very dear' or 'very sweet friend' portrayed the latter to be as close as family.[21] As soon as one left the circle of one's closest relatives, kinship could no longer guarantee the security and social protection of the individual, unless it was accompanied by circles of friendship and familiarity which allowed those who were not true relatives to be classed among one's nearest and dearest. Rotrude, the sister-in-law of St Bertha of Blangy – who retired to the monastery she founded in 686 after the death of her husband Sigfrid – was described in the *vita* of Bertha as her *familiaris amica*.[22] In this way, each looked to fill out the ranks of their 'relatives and friends', whom they called 'carnal friends': 'true friendship' – as opposed to 'fleeting friendship', i.e. political friendship – bolstered the ties of kinship.[23] In order to last, political friendships in fact had to be reinforced by deeper bonds of alliance and spiritual kinship. This can be seen in the story of the two great men of the Austrasian court, Pepin the Elder (d. 640), mayor of the palace, and Arnulf (d. 640/641), Bishop of Metz and future saint, who married their children, Begga and Ansegisel: their descendants were destined to a great future.[24] Pepin and Arnulf were thus united by two distinct traditions: that of secular friendship, and that of spiritual kinship.[25] Emotional outpourings, so characteristic of ancient friendships, were also an accepted expression of male friendship in the early Middle Ages. This can be witnessed in numerous chronicles and letters. For instance, in a letter of the Austrasian duke Dinamius to an anonymous friend, written around 580, the writer reminded his correspondent of the sweet promises of his affection and expressed his heartfelt desire through sighs.[26]

Beyond the matter of whether there was any real feeling behind the rhetorical formulas of affection, a second question concerns the nature of the bond, which was often expressed in erotic terms. As passionate as it might be in its verbal and physical expressions, such friendship aroused no suspicion of homosexuality for contemporaries. Rather, it was an esteemed bond, an honourable institution within early medieval society. Beyond concrete gestures of giving one's body, the expression of affection always employed a rhetoric which brought together elements of both ancient and Christian culture. The ideal of Christian friendship, first elaborated in late antiquity, seeped into such expressions even more when the friends – or their community, world, or circle – were close to the Church and especially its monastic climes, as was the case with Venantius Fortunatus. Christian references to *caritas*, that superior and universal love, were not absent from the language of friendship: on the contrary, they cemented it.

The opposite of *amicitia* was *inimicitia*. It could engage families and even entire clans. In Frankish society, one could not maintain a friendship with the enemy of a friend: '*Amicus amicis, inimicus inimicis*' ('Friend to friends, enemy to enemies'), as the oft-repeated medieval maxim went.[27] To be the enemy of someone, and thus also of his kin, was as much of a defining social relationship as friendship. Enmity was, in the first instance, a rupture of friendship and of peace: it incited not only hostile emotions, but also fear among those who incurred this socially accepted form of anger.[28] Conflict, a short-term configuration of forces that resulted in an explosion of essentially ritualized violent action, always called for resolution. Anger, fury, envy, and hatred seem to have motivated these breaches of peace: the social necessity of avenging offended honour gave rise to forms of exchange governed by this bond of enmity. Those who renounced violence when confronted by an injury to their honour automatically incurred shame.[29]

The most famous narrative source for the age of Clovis (d. 511) and his successors is the celebrated *History of the Franks* – or more precisely, the *Ten Books of History* – written by Gregory, a Bishop of Tours who descended from a senatorial Gallo-Roman family: it provides more than one story that attests to this bond. For instance, Clovis, having plotted the betrayal of Ragnachar, king of Cambrai (d. *c.* 510?), by his army, reproached the enemy he came to capture, tie up, and at last kill through this ruse: 'Why have you dishonoured our race in letting yourself be chained? It would have been better to die.' Next, he turned to Ragnachar's brother and said to him: 'If you had given aid to your brother, he would not be chained.' At that very moment, he struck him with his axe.[30] Far from being motivated by unhinged anger, Clovis' gesture avenged and restored lost honour, since Ragnachar, a vicious king of bad repute, had not only been a Frank but also a kinsman of Clovis. The reference to 'race', *genus*, was thus far from neutral.

For the Franks, honour was aristocratic, manly, and linked to courage. It was situated in the groin or the loins – in the genitals, in other words – and transmitted by blood. A warrior's belt, covering his loins, was thus a reference to his virility. It was why, on a quasi-physiological level, loss of honour was both a most intimate injury and one that affected the entire family: it called for the blood of vengeance, which spread within the clan as if its members were parts of the same organism.[31]

Within Merovingian society, the hostile emotions motivating these violent acts were thus far from irrational. The *History of the Franks* might seem somewhat quirky to modern eyes, but it should be approached sensitively. Such emotions and gestures must be read within the framework of values of the surrounding society; and it should also be recognized that Gregory tinted his world with emotion according to his own purposes.[32] Approached in this way, the oft-cited story of Waddon's fury can be better understood. Waddon wanted to avenge the theft of his horses, but was asked by his wife and son not to do so. He turned against his son, who was only saved from the paternal axe by luck. In order to restore his honour and thus his manhood, Waddon was prepared to risk his life by going to war rather than facing the shame of dishonour; indeed, he would come to die as a result of his vengeful campaign.[33] The code of honour legitimized vengeance provoked by righteous anger; and anger was righteous if honour was injured, as in the case of Clovis and Waddon.[34] The system of compensation provided by Salic law, the *wergeld* or 'price of honour', was only effective if anger subsided. This can be seen in another well-known episode within Gregory's work, that of Chramnesind and Sichar, a tale of vengeance that is emblematic of the complexity of social bonds.[35] These two men whose sad history Gregory described were inhabitants of Tours who became entangled in the civil war which struck the region.[36] It was in this context that Sichar killed the parents of Chramnesind. After the payment of *wergeld* by Sichar to Chramnesind, Gregory reported a rather unexpected outcome: 'Sichar formed a great friendship with him and they cherished each other with such a tenderness (*in tantum se caritate diligerent*), that they often took their meals together and slept in the same bed.' Nevertheless, during a banquet he had organized, Chramnesind was struck with anger when his 'friend' sarcastically recalled that macabre episode:

'You ought to thank me, most dear brother, for having killed your parents; since you received compensation, your house abounds in gold and in silver [...]'
   These words of Sichar aroused a great bitterness in the soul of Chramnesind, and within his heart he said to himself: 'If I do not avenge the death of my parents, I do not deserve to be called a man, but rather a weak woman.' At that instant, having extinguished the lamps, he thus sliced the head of Sichar clean off with a saw.[37]

This fatal deed was certainly impulsive: or at least, that is the impression that Gregory wanted to leave, thereby underlining the error of the two parties in earlier refusing the peaceful mediation that he himself had offered. Nevertheless, it seems that, behind the obligatory friendship that the compensatory resolution called for, Chramnesind had in no way forgotten his ultimate aim. He expedited his vengeance at the first opportunity. Not without irony, Gregory placed before his readers the two extremes of contemporary friendship between which the relationship of Sichar and Chramnesind oscillated. The display of intimate friendship between two people who were once enemies was not enough to peacefully settle their deep conflict; it could only temporarily camouflage the violence which re-emerged after injury revived their enmity.[38] The same severity already seen in Clovis' actions towards Ragnachar is again encountered. The motivation for violence was twofold: on the one hand, it related to familial affection, on the other to honour, and thus to both virility and social status. In any case, the underlying scenario integrated emotion, however spontaneous in appearance or violent, within an entirely coherent rationality of aims. Gregory himself tried to denounce the senseless passion of these aristocrats who refused the peace of the Church. But behind the harsh tones of his narrative, the coherence of the practices which characterized this world of warriors can be perceived.

In contemporary ecclesiastical circles, the value of governmental acts was also judged according to their emotional motivations: this most likely reflected the influence of Columbanus and Irish monasticism, and perhaps also represented a reaction to the political violence of the late sixth and early seventh centuries. At least this is what is suggested by a decree of the Council of Paris in 614, which stated that if a bishop removed an abbot from his post under the influence of anger (*iracundia*) or through greed,[39] the abbot could protest before the synod against such a decision, from then on deemed iniquitous. Indeed, anger and greed were considered sins within the Christian system of vices and virtues that had been developing since the time of Gregory the Great. Here, the very legitimacy of an act of good justice could be questioned if it was motivated by a vice condemned by Christian morality.[40]

And what of women in all of this?

So far, the discussion has only concerned male honour, which provoked the emotion required for just vengeance. But women also actively participated in these social exchanges. Aristocratic women, especially queens, were often active on the Merovingian public scene, even if their weapons and their motives were different from those of men. In a world where men who did not avenge an offence were deprived of their masculine honour, women were far from meek or docile. To judge by a wide variety of sources, they could be very emotional as mothers. It was an attitude that their sons rejected, or at least had little time for. In keeping with a model that went back at least as far as Augustine and which became a hagiographical *topos*, sons often fled their mothers, sometimes even violently refusing their maternal affection in order to fulfil their destinies.[41] Furthermore, women behaved differently towards their sons and towards their husbands: often affectionate and vulnerable in their relations with the former, they could act very firmly in their public dealings with their spouses.

Gregory of Tours related how Queen Brunhilda (d. 613), 'distressed by the unjust proceedings against one of her followers, *girded herself manfully* and barged into the ranks of her enemies, saying "Do not, o warriors, do not commit this crime, do not persecute an innocent, [...] nor start a fight which would waste the region's resources".'[42] In the manner underlined, Gregory described a strong woman appropriating the traits of martial and political honour. The same toughness can also be witnessed in the behaviour of Clotilde (d. 545), widow of Clovis I, who asked her three sons to avenge the murder of her parents by her paternal uncle, Gundobad (d. 516).[43]

In Merovingian society, the Christian order was still too recent to enforce the sort of gender typology that would confine women to the domestic sphere, especially given the liberty they knew in pre-Christian Germanic societies. They could be political figures just as much as their husbands. The freedom they enjoyed in these times was always very much greater *de facto* than *de jure*, however, and they would gradually lose it with the fuller elaboration of social hierarchies from the late seventh century onward.[44] By the Carolingian era, the power of women was limited to familial relationships and the reproductive cycle, even if there were some powerful queens.[45] In the interval, women played an important role, most notably within the couple – a relationship forged by tenderness and reciprocal friendship – to judge by the hagiography of the sixth and seventh centuries.[46] As the keepers of family tradition, aristocratic women reminded husbands of their duties and incited them towards vengeance: in reviving the memories of outrages that warranted revenge, they protected the good name and the wealth of the family.[47] Thus, according to the chroniclers, it was often they who put the wheels of the *faide* into motion. While they only rarely took up arms themselves, their pain, anger, spite, and resentment played a public role.[48]

The chroniclers nevertheless do relate some cases of women who themselves acted violently and thus took part in the *faides* directly. The confrontation between two legendary enemies of Merovingian history – the queens Brunhilda and Fredegund (d. 593) – provides one example: not only did they publicly display the physical signs of anger, they were quick to set the wheels of vengeance in motion. Thus, Queen Fredegund ground her teeth when Leudast (d. 583), who had dragged her name through the mud, begged for her forgiveness: in the middle of mass at the cathedral of Tours, she spurned him with tears of rage, and threw him out of the church. While trusting in the will of God, she was not satisfied with these public gestures of emotion. She had him arrested the same day, and as he resisted, he fell victim to righteous violence.[49]

Once again, the progression from emotional reaction to the act of vengeance is clear. Accepted if not obligatory, the former was governed by the social institution of the *faide*. The scripting of vengeance, from emotion to the action that it motivated, unfolded according to a social rulebook that was known to all, as seen in the case of the affair of Sichar and Chramnesind. This Frankish society, where the emotions played an active role and where violence was an accepted method of conflict resolution, was not a society of unbridled passions. Neither men nor women were permitted to become aggressive without reason. On the contrary, they made use of emotions and violence in a reasoned and calculated manner, and in forms that were socially accepted or even socially required.

The rise of heavenly emotions

The spread of Christian feeling

The Church Fathers had defined the broad outlines of the Christian economy of the emotions, and there is bountiful evidence for how it was refined and put into practice by the societies of men and women who consecrated themselves to God. It is much more complicated to establish the timing and extent of its expansion across society as a whole in the early Middle Ages.[50] On the one hand, the day-to-day reality of interactions in barbarian societies undergoing Christianization seems to have been anything but modelled on Christian norms. Even within France, however, significant regional variations can be witnessed in the Christianization of feelings over death, as well as in the use that might be made of the epitaph as a commemorative space.[51] Moreover, the influence of monastic circles made itself felt among the Frankish aristocracy from the beginning of seventh century, especially following Columbanus' arrival at the Merovingian courts. Having been expelled from Austrasia due to his opposition to Queen Brunhilda, Colombanus found lasting refuge in Neustria. There, the grand figures of the court, the counsellors and agents of the king, supported Columbanian monasticism by founding monasteries. Becoming a bishop was often the pinnacle of their careers,[52] as can be seen in the rise of figures as celebrated as Didier (d. 655), former treasurer of Clothar II (d. 629) and Dagobert (d. 639), who became Bishop of Cahors, or of Dado/Audouin (d. 686), future Bishop of Rouen, who is better known as St Ouen. In the first half of the seventh century, the correspondence of these founding Neustrian courtiers, who became clerics while remaining the king's men, employed a form of emotional expression that was very much connected to both religious feeling and hierarchical deference.[53]

Spiritual fraternity replaced familial sentiment. It was expressed in letters by declarations of joy and chaste love, sometimes mixed with a smouldering languor built on erotic tones or with terror at what lay beyond. Through how it was presented and the tone employed, emotion served as an indicator of status and social prestige, just as it had for the warrior elite, even if the methods differed in so far as the culture that codified this emotion had evolved. The difference between the world in which Gregory of Tours or Brunhilda lived, on the one hand, and that of Dado or Didier of Cahors, on the other, can be measured both in terms of generations and cultural transformation and those of emotional communities and coherent affective worlds. This can be seen in the defining influence of Columbanus' ascetic style on the emotional mannerisms of the Neustrian court and in the way Clothar II handled his frustrations. The latter, after his victory over Brunhilda in 613 and the subsequent unification of the Frankish kingdoms, seems to have tried to distinguish himself from the passionate style of the preceding generation that had caused him so much suffering.[54]

The social emotions that were soon to become vices in medieval culture – anger, envy, jealousy, hate, etc. – still played an essential role in human relationships within Western societies during this period of gradual Christian acculturation. While the game of honour and shame, of friendship and enmity, and of ritual gift exchange and violence continued to govern elite relationships throughout the period, the tone gradually shifted. The extent of this change can be witnessed in the correspondence of St Columbanus, which provides a good impression of the tone employed by this severe ascetic. Affectionate towards his brothers – the terms of love (*dilectio*, *caritas*) were the most important in his emotional vocabulary – Columbanus nevertheless showed an ambiguous attitude towards pleasant emotions. Love, contentment, and joy could only be good and commendable if directed towards God; if not they led to perdition.[55] Like St Benedict, who recommended the moderation of emotional expression in his Rule, Columbanus sought to avoid effusiveness. This can be seen in an elegant passage of a letter written to his brothers:

> I wanted to write you a tearful letter; but for the reason that I know your heart, I have simply mentioned necessary duties, hard of themselves and difficult, and have used another style, preferring to check than to encourage tears. So my speech has been outwardly made smooth, and grief is shut up within. See, the tears flow, but it is better to check the fountain; for it is no part of a brave soldier to lament in battle.[56]

Here, one again meets the attitudes elaborated in monastic circles since the time of the Desert Fathers. Through his influence, Columbanus took part in 'exporting' this sensibility to the secular world. In turn, the Neustrian court, riven with tones that were both masculine and of monastic origin, can be described as a *'monastère manqué'.*[57]

While the influence of the ascetic spirit of Columbanus was palpable among the Neustrian elite from the first half of the seventh century, the Carolingian era, which began in the following century, took things a step further. There, a whole host of evidence bears witness to the diffusion of a Christian culture of affectivity beyond those circles most closely tied to monasticism. Nevertheless, it was only visible at the highest levels of lay society, i.e. those in direct contact with clerical circles. At that time, the boundary between the clerical and lay worlds was as loosely defined as it ever would be. In the early Middle Ages, the education of well-born sons was most often left to monasteries, from which they received a solid religious and Latin culture. From then on, the courtly world would become increasingly marked by Christian culture. Spiritual friendship and affection tinted relationships amongst the elite, since they held fixed in their minds the Christian model of love and passion, uniting man to God. In their letters, clerics and monks made especial use of affectionate and familial language to address their 'spiritual sons', whether they were religious or lay.

New forms of lay devotion

This spread of Christian sensibilities made itself felt in gestures of devotion. In the eighth and ninth centuries, liturgy and prayer underwent a major transformation thanks to the Carolingian Renaissance. Liturgy was the principal setting for the lay experience of religious life. As a result, it was a major focus for the Carolingian project of Christianization. From then on, liturgy bore witness to a mounting attention to man's emotional and personal relationship with God. This upward affection was a tender and humble sentiment, expressed in prayers of request, repentance, and fear. The Gregorian sacramentary thus contained two masses asking for tears (*Pro petitione lacrimarum*), those tears of the love of God which softened the heart of the sinner and allowed him to cleanse past sins. Brought on by the action of grace within the heart, these interior tears made one worthy of redemption.[58] These masses were placed in the sacramentary immediately after two masses that asked for the purification of the heart by the Holy Spirit and then by Grace, and before two others calling for humility and patience respectively,[59] as if providing the link between divine grace and the virtues required for perfect devotion. A letter of Alcuin (d. 804) that enumerated the masses he sent to the monks of Fulda mentioned a mass *'de penitentiae lacrimis'*,[60] which is known to have been included in the sacramentary of

Tours alongside the other masses of Alcuin.[61] Moreover, the two masses previously mentioned are also present in the sacramentary of Fulda (c. 975) in an abridged form,[62] as well as in other liturgical manuscripts of the eighth to eleventh centuries; many of the prayers pro petitione lacrimarum were likewise included in the Roman missal, thus ensuring them a healthy distribution up to the present day.[63]

It was within this context of the birth of lay Christian sentiment that the trend towards composing and copying devotional manuals, generally known as *libelli precum* (prayer booklets), took root.[64] Their earliest examples are of Anglo-Saxon origin: these display an Irish influence and are often credited to Bede the Venerable (d. 735).[65] They spread from the middle of the eighth century, finding their way onto the continent by the beginning of the ninth. These little books of private prayers bear witness to the diffusion of the practice of meditative prayer, regular and solitary, among the lay elite. Serving to replace or prolong the liturgical experience, such prayers gave rise to the elaboration of an affective, interior interaction with God.[66] While composed by learned clerics, these texts were written for – or even requested by – the lay elite who, thanks to the advance of Carolingian reform, became more and more sensitive to matters of salvation. A confessional prayer, found in a collection likely compiled within the Irish entourage of Virgil, Archbishop of Salzburg, in 767 or later, gives a taste of the new atmosphere inspired by these texts. A model for a new form of prayer emerges, one which built an intimate and emotional relationship with God in almost every line:

> O Lord my God, almighty, I humbly adore you. You are the King of kings and the Lord of lords; You are the master of the world; You are the redeemer of souls; You are the deliverer of the believers [...]. I confess to you, my God, that I have sinned before heaven and before earth. Do not leave your servant alone and miserable, but help me, O Lord my God, and fill me with your knowledge. Teach me to do your will, for you are God, my master, who will reign forever and ever. Amen.[67]

Addressing God as a beloved father was original to the era: it described an intimacy with God similar to that which Augustine had felt, but which is more usually seen as characteristic of the final centuries of the Middle Ages. In the generation that followed, prayer booklets were promoted by Alcuin, a figure of the highest importance in Charlemagne's court. He compiled many of them, including one that he dedicated to his friend Arn, Archbishop of Salzburg, and another addressed to Charlemagne. These booklets placed verses from the Psalms within private prayer.[68] Thus, they served to fill the gap of a liturgical office for the faithful outside the monasteries.

Often addressed to lay lords and ladies, prayer booklets appear as practical manuals for the sanctification of the daily lives of the imperial lay elite. The prayers took up the two great and complementary lines of devotion propounded by Gregory the Great. On the one hand, they engendered an acute consciousness of sin and of the need to repent, guiding the reader towards personal penitence. On the other, they called for faith in divine love, as seen in the introduction to the Lord's Prayer in the *Libellis coloniensis*, a booklet compiled around 805–9 and conserved in a manuscript of Cologne. This example is similar to the little manual of devotion which Alcuin described in one of his letters to Arn, and it employs the same tone as the prayer previously cited:

> If you search the consciences of men, Lord, there is no one who does not stand guilty before you. If you recall the words of men, Lord, there is no one who can speak before you. If you look at the actions of men, Lord, no one is worthy to call you father. But do not give to us on account of our words, actions, and merits. Rather, on account of your great mercy, grant us eternal life, grant that we might obtain it through the prayer of Our Lord Jesus Christ, your son...[69]

While using the verses of the Psalms, these texts reflected a devotional practice which became ever more personal, individualized, and emotional between the eighth and ninth centuries. Long before the intimate tones of St Anselm of Canterbury (d. 1109) or John of Fécamp (d. 1078), these beginnings allow us to trace the evolutionary steps which led towards the blossoming of a truly emotional relationship between the praying man and God.[70]

Moral teaching

Moral teaching provides a further measure of the Christian sensibility that was taking shape: it can be witnessed in treatises on the vices and virtues as well as in texts that codified penance. In the Carolingian era, reflection on the vices and virtues spread beyond the clerical world. Developed in monastic circles between the time of the first desert monks and that of Gregory the Great, such reflections had laid out a syntax for the Christian affective life. Towards the end of his life (*c*. 801–4),[71] while Abbot of Saint-Martin of Tours, Alcuin produced a treatise on the virtues and vices – *De virtutibus et vitiis* – at the request of his 'beloved son', Guy (Wido), count of the Breton March; the author described it as a manual for day-to-day Christian morality.[72] This rather long work is proof not only of an elite lay readership for Latin texts, but also of the

Christianization of daily life and mores. Alcuin's letter to Guy, which opens the text, makes this clear:

> Do not be frightened by your lay condition and secular way of life, as if this condition might bar you from entering the doors of heaven. For just as the blessings of the kingdom of God are preached in the same way to all, so the doors of His kingdom open equally to every sex, age, and person according to their merits.[73]

Alcuin was not the first to write such a manual of morality. A little earlier, Paulinus of Aquileia (d. 802) had sent a comparable treatise to Count Eric of Friuli (d. 799), a Carolingian duke.[74] The work thus reflected contemporary tastes. While its first stirrings were present in the era of Gregory of Tours and Columbanus, the drive to moralize the lives of the lay and political elite along monastic lines only really took hold in the Carolingian era: it would subsequently become a central facet of Gregorian reform. The treatise of Alcuin was widely read and used in the centuries that followed.[75]

Taking what would later be called the theological virtues as his point of departure, Alcuin drew the reader's attention to the importance of emotional states and feelings within the practice of the spiritual life. The treatments of peace, mercy, indulgence, patience, and humility all lead back to the Pauline theme of the *homo interior* and his virtues. The reader is thus invited to meditate on their compunction of heart, that feeling of poignant regret for sins which gave value to penitential practices. The emphasis on confession and penance allowed Alcuin to underline the importance of conversion and the fear of God. Having discussed these virtuous and salutary acts and dispositions, he turned to the vices, where emotions – envy, pride, and anger – were likewise present. Some found their way into his list of the eight principal vices, detailed in the final chapters of the treatise: here the author drew in other emotions and affective dispositions, such as avarice and sloth – that ultimate monastic evil invented by Evagrius here making its first appearance in the lay world – as well as sadness and vainglory. The treatise ends by recalling the four cardinal virtues and praising the friendship which united the two men, Alcuin and Guy. Affective conversion thus represented the cornerstone of the moral conversion recommended to the count: it put the quest for inner purity into eschatological perspective.[76]

Like courtly poetry, learned and moral works naturally did not reach the illiterate lay masses beyond the elite. Nevertheless, many levels of use and knowledge of Latin and the culture that it transmitted existed at that time.[77] At their cultural level, the lay elite possessed at least a moderate knowledge of Latin, which they could and would use in their public lives, whether in writing or in speech. In terms of content or access, there was thus hardly a divide between lay and clerical culture. The boundaries remained fluid. They were all the more so given that the Carolingian political vision aimed – through Christianization – to unify the Empire and its society in a common march towards salvation.

The Carolingian vision of society: unity in love

Alcuin again proves instructive for grasping the essence of this vision and the importance of affectivity within it.[78] A most exceptional and somewhat atypical character, Alcuin always remained a deacon but nevertheless spent many years at the Carolingian court, from 782 to 796/801, acting as master of the palace school and counsellor to Charlemagne. Known for his role in the formulation of royal policy as much as his extraordinary circle of friends and correspondents, he left an impressive volume and variety of writings. His intimacy with the key personalities of the Carolingian court, as well as with the kings, princes, queens, and princesses he encountered on his travels on both sides of the Channel, render him a witness of the utmost importance to the age of Charlemagne. His position could be described as an example of 'unarticulated power'[79] in the sense that, as tutor of the royal family, his real power was much greater than his title would suggest. At the council of Frankfurt in 794, he was received like a bishop.[80]

A close look at his letters, numerous but unevenly conserved, allows one to grasp his ideas concerning human relationships and affectivity, and their direct relationship with his vision of society: 'Just like the sparks thrown up by a fire, love (*dilectio*) takes flight through the medium of letters', he wrote.[81] For him, this burning affection was central to understanding the social ties of the Christian world: the bond of love between Christ and his disciples served as a model. It infused all of his correspondence, whether it concerned friendship, consolation, exhortation, or admonition.[82] The letters served to express affectionate love and engender it within relationships, as his plea to an absent friend makes clear:

> My tender love sheds tears for an absent friend,
> Whom a vast expanse of land stops my eyes from seeing.
> Rare among men is the faithfulness that bonds dear friends.
> Amid so many occupations, he alone will be in my heart.
> Better than silver, more precious than glowing gold,
> He shines more brightly than any treasure,
> He whom all the force of my soul desires and seeks

To possess, to protect, to love and to honour.
Behold, you are this man, bonded to me by a great love
You put my spirit at ease, a sweet love you are for me
May God preserve you for all time,
May you remember Albinus [the literary surname of Alcuin] always and
everywhere. Farewell.[83]

Readers of Alcuin have long been fascinated by such warm affection, which found its way into every kind of missive: his letters are master-pieces of medieval friendship.[84] While the equation of friendship with political alliance was certainly at the root of this affection, it also drew on the aristocratic use of emotion as a mark of superiority: only the *meliores* could have such refined and exalted sentiments. Passionate friendship should thus be understood as an affirmation of the virtue, the value, and the quality of the people concerned.[85]

What is more, the Carolingian court had developed a very particular culture of friendship and love, expressed in intimate and striking terms: it drew equally from the promotion of aristocratic virtues, from the exaltation of the charisma of the king, and finally from affectionate Christian love. These ties are brought to life in a courtly poem which reflected an elite culture, written either by Angilbert (d. 814) – who took the pen name of Homer – or Alcuin, 'Flaccus Albinus'. It was addressed to King Charles, who was deemed worthy of the name of David, the great king of the Old Testament, within this circle. Alcuin and Angilbert borrowed the style of the ancient Latin poets to write songs of love to the king, which lingered on the affection that Charlemagne dispensed to the various members of his entourage. In this way, the love circulating between the king and his poets seemed to fill the court.[86]

If one can sense the realization of the ancient model of friendship within the aristocratic world in such affectionate exchanges, *caritas*, the Christian ideal of charitable love inspired by the model of Christ, was also present. Charlemagne was imbued with the charisma of a saintly Old Testament king. At times, he almost seemed to supplant Christ, thus explaining the waves of love that flowed from his breast. A letter of Alcuin written to Charles during the battle against the Adoptionist heresy bears testament to this. Here, the Church was presented as the bride not of Christ but of the king himself, who was defined as God's chosen, and even as the *son of God*: 'Arise, God's chosen man, arise, *son of God*, arise, warrior of Christ, and defend the spouse of your lord God. Consider your spouse, lest someone should dishonour her.'[87] Charles indeed assumed a ministerial, Christ-like royalty in service of the great divine plan: the Christianization and pacification of the world that would allow society to unite in reciprocal love. The omnipresence of love and affection in the style of address and correspondence had a significance that went far beyond the contours of the emotional community of the Carolingian court. It reflected the formulation of a new model of society, a model revealed to the world by the very spirit of the reforms in progress and which rendered the Franks a new elect on the march towards salvation. In 801, Alcuin praised Charles-David as a veritable priest-king, working with eschatological zeal towards universal peace and justice under divine protection:

> Blessed be the Lord and blessed be the perpetual mercy that He shows His servants, for whose prosperity and salvation, sweet David, He has led you to success and rendered you the bearer of peace; he has protected, honoured, and exalted you. On every step of your journey, He has made the light of justice and piety shine before Your Blessedness, so that the most serene splendour of your wisdom might dispel the gloom of iniquity and the clouds of perversity. Blessed is the nation to whom divine clemency has bestowed such a wise and pious guide.[88]

In Charles' day, the term *ecclesia* in fact described neither a separate domain nor the universal Church. Rather, it was synonymous with the Carolingian state, and, under its governance, the Christian people.[89] The expanding Christian society of the Frankish Empire – where the by-word for order was pacification (an omnipresent ideological leitmotif within royal ordinances amid incessant war) – was to be held together by the social bond of Christian affection. The court, with a sovereign at its head who also possessed religious authority and represented Christ who reigned in heaven, acted to lead the whole of society towards salvation.

Amid the circumstances that arose at the end of the eighth century, a new, plainly eschatological tone became apparent within the correspondence of Alcuin. For him, the Viking sack of Lindisfarne in 793, the very start of the Nordic devastation of Christian Europe, was in fact a shock comparable to what the sack of Rome had been for Augustine. On top of this, there were the numerous difficulties of 796.[90] Christian affection, the salvifying social bond modelled on the love of Christ and his apostolic community, then became the foundation of a new society awaiting the imminent end of the world, of a Christian society which had gradually taken form, but whose future seemed far from assured. In an age where unknown peoples appeared at the frontiers of the Christian West, the internal discords caused by the enthusiasms of competing elites first undermined and then destroyed the Empire, threatening its idealism. At that moment, popes and Carolingian sovereigns began to make it their essential mission to establish a Christianity on Earth that was in line with its eschatological horizons.[91] When the Empire and public power disappeared, both its symbolic and emotional bonds, on the one hand, and Christian identity itself, on the other, gained paramount importance. As for the term *Christianitas*, it took on an increasingly concrete and spatial sense from the tenth century: it became synonymous with the Christian West. Similarly, at the end of the tenth century, when public power had been entirely defeated in many parts of Francia, the notion of *pax* (peace), then spread by clerics, gained a tangible new meaning with the progress of God's peace. *Christianitas* and *pax* expressed a vision of Christian society whose cement, whose social bond *par excellence*, was affectionate love, closely modelled on *caritas*.

— 4 —

THE ZENITH OF MONASTIC AFFECTION

Leaving the Carolingian era behind, and with it the splendour of the Empire that Alcuin knew, we turn to a very different age: the turn of the second millennium AD. The tenth century, for so long described as a period of obscurity or even decline, and for which the sources are thin, now seems more like a time of transition. The reflection of the eighth and ninth centuries on the role of those affective ties that were meant to unite Christian society did not disappear with the crumbling of the Empire. Rather it returned to the monastic microcosm which had given birth to it, where it was protected from political upheavals. The monastic world, itself unified by Carolingian reform, played a major role in defining and guiding this period of transition between imperial and feudal order. At a moment where lay powers were weak, the monks still clung to the ambition of placing Christian society on the path towards salvation. Monastic reform, which became the reform of the Church as a whole, soon projected itself outwards into external Christian society in an ever-widening embrace. From the last decades of the tenth century, a time when lay powers often struggled to impose themselves at even the most local level, bishops and Cluniac monks sought to overturn a social dynamic dominated by aggression through the advancement of peace and the truce of God. Stemming the violence, putting paid to the *faide* by restrictions on warfare, extolling peace as a social glue: all were means of keeping conflict under control, and all came to weigh heavily on the values of the warrior class and even the laity as a whole. The tenth to twelfth centuries, a period where a new hierarchy of powers was gradually constructed, were a time when monks occupied a pre-eminent place in society. Emotions gained an ever-increasing importance in their discourse. The daily life of the monks favoured introspection, as well as the formation of individual and intimate bonds: among them, the flow of

69

affection from the solitary's face-to-face relationship with God towards community found immediacy. The principle of reforming oneself and society by affection thus came to lie at the heart of this monastic and ecclesiastical project.

Within this broader perspective, one can discern, around 1000 AD, the beginnings of a monastic sensibility that gave honour to emotional expressions, both before God and within human relationships. This development can be understood thanks to figures like Romuald of Ravenna (d. 1027), his disciples, and his biographer Peter Damian (d. 1072), as well as the likes of John of Fécamp and Anselm of Canterbury. The emotions they expressed, whether spontaneous or desired, or even brought about by ascetic and devotional practices, served as proofs of sincerity or the presence of grace, and as tools of communication and communion with others that acted both horizontally and vertically. The monastic efforts of these authors, who were far from out of touch with the other great figures at work in the general reform of the Church, represent a new step towards the emotional conversion of society that had begun centuries earlier. Their writings allow us to grasp the new bonds that joined affective anthropology, the project of monastic reform, and society. Approached from this angle, the famous 'renaissance of the twelfth century', often identified as a transformative moment for the inner life and moral sophistication, was no sudden revolution. Rather, it was the result of the slow maturation of an ensemble of phenomena that were at work within Western societies from the ninth and tenth centuries onward.

The origins of affective renewal

A compassionate eremitism

Within an institutional Church undergoing complete redefinition, monastic renewal allowed for the emergence of charismatic figures who could create and guide entire communities. Loving relationships with both God and one's brothers, modelled on the idea of *caritas* and sometimes rooted in severe penitential practice, reconnected with the atmosphere of apostolic-era communities. If a radical break from the world was central to their discourse, the hermits of the period were often very active men in society. At different stages of their careers, or even simultaneously, they could be spiritual directors, teachers, reformers, and abbots. While they spoke of the desert and alternated between monastic life and eremitic retreats, they were rarely alone. Whether they followed Romuald in wanting to 'make the world a hermitage', or made eremitism 'an ideal pole' for Christian society[1] their activities, like their networks, anchored them deeply within contemporary society.

Romuald of Ravenna, one of the most famous Western hermits, is only known to us from the descriptions of others, such as his disciple Bruno of Querfurt (d. 1009), and above all from the biography written by Peter Damian. The latter had not known Romuald personally, but composed his text from eye-witness accounts and made him the pre-eminent model for the monasticism he promoted.[2] Both feared and admired, Romuald lived in a very austere manner but remained close to contemporary elites. Born to a powerful family, he never truly left that world despite his choice of life. The social model he promoted indeed called on aristocrats who felt uncertain of their destiny to abandon the world as their only path towards salvation.[3] The doge of Venice, Pietro Orseolo (d. 987/997) converted under his influence; others, including Oliba Cabreta, count of Cerdanya (Catalonia), soon followed. The young emperor Otto III (d. 1002) visited him, convincing Romuald to accept the abbacy of Sant'Apollinare in Classe (Ravenna), where he had begun his monastic career. Sometime later, the emperor Henry II (d. 1024) also sought him out.[4] In his *vita*, Romuald's way of life seems far from that which the cenobitic vow of stability suggested. A true monastic leader, at no point in his life did he cease from moving from one community to another, and from one town to another. Wherever he established a hermitage, a large following gathered around him, attracted by his aura of sanctity. While the communities he wanted to reform often rebelled in the face of the extreme harshness of the practices he promoted – if one is to believe his biographer Peter Damian, he was chased out, and even threatened with assassination on several occasions – he could never give up his concern for the salvation of others. Even on a day when he had been beaten and then chased from a monastery that he himself had built, he did not lose sight of this:[5]

As he departed, an immense sadness invaded his soul. He then took this resolution, namely that henceforth, contenting himself with working for his own salvation, he would put aside entirely his concern for the salvation of others. But he had barely conceived this when a fear invaded his soul that if he stubbornly persisted in his resolution he would surely die, condemned by the judgement of God.[6]

By evoking Romuald's pangs of emotion, this passage illustrates the incessant tension between eremitism and the care of souls found in the works of Peter Damian, a tension which in turn reflected the author's own itinerant life. The *vita* of Romuald, his first work, composed at the start of his own eremitic experience at Fonte Avellana around 1042–3,

alternates between depicting the 'active' periods in the life of this inde-
fatigable traveller and monastic founder and more 'contemplative' episodes: 'The hermit displayed [...] a ceaseless concern for saving the
world which he had abandoned.'[7] Whether dealing with the terror and
joy stirred up by the saint, his anxieties and sufferings, or his moments
of intimacy with God, emotions are never ignored. They feed into the
story of his spiritual progress. Romuald was constantly tested by demons,
and often reassured by God. He addressed his God, who seemed so close
to him, in tones unheard of before *c.* 1000 AD and still fresh in the mid-
eleventh century when Peter Damian wrote his biography. When Romuald
was still a young monk, living in a swamp-bound hermitage at Classe,
the old port of Ravenna, he was tortured by demons. Entering through
the window of his cell, they threw him to the earth:

> Beating him savagely and landing horrible blows on limbs tired by long
> fasts, Romuald, visited by grace, exclaimed: 'Dear Jesus, beloved Jesus,
> why have you forsaken me? Have you given me up entirely into the hands
> of my enemies?' At these words, the evil spirits were put to flight by the
> power of God. And at once such a compunction of divine love inflamed
> the heart of Romuald that he burst into tears, like wax melting in the sun,
> and his body, bruised by so many blows, felt no pain.[8]

Here, Romuald turned to Jesus in a heartrending call of love, directly
echoing the last cry of Christ to the Father on the cross. The God invoked
by Romuald was a human god, to whom one spoke as a beloved companion, on whom one hoped to rely, and who sometimes seemed to
abandon those who loved him. The heavenly response was twofold. On
the bodily level, the demons stopped their torture. On the affective level,
divine love inflamed the heart of Romuald. Compunction, a result of
grace, was displayed through floods of tears. This intimate relationship
between Romuald and Jesus is found time and again in the text, especially in moments of solitude. Towards the middle of the *vita* (chapter
31), while living as a recluse close to the monastery he had built near
Parenzo (Istria), he 'became anxious that he should shed tears, but no
amount of effort could bring him the compunction of a contrite heart'.
Suddenly, a verse from the Psalms gave him both scriptural understanding and the grace of tears:

> Henceforth, so long as he lived and whenever he wished, he easily shed
> tears and many mysteries were revealed to him. He frequently delighted
> in such a contemplation of the divine, always in tears and burning with
> an ardour of ineffable love, that he would cry out: 'Dear Jesus, my dear,
> my sweet honey, ineffable desire, gentleness of the saints, sweetness of the
> angels', and other such things. Under the influence of the Holy Spirit, he

said these things with a jubilant soul, and we can hardly express his state with our human words. As the Apostle says: 'For we know not what we should pray for as we ought: but the Spirit himself asketh for us with unspeakable groanings' (Rom. 8: 26). That is why Romuald never wanted to celebrate Mass before a crowd, for he could never have contained the abundance of tears.[9]

It was during this defining episode that the saint, then around fifty years old,[10] proved his spiritual maturity. It was displayed through compunction, tears, and an exchange of intimate words of love with God in the altogether human person of Jesus. As reward, he received the grace of the Holy Spirit. The saint was also able to take a further step: in tears, he came to understand the mysteries of the Scriptures. His affective and intellectual bonds to God thus came as a pair. From then on, Romuald remained in a state of loving communion with God: his joyous raptures transported him into an altogether different plane of existence, his cries making clear the presence of the Holy Spirit within him. His tender and affectionate relationship with Jesus seems much closer to the way Alcuin had addressed his friends ('My tender love cries over an absent friend...') than to the veneration that had characterized the prayers of the eighth century ('The Lord my God, all powerful, humbly I adore you'). At the very moment when Peter Damian's Romuald spoke to this very human Jesus, a radical transformation of man's relationship to God, to that Other so essential to the medieval definition of the self, was taking shape.

The privilege of love: fraternal affection amongst an ascetic elite[11]

Almost as restless as their master, the protagonists of Bruno of Querfurt's *Life of the Five Brothers* ardently desired martyrdom among the pagans of Eastern Europe. They belonged to a singular group of Italian monastic reformers who all shared direct or indirect ties to Romuald: like him, the transformation they promoted was as much interior, spiritual, and emotional as it was institutional and communal.

Bruno's *Life of the Five Brothers* is in fact the earliest written witness to this circle: composed *c.* 1006–8, it predates Romuald's *vita* by three decades.[12] Bruno, born to a large Saxon family, was probably a relative of Emperor Otto III.[13] Educated in Magdeburg, he became a canon of the cathedral there before Otto called him to court in 995. During the imperial coronation of Otto in Rome, he met St Adalbert (d. 997), whose influence seems critical to this wave of monastic reform. Shortly thereafter, he left the monastery and placed himself under the spiritual direction of Romuald, who tutored him in ascetic practice. He wrote the *Life of the Five Brothers* before himself undertaking missionary work in Eastern

73

Europe from 1003 onward: he was martyred in Prussia (Lithuania) in 1009. While Peter Damian, who did not know his hero, made little effort to describe the atmosphere of the communities around Romuald (beyond mentioning the times where they rejected the saint), Bruno of Querfurt lived side-by-side with his 'master'. His narrative allows the reader to grasp both the tone of communal life and the monastic doctrine of Romuald:

> Three treasures [were] offered to those who sought the way of the Lord. For novices coming from the life of the world, there was the monastery they needed; for mature followers, thirsty for God, there was precious solitude; and for those who desired to disappear and bury themselves in Christ, there was the evangelization of the pagans.[14]

By way of this hierarchy of three monastic treasures, the text gave pride of place to missionary zeal and the martyrdom that followed. Living in an informal affective community, the brothers girded themselves with a love that was both tender and strident. Their love was shown above all to their master, Romuald,[15] but they also relied on each other, united as they were in virtue, their choice of solitude, and their desire for martyrdom. Romuald went to the Ravenna hinterlands, where Bruno was staying at the time, on his way to 'Monte Cassino, the source and origin of the monks living under the Rule. This was not, however, the sole purpose of his visit. He also desired to see his dear companion John once again, who he had not seen for so long....'[16] Citing a poem of Horace, Bruno himself said of Benedict, one of the future martyrs of his account: 'I embraced him as if he were half of my soul.'[17] Bruno's final, particularly moving encounter with John and Benedict, both subjects of his work, before their departure for the pagan lands 'beyond the Alps among the Slavs', bears eloquent testimony to the affective communion between the brothers:

> Then – I can hardly recall it without crying – as night fell, in the fading twilight before dusk, I came to talk of heavenly things with Benedict. I felt my heart beating more heavily, and loved him more intimately than ever, feeling myself closely bound to his soul. Indeed, I confess, this conversation was very sweet for my poor soul. [...] That evening then, abandoning myself in his arms, I offered both cheeks up to his holy kisses. Along the entire path which I joined him on despite my feebleness, and among the many recommendations which the last farewell suggested to us, this was the only one that has left neither my heart nor my lips (Ah, if it were possible for me to call on him now, my Lord!): 'My very dear brother, I pray of you, in the name of our common hope, through Jesus Christ, son of the Virgin Mary, remember that you will always have me with you and that

you will always be with me. When you pray or sing the psalms, always pray and implore the living God that, on account of his Name, he fulfils the one desire that he has placed in both our hearts, and that we, you and me, a poor sinner, do not die before seeing the blessed day where, having regularly shed blood, we will obtain the remission of our sins through the mercy of God. For it is not in vain what is written, "He who desires the salvation of his soul, seeks it in the name of Jesus." ' Such was the pledge of love that I, poor sinner, left with this holy man, adding and repeating in his ear that, even if our world should fall apart, I would doubtless follow behind him.[18]

Such a declaration attests to a heartfelt closeness, incarnated (in the truest sense of the term) in unprecedented physical proximity. How did physical asceticism, the desire for martyrdom, and tender affection for one's brother fit together? Such an association was emblematic of an environment that brought together more novel elements with those that were closer to the idealized model of the desert monks. In the solemn atmosphere created by the vow of martyrdom, the affective communion of two brothers, bonded by their grave decision to undertake a common mission, mirrored the intimacy of Romuald with Jesus and, beyond this, that of the apostles with Christ. Physical intimacy became possible precisely because no suspicion could be cast upon them. At least for the most part, that is. Peter Damian reported an episode in which Romuald, already a hundred years old, was accused of having carnal knowledge of a young monk: as a result, he was forbidden to celebrate mass for six months, in lieu of being burnt and hanged as some of the monks would have preferred.[19] Seen in more pragmatic terms, such intimacy was permissible, acceptable, and describable because it occurred at the moment where two brothers who had been with each other daily were separated, and amid a shared knowledge that one era had ended and that the one to follow would lead them towards the death they desired. Bruno was quick to add that the two friends never met again. The remainder of the *vita*'s narrative is built around the tension between Bruno's desire to fulfil his vow and the reasons which continually caused him to postpone his plans, and thus the anxieties and the torments he experienced because of this oft-renewed delay. While he could not join his friends, the vow lived on within him. In the end, Bruno would be martyred, just like his friends before him. But it was Romuald who had first engendered this atmosphere of spiritual intimacy around him, as shown by his links with John Gradenigo and the count of Oliba. An entire circle of friends was bound together by this 'privilege of love': Benedict and Bruno, Romuald and John Gradenigo, the latter and Benedict, Benedict and Romuald, as well as Benedict and John the Martyr.[20]

The spiritual renewal of these monks, whether reformers like Romuald or missionaries like John, Benedict, and Bruno, was clearly presented as an *affective renewal*, rooted in a strict penitential asceticism.[21] The world that the followers of Romuald built on earth was an eschatological universe of radical severity. It was directed towards the desire for heroic death, where the love of God and the love of others together supported their plan to live and die for Christ. It might be thought a rather constrictive path for the reform of Christian society, or even of monastic life: the numerous institutional defeats faced by Romuald, which Peter Damian did not flinch from describing, bear witness to this. Romuald's charisma, suggested by the success of his preaching and his exponential growth in supporters, as well as by the style of semi-eremitic and strongly penitential monasticism he promoted,[22] came into conflict with institutionalism, which was inimical to such radical expressions of reform.[23] Moreover, Romuald's *vita* states that he never wanted to lead any community; his faithful disciple, Benedict, followed him in this disavowal of leadership.[24] They preferred the romanticism of a life that mixed periods of eremitism with communal living to the strains of community administration. A true vanguard for the conquest of medieval society formed around Romuald and his disciples: they desired as much to convert the pagans as to reform the ways of Christians. As seen with Peter Damian, for them the reform of the Church began with personal reform, by rooting *caritas* in a severe penitential humility.[25]

The affective reform of monasticism and the Church[26]

William of Volpiano (d. 1031), a Cluniac monk of Italian origin, arrived at Fécamp in Normandy in 1001 in answer to the call of Duke Richard II (d. 1026),[27] having already introduced reform at Saint-Bénigne in Dijon. He was accompanied by his beloved disciple and future successor to the abbacy of Fécamp, John of Ravenna – more commonly known as John of Fécamp – who was also of Northern Italian origin.[28] John was named prior in 1017, then abbot in 1028, when the aging and ailing William retired. It was then left to him to continue at Fécamp and in Normandy the reform begun at Fruttuaria and Dijon. While William and John carried Cluniac reform into Normandy, they remained tied to the reformed monastic world of Northern Italy from which Romuald had hailed. It is thus not surprising to find a similar taste for the emotional expression of piety in their works. What perhaps most clearly distinguished the atmosphere of Norman monasticism from Romuald's world, to judge by the writings of John of Fécamp, was the absence of that ascetic extremism so characteristic of the hermits who strived towards martyrdom. Softened in this way, the affectionate monasticism which took root at Fécamp divested itself of the heroism found within the *vitae* of Romuald and Dominic Loricatus (d. 1060), written by Peter Damian at the beginning and end of his career respectively.

Nevertheless, John earnestly promoted penance, as seen in his lament over man's ultimate fate,[29] entitled *Short Verses for the Inspiration of Heartfelt Compunction, Collected from the Scriptures*.[30] Here, he reviewed the vain desires and pleasures of the world. The twelve stanzas that formed the poem are punctuated by a refrain recalling the misery of man, which drew from a liturgical formula:

> Alas man, alas man, alas, you, oh wretched man! [...] Christ, take pity on us, merciful pity. Oh you, always take pity on your wretched followers.[31]

This little-known poem is representative of the author's eloquence, literary fibre, and religious energy. It discusses foolish joy, laughter, and earthly delights, incessantly reminding the reader of the mortality of his human condition by showing him the anguish, interior confusion, and misery of worldly life. Lurking in the background, the classic themes of fear of divine judgement and decomposition as the ultimate fate of all earthly life are present. To Huizinga's ear, the tone of the poem – both lively and frightening – and the emotions that it was meant to elicit – repentance and lamentation – seemed to prefigure the smouldering emotionality of the later Middle Ages. In fact, however, the lament of the Abbot of Fécamp more closely resembles the letters of Peter Damian, his contemporary, which were likewise marked by eschatological expectation.[32] Like him, John drew heavily on questions and injunctions to lead his reader through a vivid drama of the present and future miseries that awaited those who 'slept' in temporal pleasures, instead of 'awakening' to devote themselves entirely to salvation. Nevertheless, these verses were hardly representative of the world of John of Fécamp: taken as a whole, his works were not dominated by a penitential tone, but rather by the contemplation of mystical desire.

His most personal writings – his spiritual texts and his prayers – are what truly make the Abbot of Fécamp one of the most remarkable authors of his age. Above all, he was a remarkably emotional author, crucial for grasping the evolution of the theology and Christian anthropology of the emotions. His masterpiece, the *Theological Confession*, written during his youth while prior of Fécamp (1017/18–28), makes this point clearly.[33] Both an extended prayer and a reflection on God, this text leads the reader through three ages, following the chronological path of the divine hand from creation through to salvation. The economy of salvation and that of the work itself are thus patterned after the three stages of creation/emanation, incarnation, and (desire to) return to the bosom of the Father.[34] After a sober opening, praising and professing faith in the Trinity, the second part discusses grace and redemption. The tone then changes considerably, becoming ever more emotionally charged: here, one finds a prayer for pity and grace for the sinner who admits his fear and feels himself far from heaven. The third part, by the far the longest, elaborates upon John's mystical desire and puts it into context:

> The faithful soul, burning with an immense love for Christ, ardently desiring Christ, sighing with love for Christ, hoping to see Christ, its only love, only feels sweetness by moaning and weeping, by 'fleeing, being silent, and remaining peaceful', all the while saying: 'Who will give me wings like a dove, and I will fly and be at rest?' (Ps. 54: 7).[35]

Taken as a whole, this part of the work represents an outpouring of the soul; it ends by asking for the gift of tears and assuring the sinner of the presence of God.[36] A longing for heavenly happiness dominates the text. Within it emerges the idea that only love can save: it alone enables the flight from worldly desires. John then speaks clearly of his spiritual practice, in which prayer and writing were as one and seemed to provide the sole refuge within this earthly life:

> What I enjoy most is contemplating your gifts through the soul's pure gaze and in the very sweet ardour of a holy love. I do so as much as I can down here *in the place of my pilgrimage* (Ps. 118: 54), and will continue for as long as life remains in these fragile limbs. For I have been pierced by the arrow of your love. For you, I burn with an ardent desire: it is to you that I desire to come, it is you that I long to see. [...] That is why I love so much to talk about you, to hear about you, to read about you, to write about you, to discuss you. Having entered the cool shade of your purity, I hide myself far from the passions of this world within your refreshing calm.[37]

If the mystical way was John's preferred path for the individual monk, on a collective level it could only be followed through the mediation of the Son-made-flesh. The mystery of the Incarnation is the central object of the second part, just as it was of John of Fécamp's theology, and with it came strong Eucharistic accents. He described the consequences of Christ's mediation in the first person, enriching them with his own experience:

> It is all I hope and trust in. In this Christ-man, a part of each one of us can in fact be found, our blood and our flesh. There then, where a part of myself reigns, I believe that I reign. There then, where my own blood exercises sovereignty, I recognize that it is me who exercises it. There, where

my own flesh is glorified, I know that I am glorious. While I am a sinner, because of this communion, I do not doubt grace [...] For the Lord is not so devoid of sweetness as to forget man, and to forget the man whom he carries, to not support me, given what he has taken up for me. For the Lord is not so devoid of sweetness that he does not love his own flesh, his own limbs, his own organs. In Jesus Christ Himself, our God and Lord, full of sweetness, kindness and mercy, in whom we are now resurrected, in whom we are now brought to life, in whom we are now carried to heaven, with whom we now sit in heaven, it is our own flesh that loves us.[38]

This passage presents the mystery of the Incarnation and the effects of the Passion in terms that were original to the age. Dogma, affectivity, and both the individual and communal dimensions of spiritual practice are at once distinguished and yet inexorably linked. The author spoke simultaneously in the name of all humanity and God incarnate. He expressed his faith not only in a sweet and good God, but also in the Redemption, of which he was the beneficiary as a member of the Church who carried within him the flesh of God, just as God carried the flesh of man. Such an individual affirmation of the Redemption is far removed from the anthropological pessimism of Augustine.[39] The sinful flesh, condemned by St Paul and then Augustine to return to dust amid a vale of tears, became, in John's hands, the glorious flesh of a mankind that was already saved. It is also very distant from the austere eremitic elitism of the desert. John spoke in the name of all Christians: his pronouncement was collective and communal. In his treatment, the entire Church was united in salvifying love which made each Christian an adopted child of God.[40] Love was fundamental to John's theology, centred on Christ's mediation, even if his vocabulary was not fixed: *dilectio*, *amor*, and *caritas* were used in turn. Rather than a virtue, this love was an affective movement, an emotion in the literal sense, a progression which, at every moment, united each member of the Church to Christ, and transcended their fear and the shame of their sins. Nevertheless, in the *Theological Confession*, this union was brought to fruition in the most concrete manner by the object of its demands, the divine gift of tears, just as it was for Romuald. An interior transformation was envisaged within the lachrymal process: it was described in sacrificial terms as the internal transubstantiation of the monk who had rid himself of sin and given himself up as a *living sacrifice* to God.[41]

The desire for pious tears grew at the same time as the dogma of transubstantiation crystallized in the West. This made the Eucharistic celebration the arena for a real, rather than solely symbolic, transformation of the bread and wine offered as the body and blood of the sacrificed Christ. Additionally, for both John of Fécamp and Peter Damian, individual spiritual practices and the communal rites of the Church were far from opposed. Rather, they were complementary, representing the two faces of the affective and mystical union with Christ. Peter Damian expressed the same idea in a celebrated letter devoted to hermits. Often entitled *Dominus vobiscum*, it provides a good summation of his ecclesiology:

> Truly the Church of Christ is so joined together by the bond of love that in many it is one and in each it is mystically complete. Thus, we at once observe that the whole Church is rightly called the one and only bride of Christ, and we believe each soul, by the mystery of baptism, to be the Whole Church.[42]

The bond of love gave life to the Church: it united it and embodied it within each of the faithful. This mysterious or mystical bond was renewed in the imitation of the unique sacrifice of Christ, whether it was made in the sacrifice of the mass or in the monk's sacrifice of tears. If the latter was an individual sacrifice, it had no less value for the Church as a whole. Thus, in the eyes of these authors, it was through the celebration of the sacraments and the tears which reinforced it that divine love – charitable love – was shared and propagated as the body of the Church. At the very moment when the ecclesiology of Gregorian reform took shape, religious emotion came to be invested with a new symbolic force that derived from an individual appropriation of sacramental power.

Friendship as the practice of conversion: Anselm of Canterbury

This emotional intensification of spiritual bonds reached a climax of sorts in the writings of St Anselm and his disciples. Like the rest of the men discussed so far in this chapter, Anselm was of Italian origin. He was born in 1033 at Aosta, then situated in the kingdom of Burgundy. Attracted by the reputation of Lanfranc (d. 1089), a master originally from Pavia and an adversary of Berengar of Tours (d. 1088) in the Eucharistic controversy, Anselm arrived in Normandy in 1060, at the monastery of Bec, to be taught by him. In 1063, he succeeded Lanfranc as prior and master of the school of Bec, before being chosen as abbot in 1079. In 1093, he became Archbishop of Canterbury, an office previously occupied by Lanfranc. Thanks to his writings – his corpus includes texts concerning theology, prayer, and meditation, as well as hundreds of letters – and the descriptions of his life and teaching provided by his circle, Anselm is the first author whose understanding of the emotional aspects of spirituality and monastic life can be approached with real precision.

In his celebrated treatise, *Why God Became a Man*,[43] Anselm explained how Christ needed to fully assume the human condition for man to be redeemed and that he suffered as a man in the flesh. In another text written at the end of his life, he discussed the freedom of man after the Fall.[44] The active part of liberty resided within the will, which, according to Anselm, made its presence felt through a variety of actions. He then designated 'affect' (*affectio*) as the power which acted beneath rational activity, a foundation of the will that became fully operational when reason consented to its influence.[45] To Anselm's eyes, the affective power seemed, in this sense, to be the first impulse of the will: he thus saw it as one of man's tools in his quest for salvation. Anselm remained faithful to Augustine – he did not go so far as to identify two separate forms of volition – but never before had affect come so close to taking its place as a distinct force within the soul.[46] Above all, one can see how Anselm made affect the pre-eminent force in the quest for divine conformity by placing it on theological terrain: 'my soul hungers and longs to feed upon the affection of your love, but it cannot fill itself with you'.[47] It is from these foundations that one should approach Anselm's collections of prayers and meditations. These short texts are saturated with an emotional rhetoric that strikes precisely the same chord as the prayers of John of Fécamp. Within an artfully constructed rhetorical framework, Anselm pushed to an extreme the duality of the affective dynamic that existed between the fear of sin and the glorious joy of being saved by the sacrifice of Christ. The following prayer concerning the Holy Cross serves as an example:

> With what love shall I glory in you, O Cross, when without you there would be nothing for me to glory in, and in eternity I should have the grief and misery of hell. With what delight will I rejoice in you, when by you the servitude of hell which I inherited is exchanged for the kingdom of heaven. With what jubilation shall I laud you, when without you I faced that future which horrifies me, even if it had lasted only a moment, and through you I now expect to rejoice in eternity.[48]

Indeed, it was precisely in the conversion of the affections that the path towards the beatitude of divine presence could be found. The 'conversion of tears' of Mary Magdalene, the sinner to whom the risen Jesus chose to appear first, made this clear:

> And so it is; for love's sake he cannot bear her grief for long or go on hiding himself. For the sweetness of love, he shows himself who would not for the bitterness of tears. [...] At once the tears are changed; I do not believe that they stopped at once, but where once they were wrung from a heart broken and self-tormenting, they flow now from a heart exulting.[49]

81

In this way, Anselm blended anxious impulses – which, as the very essence of the monastic sacrifice, tended to dominate such texts ('Faint within me, my spirit; be appalled, my heart; break forth and cry, O my soul';[50] 'I blush to be alive, I am afraid to die'[51]) – with the delights that his obedience to the Johannine teaching of love allowed him: 'You know, Lord, that I prize this love which you command, I hold this love dear, and long for this charity.'[52] Augustinian accents emerge in a prayer 'for friends'. This opens with an address to Jesus, whose sacrifice represented the highest form of charity that would ever be achievable by anyone: thus, the love of one's neighbour was also intimately related to Christ's Passion. Anselm recognized, however, that he did not show an equal love towards all but cherished some more than others. How could such preferences be permitted given the need for universal charity? The solution to this tension was found in the efficacy of prayer itself: 'there are many whom I hold more dear since your love has impressed them upon my heart with a closer and more intimate love, so that I desire their love more eagerly – I would pray more ardently for these'.[53] The spread of charity – or rather of that singular form of charity, *dilectio* – was assured in this manner, firstly because it was a projection of love inspired by the love of God, and secondly because love was redistributed and proliferated by prayer: 'Love them, [...] and make them love you with all their heart.'[54] In just a few lines, Anselm offered an authentic summary of his theology of friendship; he would put it into practice – in rhetorical terms, at least – in his letters.

Nearly 500 of Anselm's letters, around a third of which concern his life at Bec (1070–93), have been conserved, an extraordinary number for the period. Commentators have always been struck by the near endless reflection on spiritual friendship found in his letters, a friendship which he cultivated above all with those monks of Bec who were followers of Lanfranc, men such as Gundulf, Mauritius, and Gilbert, who had been called to fill important positions within the English Church. But the circle of friends dear to Anselm also included both monks of his monastery, to whom he wrote when they were away or when he himself travelled, and those of others. He often addressed his circle of 'special' friends in intense and passionate tones, as can be seen in a letter to Gundulf from the early 1070s:

> Whenever I intend to write to you, soul most beloved of my soul, whenever I intend to write to you, I am undecided about where exactly I should begin what I want to tell you. For everything I feel about you is sweet and joyful to my heart; everything I wish for you is the best my mind can imagine. For I see you as the sort of person I must love, as you know I do; I hear about you as the sort of person I must long for, as God knows

I do. From this it comes about that wherever you go my love follows you; and wherever I may be, my longing for you embraces you.

And do you inquire about me by your messengers, exhort me by your letters, shower me with your gifts that I may remember you? *Let my tongue cleave fast to the roof of my mouth if I cease to remember you* (Ps. 136: 6), if I do not place 'Gundulf' at the pinnacle of my friendship. [...] How could I forget you? How could someone imprinted on my heart like a waxen seal slip out of my memory? Moreover, why do you complain so sorrowfully, as I hear, that you never see any letters of mine, and why do you beg me so lovingly that you may often receive them when you have my thoughts with you all the time? Even when you are silent I know you love me; and if I am silent *you know that I love you* (John 21: 16).[55]

How should this twofold declaration of love be understood today? For in this letter one can see both the loving plea of a monk who believed himself abandoned by his friend, and the response of that friend, also a monk, who assured him that neither time, distance, nor silence itself could alter the strength of his feelings.[56] At the beginning of the 1980s, the historian John Boswell read such words as signs of a quasi-tolerance within the Church for a homosexual subculture.[57] But this explanation, founded on categories that barely made sense in the Middle Ages, fails to recognize fully the context of the contemporary rhetoric of friendship, or the way the emotional register was used within the monastic world.[58] This does not detract from the astonishing character of these exchanges, which represent a new way of expressing epistolary friendship. They are far removed from the amicable rhetoric of Lanfranc, for instance, who never expressed such an amalgamating desire.[59] Terms of friendship, such as *caritas* and *dilectio*, had long been common within ecclesiastical circles as they set about their common objectives. In the context of eleventh-century reform, this rhetorical arsenal was frequently deployed in the service of ecclesiological aims by Gregory VII (d. 1085) and Peter Damian.[60] But while epistolary friendship could serve to construct or maintain a network of allies, it does not account for the emotional intensity of these letters.[61]

The biggest clue is provided by Anselm himself, who no longer employed the same style in his letters after 1093, the year in which he became Archbishop of Canterbury. Even if some of his letters extol the blessings of friendship, their tone is more distant, more pastoral.[62] It thus becomes clear that, for Anselm, affective intensity expressed a monastic ideal and identity, perhaps even the state of a monk living under the Rule of Benedict. Thus, despite appearances, the tone did not invite intimacy. On the contrary, Anselm often ended his letters by asking for the initial recipient to bring other monastic friends into this circle of love. In the letter to Gundulf cited above, Anselm even included Osbern, a young monk who had been very close to him but had died suddenly not long before: 'Wherever Osbern is, my soul is his soul. May I therefore receive on his behalf, while living, what I could hope for from my friends when I am dead, so that they will be free of obligation to me when I die.'[63] This passage had significant theological weight since it suggested that friendship had the ability to facilitate interaction between the living and the dead: previously, this power had usually been attributed to charity, an inclusive but more dispassionate love.[64]

With Anselm, the language of impassioned friendship took on a deeply spiritual flavour. Its primary function was to maintain the unity of the community in his absence.[65] 'He who cut us off from one another taught me how much I loved you',[66] he wrote to Gilbert, a monk of Bec whom Lanfranc had taken with him. He thus continued the trend begun by Cassian, Bede the Venerable, and Alcuin. Two new features emerge, however. Firstly, this friendship became a privileged expression of the spiritual bonds of monastic community under the Rule of St Benedict. While not obvious at first sight, the letters were sometimes accompanied by gifts in cases of absence or distance, or were even framed as gifts themselves, giving material expression to the bond of friendship. The messenger thus played an important role. He carried not only the letter, but also the promise of its author, even passing on gestures of affection; in this transitive manner, he provided a presence and sensoriality that is lost when the words are read today.[67] As a monk and as an abbot, Anselm acted here in a manner appropriate to the care demanded by the Rule. But he also stood out for placing mutual affection at the heart of his relationships, even though Benedict had not only extolled affective moderation but also warned against elective affinities within the cloister. In making the monastic community a constellation of endless combinations of friendship pairs, Anselm nevertheless advanced the Benedictine project of uniting souls on a common path towards God.

A second evolution was also taking place. Anselm transposed emotional intensity into monastic sociability, whereas, even in the preceding generation, it had been reserved almost exclusively for the relationship with God and the most privileged ties amongst the friends of God. This intensity of emotion was now measured against Christ's love for man, hence the recurrent one-upmanship. The love of a friend, which reflected the love of Christ, needed to be constantly reaffirmed and augmented. Gundulf, who continually sought proofs of Anselm's love, even managed to annoy his correspondent in this little game of '*Je t'aime, moi non plus*':

> For I confess – and blush to do so – I admit, I say that my tepid charity
> is surpassed by your fervent charity, but it is not dissimilar because it is

formed by the same Rule. Just as you try hard to love me with no less ardour than you love yourself so I strive not to love you with more coolness than myself. If you demand more, indeed I neither wish to do less nor am I able to do more. Accordingly, let your love obtain for me by your prayers that I may love myself as much as I should; and your lover will so love you that you yourself will say: now that is enough.[68]

Subtly, Anselm reminded Gundulf that their friendship, while special, was merely one link within a chain which defined the connection between himself, God, and his community, rather than a solely personal bond. Within monastic letters, friendship represented the multilateral and communal aspect of a wider conversion of the emotions, whereas prayers and meditation were the individual and introspective component. Even if these different levels were linked, Anselm – like his predecessors – established a progression from the painful emotions wrought by conscience of sin, expressed in prayers and meditations, towards the comforts of spiritual friendship. Joy in Christ took the form of a joy to be shared.

The expansion of love's domain

For monastic piety, the eleventh century had been the century of emotional conversion. Here, conversion should be understood in its medieval sense, and thus not as a transition from a cold piety to spiritual exuberance, but as a movement that placed the influence of the heart at the centre of man's relationship with God. Conversion was also at work within the affective dynamic itself: an increasingly favourable evaluation of 'positive' emotions (joy, desire, enjoyment) did not so much replace traditional ascetic motivations (compunction, suffering, grief) but dovetailed with them, sometimes creating emotional compounds that seem paradoxical to modern sensibilities. Finally, it also brought about the expansion of what this intense conception of emotional power could encompass: it now ran beyond the individual relationship with God to embrace cloistral companions and even the world at large.[69]

This emotional expansion and permeability were far from inevitable within a Western monastic tradition once marked by mistrust of emotional excesses and even a desire to partition the love of God from the love of the world. They accompanied the new importance given to the Incarnation within theology and the imitation of Christ within spirituality; as a result, the sacrifice of the Passion and the conformative power of the passions became inseparable on the level of religious practice.[70] Within this far-reaching evolution, the twelfth century represented neither a beginning nor a turning point. Rather, it witnessed the seeping of this goal of love into even the smallest cracks of monastic thought and practice, where it reached dizzying heights. The dynamism of love inundated monastic discourse, where it circulated in several malleable forms: charity, friendship, and dilection (*dilectio*). This spiritual love represented neither an instinctive emotional fit, felt by a suddenly dumbstruck monk, nor a cold transposition of supreme theological principles into pious practice. Above all, it came to represent a principle of order, another notion fundamental to Christian thought, which involved liturgical developments and spiritual conversion as much as the institutional organization of communities. Love, like other emotions, could now be directed towards salvation: the *ordo monasticus* of the Church provided the vanguard for this general offensive, which found its lay counterpart in the *fin'amor*, the exalted form of love described by courtly literature.

Passionate charity as spiritual nature

The pairing of flesh and spirit held an essential place in Christian thought throughout the Middle Ages. This was especially the case in monastic circles, where the monk, if he was not an oblate, was a convert (*conversus*), whose journey of conversion was never complete. Taken in its most immediate sense, the battle against the flesh represented the soul's battle against the desires of the body. But the flesh was not solely a matter of the body: in the wake of original sin, it was also everything within the soul that barred its rise towards God, everything that stood in the way of the spirit. In taking a body, the Word had opened a path towards the spiritualization of the flesh, just as the Incarnation had opened a path towards the embodiment of the spirit. The dialectic of flesh and spirit did not, therefore, create a linear path towards salvation. The meaning of both terms did not reside as much in their objects as in their relationship: 'it was never a matter of substance, but rather of how things relate'.[71] What was 'flesh' from one angle could be 'spirit' from another: marriage was carnal in comparison to virginity but became spiritual when it inspired *caritas* within an institution designed to combat fornication. Likewise, material and bodily objects were not automatically deemed 'carnal'. Relics were thus 'completely spiritual material objects',[72] while in certain contexts, sensory stimuli (the sight of the cross, the odour of the incense, the taste of the Eucharist) took part in the process of man's elevation, reflecting the increasing attention given to the embodiment of the spiritual within religious practice.

As monks navigated between these two poles of flesh and spirit, love, which was itself a relational dynamic, was the force that set the soul in motion.[73] The path of salvation thus took on the appearance of a journey from carnal love to spiritual love. The terminology assigned to these two poles always retained a certain flexibility, where meaning depended on the articulation. Charity and dilection always tended towards the side of the spirit, albeit some expressions outranked others depending on whether their object was worldly or divine, while concupiscence was by nature the form of desire weighed down by the burden of the flesh. Love, however, remained indeterminate. Its value was partly defined by the object which it sought, but even more by the disposition of the lover.[74] As inheritors of the Augustinian ontology of love, the monks of the twelfth century, particularly those who took the habit of the reformed orders, made love the mother of all religious emotions as never before. This path of conforming one's emotions seemed to be encapsulated in that most frequently cited verse of the Song of Songs: 'He set in order charity in me' (S. of S. 2: 4). The love poem *par excellence*, the Song of Songs was one of the most commented-upon books of the Bible in the twelfth century, especially among the Cistercians, who devoted numerous exegetical treatises and hundreds of sermons to it. They followed the example of St Bernard, who produced a systematic verse-by-verse commentary in a series of eighty-six sermons.[75] Following a tradition of interpretation which went back to Origen, Bernard identified the lover with Christ and the beloved by turns with both the Church and the individual soul. At a time where love poetry reigned supreme within the princely court and where the religious themselves were often fine connoisseurs of this vernacular literature, monks revelled in the infinite allegorical possibilities it provided:

'Let him kiss me with the kiss of his mouth' (S. of S. 1: 1), she said. Now who is this 'she'? The bride. But why bride? Because she is the soul thirsting for God. In order to clarify for you the characteristics of the bride, I shall deal briefly with the diverse affective relationships between persons. Fear motivates a slave's attitude to his master, gain that of a wage-earner to his employer, the learner is attentive to his teacher, the son is respectful to his father. But the one who asks for a kiss, she is a lover. Among all the natural endowments of man, love holds first place, especially when it is directed to God, who is the source whence it comes. No sweeter names can be found to embody that sweet interflow of affections between the Word and the soul, than bridegroom and bride.[76]

Love was a gift of nature, and thus a grace placed within man by God: it accomplished its aim when directed towards its divine origin. Whether they were monks or canons, most of the great religious authors of the twelfth century – e.g. Bernard of Clairvaux, William of Saint-Thierry (d. 1148), Aelred of Rievaulx (d. 1167), and Richard of Saint-Victor (d. 1173)[77] – wrote treatises on love that simultaneously reflected on its nature and sought to render it spiritual by setting it in order. This linkage is key to understanding the originality of this monastic thought: the conversion of love did not occur without a knowledge of the soul and its faculties, creating at once a knowledge of man and a route towards his elevation. It was through this that a self-reflection which has greatly impressed modern readers took shape during the twelfth century. For instance, in his *Mirror of Charity*, written at the beginning of the 1140s, Aelred of Rievaulx included a reflection on free will and even a little essay on the affective faculty (*affectus*). Therein, it is clear that the desire for self-knowledge shown by many of the contemporary authors – in line with the famous Socratic injunction, 'know thyself' – was not carried out for its own sake, but for a higher goal, the return to God. It was from spiritual reflection on the love of God that a knowledge of the nature of man took shape. In this sense, the ordering of charity began with an interior ordering of the faculties of soul, envisioned as a balancing of reason and affectivity, of knowledge and sensitivity. Thus, Aelred thought of ordered charity as a co-operation between reason, which moderated, the will, which consented, and affect, which desired: one could love from reason, from affect, or, more perfectly, when the three faculties worked in unison towards the same goal.[78]

Another characteristic of this monastic thought on love is found in its hierarchies. The progress of the monk was broken down into a series of steps which converted carnal love into spiritual love, or elevated a love that was already spiritual towards embracing the divine. Here too, the spiritual ascent of the monk was critical. In his *On Loving God*, Bernard of Clairvaux identified four degrees of love: the love of oneself for oneself, the love of God for oneself, the love of God for God, and the love of oneself for God. Elsewhere, in a sermon, he established a hierarchy of five grades, each compared by analogy to the five senses, rising from the most carnal to the most discerning: the love of one's parents was likened to touch, social love to taste, the love of humanity to scent, the love of one's enemies to hearing, and the love of God to sight, the most noble of the senses.[79] Aelred of Rievaulx, the affective doctor of the twelfth century, identified five levels of desire within the soul – carnal affect, natural affect, social affect, rational affect, and spiritual affect[80] – and hierarchically ordered them by the objects that were loved (oneself, one's neighbour, God):

> Charity is divided into two parts: the love of God and the love of one's neighbour. Beyond that, there is charity at its beginning, charity in progress, and perfect charity.[81] In first place, God must be loved more than ourselves. Second, we must love ourselves more than our parents and family members. Third, parents and family members more than the rest of our friends. Fourth, friends more than strangers (those who are neither friends nor enemies). Fifth, strangers more than enemies. Sixth, enemies.

It is better to love one's friends than one's enemies, but more virtuous and more perfect to love one's enemies than to love one's friends.[82]

As for Richard of Saint-Victor, he devoted an entire treatise to defining the four degrees of 'violent charity' in various ways. Few texts take the symbolic framing of love so far, and none do it with such an impassioned rhetoric. Richard was not a monk, but a canon regular at the Parisian abbey of Saint-Victor, of which he was one of the most illustrious representatives. His spiritual writings are nevertheless very close in spirit and form to the mystical theology promoted by the Cistercians, especially when it came to the mystical lover of the Song of Songs:

> Great is the power of love (*dilectionis*); the virtue of love is marvellous. There are many degrees in it, and there are many forms among them. Who is capable of distinguishing them suitably or even so much as enumerating them? Of course, among these are the feelings of kindness, of friendship, of marriage and familial relationships, of fraternity, and in this manner many others. Yet beyond all of these degrees of love (*dilectionis*) is that burning and seething love (*amor*) which penetrates the heart and enkindles emotion, piercing through the soul itself to the very marrow of the bones, so that the soul may say 'I have been wounded by love' (S. of S. 4: 9).[83]

Richard imbued charity with the same erotic violence that seized the courtly lover and made him the slave of his lady: 'Love (*caritas*) wounds, love blinds, love makes one languish, love leads to weakness.'[84] The degree of love was reckoned by the intensity of its hold on one's being, based on the principle that all love binds. This discussion of love managed to simultaneously lead towards God and to oneself: it constructed an unusual psychology, unique to medieval Christianity, where affective self-conscience was found in the love of God. But Richard did not sink naively into an emotional mysticism: with the aid of processes of analogy and division, he joined together the inner man (the faculties of the soul) and the exterior man (social life), the interpretation of the Scriptures (applying the symbolism of the four degrees of charity to the Song of Songs and the Psalms) and the desire for God, in a symmetrical system which defined whether love was carnal or spiritual.[85] In the domain of the flesh, desire was more acceptable the less obsessive it was. Richard thus made conjugal affection the highest degree of carnal love, the only sort that could be virtuous. Conversely, however, in the realm of the spirit, the more violent the desire the more effective it was:

> Behold, we now have the four degrees of violence in fiery love (*dilectione*), concerning which we earlier proposed to write. Therefore, the first degree of violence exists when the mind cannot resist its desire, while the second

degree exists when that desire cannot be forgotten. Truly, the third degree exists when the mind can know nothing but its desire, while the fourth, which is also the last, exists when not even the very thing the mind desires is able to satisfy it. And so in the first degree love (*amor*) is unconquerable; in the second it is inseparable; in the third it is singular; and in the fourth it is insatiable. That which does not submit to other emotions is unconquerable; that which never retreats from memory is inseparable; that which does not take a companion is singular; when it cannot be satisfied, it is insatiable. And although several elements may be observed in each of the degrees, one should note in particular the excellence of love (*amoris*) in the first degree, in the second its vehemence, in the third its violence, and in the fourth its absolute pre-eminence. For how great is the excellence of a love (*amoris*) that exceeds all other feelings! How great, I beg, is the vehemence of a love (*dilectionis*) that does not permit the mind to be at peace! How great, I implore, is the violence of a love that violently expels all other emotion! How great is the utter pre-eminence of a jealous love (*emulationis*) that is never sufficient! Oh, excellence of love (*amoris*)! Oh vehemence of love (*dilectionis*)! Oh violence of love! Oh, total pre-eminence of jealous love (*emulationis*)![86]

The idea that charity knew variations of intensity, and that the presence of the Holy Spirit within the soul thus varied with it, formed part of a wider trend of integrating originally theological values within psychology.[87] It was a highly influential development, intertwining with the other forms of social re-evaluation that love was subjected to in the eleventh and twelfth centuries. As a result, the standing of passion received a powerful jolt. How could passion be thought of as a simple disturbance when it not only allowed for man's return to God but had also been placed within him as a mark of his likeness to God? Richard took this logic as far as it could go. For him, it was not enough that charity acted as a natural gravity which led man back to God; rather, he understood this natural feature as an imperious force. In a sense, Richard gave a place in nature to the emotional intensity that Anselm had cultivated as an experience. All love was vigorous and immoderate. As a result, man lived in a state of permanent exaltation which did not necessarily suggest failure or danger. Incidentally, Richard did not contest the ancient calls for affective moderation. Rather, he placed the nature of man on another plane, where even reasoned love (*ex deliberatione*) was strident, if only because it was always preceded by a desirous love (*ex affectione*).[88] Bernard of Clairvaux's celebrated maxim stated that, 'as for how He is to be loved, there is to be no limit to that love'.[89] Richard both radicalized and normalized this proposition: according to him, all love naturally tended towards immoderation.

The intensity of spiritual love served as a guarantee that union with God was possible. On an anthropological level, this development conferred a noetic dimension to love, which in its very action became knowledge of God. This led William of Saint-Thierry to state that, in the moment of ecstasy (*excessus mentis*), 'love itself is intellect (*amor ipse intellectus est*)'.[90] But the transformation affected the entirety of one's being according to Richard, for whom the loving soul that submerged itself in the love of God became a 'new creature (*nova creatura*)', created anew in a process the Victorine likened to 'rising from the dead (*quasi resurgens*)'.[91] If this transformation – sometimes likened by these authors to the smelting of iron – remained a distant horizon, it now seemed truly attainable thanks to love.[92] They could not have gone any further in their attempts to spiritualize the material.

Ordering the emotions

The monks remained faithful to the anthropology of Augustine, for whom all emotions were emanations of love. If love was ordered, the emotions would lead to virtue; if love was in disorder, they became vices. This same principle was deployed in turn for every emotion: each had to be directed correctly so as to act as a spiritual guide:

> These four emotions, moreover, are well known: love and joy, fear and sadness. Without these the human soul does not exist, but for certain people they bring a crown; for certain other people they bring confusion. For once purified and ordered, they render the soul glorious in a crown of virtues. Once disordered through confusion, the soul is disgraced and dejected.[93]

The ordering of the emotions was carried out on many levels. Firstly, it took place among the powers of the soul: the affective impulse was submitted to the moderating guidance of reason and intelligence. But it was also applied to the emotions in relation to each other. Bernard of Clairvaux compared them to the bride's crown in the Song of Songs (S. of S. 3: 11), which was layered in stages: first came fear, then joy, then sadness, and finally love. By layering up the effects of ordered emotions in pairs, Bernard could claim that the crown of virtues was perched on a ring of emotions: ordered fear and joy engendered prudence; joy and sadness led to temperance; sadness and love produced strength; love and fear brought justice. If the Abbot of Clairvaux's symbolic construction might seem somewhat contrived, it nevertheless shows the emergence of a moral psychology of the emotions, which took on a systematic character: 'Only grace can set in order what creation has given, so that virtues are nothing else than ordered affections [*affectiones*].'[94]

But it is in one of Richard of Saint-Victor's works, *The Twelve Patri-archs* or *Benjamin Minor*, that one finds the most thoroughgoing twelfth-century monastic reflection on the moral ordering of the emotions.[95] While hard to date, this text is one of the best known and most dissemi-nated texts of the Victorine master. It is presented as an allegorical com-mentary on the twelve sons that Jacob had by two spouses, Leah and Rachel, and their servants, Balah and Zelpha (Gen. 29–49). They per-sonify the soul and its qualities and are arranged in a spiritual progres-sion, culminating in the final son, Benjamin, who represents the union with God in contemplation. This commentary is entirely emblematic of the monastic theology of the twelfth century, which did not separate psychological investigation from spiritual goals. At the soul's summit, Jacob has pride of place: he represents the *animus*, the intellectual part of the soul. His two spouses symbolize reason and affectivity: 'Just as it belongs to Rachel to meditate, to contemplate, to distinguish and to understand; so it certainly pertains to Leah to weep, to groan, to grieve, and to sigh.'[96] The two wives are assisted by servants: Balah, the servant of Rachel, embodies imagination, while Zelpha, the servant of Leah, represents sensation.[97] Having established the necessary balance between Rachel, Leah, and their servants, Richard focused on Leah's children, likening each to an emotion:

> There are thus seven principal affections,[98] which rise by turns from the one affective disposition of the soul: hope and fear, joy and grief, hatred, love and shame. All of these can be ordered at one time and disordered at another. But only when they have been ordered are they then to be counted among the sons of Jacob.[99]

Richard explained how each of these ordered emotions arose, and how they converged towards mystical ecstasy. Penitential theology had made a deep impact on mid-twelfth-century intellectual culture: it was a major theme of theological and moral exploration at Paris. Thus, the two first sons of Leah – Reuben and Simeon – represent the fear of sin and the pain of contrition. Fear comes first, for only the preceding terror of sin could truly render the pain of repentance effective, as many contempo-rary theologians confirmed:

> For he who truly repents and truly grieves will receive indulgence without doubt and without delay. A prayer that is offered from a contrite and humbled heart is more quickly heard with favour. A heart is humbled through fear, contrite through grief.[100]

One could easily imagine how, from emotion to emotion, affectivity enlightened by reason could progress along the path of contemplation.

If the structure of the text was original, Richard was no innovator in associating spiritual virtues with ordered emotions, and thus affirming the moral value of emotions as well as their ambivalence. On the other hand, he was the first author since the Church Fathers to give such attention to the benefits of shame.[101] When he spoke of shame, Richard's meaning differed from modern definitions. In current psychological thought, shame is systematically defined as a negative emotion, a painful sentiment tied to a moral judgement, and one which is best avoided.[102] If some specific forms of shame still come with a positive connotation, they are considered distinct and labelled as such, e.g. modesty, reserve, and scruple.[103] The terminology of the Christian lexicon was more flexible (*pudor, verecundia, erubescentia*).[104] The pain that shame caused, a constant presence, was less important than its nature, its motivations, and its ends. One sort of shame could cause great suffering while remaining entirely supportable, even honourable. Meanwhile another, less trying form could be deemed detrimental, both morally and socially. This partition between good and bad shame has already been touched upon with Augustine, who, in *The City of God*, linked shame directly to sin: for him, it served both as penance and as a commitment to redemption.[105] This penitential dimension to Christian shame was linked to another meaning, drawn from classical ethics: that of shame as a fear of infamy.[106] In the Christian system, the two came together at the junction between disgust over sin and the honour of God. From the end of the eleventh century, shame was subjected to mounting attention as pastoral care became a concern of the highest order.[107] Theologians attributed an efficacy to shame, both as a disgust over sin and as a shield to guard against it.[108] This 'good' shame became increasingly conflated with what we now call modesty or reserve, eventually becoming a virtue with aesthetic qualities, as the Cistercian Baldwin of Ford (d. 1190) signalled in a sermon on the Annunciation of Mary. Here, the interlacing of noble forms of shame reached a rhetorical paroxysm, while simultaneously hinting at all the psychological complexity of the 'map of shame' drawn up by the clerics:

> The grace of her charm resides in the grace of her complexion, where paleness and blush mingle. The colour here is that of modesty (*pudor*). Modesty is twofold: it is pure (*pudor pudicus*), and it is reserved (*pudor verecundus*). Her purity (*pudicitia*) is like a white lily, her blush like a scarlet rose. Purity whitens her face, and modest reserve (*verecundia*) scatters her cheeks with red. Reserve (*verecundia*) becomes the guardian of purity; it also becomes its jewellery and ornament. [...] This holy reserved modesty is founded on blushing at depravity, purity on guarding herself immaculate.[109]

93

While this good shame was effective and virtuous, bad shame inhibited the admission of faults that made the sacrament of penance effective: it resulted from a surfeit of pride or fear over one's social esteem. It was why, in the eyes of Richard, shame was the final emotion that one had to put in order. It was personified by Dinah, the only daughter of Jacob. As a virtue, shame had been considered as the pre-eminent feminine emotion since antiquity.[110] Spurred by curiosity, Dinah fled the paternal home: left to the ravages of men, she became a victim of rape. In the exegetical tradition, Dinah was judged rather severely. Richard shifted the perspective by taking a psychological angle: the flight of Dinah symbolized the erring of the soul that blushed too much at its weaknesses. She thus illustrated a form of bad shame.[111] As for ordered shame, Richard conceived of it first and foremost as a rejection of sin. As a result, shame followed hate in the process of emotional ordering:

> Learn first to hate sin, and then you will begin truly to feel ashamed of it. If you truly hate, you quickly feel ashamed of it. That shame is known to be true when hatred of vices precedes and accompanies it. Otherwise, if you are caught in sin and confounded with shame when you are caught, I do not believe that you feel ashamed of the fault, but of the infamy.[112]

The two faces of shame – the good shame which demonstrated the rejection of sin, and the bad shame associated with fear of social ignominy – can both be witnessed here. But above all, the passage illustrates how an entirely novel conception of emotional sincerity was constructed in this period. This notion is at the core of modern psychological thought, but it was conceived differently in medieval Christian culture. What Richard called *verus pudor* – the adjective, meaning 'true' or 'authentic' was applicable to all emotions – is certainly reminiscent of that psychological interiority which we today call 'sincerity'. But the latter alone did not make something 'true': whatever was felt needed to be directed towards virtue. Sensation and moral value were inseparable in defining the intimate. Ordered shame was both a feeling and a moral conscience. Without virtuous direction, no emotion was true or sincere. This concept might seem confusing to our modern sensibilities, where psychological emotion is conceived separately from any moral substrate, indeed as the very condition of subjectivity. But it lay at the foundation of the Christian emotional system. From its earliest roots, monastic spirituality had in fact sketched the contours of what one might call an objective affectivity. Here, emotion spoke the truth both of oneself and itself, given that it was linked to morality, and, in the final analysis, to God.

Sensitive pieties

In the twelfth century, the intimate emotional encounter between the monk and God gave rise to a diverse and abundant spiritual literature. This concerned as much the affective meditations of the monk *in corde suo*, 'in his heart', as his devotion to a sensitive Christ.[113] Monks and nuns were to march their emotions to the battlefront, while Christ himself, that divine object of desire, was presented to the devout as an emotional man:

> Jesus, sweetness of our hearts
> Source of truth and light of the spirit,
> he exceeds all joy,
> and all desire
> No tongue can express it
> no hand can write it
> only he who has lived it can know
> what is the love of Jesus.[114]

In seeking the humanity of Jesus, the religious were to take stock of their own affective lives. Devotion to Christ set in motion the emotions, the senses, and the imagination – i.e. the bodily faculties in contact with the soul and the spiritual faculties in contact with the body. Hence the extraordinary success of devotion not only to the Passion, to Christ's suffering on the cross, and to his wounds, but also to the Christ Child, to the Christ who was full of compassion for Mary Magdalene and his mother, and to the Christ who formed a privileged friendship with John. Yet, according to the stereotypes of the age, a Christ who felt emotion was a Christ made feminine: the theme of the Christ-mother in Cistercian literature, as well as that of the abbot as mother, bear testament to it.[115] Incarnation and 'affectivization' came as a pair, since the two principles were tied together in anthropological representations.

The Cistercian abbot Aelred of Rievaulx was the twelfth-century author who best expressed this new spirituality. Heralding the devotion to the Christ Child, he composed a treatise entirely devoted to the childhood of Jesus, a phase of his life that was in fact little described in the canonical Gospels.[116] These considerations allowed him to elaborate a method that would become very influential, that of placing the moments of Jesus' life before 'the eyes of the heart'. Childhood was a privileged moment for Aelred, since the frailty of the child prompted affection and effusion: it symbolized a 'spiritual birth' as well as that time before the age of reason when affectivity remained untarnished by personal sin. At the end of his life, Aelred summarized the process in *The Life of the*

Recluse, which he addressed to his sister who had lived enclosed within the four walls of a cramped cell for many years. The first part of the text calls on the recluse to relive in spirit the principal moments of the life of Christ, and even to participate in them, starting with the wonders of the manger: 'Go embrace his sweet crib; slowly press your lips against his most holy feet, cover them with kisses, so that love conquers timidity, so that affection drives away fear.'[117] This rhetorical strategy, which specialists call hypotyposis, was well-worn by the later Middle Ages. But in the mid-twelfth century, it had a cutting edge, hacking through the barriers that separated the devout from Christ. It was no accident that this development is so marked in a text addressed to a woman.[118] Aelred was bold enough to encourage his sister, a virgin among virgins, to iden-tify with Mary Magdalene, an adulterous woman, and to feel her emo-tions as if they were caresses in a loving, body-to-body embrace with Christ: 'If up to now, he has denied you the approach of his feet, implore him, pray to him, raise up your eyes swollen with tears towards him. And with deep sighs and indescribable groans, grasp what you desire.'[119] The experiential qualities of participatory meditation came to a head in remembrance of the Passion. It became a moment of compassion in which, through the rising force of emotion, the devout reader not only took part in the suffering of Christ but was consumed by it:

> Who can bear to witness it? Pity now fills your heart, I know, and every-thing within you is inflamed by zeal. But, I say, let him suffer, he who suffers for you. [...] It is hardly surprising if you sadden at the darkening of the sun, if you tremble when the earth trembles, if your heart breaks with the rocks, if you cry along with the women crying at the foot of the cross. But amid these emotions, think of his most tender heart, which preserved such calm, which held so much pity. He did not concern himself with his injuries, he thought nothing of his punishment, and felt no insult. But rather, he felt compassion for the authors of his Passion, he healed those who wounded him, and gave life to those who killed him.[120]

The enclosed environments of religious life had been the proving grounds for a spiritualization of the sensitive and emotional life. Never-theless, such a direction ended up laying the groundwork for its spread beyond the cloister. In an age where historians have described the march of 'territorialization' within the Church,[121] an inverse, and doubtless complementary phenomenon can be observed in the realm of piety: the rising spiritual value of emotion and, what is more, the measuring of its worth by the quality of what was felt allowed for a form of deterritori-alization.[122] The unique communal dynamic of monasticism was far from exhausted. But by becoming more intimate, it became more universal, preparing the ground for these models to spread beyond cloistral walls.

The world as horizon: spiritual friendship and fraternal charity in the twelfth century

When it came to spiritual love, the bonds with God and one's neighbour were inseparable. Alongside the experiences seen on a smaller scale in the affective communities of the likes of Romuald and Anselm of Canterbury, the values of charity, dilection, and spiritual friendship became the very essence of monastic reform: they dominated thought on the *vita communis* within the cloister, on the bonds between monasteries of the same congregation, and even, beyond this, on Christian society as a whole. The values of spiritual friendship and charity absorbed the logics of communal solidarity which ran through feudal society. As a result, the bonds of the flesh (familial and political) came to be enveloped by the bonds of spiritual love.[123] In the process, spiritual bonds were made flesh: they became psychologized and socialized. None of these values were original to twelfth-century Christianity. Rather, their originality derived from the way they were now tied together. In the age of feudal monarchies, just as in the Carolingian era, this immersion revolved around charity. But the principle of government by network, so characteristic of feudal society, strengthened not only the political but also the spiritual foundations of friendship. On the scale of religious values, spiritual friendship enhanced the virtue of charity.

For an abbot or a monk, writing or uttering words of friendship did not necessarily signify the existence of a special affective bond with their recipient. This can be witnessed in the major collections of monastic letters that enjoyed their heyday in the twelfth century: for instance, those of the two great rival abbots, the Abbot of Cluny, Peter the Venerable (d. 1156) – nearly 200 letters – and the Abbot of Clairvaux, Bernard – more than 500 letters – as well as those of Peter (d. 1182), Abbot of the Benedictine monastery of Celle (180 letters). The vocabulary of friendship and affectionate address was part of a formal rhetoric designed to maintain or promote public ties in various contexts: it was most frequently used to accompany a request or settle a disagreement. The language of passionate friendship was sometimes directed to distant correspondents, with whom the author enjoyed no personal connection, while letters sent to those nearer might be more soberly drafted.[124] Thus, in the very public correspondence of Peter the Venerable, who led the most important monastery in the West for thirty years, half of those addressed are defined as friends or described with marks of affection: 'my dear' (*meus, mi*); 'dearest' (*carissimus*), 'beloved' (*dilectus*), 'worthy of being embraced' (*amplectendus*). Nevertheless, within this rather restrictive rhetoric of friendship, little signs, such as the use of words rarely employed, might indicate to the correspondent that he held a special place in the writer's heart. Such is the case with Peter of Burgundy, Archbishop of Lyon and a former monk of Cluny, whom Peter the Venerable described as *amantissimus* (most loved) and *dulcissimus* (sweetest), superlatives that he used only twice in his entire correspondence.[125] To a lesser degree, he also appears to have employed strategies similar to those of Anselm of Canterbury, distinguishing different circles amongst his friends by the grammatical inflection of affective terms. Nevertheless, the use of intensive forms did not always imply the highest level of attachment.

What stands out above all else in the writing of Peter the Venerable is that same rhetoric of affective inclusion which had resounded at Cluny since the mid-tenth century. During the abbacy of Aymard (943–65), a new affective vocabulary appeared in certain Cluniac charters.[126] These words were those of lay donors, who used them to express their attachment not only to their own relatives (husband to wife, parents to children), but also to the abbot and the monks. They were not consistently deployed, which shows that they had a political purpose, namely that of building an 'emotional community' binding the monastery to its lay benefactors. The love declared in the charters of donation thus participated in a political and spiritual polarization of space, also witnessed in those martyrologies that gave the title of 'friends' to the laity allied to the monastery.[127] The monastic promotion of spiritual kinship, founded to no small extent on *caritas*, should likewise not be forgotten.[128] Here, the affective connotations of charity took part in a spiritualization of the bonds of elective kinship, and even of natural family ties.[129] The twelfth-century correspondence of Peter the Venerable continued this inclusive policy, but altered its scale: from his time onward, the horizon was Christendom as a whole, even if this change de-localized a bond which was by definition personal.

The twelfth-century expansion of the rhetoric of intense charity and friendship in the conduct of monastic affairs thus speaks to the recognized capacity of the emotional register to bring correspondents together and express solidarities and communities of shared interest.[130] It was precisely because the Cluniacs and Cistercians imbued the emotions of attachment with such a remarkable aptitude to seal or renew these bonds – rendered spiritual in the process – that they were integrated into epistolary communication. The fact that the vocabulary of friendship and love primarily defined a network of relationships should not lead us to separate this register from the experience of affection by which we define emotion today. Due to the rhetorical and semantic continuity, there was no clear divide between political and personal friendship any more than there was between expressed emotion (in speech, writing, or in deed) and felt emotion. At the very least, these were the cues that shaped the emotional and affective culture of the age. Where a true divide can be see, it is between true and false friendship, between trust and treason, much more than between what was said and what was felt. Public friendships, founded on interest or gratitude, were not placed in a separate category to more intimate relationships. The former might be judged less intense, or less spiritual, but the two very much pertained to the same interpersonal context.

This idea was given clear expression by Aelred of Rievaulx, who was also the twelfth century's foremost theorist of Christian friendship. The career of Aelred is emblematic of this expansion of affective spirituality: he too moved from a monastic anchorage to take part in a broader political project.[131] He was born to a line of priests in charge of the community of Hexham, near the Scottish border, at the end of the eleventh century. His family became embroiled in the demands of Gregorian reform, which called for an end to the treatment of ecclesiastical offices as patrimony. The young Aelred was sent to the court of the king of Scotland, David (d. 1153), who became his close friend. At the age of twenty-four, he entered the monastery of Rievaulx (between York and Durham), founded two years earlier (1132) by the companions of Bernard of Clairvaux. Bequests and recruits flooded through the gates. Aelred became abbot of the house in 1147 and remained in this office until his death in 1167. This son of an English priest thus found himself at the heart of a duality which marked the politico-religious history of his place and time: the reform of the Church and the pacification of England. All his life, Aelred served these two causes. The originality of his corpus bears witness to it: it not only contains spiritual writings and sermons, but also a genealogy of the kings of England and even a life of the last Saxon king, Edward the Confessor (d. 1066). In the eyes of Aelred, who wrote a portion of his works during the civil war between Matilda (d. 1167) and Stephen of Blois (d. 1154), the most certain path towards political peace was to be found in a thorough Christianization of the ties that bound society together: the bonds of blood, alliance, and friendship. As early as the 1140s, he wrote his *Mirror of Charity*, in which the forms of spiritual pleasure found in friendship already held a key place. Twenty years later, he composed a work on *Spiritual Friendship*.[132] By choosing to approach personal relationships from this angle, rather than through the more common thematic of love towards one's neighbour, Aelred participated in the twelfth-century reconfiguration of the bond of charity. From a literary perspective, this development went hand-in-hand with an enthusiasm for Cicero's *De amicitia*, and found its place amidst a broader trend which encompassed feudal ties of vassalage and courtly literature.[133]

If the value of *amicitia* played an essential role in Christian thought from late antiquity onward,[134] it was not until the twelfth century that the notion of spiritual friendship gave rise to a truly theoretical and normative reflection. Aelred's treatise drew its framework from Cicero, the master of friendship; following this model, it is constructed as a dialogue, between the abbot himself and several monks. Over the course of a number of privileged conversations, reminiscent of the Conferences of Cassian, the great principles of Ciceronian friendship – equality, reciprocity, fidelity, striving for virtues – were discussed with reference to the thought of the Church Fathers and, of course, the Scriptures.[135] Aelred identified various forms of friendship, which are somewhat reminiscent of Aristotelian typology: carnal friendship, which rested on attraction; worldly friendship, which grew from common interest; and spiritual friendship, which was founded on virtue. If spiritual friendship had the greatest value, neither carnal friendship – provided that all sexual desire was put aside – nor worldly friendships – provided that they served honourable aims – were rejected. On the contrary, Aelred could happily conceive of a progressive journey through the ranks of friendship, which formed an accompaniment of sorts to the quest for virtue: over time, friendships could readily progress from carnal or circumstantial to become spiritual. For Aelred, each of these friendships was derived from a specific type of affection. Carnal friendship had its origin in carnal affection (*affectus carnalis*); worldly friendship was linked to the affection of gratitude (*affectus officialis*); while spiritual friendship was nurtured by rational affection (*affectus rationalis*):

> The source and origin of friendship is love. Although love can exist without friendship, friendship can never exist without love. Love develops either from nature or from duty, from reason alone or from affection alone, or from both together. We are bound together by a special affection from nature, as a mother loves her child. From duty, when introduced and accepted by reason. From reason alone, as we love our enemies, not from a spontaneous inclination of the mind but by the constraint of the commandment. From affection alone, when someone wins the love of another because of such physical qualities as beauty or strength of eloquence. From reason and affection together, as when one whom reason persuades us is lovable because of his meritorious virtue enters another's spirit through his sweetness of manner and the charm of a purer life. Reason is so joined to affection that love may be chaste through reason and delightful through affection.[136]

The text in fact says nothing of the practice of friendship. But on a theoretical plane, at least, it speaks to the links which existed between types of friendship that today are strictly differentiated. This fashion of not *a priori* separating public from private friendships went back to antiquity, to Aristotle and Cicero. For them it was meaningless to separate the quest for individual benefit, the aspiration towards virtue, and the concern for the common good, since it was part of the friendship's nature as an interpersonal bond to straddle these different levels.

While it would be naive to envision sentimental attachment at the first mention of friendship, one would be no less blind to ignore that all these authors were steeped in a literature where friendship was saturated in emotion. The emotional culture of the literate religious of the twelfth century shows that such oppositions make little sense if posed in an exclusive manner. Aelred participated in this 'affectivization' of friendship, which took place between the eleventh and thirteenth centuries: his efforts were followed up by other authors, including Peter of Blois (d. 1203), who likewise found a certain influence.[137] The English abbot was greatly attached to the emotional value of friendship, however virtuous or otherwise it might be. It was even more important since emotion, when purified and rational, came to be seen as one of the most effective paths towards divine conformity in the twelfth century. The emotional dimension of friendship had always held an important place in Christian communities; with Alcuin and then Anselm of Canterbury, it has been seen how this dimension only intensified. By theorizing friendship, Aelred pushed the joining of virtue and emotion within this bond to its apogee. While the aim of spiritual friendship was the love of Christ by way of loving one's neighbour, it remained a much more specific path, one which passed through care, sweetness, and affection. As a result, sentiment took on a specifically theological – even eschatological – dimension:

> When you have assured yourself that a friend so selected and proved desires neither to seek from you anything shameful nor, if asked, to offer you anything shameful, and when you are satisfied that your friend considers friendship a virtue, not a bargain, and that he abhors flattery, detests adulation, and has been found frank but discreet, patient under correction, and strong and constant in affection, then you will experience this spiritual sweetness: *how good and how pleasant it is for brethren to live in unity* (Ps. 132: 1). What an advantage it is, then, to grieve for one another, to work for one another, to bear one another's burdens. [...] Meanwhile, how delightful friends find their meetings together, the exchange of mutual interests, the exploration of every question, and the attainment of mutual agreement in everything.
>
> [...] Thus praying to Christ for a friend and desiring to be heard by Christ for a friend, we focus on Christ with love and longing. Then sometimes suddenly, imperceptibly, affection melts into affection, and somehow touching the sweetness of Christ nearby, one begins to taste how dear he is and experience how sweet he is. Thus rising from that holy love with which

a friend embraces a friend to that with which a friend embraces Christ, one may take the spiritual fruit of friendship fully and joyfully into the mouth, while looking forward to all the abundance in the life to come.[138]

In this fashion, Aelred brought about a remarkable shift from charity to friendship, which, by virtue of its selectivity (charity applied to all as an obligation, while friendship arose through choice), became critical to the ultimate spiritual transformation envisaged. One of the interlocutors in *Spiritual Friendship* thus raises a curious suggestion: 'To what does this lead? Should I say of friendship what John, the friend of Jesus, said of charity (1 John 4: 16), *God is friendship?*'[139] To this, Aelred replies:

This is novel indeed and lacks the authority of the Scriptures. The rest of that verse about charity, however, I surely do not hesitate to attribute to friendship, because *the one who remains in friendship remains in God, and God in him* (1 John 4: 16).[140]

The audacity of this proposal should not be underestimated: the rhetorical precaution that Aelred used to legitimize it only goes to prove the point. For fraternal charity was a somewhat loose emotional bond and the love it contained was highly rational. True friendship, on the other hand, carried with it an intensity of attachment, a taste for another who was loved by choice rather than by any moral obligation. It is thus fair to speak of an affective hardening of spiritual ties in the twelfth century. The suspicions voiced in the earliest age of cenobitic monasticism concerning the individual bonds that could develop within the cloister were long forgotten. For Aelred, these bonds, which might distinguish a pair or a little group of friends from the rest of the community, were not only to be encouraged, but represented a special path towards spiritual perfection. Thus, the monastic community as an indivisible unity of prayer no longer represented the only horizon of cloistral life. When it came to spiritual advancement, the pursuit of an individual encounter with God and the communion of all brothers in prayer were surpassed by the possibility of creating groups of spiritual friends, who grew in Christ through shared emotion.

But did the cloistral enclosure not risk losing its privileged status in the process? Were monastery walls not rendered less necessary for salvation through this monastic promotion of spiritual friendship? If this friendship today seems paradoxical, it was not perceived as such amid the religious developments that took place from the thirteenth century onward.[141] At least in this regard, it seems that the conditions were in place for a 'deterritorialization' of spiritual bonds: due to their reliance on moral qualities and the structuring power of affectivity, they would be universalized, transcending all estates and conditions. One witnesses both a widening of the symbolic space of the monastery and the surpassing of this spatial anchorage of the spiritual, two complementary phenomena that are quite emblematic of the spirit of Gregorian reform. This evolution climaxed in the following century with the release of religious from the cloister, a development which ran alongside the promotion of spiritual couples and even circles of spiritual friends. Within it, affective investment in God and in one's neighbour, now more than ever at the heart of the dynamics of spiritual formation, played a role of the utmost importance.

In the eleventh and twelfth centuries, the reorientation of Christian anthropology once again sprang from the monasteries, the hermitages and the collegiate churches, even if it quite rapidly (from the middle of the eleventh century) became part of a movement of reform which animated the Church as a whole. This groundswell was founded on the image of the Incarnation, which drew together the power of redemption and the humanization of the divine. From then on, the relationship between God incarnate and humanity, between his Passion and their passions, became the nerve-centre of Christianity. At the heart of this arrangement, the affective faculty became a capacity for conforming man to the divine, and the emotions became agents for its implementation. Human passions responded to a new paradigm, one that did not replace its ancient forbear – that of vices and virtues as the condition of post-Fall man – but added to it and took shape alongside it. It transformed their image but above all reinforced their efficacy on both a religious and social plane. The dynamics themselves were no less multifaceted. On the one hand, there was a descending model, institutional and moderated, that of the Incarnation as charity (God sent his Son to spread love); on the other, an ascending model, rather more singular and radical, that of the Incarnation as 'passion' (man grew in love through his imitation of and/or participation in the sufferings of Christ). Whether complementing or competing, they are found at work throughout the last centuries of the Middle Ages. As a result, the impassioning of Christianity could hardly be contained within monastic walls for long: this new anthropology of salvation, founded on affectivity, set out to conquer the laity. At the same time, it encountered other social and discursive logics, drawn from scientific thought on man, as well as aristocratic culture and governmental practices. We will return to all of these aspects. From these interactions, influences, and relationships, arose the emotional originality of later medieval society, on which so much ink has been spilt.

— 5 —

THE ETHICS AND AESTHETICS OF ARISTOCRATIC EMOTIONS IN FEUDAL SOCIETY (ELEVENTH TO THIRTEENTH CENTURIES)

Between the ninth and twelfth centuries, the disintegration of the imperial project and the emergence of a narrower political order within a feudal context led to profound political transformations in the West, transformations that served to place person-to-person ties at the heart of government. In this new world of fragmented powers, ties of interpersonal loyalty between lords who came from the warrior class defined the balance of power much more than they did in Carolingian times: it was a naturally unstable and fluid compound. The feudal system provided the political framework for the gradual reconstruction of sovereign authorities in the twelfth and thirteenth centuries. It relied on bonds of lineage, on engagements made publicly, on declared values of fidelity and loyalty, and on a very hierarchical structuring of warrior companionship.

In this sense, affective ideology remained fundamentally unshaken at the start of the new millennium. Much as it had been since the very early Middle Ages, it remained founded on the dialectic of friendship and enmity; it structured the relationships that defined social power in concentric circles, running from those of kinship, real or artificial, through to networks of allies. Just as in the age of Carolingian vassalage, the ties of authority and alliance of the feudal era were usually expressed in an affective register. As seen, the perception of politics in the Middle Ages as being 'hot-headed' has its roots in the power that was commonly perceived within such emotional bonds. There was no stronger bond than the love expressed by friendship or charity, since it inextricably tied together notions of service, protection, shared interest, and attachment, within an egalitarian fiction that readily accommodated hierarchical relationships.[1] The chronicles of the eleventh and twelfth centuries repeat it at every opportunity: by uniting men, homage created a friendship between lineages.

In a society where government was brought to life through interpersonal relationships, affective bonds had a *de facto* political dimension; conversely, all alliances and hostilities were formalized at an emotional level. The reasoned use of the emotions in the exercise of power thus found another source of legitimacy. At the end of the eleventh century, however, a new continent emerged within the medieval world: courtly literature, written in the vernacular by laymen, both noble and non-noble, as well as by clerics. Emotions and feelings were both named and sung; and within this field, they were legion. Naturally, love was omnipresent, but its dominance would not overshadow other courtly emotions: joy, sadness, anguish, anger, shame, and many other feelings were at the heart of poetic structure and narrative. Jean de Meun (d. 1305), in his continuation of the *Roman de la rose* (*c.* 1270), the great allegorical romance of the amorous soul begun by Guillaume de Lorris (d. *c.* 1260), both spoke of and personified the emotions: Shame, Fear, Jealousy, and even Pity conversed with and confronted Reason, adapting the tradition of ancient psychomachia.[2]

For centuries, literature had remained exclusively Latin, and was produced by clerics alone. In Western Christendom, Latin was first and foremost the sacred language of the Bible: it was the language of the Psalms, tirelessly sung in monastic churches, and the language of that love poem *par excellence*, the Song of Songs. At the start of the eleventh century, the gap between Romance languages derived from late antique Latin and Latin literature had long been so wide that those who did not know the latter could accurately be termed 'illiterate' (*illiterati*). But from the mid-eleventh century, a Romance literary culture took shape in the space of just a few decades, granting historians access to an oral poetic tradition that was doubtless already strong. It was not only one of the most beautiful fruits of aristocratic society, but formed an integral part of it. It should not be considered an essentially distorting mirror, to which one must pose the right questions to subtly reconstruct the underlying reality, but rather as an important device that played a role at the very heart of social life. Nor should one fall into the trap laid by the apparent irrationality of emotions. Behind what are justly seen as aesthetic games, the evocative power and cultural rationality of the emotions sung by the bards must be taken seriously.

The emotional order of feudal society

A society of spectacle

Whether lyric or epic, the courtly poetry that we read silently today was not written to resound quietly within the heart, but to be sung publicly, sometimes accompanied by instrumental music, before audiences that had gathered for festivities. The seigneurial court was not a world of silence and muted cohabitation. It lived according to the rules of a warrior class, founded above all on companionship, and thus on a physical proximity guaranteed by bonds of fealty and service. This was especially true for the more modest knights, who, lacking land, lived in the castles of their lords. These found their upkeep there, sometimes enjoying a salary: their social position thus depended on their proximity to their lord. Even when this physical bond was not lived out day-to-day, it remained symbolically vital, as witnessed in homage rituals that were, in some regions, sealed with a kiss on the lips. Thus, immersed within a political society where words and deeds were of vital importance, hierarchical relationships and ties of alliance and lineage had to be seen and felt in order to be recognized. The public enactment and palpable expression of political bonds were thus the preconditions for their social efficacy and, in turn, for peace.

The lyrical performances of the bards must be seen through the lens of this obligation to publicly express such bonds as a vector of seigneurial power. Beyond this, by publicly offering the spectacle of singers and jesters to the guests of the court, the lord or prince displayed an essential quality in the feudal political economy: largesse. The feudal lord was a nourishing master; he was loved for what he gave and made stronger by what he yielded. At least, that was how the bonds of vassalage were played out symbolically. In reality, a fief entered the patrimony of the vassal, who served his lord on account of the land which he held from him. Nevertheless, when the people of the court were assembled with their guests, they formed a *de facto* community. Its cohesion, albeit ephemeral and scripted, was reinforced by the various episodes that punctuated these reunions. The musical performances of courtly chant, lyric poems, or *chansons de geste*, including their sensory effects, were clearly part of this social representation. Within the moment, the courtly community was doubtless a community of feeling, joined by poetic and musical emotion. How can the historian today even grasp, let alone measure, the musical affectivity of courtly lyric, outside of which lies only a truncated human experience?

Medieval music was an art which was both analysed (it allowed the intellectual contemplation of numbers) and felt (it shaped the states of the soul). The emotional symbolism of music was deeply rooted in Western culture and formed one of the pillars of liturgical chant. Even Augustine, so critical of any sensory pleasure, laid down his arms when he evoked the spiritual benefits of sacred chant:

I realize that all the varied emotions of the human spirit respond in ways proper to themselves to a singing voice and a song, which arouse them by appealing to some secret affinity. [...] All the same, I remember the tears I shed at the Church's song in the early days of my newly-recovered faith, and how even today I am moved not by the singing as such but by the substance of what is sung, when it is rendered in a clear voice and in the most appropriate melodies, and then I recognize once more the value of this custom. Thus I vacillate between the danger of sensuality and the undeniable benefits. Without pretending to give a definitive opinion, I am more inclined to approve the custom of singing in church, to the end that through the pleasures of the ear a weaker mind may rise up to loving devotion.[3]

Since antiquity, modal melodies were associated with moral and emotional values, and these were passed down to medieval theorists. In his *Fundamentals of Music*, Boethius (d. 524) provided a synthesis of the Greek tradition, dividing music into three branches which were referenced throughout the Middle Ages. There was cosmic music, found in the harmony of celestial bodies. Human music, meanwhile, embodied the harmony of the spiritual and corporeal parts of the human compound. The final form – that which concerns us here – was instrumental music, which also included the human voice: this acted as a sensitive imitation of celestial harmonies and reflected the balance between body and soul. Boethius, following both Plato and Aristotle, assigned emotional values to harmonies. If music did not always bridle one's behaviour, it could help regulate it. Certain modes calmed, others excited: 'It is true that a sensual mind takes pleasure in sensual modes, whereby, listening to them often, it is weakened and destroyed. On the other hand, a harsher mind takes pleasure in more impetuous modes, whereby it hardens upon hearing them.'[4] Centuries later, in the age where courtly lyric found success, the authors who studied the *quadrivium* were entirely conscious of this power and could technically define the harmonic structures that produced it. For instance, in the early thirteenth century, the Bishop of Paris, William of Auvergne (d. 1249), would write:

From what has been said, it can be readily understood that [harmonies] fruitfully assist and strengthen intellectual virtue and the noble motivating powers, just as the songs that belong to the relaxed chromatic genre strongly excite and heighten lascivious and sexual motivations. Similarly, those belonging to the third genre – diatonic – lead human souls to hardness, and incite and arouse ferocity. Because of this advice from the musicians, they tend to be employed in battle and to rather remarkable effect, since they even incite horses to war, stimulated by the sound of the diatonic form.[5]

It would be hazardous to extrapolate an interpretative framework for emotional lyricism from such theories. The medieval theorists did not always attribute the same emotional values to the eight Gregorian modes. Far from it: while one person might reserve a particular harmony for serious emotions, another thought the same to be appropriate for joyous scenes! Nevertheless, contemporary musicologists have attempted to explore the matter.[6] The difficulties of reading that result from the absence of rhythmic indication in melodic notation will not be dwelt on here. The neumes give the pitch of sounds, but not their length: specialists thus openly recognize that modern attempts to restore modal chant are at best hobbyism and at worst parody, rather than serious interpretations. Nevertheless, contemporary guidance is not entirely lacking: for Remigius of Auxerre (d. *c.* 908), in the tenth century, the complete chant had to provide a harmony of sound, words, and dance.[7] To seek the connection between meaning and sound, and to see both as part of the same emotional expression, is thus not in vain. Verses and rhyme framed the melodic form. But did the melodies chosen to sing the *planh* – the chant of lamentation – or the *canso* – the chant of love – make use of distinct forms to provoke emotions of pain or empathy in the audience? Or was the melodic form arbitrarily perceived as signifying sadness or love?

While it is prudent to resist the temptation of viewing courtly music as an amplification of the emotional value of the text, it is certain that the melody served the text, 'calibrating' its emotional perception. One can sometimes glimpse how contemporaries perceived the evocative power of music, such as in the following description drawn from the *Roman de Tristan* of Thomas of England (active *c.* 1170–80). Here the writer drew on the well-known motif of the 'eaten heart' to describe Iseult singing a lament:[8]

> *En sa chambre se set un jor/ E fait un lai pitus d'amur :/ Coment dan Guirun fu supris,/ Pur l'amur de la dam ocis/ Qu'il sur tute rïen ama,/ E coment li cuns puis li dona/ Le cuer Guirun a sa moillier/ Par engin un jor a mangier,/ E la dolur que la dame out/ Quant la mort de sun ami sout./ La reïne chante dulcement,/ La voiz acorde a l'estrument./ Les mainz sunt beles, li lais buons/ Dulce la voiz, bas li tons.*

> One day she sat in her chamber/ and composed a tragic lay of love:/ how my lord Guirun was taken unawares/ and killed for the love of a lady/ he loved beyond all else,/ and how the count her lord one day/ tricked his wife by giving her/ Guinrun's heart to eat,/ and of the sorrow the lady felt/ when she learned of the death of her loved one./ Iseult sang so sweetly,/ her voice in tune with her instrument./ Her fair hands played, the lay she sang was good,/ her voice soft-pitched, the tone of her instrument low.

Rather than being entirely defined by the words or the melody, lyrical emotion was a product of performance; and each performance was uniquely accented by the rhythmic judgements and dramatizations of its interpreters. Courtly lyric conformed to rhetorical frameworks and melodic conventions. The audience knew by heart the adventures of Lancelot and the tragic outcome of the romance of Tristan and Iseult, and were no less familiar with the repetitive melodies of the songs. Doubtless, spontaneous emotion could arise from hearing a voice as moving as that of Iseult: one might note the artful *mise en abyme* of the poet Thomas, who tempted his readers to recall moments when they too had been particularly moved by chant. Above all, however, lyrical performance cast a 'vocalized image of emotion' over the gathering,[9] which could be identified by the audience and reinforced their sense of belonging to a community of shared aesthetic and moral values. Emotions may well have been stirred by way of lyric, but that was not the primary aim of such courtly spectacles. To be more precise, one must cast aside the modern habit of dissociating emotions that are felt from those that are recognized. Rendered unique by the context of its execution – place, time, type of audience, the cause of gathering – lyrical emotion resided entirely in the performance: through a spectacle that mobilized the senses, emotions, and intellect, it appealed to and reinforced the shared cultural and ideological touchstones of aristocratic community.

Revolutions of love

The modern enthusiasm for the profane literature of the Middle Ages, which has hardly diminished over the last two centuries, is largely derived from the thematic of love. To some eyes, the twelfth century might even seem to have 'invented' passionate love.[10] The modern mythology of love is indeed still inhabited by the legendary affairs of Tristan and Iseult, Lancelot and Guinevere, and even the real, but no less romantic passion of Abelard (d. 1142) and Heloise (d. 1164). And even if the evaluation of charitable love and friendship in the Carolingian era and the eleventh century rebirth of love in Latin literature is now better appreciated, the obsession of the medieval poets and romance writers with love remains no less striking.[11] Literary genres did not always handle it in the same way, but few escaped its grasp. Where medievalists, philologists, and social and literary historians showed an interest in affective matters prior to the emergence of the 'history of emotions', it was through this amorous prism.[12] Moreover, this interest has been perpetuated by a very specific literary figuring of love: 'courtly love'. Yet courtly love is a rather recent invention: it was first theorized in the 1880s by Gaston Paris, a philologist and professor at the Collège de France. Through that expression, Gaston Paris described an ethic of love that, for him, characterized a portion of the poetry and romances produced in the twelfth century. For their own part, medieval writers never really theorized their poetic output. That is not to ignore the famous work of the cleric Andrew the Chaplain (active at the end of the twelfth century), *De amore*, written in Latin around 1184 and probably at the court of Marie de Champagne (d. 1198). It is the only attempt to theorize courtly love written in the twelfth century, albeit late within it and produced at a Northern French court. The structure of the text is rather unusual. The work has three parts. The first two represent a true medieval *ars amatoria*, interrogating the nature of love, the means of obtaining it, and the many ways of keeping it. But the third book tears this entire edifice down in one fell swoop, admonishing the reader not to make use of this manual of seduction but to turn towards God and eternal rewards. This last part is imbued with the exuberant misogyny that one finds in some courtly literature. Was it a tribute to the poet Ovid, who offered his *Cure for Love* in the wake of his *Art of Love*? Was it the result of a taste for paradox and irony? With all things considered, *De amore* should be read as an exhilarating rhetorical exercise, bridging the gap between the twelfth-century Latin renaissance and courtly life, rather than a theorization of romantic literature.

In considering courtly love, Gaston Paris drew on troubadourian lyric poetry as well as *The Knight of the Cart*, a romance by Chrétien de Troyes (active during the second half of the twelfth century). At least as he defined it, courtly love represented a rather limited form of romance, the sort which occurred between a married woman born into the upper nobility, the *domna* of the troubadours, and a knight of more modest social rank. It was a relationship of adultery and social inequality. Desire was at the heart of the romantic bond. But it was a desire seldom satisfied, distancing the man from the lady and delaying their embrace, as witnessed in the well-known troubadourian theme of *amor de lonh*, love from afar, made famous by Jaufré Rudel (active around 1130–70). Taken in this sense, courtly love found its fullest realization in the Occitan motif of the *fin'amor*. This described an ideal of loving harmony between the *domna* and her lover that was only attained at the end of a long road. The path was punctuated by emotions; they accompanied or even brought about the transformation of the suitor (the *fenhador*) into a beggar (*precador*) – when the *domna* gave him a glimpse of hope – until finally he received his reward, a passionate embrace that made him the *drut* of his lady. As the *fin'amor* was above all an 'erotica of mastering desire',[13] the emotions on which it was founded served a dramaturgy of absence and longing. Sorrow, melancholy, and languor were all accompanied by abundant tears, which medieval heroes were never stingy with:

110

Dous' amiga, no'n puesc mais :/ Mout me pesa qar vos lais,/ E ver dol mein et esmais,/ E teng m'o a gran pantais/ Qar no-us abras e no-us bais/ E departen nostr'amor.

Sweet friend, I cannot go on:/ My heart too heavy to leave you,/ I am in mourning and tears,/ I find it a cruel torment/ to not embrace or kiss you,/ to turn away from our love.[14]

The literary origins of the *fin'amor* have been debated extensively without any satisfying answer having been put forward. This is precisely because the cult of love which imbued courtly lyric was only one face of a longer-term tendency that deeply affected Western, Christian, Hebrew, and Muslim culture, and cleric and layman alike. It became visible in new forms as the upper edges of lay society gained access to writing and learned culture. From then on, and more than any of the many other rhetorical forms in which the power of love was expressed, lyric poetry presented a configuration of emotion that was both original to and emblematic of the affective sensibility of the feudal era. It was character-ized by three essential elements. The first was the *mezura*, which stood for the harmonious use of emotions: it stopped one from becoming submerged within the destructive ardour of passions. This rule of courtly prudence in fact somewhat recalls the moderation of the passions already proposed by antique philosophers, which they called 'metriopathy'. In sum, the *mezura* expressed a mastery which allowed emotional excesses to be contained, without entirely bridling them: the right dosage of pain, of anguish (or even anger) in the face of loss, and of restraint made the knight worthy of the lady. The second emotional principle which guided the lyrical *fin'amor* was *joy*, the hope of every lover. The word sounds familiar to our ears, but back then, it pointed to a more elusive horizon. At times, *joy* expressed something similar to 'joy', when it represented loving contentment. But it also expressed the lovers shared enjoyment of each other or even a form of delight in the chase:[15]

Tant era l'amans cochatz/ De la deziran ardor/ Del joy que l'er autreyatz,/ Qu'elh se dava gran temor,/ Qu'al ser non atendes víus.

So much was the lover pressed/ by his desirous ardour/ for the *joy* that he might gain,/ That he feared himself unable/ to survive 'til the evening.[16]

Through its ability to draw together the hopes of a relationship, the idea of *joy* bears witness to the anthropological weight that medieval poets found in emotion. *Joy* was certainly an emotion in the modern sense, or more exactly, a composite of emotions; but at the same time, it also served as an ethic for amorous relationships, and even as an expression of lyrical pleasure. Even if it most often remains impossible

111

to untie these different aspects from one another, they recall the historical link in Western culture between *emovere* as a rhetorical category and psychological conceptions of emotions. Finally, as its third remarkable characteristic, courtly love was driven by an emotional dynamic of anticipation which stemmed from the distance, or even the inaccessibility, of the beloved. Medieval theologians had an expression to describe this form of pleasure, born from long anticipation of joys to come: they spoke of 'morose delectation'.[17] The epithet 'morose' should not be interpreted as derogatory: it did not refer to a regular form of sullenness or an attack of sadness. *Morosa* derived from *mora*, 'delay'. Thus, 'morose delectation' described a form of pleasure in anticipation where the imagination played a vital role, presenting the spirit with a premonition of enjoyment. Since the time of the Church Fathers, Christian theologians had debated the value of the pleasure that preceded the possession of a coveted object. For 'delectation' was perceived as an imposing emotion, practically impossible for the will to control, i.e. the mere thought of an object of desire makes one feel a first movement towards that object, alongside an enjoyable sensation. Delectation had always played a vital role in Christian anthropology, in so far as it related to the contentment that resulted from simple desire, which included the spiritual desire for God. The dynamic of pleasure in desire thus held a central place within medieval culture, as much in religious literature as in courtly life. It was because all the desires were accompanied by a form of anticipated enjoyment that they were sweet and powerful to those who felt them. This could be both a benefit to the soul, when that desire-pleasure was directed towards God, and a danger, when it took the form of temptation towards sin.

The grip of this desire-pleasure took many forms in the emotional culture of the medieval literati; so commonly recognized was its value, however, that it is not worthwhile to try to trace lines of descent.[18] Even if poets did not refer explicitly to 'morose delectation', these writers played with the codes and norms pronounced by the learned. A matter that was treated as serious among the theologians was redirected and exalted through the pleasure of words and rhythm in courtly lyric:

> *C'aissi vauc entrebescant/ los motz e.l so afinant :/ lengu'entrebescada/ es en la baizada.*

> Thus I will come to entwine/ the words and polish the sounds:/ the tongues will come to interlace/ just as in the kiss.[19]

The *fin'amor*, founded on delay and the expectation of pleasure, allowed for a whole dramaturgy of opposing emotions (pleasure and pain, hope and anguish, contentment and melancholy, etc.), since 'morose delectation' was simultaneously an anticipatory pleasure in enjoyments to come and a suffering derived from current absence. The sighs of distant love tasted sweeter than laughter, wrote Bernard de Ventadour (d. end of twelfth century).[20] Such lyrical games indeed reached something of a climax when the poet directly extolled the sweetness of suffering inflicted by absence:

> *De dezir mos cors no fina/ Vas selha ren qu'ieu pus am ;/ E cre que volers m'enguana/ Si cobezeza la-m tol ;/ Que pus es ponhens qu'espina/ La dolors que ab joi sana ;/ Don ja non vuelh qu'om m'en planha.*

My heart will always desire/ her alone, above all others;/ And I believe my will fails me/ if lust draws her off from me;/ For it stings more than a thorn/ the pain that is healed by joy/ So no one need pity me.[21]

To isolate this familiar motif of the *fin'amor* from the other schemas found in lyric poetry (such as the *bone amor* or the *fole amor*)[22] risks doing a disservice to the creativity of these poets. The emotional resources of vernacular literature ran much deeper. In this dance of courtly love, lovers ceaselessly interrogated their emotions, debated them, and strived amidst their goads. But beyond the 'literary psychology' that resulted, the motif of courtly love reflected an unprecedented preoccupation with the 'loving couple'. Between the eleventh and thirteenth centuries, the tales of the poets went hand-in-hand with the emergence of a new vision of the ideal emotional relationship between men and women, a vision that would enjoy influence for centuries to come.

The loving couple and its twin

The naturalization of love

Behind its glittering attire, might courtly love not also bear witness to a bitter competition with other models of love that raged in the twelfth to thirteenth centuries? This hypothesis stems from a simple observation: the *fin'amor* was a form of love that could only apply to a male-female couple. It was an observation that Andrew the Chaplain somewhat mischievously transformed into a self-evident conclusion: 'Love (*amor*) is a certain inborn suffering (*passio innata*) derived from the sight of and excessive meditation on the beauty of the opposite sex.'[23] Historians have long since remarked that courtly love, by borrowing liberally from the norms of feudal service, created a love triangle of sorts: behind the lady courted by the young knight, there was often a husband who was also an established lord, a dominant figure. The service of love and that of vassalage thus tended to become confused: in seducing Guinevere, was

113

Lancelot not experiencing his own love for King Arthur (see Figure 4)? But even if one can recognize 'homosexual tendencies within the framing of courtly love poetry',[24] as Georges Duby put it, the chant of love nevertheless put the heterosexual couple centre-stage. While the *domna* might appear as the prize in a politico-affective competition between males, the woman in the *fin'amour* remained at the centre of the courtly circle. This also signifies – and this is a point of the utmost importance – that sexuality took part in the game of love. Whether or not sexual fulfilment was present at the end of the journey ultimately mattered little: its possibility consumed the relationship. The convergence of love and sexual pleasure, whether realized or idealized, was nevertheless a real novelty for medieval culture. Up until then, clerics, who claimed an exclusive right to define the contours of true love, had been careful to keep the two registers as separate as possible. And since, according to them, the quest for carnal pleasure was one of the stigmas of original sin, sexuality was presented first and foremost as a menace: this was even the case in the conjugal setting, since it had the potential to distort the purity of dilection (*dilectio*), the pre-eminent form of spiritual love.

One can imagine the clerics' shock at the sight of courtly manners: there, sexual pleasure was no longer an obstacle to true love, and could even provide its crowning moment. Speaking in the voice of Tristan, Thomas of England would express this in the frankest terms:

> *Issi cum l'amur vient del faire,/ Si vient la haür del retraire;/ Si cum l'amur del ovre vient,/ E la haür ki s'en astient.*

> Just as love comes from love-making, so hatred is the result of abstention; as love ensues from the act, so hatred is felt for the man who abstains.[25]

Within this switch, there was of course a certain mockery of the moral rigour preached by so many priests.[26] What could have been more subversive than to celebrate adulterous love just as the Church cemented its control over the institution of marriage? That said, the codes of courtly love soon left the niche of adulterous pleasure. In the romances of Chrétien de Troyes, Yvain and Erec put the values of courtly love to work in service of the marital relationship. Looking beyond the issue of transgression in love, it was indeed the loving male-female couple that the courtly model served to glorify.

As a counterpoint to this triumph, however, a major transformation was beginning to take place: outpourings of affection between men were gradually being brought into disrepute.[27] Within lay and ecclesiastical elite culture, heartfelt effusions had long been the province of men amongst men (see Figure 5). An aspect of this masculine sociability has already been touched upon: the importance of *amicitia* for political relationships among the Merovingian and Carolingian aristocracy as well as at the heart of the institutional Church. The friendship cultivated in these secular and ecclesiastical networks was just as much a political or religious bond – an expression of hierarchical or communal solidarity – as an affective bond: the two aspects were inseparable. Unlike courtly love, which was an 'invention' of the eleventh and twelfth centuries, affective homoeroticism was backed by age-old tradition within medieval Latin culture. Alcuin and the literary circles of Charlemagne's court bear witness to it. Thanks to a great tide of classical Latin rediscoveries, the poetry of eleventh- and twelfth-century churchmen would happily revisit the codes of ancient male eroticism. Marbodius (d. 1123) – a great man of letters trained at the cathedral school of Angers, which he led before becoming Bishop of Rennes – provides a striking example:

> Horace composed an ode about a certain boy/ Whose face was so lovely he could have been a girl,/ Whose hair fell in waves against an ivory neck,/ Whose forehead was white as snow and his eyes as black as pitch [...]./ But this boy, so lovely and appealing,/ A torment to all who looked upon him,/ Was made by nature so cruel and unyielding/ That he would rather die than yield to love./ Harsh and ungrateful, as if born of a tiger,/ He only laughed at the soft words of admirers,/ Laughed at their vain efforts,/ Laugh at the tears of a sighing lover.[28]

Building on such homoerotic poetry, the vernacular literature of the twelfth and thirteenth centuries was full of male couples seized by intense love: Floovant and Richier in *La Chanson de Guillaume*, Balan and Naimes in *La Chanson Aspremont*, Ogier and Kataeus in La *Chevalerie d'Ogier* by Danemarche, and the dashing Roland and the wise Olivier in *La Chanson de Roland*.[29] While Olivier lies mortally wounded at the feet of his companion, the latter barely has time to tell him how much he loves him before fainting, overcome with emotion (v. 2001). Charlemagne likewise collapses when he in turn learns of the death of his nephew Roland: 'Never will there be a day when I do not ache for you' (v. 2901), he says, beginning a poignant lament of 'faith and love' (v. 2897) of over forty verses. Chivalrous heroes spoke of their love at length and mourned the pain of surviving their companions. 'We have been together for days and years', said Roland, leaning over the lifeless body of his friend: 'It grieves me to live' (vs 2028 and 2030). But on the other hand, their promises were sometimes strangely broken.[30] The *Chanson de Roland* is an epic of blood and emotion in which even traitors seal their betrayal with kisses of false friendship.

Ami and Amile – a *chanson de geste* which had many versions in Latin, Old French, English, and German – is even more emblematic of later medieval chivalric friendship. Ami and Amile were born the same day and look alike, as if two drops of water. While not relatives, the two men are, in essence, spiritual twins: even before they meet, each felt the desire of the other. The romance begins with that first quest, one of kindred spirits who predictably become friends at first sight:

> *Le cheval broche des esperons doréz,/ Isnellement est celle part aléz,/ Et cil le vit qui l'ot ja avisé./ Vers lui se torne quant il l'ot ravisé,/ Par tel vertu se sont entr'acolé,/ Tant fort se baisent et estraingnent soef,/ A poi ne sont estaint et definé.*[31]

> With a kick of his golden spurs, he [Ami] rushed toward him [Amile], and Amile, who had seen him from afar, recognized him in turn. He raced forward and the two met in a tight embrace, so mighty was their kiss and so tenderly did they clasp each other, they almost fainted dead away.[32]

The *c.* 3,500 verses which make up the *chanson* detail a succession of events that stretch their friendship to the limits. Ami perjures himself and is struck by leprosy, while Amile kills his own children to care for his companion by bathing him in the blood of his two sons (God later resurrects them). At the end of the song, having completed a pilgrimage to the Holy Land, the two men die together and are buried in a common grave. At the end of the Middle Ages, the latter practice became a reality for 'sworn brothers', companions in arms who were bound by an oath of friendship.[33]

It is little surprise that emotional relationships between men were exalted in the literature of the feudal era. Their prevalence, which carried forward the traditions of the aristocratic and Christian culture of the Carolingian age, resulted from the conjunction between the dominance of men in relationships of authority and the perceived cultural utility of emotions in social communication.[34] Literary models found reflections in real behaviour, at least according to the chroniclers. One need only cite the example, reported by several contemporary chroniclers, of the affection that the young Richard the Lionheart (d. 1199) felt for the king of France, Philip Augustus (d. 1223):

> Richard, then duke of Aquitaine, son of the king of England, passed a spell with Philip, king of France, whom he had long held in the highest esteem. Thus, he ate with him each day from the same table and the same plate, and at night, they did not use separate beds. And the king of France loved him like his own soul; and they cherished each other so much that, on account of the passionate attachment that existed between them, the dumbfounded king of England wondered what was going on.[35]

In view of the customs that governed medieval political society, such behaviour, combining emotional demonstrations and physical intimacy

116

(at the table and in the bed) was hardly surprising. The intensity of the gesture made Richard's father anxious, but only over his son's political intentions, rather than his intimate desires.[36]

Much as in the closely related context of spiritual friendship, such praise of aristocratic homo-affectivity left no room for sexuality except as a foil: it represented the vulgar and vicious opposite of a noble, manly, and spiritual love. This does not mean that the historian should dismiss the possibility of homosexual acts. But one must be careful not to project anachronistic categories onto medieval conceptions, within which the conflation of emotional effusiveness with sexual desire was far from automatic. While condemnations of homosexual practices were present in the early Middle Ages – in legal codes, penitentials, and in the writings of theologians – repression was not a priority for the lay or ecclesiastical authorities before the end of the twelfth century at the earliest. It can easily be supposed that some of these men not only declared their love but also took pleasure in making it, without necessarily becoming anathema to their contemporaries. Some loving relationships doubtless found a place within this homo-affective political and religious culture. By enjoying their lover's body, they enjoyed the presence of a friend. But this link cannot be deduced from the texts themselves, which never refer to carnal union as an outcome of friendship. Literary expressions instead appear to have created an invisible partition between the registers. In short, all remained encompassed by the inherited framework of ennobling love, within which it was characteristic to use the homoerotic register while keeping sexuality at bay: to even speak of the danger would mean dishonour. The model of love between knights rested on entirely different foundations to the heterosexual lyricism of the *fin'amor*, where carnal union openly held its place in the dynamics of love.

Such were the major models which underpinned courtly literature in the twelfth to thirteenth centuries. On one side, there was a masculine model, which exalted the values of friendship, fidelity, and service, the characteristics of the feudal ideal. This literary valorization was nothing new. On the rhetorical plain, it echoed a clerical poetry which was inspired by the homoerotic odes of classical poets, but also a religious veneration of the spiritual friendship that defined Christian sociability. Even if the affective rhetoric was highly effusive, even if it encouraged contact through kisses and embraces, it remained separate from the register of sexual desire. On the other side, courtly love shined a spotlight on a heterosexual model of love. This was certainly not without precedent either: for example, one might think back to the Carolingian celebration of love between spouses. But it was in vernacular literature that it truly exploded. In its different forms, whether adulterous or marital, the courtly love that the poets wrote of made the connection between true love and sexuality. On the rhetorical plane, these two models of love generally drew from the same emotional registers, with a fluidity unique to courtly literature. Only the question of sexual enjoyment stopped the two models from overlapping one another. In the male context, it was out of the question, while for male-female couples, it could well be part of what they sought to accomplish.

A question remains concerning the connection between the two rhetorics of love. Some have perceived courtly literature as the venue for a clash between the 'traditional' model of manly love, which was an expression of chivalry, and a 'new' predatory heterosexual culture.[37] Such a total dichotomy may be misleading, however. The loving service of a lady took its place within the context of chivalric service and thus did not harm the valour of a warrior. In addition, many attitudes described as courtly (hospitality, the sharing of the bowl or the bed, the exchange of words and gestures of affection) were no less pertinent to the relationships between men and women than they were to men among themselves or women among themselves. There were occasional tensions, of course, such as in Chrétien de Troyes' *Yvain, the Knight of the Lion*, where Yvain, having left to take part in tournaments, breaks his promise to his wife Laudine not to leave her for more than a year. Ashamed of having gone back on his word, worried that he has lost the love of his lady, Yvain slumps into a madness that might seem to embody the dilemma facing the perfect knight: he had to leave his lady to prove his valour in combat, and yet, no less importantly, he had to renounce his search for adventure to remain at the service of his lady. Perhaps more than a sign of a problematic opposition between two worlds, it represented the literary illustration of the intrinsic tensions of courtly culture, tensions which provided the very thrust of the romantic dynamic. There was a genuine coherence behind this paradox, for it was only in offering the lady a spectacle of his bravery that the knight could earn her love. Thus, the pinnacle of chivalric valour was to render arms in the ultimate battle, the battle of love, as Chrétien explains at the end of *Yvain, the Knight of the Lion*:

Or a messire Yvains sa pes ;/ Et pöez croire c'onques mes/ Ne fu de nule rien si liez,/ Comant qu'il ait esté iriez./ Mout an est a boen chief venuz/ Qu'il est amez et chier tenuz/ De sa dame, et ele de lui.

And now Yvain had his peace,/ And surely, believe me, nothing/ Had ever pleased him better,/ However miserable he had been./ It had all come right in the end./ His lady loved him again,/ And cherished him, and he cherished her.[38]

The impossible innamoramento *of same-sex lovers*

Nevertheless, it seems undeniable that the foundations of the homo-affective model were attacked in the twelfth century, and that the elaboration of the ideal loving couple had played a role in undermining it. Many things came together within this process. The first was the hardening of attitudes among both ecclesiastical and lay authorities against the 'vice of sodomy' (*vitium sodomiticum*). During the early Middle Ages, the term 'sodomites' (*sodomita*) – frequent, for example, in penitentials – was applicable to people accused of any number of faults essentially derived from fornication or non-reproductive sexual practices. The sin of sodomy thus encompassed homosexual practices but was not limited to it. But in the vast enterprise of reform led by the Church from the middle of the eleventh century, some of its more zealous activists chose to make the fight against the crime of sodomy their battle cry. It is Peter Damian who has the dubious honour of having written the first work entirely dedicated to the denunciation of homosexual activity, the *Book of Gomorrah* (*c.* 1051). It is in this treatise that the word 'sodomy' (*sodomia*) appears for the first time and it came with a much stricter meaning: homosexual practices.[39] Moreover, Peter Damian proceeded to draw together the concepts of sodomy, heresy, and behaviour that went 'against nature'. This marked the beginnings of a correlation between these three notions, one that would provide the ideological grounding for the repression of those accused of homosexual practices from the thirteenth century onward. Not content with simply denouncing the vice of sodomy, Peter Damian used his treatise to accuse bishops of protecting sodomites in their dioceses, giving credence to the idea that not only was the practice widespread, but that sodomites also formed organized and solid communities. Here, the message slipped almost imperceptibly from the denunciation of the act towards the idea that sodomy could define an individual or groups of individuals. Care should of course be taken not to transform the invective of one censorious individual, as influential as he was, into a refrain that the ecclesiastical authorities took up in chorus. Pope Leo IX, to whom the work was dedicated, wisely left Peter's manuscript to gather dust, judging that the papacy had bigger fish to fry. Nevertheless, the accusation of sodomy was deployed more frequently in the twelfth century, especially as a political weapon: it was a sign that this vice was coming into clearer focus than others. Similarly, the development of naturalistic thought among the learned had repercussions for the vilification of behaviour considered to be against nature.[40] The natural order in question was not only that of reproduction but also of the human social order ordained by God. Sodomy could thus be seen to go against both the natural law of procreation and against sovereignty, whether it be divine or terrestrial: the accused was thus exposed to the simultaneous charges of heresy and lese-majesty. The 'suspicion of sodomy'[41] was spreading, and forms of behaviour which previously contained no sexual connotation for contemporaries – such as certain forms of warmth between men – were now liable to condemnation.

The romantic genre was certainly not immune from these changes. From the end of the twelfth century, it became possible to impugn a knight by laying the suspicion of sodomy on him. In the *Roman d'Énéas* (*c.* 1160), a re-telling of the *Aeniad*, Lavinia is in love with Aeneas, but her mother, Laurentia, has other ideas. When she learns that the heart of her daughter is set on the Trojan, she makes clear her anguish. She launches into a particularly crude and violent diatribe against Aeneas, no small part of which is taken up by the accusation of sodomy: this is brought up well before any suggestion of cowardice, the latter being little mentioned despite being the worst infamy that could befall the reputation of a knight. Furthermore, the argument that such actions imperilled the species makes one of its earliest appearances here. Not content with offending God and nature, the sodomites now menaced the survival of society:

> *Cil cuivers est de tel nature/ qu'il na de femmes gaire cure./ Il prise plus le plain mestier,/ il ne veult pas bice chaucier,/ moult par aime char de mallon ;/ il prisera miex son garçon/ que toy ne autre acoler./ A fumelle ne set voller,/ ne passera mie au guicet ;/ moult aime fraise de varlet. […]/ Il n'aime point piau de conin./ De cest siecle seroit tost fin/ se tous les hommes qui i sont/ estoient tel par tout le mont :/ jamais femme ne concevroit,/ grant souffraite de gent seroit ;/ l'en ne feroit jamais enfant,/ ffaudroit le siecle a ytant./ Fille, moult as le senz perdu/ quand de tel homme fais ton dru,/ qui ja jor n'avra de toy cure/ et qui si fait contre nature :/ les hommes prent, les femmes let,/ le naturel couple deffait./ Garde nel me dies jamais,/ ceste amistié veul que tu lais/ du sodomite, du couart.*

This wretch is of the sort who have hardly any interest in women. He prefers the opposite trade: he will not eat hens, but he loves very much the flesh of a cock. He would prefer to embrace a boy rather than you or any other woman. He does not know how to play with women, and would not parley at the wicket-gate; but he loves very much the breech of a young man. […] He does not love the coney fur. It would quickly be the end of this life if all men were thus throughout the world. Never would a woman conceive; there would be a great death of people; no one would ever bear children, and the world would fail before a hundred years. Daughter, you have completely lost your senses, since you have taken as your love such a man, who will never have a care for you, and who acts so against nature that he takes men and leaves women, undoing the natural union. I wish you to give up the love of this sodomite, of this coward.[42]

From then on, it was as if the love of men and the love of women were in direct competition within this knightly world, an unthinkable notion at the beginning of the century. In the 1180s, Andrew the Chaplain was quick to head off this issue in the introduction to his work:

> Now, in love you should note first of all that love cannot exist except between persons of the opposite sexes. Between two men or two women love can find no place, for we see that two persons of the same sex are not at all fitted for giving each other the exchanges of love or for practicing the acts natural to it. Whatever nature forbids, love is ashamed to accept.[43]

What one might call the perverse effects of the rise of loving marriage in the twelfth century only added to this growing culture of suspicion: this ideal served to reinforce the social correctness of the *naturel couple* that Laurentia invoked in the *Roman d'Énéas*. The spiritual control of the matrimonial institution had been one of the great victories of the medieval Church. Since the Carolingian period at least, this long-term enterprise had been driven in the name of love between souls. Seen from the clerical side, the cultural history of marriage is a history of loving marriage. The affection which joined spouses was certainly not the passionate love which left hearts dumbstruck and enticed the flesh, but a spiritual love that made two souls one. For the theologians and the canonists, conjugal love was a mixture of affective attachment, loyalty, moral fidelity, and accord between wills, all sealed within a relationship which nevertheless remained strictly hierarchical.[44] For the Roman jurists, *affectio conjugalis* was one of the conditions of marriage. For the canon lawyers, it was a key pillar of the same, here accompanied by a strong 'sentimentalization' of the value of *affectio*, which had initially signified more of a respect for the rank of wife, and thus of her *gens*, than an emotional attachment to her person. By the twelfth century, the ecclesiastical control of marriage had never been stronger.

Certainly, the Church did not decide everything, far from it: it fought against clandestine unions, and had to deal with the strategies of families who had their own interests in making and undoing alliances, just as they had always done. Nevertheless, its instructions had never been as well understood. To achieve this, it had put in place a tool of remarkable social and symbolic efficacy: by the end of the century, marriage had become a sacrament, delivered at a solemn ceremony conducted by a priest. The matrimonial union was thus no longer merely a method of channelling sexual impulses and ensuring reproduction: it sanctified the loving couple, setting them on the road to salvation. The result was an encounter between sexuality and spiritual love, unprecedented in Christian cultural history. Some clerics (albeit only a few) even thought that the spiritual benefits of marriage made the search for sexual enjoyment forgivable.[45] The ideal marriage remained chaste, through either the absence or parsimonious practice of sexuality, and the couples sanctified by hagiography were almost always those who had renounced any sex life.[46] It should not be forgotten, however, that carnal consummation was also a validating element of marriage, as the theologian Alan of Lille (d. 1202) stated: 'We admit that marriage cannot be consummated without sexual union (*carnali coitu*), and thus that sexual congress is not always a sin.'[47]

As timid as this reconciliation was, it unintentionally helped to usher in secular developments that shared the same spirit as the values of romantic love. From then on, sexual pleasure could be the crowning achievement of the union of hearts; conversely one was only to sleep with a soulmate, duly chosen from the opposite sex and outside the circle of consanguineous relatives. Such was the vision of sentimental sexuality which took shape between the eleventh and thirteenth centuries, both within courtly lyric and clerical discourse. The indirect consequence of this development was to weaken the divide between homo-affectivity and homosexual acts. For if sexual eroticism and love were now compatible for heterosexual couples, why couldn't the same *rapprochement* be applied to the old patterns of male love? Nevertheless, such a conflation was inconceivable. The twelfth century created the right conditions for a 'loving homosexuality', a culture of love where men slept together. But the moral and legal dictates that governed medieval Christian societies vilified homosexual practices by placing them at the heart of the vice of sodomy: this possibility was thus nipped in the bud. On the contrary, as the heterosexual ideal of the loving couple took shape, masculine homo-affectivity, at once so similar and so different, was brought into disrepute. At the beginning of the twelfth century, two men who loved each other truly, such as Olivier and Roland, could not be suspected of an attraction 'against nature' so long as their love was recognized as true, and therefore solely spiritual. By *c.* 1160, in the fictional economy of the *Roman d'Énéas*, Laurentia thought she could shake her daughter's love for Aeneas – a man who described his friend Pallas as the 'most handsome young man in the world' – by painting him as a sodomite eager for pleasure. In the space of a century, this social outlook had been upturned.

The combined effects of hardening attitudes against the vice of sodomy and an unprecedented promotion of 'heterosexual love' had demoted homo-affectivity. It was relegated into second place, behind the model of the male-female couple, and could even arouse suspicions of a vice against nature. This process was amplified by the transformation of political structures within Western Europe: almost everywhere, sovereign authorities overpowered aristocratic systems. From then on, within the context of rising monarchical power, the values and rituals of symbolic equality specific to feudal society (friendship, physical closeness) gave way to hierarchical values (fidelity, service). By the thirteenth and fourteenth centuries, political theories of friendship would take account of the question of hierarchy ('Can the king have friends?'[48]). Echoing this, the Church, using the same accusation of sodomy, put pressure on a military culture whose violence it wanted to redirect.

The twelfth century marked a turning point for the Western culture of love. On the one hand, in its best-known aspect, the erotic love of courtly culture intertwined with the ecclesiastical promotion of conjugal love, albeit not without friction. The result was a model of the male–female relationship founded on the conjunction of what Michel Foucault called 'the axis of love culture' and 'the axis of sexuality'. On the other hand, such a conjunction was denied to same-sex relationships. One can hardly mourn the death of some sort of homosexual subculture, since it had never existed in institutional circles (whether secular or ecclesiastical). Nor can one deplore the end of tolerance towards homosexual practices, since these had always been entirely outlawed within normative discourse. On the other hand, the 'courtly moment' had by chance created conditions that might have allowed for an *innamoramento*, for an acculturation of homosexual practices within love, if all the while preventing it from happening. The outcome was twofold: it placed homo-affectivity under suspicion and deprived same-sex couples of a culture of love, or at least condemned them to secrecy and a marginal existence. The subsequent disjuncture of the two models became such that, even today, it is difficult to interpret the medieval sources in which they had long lived side-by-side. Deprived of a culture of love to ennoble them, homosexual practices could only be socially perceived through the prism of the 'crime of sodomy'. Through this process of deculturation, same-sex lovers were transformed into individuals of pure sexuality.

Literary emotions and aristocratic values

Epic emotions

If love was undoubtedly the summit of literary emotions, the emotional palette of medieval authors possessed an impressive variety of registers and nuances. And since one of the functions of rhetoric in the Middle Ages, as in antiquity, was to arouse emotion so as to better convince others, it is legitimate to treat the content of medieval poems and romances as a poetry of the emotions. Those medieval literary scholars who have studied laughter and melancholy in courtly romances,[49] the fear of the chivalric hero,[50] and jealousy in troubadourian lyric poetry[51] have long done just that. Today, studies tend to avoid typological approaches, which presuppose that emotions can be isolated from one another, preferring to question how the emotional anthropology of the authors informed the style and art of their writing.[52] Thanks to contributions both old and new, the historian can now explore the medieval literary representations of the emotional man and the framing of emotion within social relationships. The emotions of courtly heroes portray the values of feudal society in song. When they clash within the same character amidst the twists and turns of the tale, they express the complexity and tensions induced by these idealized virtues, or conversely, the stigma attached to those who failed in them. Epic literature was a 'sounding board' for the social values and aspirations of courtly society: it not only restated its hopes and fears, it amplified them.[53] When set within a narrative, emotions also provide the energy for fictional action: they lead the way towards explosive action, and push the characters to fulfil or otherwise revise their original intent. In doing so, they inform the reader or listener of the underlying tensions, sharpen the attention, and foreshadow plot reversals. In so far as courtly literature was also a work of self-representation within aristocratic circles, this game of emotions has much to tell the historian about their ideal use within society and their role in individual and communal relationships.

It is impossible to provide an overview of such a broad field in just a few pages. Some pointers can nevertheless be offered to highlight the interactions between literary production and the social ramifications of emotion. In recent years, the *chanson de geste* has benefited from some insightful studies into the emotions of the epic heroes.[54] For example, historians and scholars of medieval literature have shown interest in 'epic fear' within a genre where heroes are usually thought of as models of unfailing courage and moral virtue, qualities that built the stereotype of the fearless and irreproachable knight. There are many heroes who fit this portrait, beginning with Roland himself. Fear, however, signified by different words (*paor, doutance, freor*) and graded according to its intensity (*effroi* or *hide* usually signified a violent fear), is also present in epic. It primarily serves as a counter-value. Sometimes it underlines the moral weakness of the traitor or the non-knight (the phrase '*couart comme vilain*' thus became almost proverbial). Sometimes it draws the mind to the humanity of the hero secretly seized by fear.[55] In line with the medieval anthropology of emotions, fear serves as a marker of the moral value of the characters. It provides the motivation for action at key points of the narrative: the coward chooses to flee, while the brave man redoubles his courage. The emotion of fear in the *chansons de geste* is brought to life in a bodily manner. When the usurper Fromont, in *Jourdain de Blaye*, sees the arrival of the assailants led by Jourdain against Blaye, he trembles in terror: '*Toute la chars* [the flesh] *me tremble*' he said to his companions.[56] In keeping with medical tradition, fear makes hearts and stomachs convulse. The motif of epic fear thus had didactic and literary functions. It was didactic in the sense that authors evoked fear to convey messages of a political, ideological, religious, or moral nature. For example, the cowardice of Louis, the son of Charlemagne, in *Le Couronnement de Louis*, suggests that fear cast doubt over the legitimacy of a sovereign. Conversely, the fear of God recalled the Christian values at work within the saga. Literary functions emerge when fear is evoked to intensify the narrative, when it establishes a contrasting backdrop for the primordial virtue of courage, or where it acts, like all emotions, as a 'clutch to shift the narrative'.[57] In the latter case, it follows a recurring tripartite pattern: first comes the presence of fear, then a discursive intervention (provided by a harangue or prayer), and finally action or combat.

If fear appears to be an 'epic counter-value', such is not the case with anger, another very common emotion in this literary genre. Like fear, it can be graded according to different degrees of intensity, from ire to devastating fury, and it possesses precise functions within the narrative economy of the *chansons de geste*. It could mark a beginning. In keeping with Homeric epic, the wrath of a rebellious baron sometimes initiates the cycle of action. *Le Charroi de Nîmes* opens with the anger of its hero William of Orange, who reproaches the king for his ingratitude: this foreshadowed his request to possess the cities of Nîmes and Orange should he succeed in taking them back from the Saracens. Anger assumes a structural function in the sense that it reflected the political tensions of feudal societies. The king's anger against his disloyal vassals demonstrated the strengthening of royal power. Conversely, for the aristocrats, anger could mark the dissatisfaction of vassals who considered themselves insufficiently rewarded, as in the case of William of Orange: 'What a long wait for a poor boy who has nothing to take nor to give to others!'[58]

In these examples drawn from the epic genre, it is easy to see how the literary functions of emotion echoed anthropological ideas in which emotions revealed the moral qualities that directed and predisposed people towards action. To be moved was to make a choice, in the fullest sense of the term. Emotion had a discriminating power: without requiring long description or explanation from the narrator, it signified what the character wanted or rejected. Whether spoken or displayed by the body, emotion also foreshadowed explosive action by providing motivation. Beyond their aesthetic function, moreover, literary emotions revealed social aspirations, in the way that authors characterized the balance and imbalance of society.

Looking upon another, another looking upon oneself: jealousy and shame

This is most perceptible when those emotions which are naturally inter-subjective are considered.[59] Take, for example, the case of jealousy. While not omnipresent in the romantic literature of the twelfth and thirteenth centuries, jealousy nevertheless holds a special importance within it: in the Occitan tradition, it gave rise to a specific character, the *gilos*, and several southern works – *Las Novas del Papagay* by Arnaut de Carcassès (thirteenth century), the well-named *Castia Gilos*, the 'chastising of the jealous man', by Raimon Vidal de Besalù (active in the first half of the thirteenth century), and the great anonymous romance *Flamenca* (end of the thirteenth century) – can be seen as romances of jealousy. Jealousy could affect any character, women included. It is out of jealousy that Iseult of the White Hands leads Tristan to believe that the sail of the ship he expected was black, the agreed sign that his mistress had refused to come to him. Upon learning the news, Tristan immediately dies of despair. Nevertheless, the jealousy most emblematic of courtly literature is that of the husband. It is sometimes ridiculed, for instance in those erotic *fabliaux* where the cuckold husband is beaten up. But conjugal jealousy is also revealing for the dysfunctions of courtly life. In courtly literature, jealousy is always a negative, destructive emotion, even though Andrew the Chaplain had conceived a form of jealousy indispensable to courtly love, the *vera zelotypia*, a term closely related to the biblical meaning of *zelus*. In religious vocabulary, *zelus* described a form of anger, and in particular the divine wrath of the Old Testament. Where it was found in men, *zelus* could signify a powerful and exclusive attachment, perceived positively when directed towards God. This 'zeal' was thus synonymous with ardour and fervour. For clerics, the negative jealousy *par excellence* was envy, coveting the things of others.[60] From this aspect, literary *gelosie* is the corollary of envy, itself embodied in another typical character mould of courtly literature, the *enveios* or *losangier*, the slanderer who sews doubt over the wife's probity and provokes the husband's jealousy. Within the courtly environment, jealousy was thus the symptom of a crisis or a decline in chivalrous values, especially the primary virtue of love. It is why the jealous husband always played a wicked role, and why jealousy never paid, only pushing the virtuous wife into the arms of the lover unjustly ascribed to her from the outset. This is what happens in *Castia Gilos*, where King Alfonso of Barbastro, made jealous by the slanderous remarks of the *losangiers*, sets a trap for his wife to catch her red-handed. The latter, discovering the subterfuge, succeeds in escaping and, in revenge, commits the adultery of which she was unfairly accused. Jealousy could not be rewarded because it went against courtly service, which relied upon a blind confidence in the virtue of the wife. Jealousy thus became a sign of a transgression, an attack on the *mezura*, the harmony of emotions so essential to courtly life. The jealous man, meanwhile, was always depicted as impulsive. Such is the portrait painted of the jealous Archambaut in the *Flamenca*:

> *Soen vai dins, soen defora ;/ Defora art, dedins acora ;/ Ben es gelos qui aisi bela :/ Quant cuja cantar et el bela,/ Quant cuja sospirar, bondis.*

> Often he went in and often out;/ outside he burned, inside he froze;/ he is jealous indeed who stares so foolishly./ When he imagined that he sang, he bellowed;/ when he thought that he sighed, he yelled.[61]

Since the values on which the stability and harmony of courtly society were founded were fidelity, prodigality, and, in its literal sense, the nobility of sentiment (i.e. the absence of suspicion), jealousy meant disorder. This is witnessed, for example, in *La Mort le roi Artu* (written about 1200), the last part of the *Lancelot en prose* cycle, which portrays Arthur and his court in an unfavourable light. At the beginning of the thirteenth century, the criticism of monarchical sovereignty was no longer rare in romantic literature. Here, the poisonous jealousy of the king became a symptom of the decline of courtly society. On the level of literary aesthetics, jealousy opposed the virtue of love. On the anthropological level, it was the symptom of disorder within the emotional equilibrium. Finally, in so far as reflections of social tension can be found within the literature, the emotion of jealousy appears related to the practice of power, signifying the disturbance of political harmony: it could signal the knight-vassals' loss of confidence in the rightful distribution of honours, or even the failure of a sovereign (or lord-husband) who could not fulfil the decisive role demanded of him.

Another social emotion was yet more essential to the workings of a courtly world founded on warrior companionship: shame. The very term for shame – *honte*, or *hunte* in Old French – derived from the Frankish vocabulary of honour and dishonour; it is used more frequently than its equivalent of Latin origin, *vergogne* or *vergoigne* (from *verecundia*) in courtly texts.[62] Within them, the emotion of shame is an emotion of suffering; it is linked to experiences of social disapproval and the fear of being exposed to the same. Therefore, escaping situations of shame is a powerful driver of choices and actions: 'I fear shame and sin', says Tristan, fearing public ignominy if he refused to consummate his marriage with Iseult of the White Hands.[63] Nevertheless, shame is also an emotion that could elevate the courtly hero. This is the case in the well-known story of Lancelot, who, deprived of his mount but hoping to receive news from Queen Guinevere, decides to ride in a cart – of the sort in which, as Chrétien de Troyes described, thieves were usually displayed for pillory. In an environment where honour was most precious, accepting the humiliation of shame was the ultimate sacrifice one could make for love:

Tantost a sa voie tenue/ Li chevaliers, que il n'i monte ;/ Mar le fist et mar en ot honte/ Que maintenant sus ne sailli,/ Qu'il s'an tendra por mal bailli ;/ Mes Reisons, qui d'Amors se part,/ Li dit que del monter se gart,/ Si le chastie et si l'anseigne/ Que rien ne face ne anpreigne/ Dom il ait honte ne reproche./ N'est pas el cuer, mes an la boche,/ Reisons qui ce dire li ose ;/ Mes Amors est el cuer anclose/ Qui li comande et semont/ Que tost an la charrete mont./ Amors le vialt et il i saut,/ Que de la honte ne li chaut/ Puis qu'Amors le comande et vialt.

[...] The knight/ Followed along behind/ For several steps, not climbing/ Right up. But his hesitant shame/ Was wrong. Reason, which warred/ With Love, warned him to take care;/ It taught and advised him never/ To attempt anything likely/ To bring him shame or reproach./ Reason's rules come/ From the mouth, not from the heart./ But Love, speaking from deep/ In the heart, hurriedly ordered him/ Into the cart. He listened/ To Love, and quickly jumped in,/ putting all sense of shame/ Aside, as Love had commanded.[64]

Such a confrontation between Reason and Love is a hallmark of courtly literature. Behind it, however, the original features of the medieval psychology of emotions are clearly distinguishable. A superficial reading might lead one to think that, for Lancelot, the intelligence of reason, which carefully determines the most appropriate approach, is entirely set against emotion, impulsive, unthinking, and blind. Looking deeper, however, Reason and Love represent two kinds of evaluation: each has its own rationality but they nevertheless point in different directions. Both seek to evaluate the same emotional signal: fear. Is it in the interest of Lancelot to give free rein to the fear of shame which spontaneously consumed him? That is the choice that must be made. In response, two forms of discursive rationality clash. The voice of reason is that of social norms and behavioural conformity to the direct demands of honour. The voice of the heart delves into another, more complex level of interest: does the service of love require his exposure to a situation in which he might lose that love? In a certain sense, *Raison* here represents a weak rationality, obedient to social 'routine': thus, one was to flee all situations of dishonour. Love, on the other hand, proves the more subtle advisor: Chrétien indeed intervenes in the narrative to indirectly render homage to it. The victory of Love is a matter of the imperious power of passion over the will: this follows a dialectic of Stoic origin, contrasting with an Augustinian orthodoxy in which passions were acts of the will.

Nevertheless, it would be misleading to understand this love as pathological, as overriding free will: such was a contemporary interpretation that certain theologians attempted to impose to condemn any cult of passionate love.[65] On the contrary, this passage shows that, despite the schema of apparent opposition between the rational and the irrational, the analysis that precedes the choice and action of Lancelot results from a remarkably efficient affective rationality, one that is able to encompass individual subjectivity. Love also argues that shame would not hinder the conquest of the lady, but on the contrary, make it more likely. Thus, while Reason proves unequal to the situation and is confined to the role of a simple mouthpiece of social conformity, Love proposes a transgressive response, adapted to the uniqueness of the circumstances. It stands as a fine example of the emotional rationality of courtly life, but also of Chrétien's utter mastery of the rhetoric of emotions.

The profusion of emotions in literature was no matter of chance. Emotions, in medieval anthropology, made moral choices. It was they that bound the body and soul together, it was they that motivated action within a cultural, political, and social environment where love was made the ultimate bond (expressed politically through faith, religiously through the love of God, and socially through charity). In addition, emotion was what made relationships (the unique quality of love), drove events, and brought about change. Late medieval courtly literature undoubtedly contributed to shaping emotions such as they were employed personally and in society. On the other hand, poetry can also be thought of as a configuration of emotion in language. The bond between anthropology and the rhetoric of emotions had been vital within Western culture as far back as Aristotle and Quintilian: the *literati* of the medieval period did not depart from their ancient heritage in this regard. Is what we call literature not simply the language of emotion in Western culture? Is literature not simply emotion that has entered into discourse, and not only the sort of discourse which directly concerns emotional matters? The end of the Middle Ages witnessed both a major rhetorical inflation within courtly literature and a decline in the social significance of courtly life. At its core, the ritualization of emotions became greater, but in a manner that was less connected to social and political needs, in line with the consumption of the feudo-vassalic regime by the monarchical state. Even when politically devalued, however, the rituals of courtly life went on to form the basis of court etiquette. Above all, they would permanently leave their mark on the Western imagination of love.

THE EMOTIVE NATURE OF MAN
(ELEVENTH TO THIRTEENTH CENTURIES)

Are emotions part of human nature? Or do they pass through it, like fleeting tempests, in response to external influence? The philosophical schools of antiquity had considered this question repeatedly and found a quandary within it. Plato and Aristotle saw an ontological value in the passions, whereas the Stoics saw them as disturbances of one's being that paralysed judgement.[1] The most tried and tested men could rid themselves of them, or at least stop this passionate illness from rooting itself in the soul. The Christian intellectuals of the religion's first centuries had readily appropriated this way of thinking about emotion, i.e. as a disturbance of the soul. At the same time, they moralized over passionate occurrences. Passion was not in the nature of man that God had created, at least not in the form of an appetite that could overwhelm reason and the will. It only became the unstable element within him in the wake of original sin, the new condition of man following his expulsion from terrestrial paradise.

This outlook lived on throughout the early Middle Ages. It is why ecclesiastical authors had long been less concerned with the psychology or physiology of passions than with the struggle between vices and virtues, where the real stakes seemed to lie. Yet in the space of just two centuries, between the eleventh and thirteenth centuries, the learned outlook on man underwent a profound transformation. Amid a general evolution of mentalities, an unprecedented naturalism thought of the body and the soul, the macrocosm and the microcosm, as a unity.[2] Founded on methodical commentary and the technique of contradictory argumentation (the *disputatio*), the culture of the urban schools and then of the universities, known today as scholasticism, was fascinated by systematization and classification. The ordering of discourse was meant to reflect the harmony of the created world, which was left open to exploration by human intelligence. An understanding of the divine order that expressed itself throughout physical nature came to the fore and broke free from the austere dialectic that had placed the spiritual man and the carnal man at opposing ends of the path towards salvation. Faced with the dualist tensions that had characterized the early Middle Ages, both schoolmasters and certain monks sought to gather up the pieces of a humanity that had been shattered in the wake of original sin. To think of man by way of his physiological faculties, to think of him as a unity of body and soul, and to entirely re-evaluate him within a new anthropology of salvation: these were some of the challenges that the intellectuals collectively turned their hand to.[3] Within this transition, which some have described as the 'invention of anthropology',[4] reflection on the emotions – described in learned language as 'affects', 'passions', 'movements of the soul' or 'accidents of the soul' – played a role of the utmost importance. Weaving between the drives of the body and the urges of the soul, the forces of feeling and desire held a pivotal position in tying the human compound together. Nevertheless, the moral direction inherent in emotional impulses was far from neglected. Systematic thought on the emotions took shape in the twelfth and thirteenth centuries precisely because they were at the heart of an anthropological outlook that saw the human being and the ethical course that mapped out the virtuous path as a unity. It is this twofold dynamic, at once ethical and ontological, a dynamic that made man a 'restless subject'[5] in later medieval learned culture, that this chapter seeks to bring to life across some of its key junctures and most defining thinkers.

A traditional divide, still commonplace within intellectual history, separates the so-called 'scholastic' period, beginning at the end of the twelfth century, and the century that preceded it. The influence of new translations of Aristotle and Avicenna (d. 1037) in the later period has framed the great intellectual figures that came immediately before, whether drawn from monastic circles or the urban schools, as precursors: at best, they seem to prepare the ground for a systematic reflection for which they could only formulate the premises, however much we might speak of a 'twelfth century renaissance'. But while the translations made a critical contribution, opening up new perspectives on knowledge and providing new intellectual tools, they also satisfied a need and responded to a pro-active scholarly effort that had been triggered by new questions about human nature. By tracking the emergence of a science of the emotions from the eleventh century onward, it becomes clear that the integration of affective categories within human nature pre-dated the 'rediscovery' of Aristotle at the end of the twelfth century. It was the result of innovative investigations founded on a library of knowledge that, medical writings apart, was scarcely different from what had been available to

131

Carolingian scholars. That is what is so remarkable. The course of high medieval intellectual debates did not follow the convulsive pattern so often ascribed to them. Rather, it was more like a deep breath, which, in one continuous motion, brought about a revolution in anthropology, in reflection on man, between the eleventh and thirteenth centuries.

A prelude: the controversy over the 'first movements of the soul'

To take stock of the debates that crisscrossed twelfth- and thirteenth-century thought on the emotions, we begin with a controversy that had exercised learned circles for several generations, one which we have already mentioned.[6] It is the famous question of prepassions or pre-affects, those first movements of passion that remind us of modern conceptions of emotion. As seen earlier, the anthropological edifice bequeathed to monastic authors by the Church Fathers was founded on the principle that the 'movements of the soul' were directly dependent on the will. The body was certainly subjected to natural influences that were exempt from any moral judgement, such as feeling hungry or thirsty, but any desire, anything felt positively or negatively involving the soul, entered the purview of the will. Feeling a certain pleasure in tasting a dish or a drink, even if this pleasure responded to a natural necessity, thus contained a potentially sinful dimension.[7] But despite the prolonged dominance of patristic responses, these questions returned to the fore at the beginning of the twelfth century, against a background of renewed reflection on the role of the faculties of the soul in the commitment of sin.[8]

It was in this context that, at the end of the 1130s, Abelard, then at the height of his art and renown, wrote a treatise on ethics, *Know Thyself* (*Scito te ipsum*). Here, he argued that there could be no sin without conscious consent: 'It isn't a sin to lust after someone else's wife, or to have sex with her; the sin is rather to consent to this lust or to this action.'[9] This morality of intention led Abelard to reject the idea that sin lay at the first suggestion of desire, or in the pleasure of *delectatio*, that involuntary joy inherent in desire. While the spontaneous sensation of pleasure might lead the soul towards sin, sin was not in any way present within it, not even surreptitiously, without the soul's consent. And for consent, there had to be intention: in other words, a commitment of the will enlightened by reason. At first sight, Abelard's proposal does not appear revolutionary. For Augustine, only those movements that engaged the will could be qualified as sinful. Nevertheless, for the latter and his monastic readers, even the spontaneous pleasure which accompanied temptation concealed an element of consent, a hangover from original sin. Abelard argued instead for a narrower definition of the subject, freed from the spectre of a will that could lose control over itself. This was the meaning of the notions of intention and consent: they represented a will that was fully conscious and freed from itself.

At the same time, Abelard distinguished the vice present within nature and the vice derived from consent: the first inclined one towards evil but was not a sin, while the second was clearly sinful. This doctrine had significant consequences for the way emotions were understood: without being freed from their moral connotations, they could now benefit from a subtler and more complex evaluation. Thus, for Abelard, a wicked act committed in the grip of anger was certainly a sin, but being angry – i.e. having an angry temperament – was not in itself a sin, even if it was, in the truest sense of the term, a natural defect of the soul just as a limp was a natural defect of the body:

> This kind of mental vice isn't the same as a sin. And a sin isn't the same as a bad action. For instance, being hot-tempered – that is, disposed or easily given to the turmoil that is anger – is a vice. It inclines the mind to doing something impulsively and irrationally that isn't fit to be done at all. Now this vice is in the soul in such a way that the soul is easily given to getting angry even when it isn't being moved to anger, just as the lameness whereby a person is called 'lame' is in him even when he isn't limping around. For the vice is present even when the action is absent. So also the body's very nature or structure makes many people prone to wantonness, just as it does to anger. But they don't sin by the fact that they are like this ...[10]

This advance might seem modest, but it was actually rather significant. While retaining an ethical aspect, the emotional personality of every human was now a matter of nature rather than of fault. If men were entirely culpable for the actions their emotions drove them to commit, emotion itself, as a constitutive disposition within human nature, was released from the drama of original sin.

William of Saint-Thierry had clearly recognized its significance when he alerted his friend Bernard of Clairvaux to this conception which found moral responsibility only in consent. When the Abbot of Clairvaux accused Abelard before his judges at the Council of Sens in May 1141, he made certain that this proposition featured among the nineteen that were denounced.[11] For Bernard of Clairvaux, whose position accorded with Augustine and Gregory the Great, responsibility began from the first suggestion of sin: 'We must crush the head of the serpent, that is, suffocate within ourselves the first movements.'[12] To reprise the example of adulterous lust cited by Abelard, to feel desire for the wife of another was to have already committed to the path of sin. Nevertheless, on this question of responsibility for the first movements, it would be glib to cite a direct opposition between the world of the monks and that of the schools, as if the former was hell-bent on a sombre vision of the concupiscent will and the latter the promoter of a naturalistic understanding of emotion. The Cistercian Aelred of Rievaulx in fact drew close to the positions of Abelard when he discussed these same questions: he affirmed that being troubled by the first movements was neither commendable when they were good nor prejudicial when they were bad.[13]

In the second half of the twelfth century, two understandings of the first movements can be distinguished. Certain masters, influenced by the logic of Abelard, like Simon of Tournai (d. 1201) or Alan of Lille, upheld the idea that the first prick of desire (*titillatio carnis*) could not be a sin – not even a venal one – since it was entirely outside of the will's control. This thesis would still occasionally find adherents in the first half of the thirteenth century. But most authors, the influential masters Anselm of Laon (d. 1117) and Peter Lombard (d. 1160) among them, upheld the classical position bequeathed by the Church Fathers, namely that of an immediate moral responsibility for the first movements. It is this answer that dominated at the beginning of the thirteenth century: it was notably reprised by Thomas Aquinas (d. 1274).

It might be concluded that the attempt of Abelard's 'school' to naturalize emotional currents had failed. In fact, the debate had led to a shift in how the power of feeling was mapped within scholastic anthropology. In the patristic tradition, man's appetites were divided between the perception of the physical senses, which involved the body and the animal soul – the *anima bestialis* as defined by Jerome – and an affective sensitivity, made up of desires and aversions, which corresponded to the rational soul, the *anima rationalis*. Until the twelfth century, the first movements had the unique quality of residing at both of these two levels of the soul. This came at the price of an ambiguity which the masters of the schools and then of the universities tried to clarify through the definition of a dual sensitivity (*duplex sensualitas*). On the one hand, they noted a strictly animal sensitivity. This was stimulated by what Gilbert of Poitiers (d. 1154), a contemporary of Abelard and master of the cathedral school of Chartres, called 'primary first movements', such as feeling hungry or thirsty. On the other, there was a rational sensitivity. It was rational in the sense that reason could intervene to control it, and it responded to the influence of 'secondary first movements'. The theory of a dual sensitivity, animal and rational, synthesized the two options explored in the twelfth century. The first pang of emotion brought about by the 'secondary first movements' was involuntary; as such, it corresponded to the natural dimension of emotivity, which was closely linked to the body. But as this movement also set the rational soul in motion, it could potentially be controlled by reason. In this way, theologians conceived that emotion could arise from an involuntary impulse, produced in part by the body, but that it also remained under the control of reason, and thus, of the will. The beginnings of desire and the impulse of anger were irrepressible, as were the pleasures of imagining the satisfaction of these urges. No one could escape them, but one could still be morally culpable on their account, since reason, which presided in the soul, was meant to intervene to repress improper emotion. The weakness of nature created by original sin thus did not disappear from discussion. But it now tended to be understood as a specific fault of reason, which was unable to master an affective sensibility that had been placed in its care.[14]

The twelfth- and thirteenth-century controversy over the first movements of the soul thus partially naturalized emotion, without necessarily exonerating man of responsibility for the acts his emotions drove him towards. Characterized by its technical nature, this debate is emblematic of the evolution of scholarly thought towards a natural philosophy of the emotions. Within it, man's moral path lay in fulfilling his nature, in being an emotive creature endowed with reason.

Accidents of the soul and of the heart: the medical science of emotion

The emotional mechanism

The rise of a medieval science of the emotions cannot be separated from the renewal of medical thought in the Latin West that took place from the eleventh century onward: the latter represented the first new import derived from contact with Greco-Arab knowledge.[15] In the monastic environments of the early Middle Ages, medical knowledge contracted, and came to rely on a reduced set of repetitive theories. As in many other areas of thought, the role of translations was critical. Around 1077, Constantine the African (d. late eleventh century) arrived in Southern Italy, where Latin, Greek, and Arab cultures had intermingled for generations. As a man, he is little known to us. He probably came from one of the Christian communities that still existed in the Maghreb after the Muslim conquest. Constantine joined the monastery of Monte Cassino where, over the years, he translated a number of medical texts from Arabic into Latin.[16] Among these were the *Isagoge* of Ḥunayn ibn Isḥāq (called Johannitius in the Latin West), which remained the textbook for all those who studied medicine up to the end of the Middle Ages, and, first and foremost, the *Pantegni*, adapted from a work written at the end of the tenth century by the Persian doctor 'Alī ibn al-'Abbas al-Maǧūsī. They contained a significant portion of the teachings of Hippocrates and Galen, adapted by the Arab medical tradition which transmitted them.

While Constantine the African worked at Monte Cassino, at nearby Salerno, a great seat of medical learning, the Bishop Alfanus (d. 1085), himself a former monk of Monte Cassino, translated *De natura hominis* by Nemesius of Emesa (active at the end of the fourth century); this treatise on the nature of man contains some significant reflections on the passions of the soul. The passions were also discussed by John of Damascus (d. 749) in his *De fide orthodoxa*, which would in turn be translated by Burgundio of Pisa (d. 1193) in the mid-twelfth century. The medical science of the emotions that grew in the eleventh and twelfth centuries was just one plank of a much broader investigation, one that made no separation between physiology and the psychology of the emotions. Medical thought was thus not detached from natural philosophy. It was man in his entirety that was being explored and mapped. Within the space of a few decades, the impression of human affectivity shifted from a psychomachia, a moral battle between the vices and the virtues in the soul, to a psycho-somatology of the emotions, which took part in the natural movements of body and soul.

In the *Pantegni*, emotions appear as movements of the breath of life, originating in the heart and flowing out into the whole body. The dynamics of the emotions were like a respiration of natural warmth: they were carried by the blood (a fluid in which the humours mingled and which was itself one of the body's four humours), which flowed from the body into the heart, the pre-eminent emotional organ, and then spread from the heart to the limbs. Emotions nevertheless originated in the soul: they were thus actions of the soul which caused somatic modifications (pallor or blushing as the blood ebbed and flowed, changes in heart rate, warming or cooling according to the displacement of humours, etc.). Emotions were active; that is why Constantine and those inspired by him preferred to call them 'accidents of the soul' – suggesting that emotion was a movement born from external influence – rather than 'passions of the soul', even if the latter expression was also used by doctors.

Ancient medicine was founded on the conviction that everyone's behaviour and way of life had implications for their health, which relied on an equilibrium of the humours that guaranteed a good 'complexion' (*complexio* in Latin). Since late antiquity, this tradition defined 'six non-natural things' (thus distinguished from the three 'natural things' of Galen, which were the limbs, the natural spirits, and the blood) on which one could draw in conserving or recovering good health: air; food and drink; movement and rest; sleep and wakefulness; retention and evacuation of wastes; the passions of the soul; or, according to other authors, sleep and wakefulness; exercise and rest; hunger and thirst; food and drink; retention of wastes; bathing and emotions.[17] The section that discussed the emotions in the *Pantegni* mirrored this structure of 'six non-natural things'. Constantine identified six accidents of the soul: anger, joy, sadness, anguish, fear, and shame. Certain emotions, such as anger and joy, resulted from the warming of the blood: this produced a centrifugal force within the heart that reached out towards the exterior limbs. Others, such as anxiety and fear, brought about the opposite, a centripetal movement which drew blood from the members towards the heart. The somatic manifestations that resulted from these movements varied in intensity depending on whether they were slow (as in the case of joy or sadness) or fast (anger and fear).

As seen, the emotions worked according to a mechanism of spirits and fluids which led to reactions throughout the body; some of these, such as the reddening of the skin, were more noticeable than others. Joy was thus a slow release of the natural warmth of the body towards the members. This centrifugal movement was accompanied by the dilation of the heart and an internal cooling. If joy was moderated, the movement retained its gradual characteristic, and it brought only benefits to the body and soul. On the other hand, a joy that was too intense caused a sudden expulsion of the heart's entire vital force and risked provoking fainting or even, according to Constantine, sudden death. Excessive fear could equally cause a fatal reaction, due to an inverse movement, a violent rush of the vital spirits towards the heart.[18]

Up to the end of the Middle Ages, this dynamic scheme, founded on the theory of humours and temperaments (choleric, phlegmatic, melancholic, bilious), remained the foundation for the conception of the emotions among physicians. It was enriched by the new imports of the second half of the twelfth century, particularly the *Liber ad Almansorem* of Abū Bakr al-Rāzī (Rhazes), and the *Canon of Medicine* and *De anima* of Ibn Sīnā (Avicenna). From the end of the twelfth century, these medical theories of the passions spread to scholastic thought and learned culture more broadly, in line with the medicalization of medieval society and the professionalization of medicine at the universities.[19]

In this process, the teachings of Avicenna were defining. Thanks to the Latin translations of his writings, Westerners took a new step towards a psychosomatic theory of the emotions that would influence both physicians and philosophers.[20] According to Avicenna, the emotions began as mental states brought about by an exterior object that contained, for the one who perceived it, a certain tendency (*intentio*). Through sensory perception, this objective 'intention' was submitted to the judgement of the 'estimative force' (*vis aestimativa*), found in the frontal cortex of the brain. Properly described, emotion was the combination of this perceptive judgement that man shared with the highest animals, and the somatic reaction that accompanied it.

In this sense, emotion formed part of a decision-making process that took place over a number of stages: the felt perception of form, the perception of the particular intention of an object, the evaluation of that intention, the bodily movement of attraction and aversion (that is, emotion in its strict sense), the decision, and the bodily action executed through the nerves and muscles.[21] Thus, for example, even a lamb that had never seen a wolf in its life would upon doing so immediately understand that the wolf was hostile. It would perceive straight away the bad intention inherent in the nature of wolf, become fearful, and take flight.[22] Emotion was thus an instinctive response whose cause was found in an external object. It could nevertheless draw on experience: a dog once beaten would always fear the club, which took on a 'hostile' intention for it. The difference between human and animal emotions did not lie in their nature, but in the fact that man, through his use of reason, could intervene to moderate, control, and even counteract the inclination that emotion carried him towards. The animal, however, lacking rational judgement, could only instinctively obey its emotions.

Emotions and healthy living

For both philosophers and physicians from the eleventh century onward, the search for physiological causes to psychological states took on a paramount importance in the study of man. Since emotions expressed a change in the equilibrium of the humours, produced and moved around the body by the force of certain organs, it now seemed possible to manage them medically. It was up to the physician to correct their dysfunctions, which meant both intervening on account of emotions and using emotions as remedies. Emotional therapy was certainly not new, since it had existed in ancient medicine. What arose with force at the end of the Middle Ages, however, was the principle that disturbances generated through excessive or bad emotions could be cured by medication and changes to one's diet and lifestyle which did not solely relate to the religious policing of vice and virtue.

In the last centuries of the Middle Ages, physicians became ever more present at court, mingling with princes and prelates, as well as in the cities, where they were fostered by the wealthy.[23] Medical knowledge became vernacularized and more accessible to the laity. From the end of the thirteenth century onward, doctors wrote personal prescriptions, *consilia*, for their protectors and patients, which they subsequently compiled. They also wrote treatises on hygiene and healthcare based on the theory of six non-natural things.[24]

The *Regimen sanitatis*, written by the celebrated Catalan theologian and physician, Arnold of Villanova (d. 1311) and dedicated to the king of Aragon, James II (d. 1327), represents an example of this latter genre. This complemented his *Speculum medicinae*, which also dealt with the medical treatment of the emotions.[25] Through the eclectic nature of his scientific thought and political activism at the courts of Southern Europe – he was the personal physician of Pope Clement V (d. 1314), with whom he pressed the cause of the dissident Spiritual Franciscans – Arnold of Villanova heralded the emergence of a new sort of late medieval intellectual. His life also bears witness to the rising power of medical practice. Arnold of Villanova's conception of the passions drew faithfully from the dynamic model transmitted by Constantine the African, and enriched it with the teachings of Avicenna. If emotion had its origins in the soul, its very existence resulted from changes within the body. In this sense, Arnold proposed one of the most elaborate theories of the causes of emotion. He distinguished two sorts of causes: external, derived from an object perceived by the senses, and internal, which depended both on the evaluation of the estimative force and the way in which different bodily factors (the complexion of bodily members, the mixing of the humours, the circulation of vital currents) made one predisposed to different emotions. On the physiological plain, passion was a process of change within the members and within the heart. Thus, for Arnold and his cohort, it now seemed possible to cure the harmful effects of certain emotions by working on one's physical complexion.[26]

The remedies proposed were of various natures. Taking influence from the classical theory that the clash of opposites helped to restore inner harmony, several doctors recommended combating a damaging emotion with another emotion. For example, Maino de Mainieri (d. 1368), while denouncing the harmful effects of anger on health, thought that an outburst of anger could be beneficial to people of a cold and wet complexion, through the sudden heat that it then released into the body.[27] Salt-water baths were recommended to counteract certain forms of sadness.[28] A change in diet was often prescribed for those who suffered from emotional difficulties. As fear was shown by a cooling of humours – resulting in pallor, trembling, and even diarrhoea (since heat was concentrated in the abdomen) – wine was considered a good remedy, since it warmed the blood.[29] Wine also helped to fight sadness, which was thought to create dryness and coldness due to a contraction of the heart. Arnold of Villanova recommended a diet of white meat and other delicate foods to stimulate a moderated joy, once again a guarantee of good health. For one of his patients suffering from anxiety and melancholy, Gentile da Foligno (d. 1348) prescribed a soothing syrup, which consisted of cinnamon, fennel, and a liqueur made from lemon, citron, and cloves.[30]

Nevertheless, medical writings tended to prefer general recommendations for one's way of life. Above all, it was a matter of avoiding strong emotions and the ravages of passions like anger through leading a moderate and refined life, surrounded by fine things and good company, as the Italian physician Barnabas da Reggio (d. *c.* 1365) counselled: 'Listening to smooth singing and the delectable music of many instruments, and reading and listening to the reading of tasteful works, not only calms anger but helps combat pain and sadness.'[31] The benefits of music were constantly cited by physicians, who seemed much less ignorant of ancient wisdom on this matter than certain theologians, such as William of Auvergne, liked to claim: 'Within the harmonies, many affections have only been treated haphazardly and fortuitously by physicians, who are ignorant of the identity and quality of the harmonies that have such a force.'[32] From reading Boethius, the physicians, just like the theologians, had learned that the union of the body and the soul had a musical structure to it: the heart emitted pulses, provoked by the emotions, just like a musical instrument.[33]

Emotional therapy was one of the battlegrounds in the growing rivalry between theologians and physicians that followed the Fourth Lateran Council (1215). This had required doctors of the body to urge their patients to first consult a doctor of the soul: by refusing to divide the patient into two parts, body and soul, each side claimed that the whole man lay within their field of competence.[34]

Remedies for melancholy

It is difficult today to study objectively the place that melancholy occupied in medieval culture and representations, since this affective state, under its many names and guises, has fascinated the modern and contemporary imagination, retrospectively altering its historical meaning.[35] By the end of the Middle Ages, *melancholia* was already one of the most treated emotional disturbances in the *consilia*.[36] In Hippocratic medicine, melancholy was materially tied to one of the four humours: black (*melaina*) bile (*cholè*).[37] In this sense, melancholy resulted from an excess of black bile in the organism. This could be the source of many ills, all essentially leading to excessive sadness, insomnia, languor, and/or a general distaste for things. A disturbance of reason as much as of the emotions, sadness could lead to madness, bringing with it not only crazed thinking but also the rise of fury and anguish.

In the early Middle Ages, melancholy was not a distinct state. Rather, it was subsumed under the label and form of 'sloth', that high evil so greatly feared by the desert hermits who called it 'the noontide demon'. The return of the sickness of melancholy coincided precisely with the translation of medical texts, in particular the *De melancholia* of Ishāq ibn 'Imrān, translated by Constantine.[38] A little later, *Cause and Cure*, attributed to Hildegard of Bingen (d. 1179), devoted significant attention to melancholy. There it was described as the defining humour of sinful man, the material component of the sadness that conquered him after the Fall, which transformed his physiology and therefore his emotions.[39]

In the twelfth and thirteenth centuries, learned discourse on melancholy drew simultaneously from religious and medical thought, even if the latter gained ever more autonomy. At the end of the thirteenth century, Taddeo Alderotti (d. 1295), the first physician to write *consilia*, treated the case of a merchant who complained that he had not been able to fall asleep for two years. The treatment Alderotti prescribed was entirely characteristic of this evolution, combining a change of diet and practical counsels: the merchant was told, for instance, to wear attractive clothes, listen to music and enjoy fine things of every kind. The satisfaction they provided would rewarm the heart and help to drive away sadness.[40]

In the centuries that followed, the prescriptions for combating melancholy remained the same: they insisted upon the importance of avoiding violent emotions and sombre thoughts, and of surrounding oneself with pleasant friends, so as not to fall into lonely bitterness. The physicians even treated post-natal melancholy in the same way.[41] The medical treatment of the passions does not seem to have been a matter of gender, or at most only marginally so.[42]

If melancholy could take different forms, there was one sort that was frequently reflected upon: lovesickness. Courtly literature had already played with mixing medical melancholy into the theme of amorous suffering that led the protagonist to the edge of madness:[43]

> He desired nothing except death. He said it himself, he could not find relief from his sufferings except by dying. The sire Tristan was extremely sad. He was such a vision of suffering, and lamented so deeply that anyone who saw him would have taken him for a madman. He screamed and wailed so loudly that his voice echoed near and far throughout the whole forest.[44]

In medicine, this illness took the name of 'heroic love'. According to Arnold of Villanova, who was the inventor of the expression *amor heroicus* (derived from *amor ereos*), the illness of love could be described as heroic since the sentiment not only primarily affected nobles, but conquered the one who felt it.[45] According to a tradition that went back to antiquity, the melancholy of love was a distinctive characteristic of extraordinary people.[46] On this basis, Arnold explicitly made the connection with the aristocratic passion of courtly love. If the medical interest in lovesickness was ancient, Galen did not apply his somatic interpretation of the passions to this disease. This was done by Constantine the African, in his translation of *De melancholia* and in the *Viaticum*, adapted from an Arabic treatise of the tenth century by Ibn al-Jazzār, who produced the first real theory of lovesickness and made the link with melancholy.

For Constantine, heroic love had two causes: one was physiological (caused by an excess of black bile), the other psychological (when thoughts of love became an obsession). Remedies were to be found in distraction, wine, music, or even the company of another beautiful woman... At the end of the Middle Ages, medical discourse led to an increasingly physiological reading of this theme: love and its disorders become a matter of fluids. For Arnold of Villanova, the fixation of desire warmed the heart, and the heat spread to all the members, including the brain, the seat of judgement. Thus, if the problem was born from an error of evaluation, from that point onwards an entirely physiological process entrenched lovesickness and made it self-sustaining. By drying out the organs, it caused insomnia, loss of appetite, discoloration of the skin through the effects of yellow bile, changeable moods, and so on. As for remedies, Arnold was no innovator and always proposed the same derivatives.

From the end of the eleventh century, medical discourse took up the task of reflecting on the emotions, advancing explanations that spanned the physiological and the psychological, and maintaining a tight bond between organic life and psychological life. This process participated in the general movement towards the naturalization of emotions. It is all the more interesting to follow in this domain given that it ran alongside the popularization of medical knowledge amongst a rather diverse population of merchants and urban magistrates: if they were still an elite, they were also lay.

This accessibility nevertheless had its limits. By adapting their counsel to the social and cultural station of their patients, the physicians had in effect made emotional harmony conditional on a rather expensive way of life, unobtainable for the vast majority of people. If it was necessary to listen to delicate music, to read poetry, to drink good wine, to eat refined foods, and to wear flashy clothes to be in good emotional health, the labouring classes had little chance of gaining it. The stereotyping of the emotional agitation and instability of the common folk would only grow stronger as a result. Conversely, certain emotional conditions (such as melancholy) themselves became marks of elite status. From this perspective, the medicalization of well-to-do urban society at the end of the Middle Ages accentuated the discriminatory function of emotion.

Through the way in which emotion was understood and lived out in society, it came to serve as a tool of social distinction.

Monastic anthropology in the twelfth century: the challenges of a spiritual psychology

Affect as a power of the soul

As has already been seen with the first movements of the soul, until the last decades of the twelfth century at least, the urban schools did not have a monopoly on psychological theory. It developed just as much in the monasteries, where such ideas were first formulated. Despite the dichotomies which historians have at times preferred, the twelfth century was marked by a great fluidity in how knowledge was distributed.[47] Indeed, from the 1130s – or even earlier, if one counts the monastic school of Bec – the Cistercians and the masters of the Parisian abbey of Saint-Victor collectively produced a human science that wove affective and speculative thought together. In the twelfth century, one of the main psychology textbooks used by university teachers was an anonymous treatise, *De spiritu et anima* (*The Spirit and the Soul*), written in the 1170s and probably by a Cistercian. This treatise drew on a variety of written sources, some of which were contemporary. It offered a synthesis of such quality that the text was soon attributed to Augustine. The Cistercians likewise soon became masters of a genre that had fallen into disuse at the end of antiquity, that of treatises on the soul. William of Saint-Thierry, Aelred of Rievaulx, and Isaac of Stella (d. *c.* 1170) each wrote one.

Why did these men, who warned against the arrogance of the philosophers and the materialism of Hippocrates' disciples, nevertheless devote themselves to mapping the human soul and even the body in their powers and their qualities? It was precisely because they had taken up the challenge of joining monastic introspection with those new brands of knowledge that gave pride of place to observation and logic. The aim of this reflection on the nature of the soul was thus to bring the science of man into synergy with his spiritual destiny. It followed the Augustinian path, revived at the end of the eleventh century by Anselm of Canterbury, of combining philosophical reflection on the powers of the soul with a spiritual perspective.

The decisive Cistercian contribution to medieval anthropology was to add affectivity to the pantheon of the soul's powers.[48] In thinking of the soul, they drew on the Platonic and Stoic philosophical traditions transmitted by the Fathers, and began by dividing it into three powers. As Isaac of Stella reminded his readers: 'The soul is rational, concupiscible,

and irascible, thus forming, so to speak, its own trinity.'[49] On this foundation, they affirmed the Stoic tradition of the four affects. Joy and hope
were the fundamental emotions of the concupiscible part: in other words,
it was the faculty of desire. Pain and fear, meanwhile, were associated
with the irascible faculty, which thus resembled hatred in so far as it
fostered rejection:

> The affective capacity (*affectus*) is understood to have four parts. Accord-
> ing to what we love, we either rejoice in the present, or hope for the future.
> According to what we hate, we either suffer in the moment, or fear future
> suffering. In this way, joy and hope depart from the concupiscible faculty,
> pain and fear from the irascible faculty.[50]

The lists of affects defined by these authors would go into much greater
detail. Isaac also connected the irascible faculty with compunction, heartfelt penance, boredom, fear, sadness, worry, sloth, jealousy, anger, indignation, and so on. Beyond joy and hope, the concupiscible faculty also
encompassed delight, rejoicing, exaltation, charity, and much more
besides.[51] Bernard of Clairvaux likewise created his own lists, again
dividing the emotions between the irascible and concupiscible:[52] these
were of particular influence for the author of *De spiritu et anima*.[53] These
legions of inclinations, which all grew from the heart – hence their frequent description as *affectus cordis*, affects (or attachments/desires) of
the heart – were responsible for the motion of the soul: 'even if [the soul]
does not move locally, it does move through desire [*affectus*]'.[54] Isaac
would affirm that the affective capacity of the soul, the *affectus*, and its
ability to know, the *sensus*, together constituted the two poles of the
human dynamic. What was initially a tripartite system thus became
binary:[55]

> It is still useful, brothers, to determine, by spiritual discernment and atten-
> tive observation, the source of everything that arises within us: the origins
> of thoughts and affects, the roots of desires and wants, as well as of sug-
> gestions and delights.[56]

Aelred of Rievaulx reached a similar conclusion. For the English
abbot, *affectus* was a 'spontaneous, pleasant inclination of the spirit
towards someone'.[57] This definition did not encompass all forms of
emotion, rather just those that engendered interpersonal attachment.
By insisting on the spontaneity of emotional movements, Aelred continued an evolution already begun by Anselm of Canterbury, who had
made affect a specific form of wilful action: 'Now this inclination of the
mind is opposed to the will of man in the soul: it resists reason in every
respect.'[58] The monastic anthropology inherited from Augustine had

defined three faculties in the soul: memory, reason, and will. Without ignoring this schema, Aelred subtly moved towards a new proposition, proposing a new tripartite model: affect, will, and reason. In so doing, he recognized the possibility of competition, or even open conflict, between affect and will:

> Therefore, as we have said, no spiritual person fails to realize that the love of God should be appraised, not according to these momentary attachments [*affectus*] which are not at all dependent on our will, but rather according to the abiding quality of the will itself.[59]

By stressing repeatedly that affects were momentary inclinations, and thus describing them as impulses (*impetus*), Aelred argued for a division between the rational will, which allowed for the control of action over time, and affect (or attachment), unpredictable and ephemeral. Affect and will waged war in the soul. The opposition between affect and reason often appears similar. For Aelred, the biblical example of Rachel's pain illustrated this inner struggle: 'Attachment [*affectus*] demanded sons, but reason resisted attachment, so that [the sons] might not be recalled. Divine providence delayed taking her up.'[60] By contrast, their collaboration was fruitful when it helped to engender an orderly love:

> Love arises from attachment [*affectus*] when the spirit gives its consent to attachment, and from reason when the will joins itself to reason. A third love can also be brought about from these two when the three – reason, attachment and will – are fused into one.[61]

Thus, according to Aelred, there were loves solely driven by reason and loves that were solely emotional. But they seemed incomplete so long as reason and emotion did not combine their forces within the same momentum. While affect was phagocytosed by the will in traditional Augustinian anthropology, Aelred clearly identified a specific field of activity in the soul for each of these three powers. In this way, he shifted the model significantly, allowing appetitive feeling an autonomy within the soul. Moreover, by distinguishing affect, on one side, and the rational will, on the other, he too helped to propagate a binary pattern for the dynamics of the soul.

For better or for worse: the affective union of body and soul

Emotions were also critical to the ties between body and soul. Man consisted of two distinct substances: the soul, which alone represented the being truly created in the image of God, was not blended with the body that it animated. Nevertheless, the two substances formed a natural

145

unity (*unitas naturalis*) which was indispensable to life and eternal beatitude, as St Bernard described when defending the dogma of bodily resurrection.[62]

To explain this unlikely union, Cistercians explored several leads: formal analogies between the body and the soul, the existence of a median element uniting the two substances, the modalities of the presence of the soul in the body, etc. The affective faculty was often cited as evidence for these forms of association between body and soul, due to its intermediate position and dynamic quality. Bernard thus characterized the attachment which the soul retained with the body after death as a 'natural affection' (*affectus naturalis*), necessary to the *unitas naturalis*.[63] The two substances appeared to be joined at their edges, represented by the superior bodily faculties on one side, which were in close contact with the soul, and the inferior spiritual faculties on the other, which required bodily functions to act. For example, Isaac of Stella, inspired by Hugh of Saint-Victor (d. 1141),[64] made imagination and sensation the two perfect intermediaries between the body and the soul: the union of the human individual depended on them.[65] Other authors appealed to affective power in more unexpected ways. Aelred of Rievaulx, for instance, described how the soul was brought to life in the body at the moment of conception through the action of paternal and maternal affection, a spiritual force conveyed by the sperm.[66]

William of Saint-Thierry went the furthest in attempting to align physiological knowledge with the spiritual doctrine of the Fathers in his unparalleled treatise, *On the Nature of the Body and the Soul* (*c.* 1140).[67] This text has a unique bipartite structure. Its first book is a physical analysis of the body, which synthesized the medical knowledge of its time, leaning heavily on the translations of Constantine the African and Alfanus of Salerno.[68] The second is devoted to the soul. The two books seem almost unrelated to each other. It is as if William, having written a treatise on the soul, simply appended another chapter devoted to the body. It is plausible that, in so doing, he sought to respond to contemporary philosophers, some of whose assertions he contested and judged to be materialistic.[69] William tackled the passions (*passiones*) in the second part of the treatise but he attributed them as much to the body as the soul, depending on the context and the author he drew from.[70] In fact, he found several tiers of passions that moved from the body to the soul. Among them, physiological passion related to an illness or an injury of an organ.[71] But above all, passion, understood as the capacity to suffer, was what bound the soul to the body: it was the presence of the soul in the body and the means by which the body acted upon the soul. William made this passability a distinctive characteristic of the soul, one that distinguished it from all other spiritual substances: 'No other spirit receives the flesh or body to share its sorrows and joys.'[72] William then stated that there were both passions of the flesh and those of the spirit. The former were irrational and worked in connivance with the body. The latter were rational and participated in the elevation of the spirit. When 'the spirit [followed] the natural desires of the flesh or the senses', the animal passions became vices of the soul:

> For, as has been said, what is natural in beasts is vice in man. For carnivores are driven by ferocity, the love of pleasure serves the fertility of animals, fear protects the weak, fright *a fortiori* the weaker, gluttony the corpulent. From none of these do animals or beasts suffer passion, because none of these things which flow from libido are matters for sorrow in irrational beings. But human misery, admitting these passions with an open heart and augmenting their beginnings both in number and strength by its deliberate cooperation, produces a most turbulent and undescribable generation of vices.[73]

William thus defined an anthropology of how passion became vice. It started as a bodily impulse, but 'ascended' through capillary motion towards the spirit, degrading it as it went. The irrational passions ultimately contaminated one's thoughts, completing their mutation into vices.[74] In this way, he drew from an outlook similar to that of the Church Fathers, especially Gregory the Great, since he placed the origin of vice in the impulses of the bestial soul. But William also pushed the game of analogies between the qualities and functions of the body and those of the soul to new extremes.[75] By speaking of spirits and virtues in describing the principles of life, whether it be digestion or rational activity, and by locating the faculties of the spirit in the lobes of the brain, William ended up creating a tension over the boundaries of body and soul. His description of the passions and their activity leaves the same impression: he aimd to convince the reader of a closer union between the body and the soul.

Monastic anthropology in the twelfth century was thus emancipated from the pessimism of the Church Fathers, for whom human nature was fatally oriented towards sin. While continuing to draw on this heritage, monks were rethinking the ties between soul and body, freedom and moral responsibility. Even before the Aristotelian theory of the inseparable union of body and soul began to colour Western thought, they experimented with an innovative path. They did not place much value in the body, which remained a problematic 'other' for them. Nevertheless, by describing the 'inferior' faculties of the soul, those which came into closest contact with the body, as open to its influence, they took the first step towards its rehabilitation. These faculties – sensitivity, imagination, and of course affectivity – were those on which spiritual activity relied. While less celebrated than those undertaken by the contemporary masters of urban schools, these monastic explorations of the human microcosm suggest that a powerful transition was taking shape from the early twelfth century. Under pressure from a variety of intellectual influences, the traditional conception of passion as a disturbance of reason and of the will began to falter. Increasingly, it was seen as a constituent force of human nature.

Towards a university science of the passions of the soul: the thirteenth century

In medieval thought, two major strands of psychological discourse can be discerned.[76] One was spiritual: here the emotions, as actions of the will, had immediate moral connotations. The other was scientific, where the emotions were discussed as part of a reflection on human nature. If the dominance of the spiritual approach had initially gone unchallenged, it would be wrong to describe the Christian intellectual history of the emotions as a journey from a moral discourse to a scientific outlook. When the Church Fathers placed the passions of the soul within the framework of vices and virtues, they in fact relied on a scientific psychology, influenced by medical thought and natural philosophy. Conversely, the rise of naturalistic thought from the end of the eleventh century did not lead to the decoupling of emotions from moral reflection, but rather to the integration of that outlook within natural philosophy. The two discourses had always lived side-by-side, and constituted the twin poles of the same cultural edifice.

The mid-twelfth-century anthropological treatises of the canons Hugh and Richard of Saint-Victor and the *De anima* writings of the Cistercians represented a state of equilibrium. At the end of the century, a renewed reflection on the passions of the soul took place as Western thought became open to the *logica nova* and the ethics of Aristotle, as well as to the philosophical and medical writings of Avicenna. From schools to universities and princely courts, from ecclesiastical to lay circles, the social contexts where knowledge was produced evolved in lockstep. It was in the eleventh and twelfth centuries that the essential questions concerning emotional anthropology were posed. Was affectivity a power of the soul? What was the role of the passions in the union of body and soul? Was man responsible for his spontaneous emotional urges? Could the emotions be ordered in such a way that they became virtues? These questions, which blended spiritual concerns with scientific investigation, called for the elaboration of an integrated intellectual approach. In the mid-twelfth century, this could not yet be effected, as witnessed in the strange co-habitation of body and soul in the work of William of Saint-Thierry. Yet, within the space of two generations, between the end of the twelfth century and the middle of the thirteenth, a truly scientific study of the emotions took shape: it came to situate itself midway between theology, on the one hand, and medicine and natural science, on the other.

Emotions and individuals between psychology and morality: the early thirteenth century

The thirteenth-century scholastic science of the emotions was framed within what historians of philosophy call the 'psychology of faculties': here, psychical phenomena were considered as faculties of the soul.[77] The groundwork for this psychology was laid in the twelfth century, but it was only through the reading of the works of Aristotle, Avicenna, and subsequent Aristotelian commentaries that it reached maturity; at the same time, the work of combining Augustinian heritage with Greco-Arab medical knowledge continued at a pace. In the first decades of the thirteenth century, the task of systematization drew from the newly accessible sources in a syncretic manner. A strong moral orientation was maintained in the very manner of constructing this psychological knowledge.

Some psychological treatises, such as those written by David of Dinant (d. *c.* 1217), Alexander Neckham (d. 1217), John Blund (d. 1248), as well as a host of anonymous authors, were particularly focused on the classification of the emotions: here they were understood from an Avicennan perspective as actions of the estimative faculty. In his *Tractatus de anima*, written around 1210, the English theologian John Blund elaborated a system where the concupiscible and irascible emotions formed opposing pairs, i.e. love vs. hate, joy vs. pain, desire vs. disgust. Alongside several other contemporary authors, he enhanced a schema drawn from the Church Fathers, where the concupiscible emotions brought virtue, and the irascible ones drew one away from vice. Two distinct paths towards moral good were thus defined.[78]

Other works of moral theology written in the same period, such as the *Summa aurea* of William of Auxerre (d. 1223), and the *Summa de bono* of Philip the Chancellor (d. 1236), allowed room for original proposals concerning the relationship between affective psychology and the virtues. For example, the anonymous treatise *De origine virtutum et vitiorum*, written in the first third of the thirteenth century, put forward a unique emotional model.[79] Its author, possibly an English monk, conceived of the passions – joy, hope, sadness, fear – as products of one of the four spiritual powers: that of 'alacrity' (*alacritas*), which represented a sort of strident desire. The passions were echoed in the actions of the will, itself a power of the soul: these actions were defined as love, desire, hate, and defiance.[80] The passions of alacrity and the actions of the will conditioned the movements of the soul that led to virtue. Conversely, the author made *affectus* one of the four forces of the flesh which rapidly drew man towards vice.[81] In the decades that followed, an academic process of standardization gradually put an end to such unique classifications. Nevertheless, their originality bears testament to the fluidity of notions and vocabulary, as well as reflecting the primarily pastoral concerns of their authors.

The overlapping of scientific and pastoral concerns can be better grasped through the moral writings of William of Auvergne, one of the major authors of the first half of the thirteenth century. A canon of Notre-Dame in Paris who subsequently became bishop of the city from 1228 until his death in 1249, William never lost sight of his pastoral mission in his works. Seeking to reconcile Augustine with Avicenna, he identified three powers within the soul. There was a cognitive faculty and a motor faculty, the latter divided into two parts: one commanded movement, the other effected it.[82] Emotions were manifestations of the commanding motor faculty, albeit that the will controlled and directed every movement of the soul.[83] Within emotion there was thus a passive dimension, which reacted to the stimulation of the senses, and an active dimension, when desire was taken up by the will. Here we find a chain of interventions which is not so distant from what Aelred of Rievaulx had proposed a century earlier. Emotions were 'within man' (*in nobis*), as movements given form by the cognitive faculty and carried forward by the will. But they did not come 'from man' (*a nobis*), since they were provoked by external impetus. For William, this process transformed passion (*passio*) into affect (*affectus*).[84] But behind this reasoning he was keen to show how virtuous action was possible. Indeed, virtues, like vices, were nothing other than instances of *affectus* that had become lasting: they were *habitus*, ways of being, whether good or evil. Thus, love and hatred, pain and joy, anger and clemency, and all other associated emotions became the building blocks of vice and virtue whenever they became durable dispositions.[85]

On the psychological level, William clarified an idea that became central to the understanding of virtue in the thirteenth century: it was thought of as a passionate *habitus*. Ways of being were motivated and given moral meaning by the emotions; the initial affective impetus of the movement did not disappear within this *habitus*. William here expressed all the originality of Christian thought on emotion. Not only was emotional intensity not denounced in and of itself, but virtue did not demand that emotion was eliminated or even transformed: it simply had to become a lasting state. William gave his readers a taste of this complexity when he treated confession and penance.[86] Of the three phases of penance (contrition, confession, satisfaction), the first was considered the most emotional: theologians generally associated it with the pain of repentance. Yet, for William, the emotional palette of contrition was even more expansive: emotions of fear, shame, indignation, hatred, and so on, were all contained within it.[87] Contrition was thus conceived as a virtuous process marked by a certain consistency, one that blended the pain of sin with shame and disgust over the deed, alongside other emotions.[88] The challenge thus lay in finding the right balance between the emotions, which were unstable by nature. This is why William devoted so much space to the use of shame in penance: he distinguished prideful shame, which he judged as harmful or even diabolical, since it stood in the way of confession, and virtuous shame, which had to accompany contrition and was a gift of God.[89]

When it came to defining the right paths for every Christian, one can sense the challenge that this transition from *affectus* to *habitus* represented for preachers and confessors. They not only had to encourage their flock to evaluate their emotions according to some rather complex criteria, but also to ensure that certain emotions were felt in an almost permanent manner, since they were the foundation of the virtues.

John of La Rochelle: the turning point of scholastic anthropology

We are indebted to a master of the University of Paris, John of La Rochelle (d. 1245), a contemporary of William of Auvergne, for the most successful attempt to elaborate a systematic psychology of the emotions in the first half of the thirteenth century. John numbers among the first generation of Franciscans who went to university. Of the two works he devoted to the soul and its powers in the 1230s, the *Summa de anima* had the greatest impact, exerting a direct influence on the greatest theologians of the thirteenth century:[90] the Franciscan Alexander of Hales (d. 1245), master then peer of John; Bonaventure (d. 1274), who was his student; as well as the Dominicans Albert the Great (d. 1280) and Thomas Aquinas. John's treatment of the passions of the soul offered a synthesis of available learning, both old and new. Alongside Augustinian tradition represented in the treatise *De spiritu et anima*, he drew on the teachings of John of Damascus and above all the *De anima* of Avicenna. John intentionally made this framework visible, giving the *Summa de anima* the feel of a compilation. In the second half of his work, he described in succession the theories on the soul of Pseudo-Augustine, John of Damascus, and finally – and at length – that of Avicenna. He also integrated the medical knowledge available to him within his synthesis: he found, for instance, part of the explanation for variable affective dispositions in bodily complexion (i.e. in the movement of humours).[91] John of La Rochelle thus formalized the scholastic idea of emotion, which was conceived as an act of the appetitive power accompanied by changes within the body:

> It should thus be noted that, according to Avicenna, there are two parts within the appetitive power: the concupiscible power and the irascible power. The concupiscible power controls those movements through which one approaches whatever seems necessary or useful in satisfying the appetite. The irascible power commands motion to repel whatever the appetite to conquer deems harmful or corrupting.[92]

On this foundation of attraction and rejection, John rolled out a list of twenty-three passions. Eight were of the concupiscible part and revolved around the pleasure-pain distinction (joy, desire, love, hatred, disgust, envy, sadness, mercy) and fifteen were of the irascible part, corresponding to the duality of weakness and strength-building (ambition, hope, pride, domination, contempt, audacity, anger, insurrection, poverty of spirit, despair, humiliation, respect, penance, impatience, fear).[93] The eclectic nature of this taxonomy may be disconcerting at first, but it must be remembered that the final lists of passions and affections were not of primary importance. What mattered were the principles of classification which governed the appetitive powers in their relationship with the soul's powers of judgement and command, on the one hand, and the body, on the other.

Above all, this taxonomy should be understood in light of John's critical reflection on the passivity of the soul found in the first part of the text. After dealing with the union of the soul and the body, he asked why this union existed: in other words, what, ultimately, was the reason for the Incarnation? In his answer, he affirmed that the natural union between body and soul had been effected when the former was not yet tainted by sin. But he immediately added that, in the post-Fall human condition, the union between body and soul could still bring reciprocal benefits, even if it also brought difficulties. It was in this context that John questioned the origin of passions: did they come from nature or from sin? His answer distinguished natural passion, which derived from human nature, from unnatural passion, which resulted from fault.[94] John understood the phrase 'natural passion' in several ways. He did not in fact deny that its movement might be unstable or immoderate. The fact that the soul could undergo the assaults of passion was not in itself an effect of sin. It was its nature. This could be thought of as a type of imperfection – a 'defect' (*defectus*), as John called it – but it was certainly not an evil. It was original sin that had transformed this weakness into a constitutive part of all human existence. Before the Fall, unstable passion was a possibility; afterwards, it became inescapable.

In appearance, the schema bequeathed by Augustine that linked emotional disturbance to sin went unchallenged. But John introduced a change in weighting. A naturalistic facet that was completely alien to the Augustinian conception was added, since he refused to see the symptoms of sin in the instability of the passions. There was, he said, a natural emotional vigour, common to all men before and after original sin, and there was a susceptibility to misfortune that followed the Fall: 'In the first way, susceptibility precedes the fault; in the second, it comes after the fault.'[95] In the scholastic anthropology of the Franciscans, the emotions expressed both the fragility and the freedom of human existence. In this sense, passion had become an essential part of man.

Thomas Aquinas: a psychological science of the passions

By the mid-thirteenth century, the conditions were in place for university masters to give specific treatment to the passions of the soul in their theological works. This can be seen with the Dominican Albert the Great, who addressed the matter in many of his writings. He employed a variety of perspectives in order to integrate the subject within Aristotelian contexts.[96] Thus, in his treatise De motibus animalium, a commentary on Aristotle's work of the same name, the passions were considered in their purely physiological dimension, while in his Summa de bono and in his commentary on Aristotle's Nicomachean Ethics, they were viewed from a moral perspective: 'Passion is a movement of the sensitive appetitive power, and derives from the representation of a good or an evil.'[97] Albert, who gained access to a complete translation of the Nicomachean Ethics in the 1240s, was the first to draw together all the different aspects of the Aristotelian science of the passions. Nevertheless, he remained closer to the moral theologians of the beginning of the century than the likes of John of La Rochelle, since his analysis of the passions remained subordinated to the discourse on virtue.[98] In the Summa de bono, he inserted his long delineation of the system of the passions into the section devoted to the virtues – between temperance and prudence specifically – as if the psychology of the passions could not be understood in a truly autonomous manner.

That ultimate step was taken several years later by the best-known of his students, Thomas Aquinas. The latter is often presented by historians of theology as the author of the first medieval 'treatise on the passions'. The honour does not seem undeserved when one considers the twenty-six questions that the Dominican devoted to the passions of the soul in his master work, the Summa theologiae.[99] The collection, written around

1270, forms a substantial and coherent treatise, and precedes the section devoted to *habitus* and the virtues. Thomas Aquinas defined the passions as motions of the sensitive appetite of the soul: they responded to external influences and were accompanied by transformations within the body. In this manner, he identified eleven principal passions, which he defined as either concupiscible (love, hate, desire, aversion, joy, sadness) or irascible (hope, despair, fear, boldness, anger). Among them, he established hierarchies and synergies. Here, he was particularly fond of the dynamic of opposite emotions, placed in pairs. Love and hate stood at the pinnacle: Thomas, just like Augustine, made love the mother of all passions. They were followed by desire and aversion, joy and sadness, and finally anger, the only passion without an opposing partner.

At last, an autonomous science of emotion – which presented itself as both psychological and physiological – could be envisaged at the very heart of theological discourse. From this perspective, the *Summa theologiae* crowned a century's worth of progress in that direction.

Nevertheless, it should not be forgotten that Thomas in fact introduced few new considerations. He drew from the same sources as his masters, and his taxonomy, as well-developed as it was, was narrower than that of John of La Rochelle. Thomas' analysis is remarkable primarily for its synthetic and systematic qualities. His work underlined the principal teachings of scholastic thought, not least the bodily implications of the passions. Thomas Aquinas, a supporter of Aristotelian hylomorphism, set himself against the dualism of substances that characterized Augustinian thought. He paid equal attention to the twofold nature of the passions, which were at once psychical and somatic. The bodily changes that accompanied passion were not only effects of the soul's movement, but themselves participated in the passionate process. Passion was a psychosomatic phenomenon, within which a formal element (the momentum of the soul) was combined with a physical element (physiological change).[100] As an immediate consequence of this conception, medical theory could be entirely integrated within thought on the passions.

Another original characteristic concerned the cognitive dimension of the passions. The passions were movements of the sensitive appetite. They thus escaped reason, at least at first. Nevertheless, they were not simple sensations, but rather actions which depended on a form of sensitive cognition, which resulted, as Avicenna had already suggested, from the evaluation of the thing perceived. Every emotional movement required the perception of the tendency objectively contained in the cause of emotion.

A third original trait concerned the ethical implication of the passions. In carefully separating his 'treatise on the passions' from his 'treatise on the virtues', the Dominican departed from the way Christians had thought of the passions for centuries, i.e. as symptoms of vice or virtue. The ground for this was already well-prepared of course, but it was Thomas who truly capped this fundamental transformation: as natural movements of the soul, the passions themselves held no moral value, either good or bad. On the other hand, they fell within the grasp of moral evaluation to the extent that the rational powers were meant to manage the passions. From this, Thomas could affirm that all passions served virtue, so long as they were submitted to reason: 'The passions of the soul, in so far as they are contrary to the order of reason, incline us to sin: but in so far as they are controlled by reason, they pertain to virtue.'[101] While Thomas rehabilitated passion, he had done so through an absolute confidence in the capacity of man to act according to reason, whether by guiding passion when it led to moral good, or by neutralizing it when it might cause harm. In both cases, it is fair to say that passion was always directly or indirectly 'a matter of virtue'.

Thomas Aquinas possessed a real zeal for psychological investigation and thus bears witness to the new outlook on emotions at the end of the Middle Ages; this was surely not unrelated to the primary Dominican mission of preaching. It is notable that his exposition of the passions in the *Summa theologiae* is twice as long as his treatment of the virtues. Above all, the twenty-six questions it contains are full of details, nuances, and very concrete considerations over feelings and their complexity. If individually they were not original, they allowed for a very attentive reflection on the little quirks of the soul and the body. The largest part of the treatise is devoted to specific emotions and their intricacies. How did they arise? Through what physical symptoms did they make themselves known? What were their effects? How could the benefits they brought be cultivated and the dangerous inclinations they engendered be fought off?

For example, Thomas devoted three questions to anger.[102] His generation took a more complex view of anger than the monastic thinkers of previous centuries. The Christianization of chivalric ideology, the affirmation of the principle of sovereignty, and the turn towards Aristotelian ethics all presaged the transition from the ecclesiastical condemnation of human anger towards a more nuanced evaluation, including on the psychological level. Thomas defined anger as 'a shock to the soul provoked by outrage'.[103] It was a passion that necessarily relied on reason, since it presupposed a mental representation of the offence, and on a certain moral sensibility, even if misapprehension could cloud one's judgement. One did not get angry without a sense of what was just and unjust. Otherwise, the anger was simply instinctive, as with animals whose behaviour sometimes appears rational without truly being so. Animal anger was simply a warming of bile, an aspect of anger. Human anger was not a simple passion, but rather a mixture of feelings that combined sadness (experienced when affronted), hope (that justice might be restored through vengeance), and burning desire (which motivated one to act).

Thomas loved to compare the passions with each other, to contrast them through their similarities and their differences, to establish hierarchies, and to show how the mingling of primary passions could produce an infinite array of derivative passions.[104] He compared the physical effects of anger to those of love, since they were two forces which led to the bubbling of the humours. But love was a warming of the blood, producing a sweet and smooth heat within the body, while anger inflamed the venomous bile and led to a feeling of bitterness. Thomas linked anger with hatred, in the sense that these two passions wished ill on the person they were aimed at. The difference resided in the fact that the act of anger sought restitution for an injustice, whereas hatred did not concern itself with moral judgement. Having reviewed the causes of anger, which all led back to an injury against honour (thus confirming that anger implied a moral evaluation), Thomas asked a bold question concerning pleasure: did one feel pleasure in getting angry? Yes, Thomas responded, and indeed in two ways: there was a pleasure in imagining the satisfaction of one's desire for vengeance, and another in its fulfilment. Nevertheless, in the first phase (desire for vengeance), the pleasure of anticipation was accompanied by a form of sadness, since the angry man suffered from the fact that the injury inflicted was not yet redressed. As a result, such a man experienced pleasure and sorrow successively, or even at the same time: 'Thus sorrow seems to be the beginning of anger, while pleasure is its effect or conclusion.'[105]

Thomas Aquinas did not revolutionize learned thought on the passions. Rather, he produced what became its defining monument, both for the later Middle Ages and even beyond. At the end of the thirteenth century, the debates over the psychology and ethics of the passions continued within university environments, only strengthening the tendency to grant greater autonomy to the affective power. This was especially the case within those currents marked by the thought of Augustine and Bonaventure, who always saw immense power in the will, the true summit of the soul.[106] Such was the position held, for instance, by the Franciscan Duns Scotus (d. 1308): in his conception, passions no longer acted against the will but were a 'competing (or concurrent) force' within it.[107] Despite being opposed to metaphysical Thomism, on this point Duns Scotus held a position on the moral value of emotions which was not so dissimilar from the thought of Thomas Aquinas. For him too, so long as the spirit learned to moderate the passions, they were related to good will: 'Where there are passions, there is virtue',[108] he wrote, highlighting an idea which has already been seen in Thomas' work. All in all, it was a happy reversal for a much-maligned part of human nature, one that had been the subject of so much suspicion among medieval thinkers.

In the twelfth and thirteenth centuries, a science of the emotions took shape. If we have followed it here from the perspectives of psychology and physiology, it also found expression in other fields of knowledge.[109] It bears testament to a long-term softening of Christian attitudes towards passionate man. At least within learned culture, a calmer anthropology can be detected, which naturalized the body and emotional life. This reflection began in the reformed monastic circles of the eleventh century and continued within university colleges during the thirteenth and four-teenth centuries: amid shifting frameworks of thought, it evolved con-tinuously. In taking its place within human nature, emotion was normalized, and yet it continued to occupy a strategic place within the human disposition. Thomas Aquinas provides a good witness to this evolution, in which theological discourse came to accept the passions and sought to domesticate them through reason. The rational mind – the noble part of the soul which Augustine called *mens* – henceforth had to make peace with the auxiliary forces of sensation, imagination, and emotivity, all of which were connected with the exterior and alterity. The empire of the spirit remained unchallenged, but a change of regime had occurred. A 'federal conception'[110] of the self had taken charge: a more efficient self, without doubt, but also more unstable, exposed to internal revolts as well to foreign invasions, both divine and devilish.

— 7 —

THE POLITICS OF PRINCELY EMOTION (TWELFTH TO FIFTEENTH CENTURIES)

Modern historians and political scientists have only recently begun to take the emotional dimension of the art of government seriously. If we begin from the presumption that politics is founded on calculated anticipation and cold rationality, how can we be anything but contemptuous of actions that suggest emotional agitation? Seemingly incompatible with the rational exercise of power, emotion appears only to disturb the judgement of the strong and to motivate the impulses of the weak, rendering them vulnerable to manipulation by the more astute. This principle has been all the more unshakeable given that it has guided the very construction of political history in the West since the end of the Middle Ages.

For how can one ignore Machiavelli's (d. 1527) *The Prince*, surely one of the most celebrated political treatises in European history? The fact that the Florentine's work has given rise to many misunderstandings is neither here nor there: the rise of modern states would be accompanied, we are told, by the gradual expulsion of emotion from the political domain. It was good politics to become a cold-blooded creature. But this conception, which at some point came to be taken for granted, is the result of a rather recent historiographical fiction: it goes back no further than the end of the nineteenth century. It is enough to return to the sources and content of *The Prince* to see that the latter is far from being as blandly 'machiavellic' as the author's name would suggest.

In this text, written at the dawn of 'modern' times (1513) and dedicated to Lorenzo II de' Medici (d. 1519), Machiavelli in fact encouraged the prince to make good use of the emotions, both his own and those which he aroused among his people, by adapting them to his goals. Machiavelli said that the prince should make sure that he was loved by his people, for happiness was a source of peace: if it was right that he was feared as a master of war, he had to make sure, above all, that he was not hated.[1] Machiavelli swapped the legendary *bon mot* of Atreus, king of Mycenae – 'Let them hate me, so long as they fear me' – for a far more subtle demand: 'The prince must nevertheless make himself feared in such a way that he will avoid hatred, even if he does not acquire love, since one can very easily be feared and yet not hated.'[2] This policy only appears cynical if one presupposes that emotions are external to the rational sphere, and thus only make trouble for it. As soon as that presumption is lifted, it is easy to conceive of how the emotions might work in complete harmony with the rationality of governmental strategies.[3] Indeed, they can no longer be left at the margins of political history.[4]

Sovereign emotion

From the political body to the princely body, and back again[5]

At the end of the Middle Ages, political thought was dominated by the metaphor of the human body. In 1159, John of Salisbury (d. 1180), an Englishman, wrote his *Policraticus*, a political treatise that would go on to enjoy significant influence. Here, one finds the first instance of society being imagined as a human body, where the king was the head and the people its members.[6] This organic political metaphor had ancient origins, but in the Christian West, until the *Policraticus*, it had only been used to describe the 'mystical body' of the Church, with Christ at its head and its various spiritual and temporal powers as its members. By way of this image, ecclesiastical intellectuals began to transpose the Pauline conception of the community of the faithful as the mystical body of Christ into the domain of the *regnum*. In a society increasingly marked by naturalistic thought which linked microcosm and macrocosm through a prolific system of analogies, the political body would itself be conceived as one and the same organism. This outlook was reinforced by the theory of the humours, which governed understanding of human life in the Middle Ages. The personal body of the prince and the social body of the kingdom, the natural organism and the political organism, were thus conceived as part of an interconnected network. The complexion and temperament of the king's person determined to no small extent his ability to govern; while, conversely, his practice of government had an influence on his physical state. The movements of the humours led to temperaments that were nothing other than emotional personalities: an excess of yellow bile produced an angry temperament, black bile a melancholy temperament, blood a sanguine temperament, and phlegm a phlegmatic temperament. Associated with primary characteristics (warm, cold, dry, humid), these basic configurations could be freely combined, allowing for kings who were angry-sanguine, angry-melancholic,

159

sanguine-phlegmatic, and so on. The social body could be brought low and afflicted by diseases, which in turn afflicted the body of the prince himself, just as the prince's government impacted the health of the social body. The result was a multitude of potential interactions, in which the passions had an essential role to play.

It is thus hardly surprising that medieval historians have begun to devote significant attention to the body of the prince, which was at once a vehicle and an interface for emotion. A kind of morphological rule-book defined the emotional temperaments that were best suited to the principles of government. The prevailing rule was one of proportionality, of harmony between the members. The prince had to be sufficiently tall, with well-proportioned limbs, and a broad chest in which to house his heart, given that the latter was the organ from which many of the emotions associated with power were derived, first and foremost those 'blood' emotions like anger and impetuosity. The face was a strategically important canvas for emotion.[7] Ideally, it was to be lightly coloured, signifying a moderate excess of blood that announced authority: the chronicler Georges Chastellain (d. 1475) thus points to the 'thick veins, full of blood' on the face of Philip the Good, duke of Burgundy (d. 1467).[8] A ruddy face was also synonymous with a joyful temperament. His hair was another important feature: in the later Middle Ages, having long hair and a beard, provided they were well-groomed, were signs of a natural warmth. Conversely, a pallid complexion and clean-shaven skin suggested a predisposition towards fear. Naturally, these general characteristics, drawn directly from the principles of ancient physiognomy, were frequently adapted by the chroniclers.

For example, the portrait of Charles V (d. 1380) given by Christine de Pizan (d. c. 1430) conforms to the ideal proportions, bodily features, and emotions appropriate to a 'wise' sovereign:

> Sa phinozomie et sa façon estoit sage, attrempée et rassise, à toute heure, en tous estas et en tous mouvements; chault, furieus en nul cas n'estoit trouvé, ains agmodéré en tous ses fais, contenances et maintiens.

> His physiognomy and his manners were marked by wisdom and measure at every hour, in every circumstance, and in every movement. He never became heated or violent on any occasion; rather, he remained moderate in all his actions, behaviour, and manners.[9]

While she recognized the sovereign's face to be a little paler than was ideal, Christine de Pizan wrote it off as merely the effect of a lingering disease, rather than any weakness of constitution. She was thus careful to quickly reintegrate this potential sign of imbalance – which, in other circumstances, might have suggested an emotional coldness (suggesting cowardice, for example) – within the model of complexional conformity between the body and emotional temperament.

A prince who lacked the favour of his chronicler was liable to find himself saddled with a disharmonious body and an emotional temperament contrary to the characteristics expected of a sovereign. Louis XI (d. 1483) fell victim to this in the unflattering caricature drawn up by Thomas Basin (d. 1491). His absence of royal dignity translated into an inelegant physique: saggy legs, a lean face, a long nose, and sunken eyes. This went hand-in-hand with his skill in dissimulation and emotional manipulation, which was not seen as a positive political quality...

Charles the Bold, the last of the Valois dukes of Burgundy (d. 1477) provides an almost complete contrast. He was given a morphology that conformed to the choleric temperament that all the chroniclers saw in him: sturdy and robust, he had powerful thighs and a roughened face, with a black beard and strong jaw. His complexion was ruddy, indicating his susceptibility to outbursts. The features of his father, under the pen of Jean Molinet (d. 1507) or Thomas Basin, were far from dissimilar (large lips that were full of blood, eyebrows that stood up 'like horns when angered'), likewise signalling a choleric temperament. With Philip the Good, the predisposition to anger suggested a controlled wrath, in line with what was expected of princely authority. But with his son Charles, this choleric propensity was excessive to the point of overflowing, and sent him tumbling towards a disorder of the humours, always harmful to the exercise of the government. This divergence in how father and son were perceived shows that while descriptions were always stereotyped, they were no less subtle and ambivalent for it.

While often found in later medieval historiographical writings, such galleries of princely portraits would only be of anecdotal interest if the emotions described did not participate in political communication, i.e. the very act of governing. This was ultimately what was at stake: the emotions of princes directly participated in government. In this sense, the physique of the prince reflected his innate abilities but also the story of his reign. And the political use of princely emotions resulted from a combination of natural predispositions and learning.

The prince in the mirror of his emotions

The art of ruling in the later Middle Ages relied on what Michel Foucault has called 'governmentality', that is to say, a tight dovetailing between one's relationship with the self and the exercise of power over others.[10] Derived from the ancient model of the wise king, this timeless requirement would only be reinforced in the Middle Ages by the Christian understanding of worldly power. Gregory the Great had theorized its

161

foundations at the turn of the sixth and seventh centuries. As they had been created by God, all men were equal. From that perspective, no man had a right to exercise power over another. But this rule was valid only as long as men did not commit sins. It was vice – rather than nature – that rendered men unequal in worth.[11] Just as men exercised natural dominion over animals due to their possession of reason, lines of power had become a necessity within human communities due to sin. This notion was still in force during the last centuries of the Middle Ages, as can be seen in the treatise that the encyclopaedist Vincent of Beauvais (d. 1264) dedicated to Saint Louis (d. 1270), *De morali principis institutione*: 'That a man commands other men in this life is not the result of nature, which has created all men equal, but rather the result of sin.'[12]

This ecclesiastical conception of power implied that a prince must be educated in the virtues, since he could not derive his legitimacy from his blood alone. This led directly to the matter of the passions. Just as man had 'a right to rule over brute beasts', as Vincent of Beauvais wrote, so the authority of the prince was only legitimate due to men having become 'beings without reason', that is, beings subject to their evil passions. The king was only truly a king to the extent that he had mastery over human passions – his own to begin with, and then those of his people. At the very root of this ecclesiastical ideology of power lay an organic link to the matter of the passions, by way of the dialectic of vice and virtue: virtue led to wisdom, which relied on a temperate use of the passions. Conversely, any disorder among the passions would derail the exercise of power: 'Power in the hands of a man who is devoid of wisdom or wicked can only be likened to a sword in the hand of a furious madman.'[13]

The matter of educating the prince in the correct use of passions, i.e. making them sources of virtue – was at the very core of a political literary genre alive throughout the Middle Ages, a tradition commonly lumped together under the label of 'mirrors for princes'. Texts of this sort were 'mirrors' precisely because they concerned providing the prince with an ideal image to which they were meant to conform. These writings, which first appeared in the Carolingian era, were rooted in patristic thought, particularly that of Augustine and Gregory the Great. For them, the king was essentially one who 'ruled', the *rex rector*, as Thomas Aquinas put it, i.e. the one who conducted himself and led others with rectitude. Someone could only be king if he acted wisely and in an upright manner: from this premise, attention was turned first towards his personal merits, and then to his capacity to inculcate virtues among the ruled, those most in need of correction. From the twelfth century onward, the organic metaphor would only serve to reinforce the tight bond between the personal virtue of the prince and the collective virtue of his subjects.

162

As a result, while training the passions is an ever-present theme in 'mirrors for princes', the subject is rarely given specific treatment within them, since their discourse focuses directly on the goals of such education – the virtues that had to be cultivated, and the vices that had to be avoided. Emotions are certainly present, but only underlying the narrative, in the sense that the vices and virtues lodged in a man's heart largely resulted from the good or bad government of the passions. Sometimes the categories are conflated: for instance, envy appears simultaneously as a vice and a wicked passion, while hope and charity are presented as both virtues and good passions.

Among these treatises of princely education, there is, however, one text that lingers over the 'movements of the heart', and indeed a rather important one: *De regimine principum* ('On the government of princes'), composed between 1277 and 1279 by Giles of Rome (d. 1316) and dedicated to the future king of France, Philip IV ('the Fair', d. 1314), who was then just ten years old. This treatise enjoyed considerable influence: it was the most widely disseminated political work in the Middle Ages, in part because Philip the Fair asked Henri de Gauchi to produce a French translation of it.

Giles of Rome, a scholastic philosopher at the University of Paris, saw political science and rational science as inseparable.[14] This view, influenced by the thought of Aristotle and Thomas Aquinas, placed great emphasis on the king's moral virtues as prerequisites for his capacity to govern. It shows us how the theory of passions, descending from the university to the princely courts, served to tie together thought on man and society as part of the same ordered world in the late thirteenth century.[15] The treatise of Giles of Rome is divided into three parts, a testament to the overall political project of the work: in the first the king is considered as a private person, in the second as the head of the family, and in the last as the head of the political community, the three levels corresponding to the three Aristotelian fields of ethics, economics, and politics. Thus, in its attempt to make sense of sovereign legitimacy, it treats private and public life, the domestic circle and the political circle, as parts of the same progression. Just as the natural body of the king was intrinsically tied to the body politic, his qualities as a private person would determine his ability to govern.

The passions of the prince are considered chiefly in the first part of the work, which is devoted to self-government, and hence to ethics. Giles of Rome defined the criteria by which the king's actions would be assessed, namely the quality of the ends envisaged, the virtues he acquired, the passions that supported them, and those good habits defined in light of this system.[16] The passions of the soul were morally beneficial, provided the prince made good use of them. They then became the bedrock of the virtues. Giles of Rome identified twelve passions required for good government, just as there were twelve virtues. Thus 'kings and princes must understand the movements of the soul, for they can do great harm to the kingdom when they are poorly directed and run counter to reason, or the greatest good if they are properly conducted according to reason.'[17] Giles owed his nomenclature of the passions to Aristotle's *Rhetoric*, on which he had written a commentary that drew inspiration from the analyses of his master, Thomas Aquinas.[18] At the top of the passionate edifice sat love, which was the 'first movement', the *primus motus*, from which all others followed. This first passion, which could in turn become a virtue, was presented as one of the foundations for the art of government, as well as the political bond *par excellence*.[19] If politics was the expression of the ordering relationships within the body politic, then love was their driving force. From love, defined as a movement of attraction, and hatred, a movement of repulsion, were derived all the other passions that one had to learn about. They were divided into five principal pairs: hope and despair, desire and disgust, fear and boldness, affability and anger, joy and sadness. To these Giles added a number of secondary passions, such as jealousy, envy, and shame.

If kings had to study these movements, it was because the majority were neither good nor bad in and of themselves. They had thus to be avoided or explored depending on the circumstances and aims envisaged, while always respecting the requirements of good measure and control. Kings were to avoid excessive fear, for fear emptied the heart of blood and paralysed the limbs: a prince who was too fearful was incapable of action, and thus, in its literal sense, of governing. On the other hand, a moderate fear would illuminate judgement: it was, of course, desirable to fear what might harm the kingdom. Again and again, an organic bond was cited between emotion and action, between being moved and putting things in motion. Passions were the foundation of every act of government – whether the government of oneself or of others – since they provided the efficient cause of action (or what paralysed it).

To an extent, Giles of Rome's exposition of the good and bad use of passions merely reiterated the advice of all moral literature since Aristotle. Passions were to be used in an orderly and measured manner so as to place them at the service of the virtues. In this sense, the government of the passions required of a king carried the same obligations that were imposed on any reasonable man. The rubrics concerning joy, sadness, and jealousy thus drew from shared moral foundations. However, having to direct the conduct of others implied specific requirements. The king was called upon to be an example in the field of virtue, just as in his righteous use of passions. The king idealized by such 'mirrors' was thus to be at once an ordinary man and a unique being, animated by both common and exceptional emotions. Such was the case, for instance, with hope. Giles of Rome stated that hope stemmed from the desire for a good thing: the greater the good, the greater the hope. Yet unlike lesser people, who were limited by their status, the king could attain great wealth and great honours. As the guarantor of the common good, of the happiness of all, the king had to be animated by a hope that was in proportion to what was in his power; conversely, despair was practically forbidden. His 'grandeur of heart' depended on the princely capacity to hope.

The teachings of Giles of Rome directly influenced many of the later medieval works on political morality, thus assuring the transmission of scholastic thought on the passions from the university to the princely court. Their impact can certainly be felt in another important treatise, the *Livre des fais et bonnes mœurs du sage roy Charles V* (The Books of the Deeds and Good Character of King Charles V, the Wise), written by Christine de Pizan in 1404 at the request of Philip the Bold, duke of Burgundy (d. 1404). But in one way or another, every text on princely education took an emotional point of view on political relationships. On the moral plain, the orientation towards vice or virtue was played out at the level of emotional reactions. One could not be a wise king while acting under the influence of disordered emotions. Certain powerful emotions – such as the hope for good things or the hatred of evil – were nevertheless not incompatible with the virtue of temperance, the act of conforming one's desires to reason. A wise king was not a placid king, still less a king who was never perturbed. If righteous emotion was to be found at the mid-point between too much and too little, the correct intensity depended on the situation. Thus, for Giles of Rome, the affability required of a prince was not synonymous with a gentle and indulgent mood; rather it was a virtuous passion which allowed for the well-judged use of anger. An affable prince was thus still expected to be angry at injustice, to suffer with those who suffered undeserved ills, and to rejoice at the punishment of the wicked. Each emotion, through its motives, its intensity, and its ends, showed the prince the path that his actions would follow. He could thus evaluate whether his desires or aversions were in line with the good of the realm at the very moment that he felt them. In this sense, emotion was not simply a moral indicator, at the root of virtue and vice, but could also be a good counsellor or a bad one. Finally, emotion acted as a stimulus towards action. A decision would be just if the emotion behind it was correctly directed towards virtue. But it was likely to become a mistake if that emotion was not mastered. Thus, while the emotional education of princes relied on the same behavioural requirements that were imposed on every good Christian in the late Middle Ages, it was no less unique as a result.

The emotional portrait of Saint Louis

If there is one medieval king whose 'emotional government' has left a lasting impression on common memory, it is indeed Louis IX. The holy king was described as the 'roy piteus' ('the king of pity') by his companion and biographer Joinville (d. 1317),[20] and had been, according to Voltaire, 'as compassionate as if he had always been unhappy'.[21] Jacques Le Goff was not mistaken when he chose to close his monumental biography of Saint Louis with a chapter entitled 'The Suffering King, the Christ-king': he was at once a man who suffered in body, from the pain of chronic diseases, and a Christian individual, who, in penance, voluntarily inflicted suffering upon himself.

The English chronicler Matthew Paris (d. 1259), a contemporary of Saint Louis, emphasized the king's sadness on his return from the crusade in 1254: he was 'cast down in heart and look', he sighed frequently, and seemed unmoved by distractions. Saint Louis showed all the signs of depression. It was not only sadness that overtook him, but also the shame of having failed in his mission as a Christian king: 'Woe is me, through me the whole of Christianity was enveloped with confusion and shame.'[22] This represents something rather exceptional: a circumstance in which royal shame was permissible, since it came from the shame of penance. Following the example of Michelet,[23] Jacques Le Goff took an interest in the king's tears. These flowed profusely in his biographies, bearing testament to his devout piety and his love for his people. But as described by his confessor Geoffrey of Beaulieu (d. end of thirteenth century), he also prayed for tears as a mark of grace, a gift from God, even if they did not always come:

> He greatly longed for the grace of tears, and he would piously and humbly lament this shortcoming to his confessor, saying to him in confidence that, when in the Litany it was said 'that you may bestow upon us a fountain of tears,' he would earnestly say, 'O Lord, I dare not ask of you a fountain of tears, but a few scant drops of tears would do to water the parched hardness of my heart.' Once, in private, he revealed to his confessor that when the Lord had given him some tears in prayer, which he felt pleasantly flowing down his cheeks into his mouth, their flavor was most sweet, not just to his heart, but to his taste also.[24]

The figure of the king in pain, of the self-sacrificing Christ-king, drew on a political ideology and practice that was deeply rooted in the emotions. The king's contemporaries were perfectly aware of this: 'Saint Louis loved God with his whole heart and it was on Him that he modelled his actions. This could be seen in that, as God died for the love of his people, so did the King more than once put his own body in danger of death for the love he bore his people.'[25]

Among contemporary historians, Joinville – who had accompanied the king in the Holy Land – stands out as being the most attentive to this side of his personality. He bequeathed an emotional portrait of Saint Louis that is both subtle and complex. He portrayed a king who was by turns the master of himself and impulsive, lenient, and wrathful. Above all, Joinville, who never failed to point out the king's great affection for him ('Seneschal, you know that I have loved you well'),[26] testified to the truly political dimension of royal emotivity.

It was usually matters of religious morality that provoked Louis' impulsive reactions; they suggest that he brooked no argument on such issues. The holy king's distaste for games of chance, which he regarded as an insult to God, is well known. While sailing towards Acre, Saint Louis reacted sharply upon learning that his brother, the count of Anjou, was playing 'at the tables': he 'se courouça moult fort a son frère' ('was very angry at his brother')[27] and threw his dice and chips into the sea, vehemently reprimanding him.[28] The king had little hesitation in unleashing his belligerent fury whenever he fought against the Saracens.[29] On the other hand, when warlike anger stirred among his barons, who wanted to go and besiege Avignon, it was he who held back their impetuosity, which he deemed poorly directed: 'The king with difficulty restrained their fury, and said to them: "I go from France, not to avenge my own injuries, or those of my father, or mother, but those of my Lord Jesus Christ." '[30] Thus the political anger of Saint Louis, which was by necessity rare, conformed with what was expected of a prince, but also served to delineate precisely the personal style of his government: that of a man particularly sensitive to religious ethics and the defence of the faith. This did not stop Joinville from concluding that the king could get carried away too easily, nor from telling him about it: 'I want you to have a contract with me that if I ask you for anything all this year you will not be angry; and on my side I will not be angry if you refuse me.'[31] Saint Louis, who could occasionally appear a jovial king,[32] burst out laughing. A little later, he did not forget to show his sense of humour by yielding to Joinville's friendly request: 'You may say what you please, but I am not getting angry!'[33] Louis could even laugh along when Joinville teased him for his reputation for holiness. On receiving a request from a group of Armenian pilgrims who hoped to meet the 'holy king' on their way to Jerusalem, Joinville conveyed their message, but not without ribbing his king: 'Sir [...] there is a crowd of people outside from Greater Armenia. They are asking me, sir, to let them see the holy king; but I do not want to kiss your bones just yet.'[34] The joke was met with guffaws by the king.

For Saint Louis, governing with the emotions meant making use of both royal emotions and those aroused in others. This becomes clear, for instance, in his exercise of justice. Shame, whether cited explicitly or wrapped up within rituals of redemption, was an essential instrument of the king's justice. Joinville provided many examples. For instance, the four judgements he recalled witnessing while in the king's presence at Caesarea all contained a form of humiliation or the threat of humiliation that might stir the shame associated with dishonour. The first concerned a knight whom the king surprised at a brothel in the throes of passion. Saint Louis gave him a choice. He could either be dragged all over camp dressed only in a shirt (i.e. in his underwear, a state considered similar to nudity) by means of a rope tied around his genitals and pulled by the prostitute, in line with a judicial practice found in Southern Europe;[35] or he could hand over his horse and weapons to the king and then leave the camp. In both cases, the real punishment was infamy, an affront to chivalric honour, impugning either his manhood or his social status. Unsurprisingly, the knight preferred the second proposition. The second judgement settled a conflict over spoils between Joinville's men and the brothers of the Hospital. Joinville won the case and the master of the Hospital made his brothers eat off a blanket on the floor (and not at a high table, as befitted their rank) for as long as Joinville desired. The third judgement concerned a sergeant accused of having struck a knight in the service of Joinville. The king granted to Joinville that the sergeant should go barefoot in his underwear to the knight's tent, and kneel before him to offer reparation.

The last act of justice was the most spectacular. It became known that the marshal of the Templars, Hugues de Jouy, had entered negotiations with the sultan of Damascus without first deferring to the king. The latter was extremely angry and inflicted a humiliating sentence on the master of the Templars, Renaut de Vichiers. The king forced him to come barefoot to the royal camp and there, with everyone watching, recant before the sultan's emissary. Finally, he was compelled to kneel and make honourable amends for his act of disobedience.

These scenes of public humiliation are emblematic of the practice of the *amende honorable* enforced by sovereign courts at the end of the Middle Ages. The term referred to rituals of public penance that had been translated into the context of lay relationships: their function was to restore the injured honour of the victim – as well as that of the king, in his role as the guarantor of justice – without recourse to physical punishment. Instead of exercising a vengeful justice, the king imposed a shame that served as reparation for the offence: in the context of the crusades, where every armed man was precious, it was indeed an act of *realpolitik*, its efficacy guaranteed by the playing out of ritualized emotions. It must be noted that the sequence often began with the anger of the prince: learning of the fault, the monarch would feel discontent and indignation, which signified an affront to his honour. The shame within the reparation thus responded to an expression of anger which had made the crime public.

The king's private character and exercise of power were thus indivisible, as these examples taken from Joinville's *Life of Saint Louis* make clear. The political person and the private person were never separated. This interweaving of these registers contributed to the construction of the royal portrait. Joinville's Saint Louis was at once an extraordinary figure and an ordinary man who had to put his passions in order. Through the affective psychology of the sovereign, an ideology of royalty was played out that straddled sacrality and humanity, the political body and the natural body.

Governing through emotion

Ira regis

Wrath would seem to be the royal and princely emotion *par excellence*.[36] In the Bible, it often serves as an expression of divine power. The wrath of medieval kings, the *ira regis*, presents an obvious analogy, striking when an affront to majesty occurred. It resulted from an offence against the foundations of *potestas*. Thus it was comparable to divine anger, even when the king was not directly presented as the strong arm of God's wrath.[37] In chancery writs, the threat of *ira regis* was usually expressed by phrases like 'under the pain of incurring our indignation',[38] and served a similar function to the comminatory clauses found in ecclesiastical acts: a curse, placed on the same plane as divine wrath, would fall on anyone who might transgress the will of the prince.[39] This comminatory anger was often all that was required to make the point. But the *ira regis* could also be expressed through the prince as a physical person, by way of gestures, words, and bodily signs.

Since antiquity, moral literature had discussed the conditions under which a prince's anger was permissible. Nevertheless, positive perceptions of anger, even of the royal variety, took a long time to gain currency among the literate Christian elite. While Gregory the Great distinguished between sinful and zealous anger, the latter motivated by the defence of virtue, moralists still placed it on the list of principal vices.[40] The only exception was the wrath of God. As for the anger of the great aristocrats, it was too closely associated with customary practices of vengeance and endemic violence to receive clerical blessing. Thus, all the chroniclers deplored the wrath of Henry II of England (d. 1189) against his sons

169

Richard and John (d. 1216), who in turn inherited the temperament of their father.[41] Because of their belligerent ferocity, the Plantagenet kings were called 'sons of wrath' by their detractors.[42]

During the last centuries of the Middle Ages, the evaluation of anger became more nuanced: it benefited from the increasingly 'naturalistic' discourse on the passions, and especially from the rediscovery of Aristotle, who cited it as one of the sources of courage. As such, it was closely linked to martial qualities, such as boldness and belligerent zeal. It nevertheless remains difficult to identify within surviving texts: it appears under various guises – wrath, ire, or fury – depending on its origin and intensity, but these terms remained without precise definition.[43] It was mixed up with other affective states, such as sadness, pain, or bitterness, and it is sometimes difficult to say which tone is dominant. Far from becoming rarer, the political invocation of anger would only gain ground in the final centuries of the Middle Ages. It can be witnessed at all levels of power amid the restoration of public authority in Western Europe: the *ira principis* of the counts of Toulouse in the twelfth century was as formidable and sacred as that of the Spanish kings or the contemporary Capetians.[44] It also responded to a number of different political logics: the flamboyant anger of the feudal lord directly recalled his martial vigour, while the anger of sovereigns, terrible but restrained, could serve as an act of justice.

In its strict sense, anger was defined as a response to a perceived offence, i.e. an unjust insult, usually one made in public. This is why it was so often related to tarnished honour.[45] In the eyes of those who beheld princely anger, its value was primarily defined by its moral nature. Some anger was good, some was bad. More precisely, there were good and bad reasons for getting angry; and when that anger was legitimate, there were good and bad ways of showing and deploying it. Good anger arose from righteous causes, was expressed in a correctly measured manner, and produced reactions proportionate to the offence.

But how could a reaction that appeared spontaneous – indeed, one wrought by the humours – be political? To the extent that princely anger reacted to an offence, it revealed the values that had to be defended. Thus, through the act of anger, the nature of government was expressed. The prince was supposed to become angrier when the honour of his kingdom was offended than when it was the honour of his own private person. But the two were not separated: the body of the king was supposed to give flesh to the signs of indignation found in the body politic. *A contrario*, the chroniclers maligned the choleric temperament of Charles the Bold because they saw only individual passion within it, which he sated in defiance of the people's interests. The primary political function of anger seems to have been to guarantee stability and rightful order. The personal passion of anger led to disorder, while the *ira regis* repaired an imbalance that had arisen to the detriment of the common good. The good prince had to deploy anger parsimoniously, not only for moral reasons, but also, from a political perspective, to ensure stability and respect for his authority. Tyrants, on the other hand, were presented as furious madmen. These political demands were piled on top of each other without effacing the personal traits to which the chroniclers were also attentive. They have bequeathed emotional portraits that can seem complex or even paradoxical, at least if we insist on judging them by our contemporary psychological criteria.

Anger as verdict: the murder of Thomas Becket

Whether expressed or repressed, royal and princely anger was not only suggestive of political ideology and values; it also participated in acts of government in a way that would today be described as 'performative'. That is, it reinforced the validity of an action within a culture of political communication where publicity was always desired. Thus, when a ruler gave voice to wrath – and especially when it was also made visible on and within the body of the prince by changes to skin colour, staccato breathing, a booming voice, facial twitching, and sweeping, disorderly gestures[46] – those assembled, and indeed, symbolically, the entire kingdom, were warned that a person or a group was temporarily or permanently withdrawn from the protection and love of the prince.

Anger accompanied and executed royal justice. The anger of the Plantagenet kings thus participated in a sort of political protection racket: someone deprived of its assistance was exposed to the rapacious assaults of his enemies. One of the most famous examples is that of Henry II, in December 1170, calling his barons traitors for failing to rid him of Thomas Becket (d. 1170), the Archbishop of Canterbury. Henry II's public anger against his former chancellor, who since 1164 had been opposed to the royal domination of the English Church, was an old affair.[47] In the wake of the Assizes of Clarendon, which, in January 1164, had established close royal control over the Anglo-Norman Church, Thomas Becket had already provoked the king's fury. When the archbishop attended a council of bishops that met a few months later, he carried a processional cross to signify the abuses of royal power. As the chronicler William of Newburgh (d. *c.* 1198) wrote, 'The king, who was already very angry, had yet another reason to be enraged.'[48] In July 1170, Henry II had refused to give Thomas the kiss of peace. For the four knights who murdered the archbishop in December 1170, it was self-evident that the *ira regis* had withdrawn all legal protection from the prelate. The anger of the prince could serve as a death sentence, without the actors or the chroniclers who reported their deeds having to delve any deeper for justifications. This anger was a political act, codified and interpreted as such. It was in fact an act of summary justice, of which the barons, who premeditated the murder and prepared for it in every detail, would be the executors (see Figure 3).

The rest of the story might seem astonishing. Indeed, the chroniclers state that, upon hearing the news, the king became overwhelmed and collapsed. He had never wanted the death of Thomas Becket. How was such a misunderstanding possible? Was it simply the result of grave hypocrisy playing out in full? Henry II would seem to have knowingly manipulated the rules of the *ira regis*. By repeatedly acting out his anger over many months and years, through both his behaviour and his words, he had allowed the idea that he authorized the archbishop's murder to become well established among his entourage. In the same way, the barons, whether sincere or not, knew that they could call upon these royal signals as justification for their actions. Even before the fateful words that led to the assassination were spoken, the 'misunderstanding' had long been building due to Henry's repeated angry gestures against Thomas. The physical signs of anger, as well as the meanings of the words he pronounced, led to an eruption, the climax of a long process of emotional persuasion. Nevertheless, like all human communication, emotional communication is never unequivocal. The king's words could be misjudged, just like his mood. This measure of uncertainty (or flexibility) also contributed to how political bonds developed, allowing them to adapt to changing patterns of power. Whether the assassination of Thomas Becket was the result of a cynical strategy of manipulating public emotion, or of the 'failure' of emotion as a tool of communication, the episode provides a particularly emblematic example of the capacity of princely emotions to drive political action.

Casting shame and being ashamed

From one angle, shame appears to be the exact opposite of anger. Anger was conceived of by medieval people as a strident movement of desire; shame was accompanied by retreat, or even flight. The former granted the satisfaction of behaving in accordance with one's values; the latter provoked self-disgust, wrought by the pain of having failed in the same. Nevertheless, resemblances were perceived which could help to reconcile the two, especially in their somatic expressions. Both anger and shame brought on blushing, and it was thus not thought uncommon for blushing in anger to lead to blushing in shame, and vice versa. Above all, these two emotions brought the same value into focus within the context of royal and princely courts: honour.

If shame was perceived within princely entourages, it was most often the shame of others, of those who had committed treason or had been derelict in their duties. Could the king himself feel and express shame? Giles of Rome advised the prince to steer clear of all forms of shame. Shame was an emotion unworthy of a king. For the Parisian master, this advice even encompassed the only form of shame that was usually considered praiseworthy: *verecundia*. According to Thomas Aquinas, who took influence from Aristotle, *verecundia* was the emotion of those who feared exposure to public disapproval. It was a moderate form of shame, felt in anticipation so as to guard against the agony of misdeeds. According to tradition, *verecundia* was especially appropriate for women, for whom such risks were considerable, as well as for young people who were still learning to discriminate between good and evil. On the other hand, the king was exempted from its demands, given that he was meant to embody authority and wisdom. To feel *verecundia*, an unmanly virtue, would be a failure to embody majesty.

The French and English chronicles of the twelfth and thirteenth centuries speak very little of the king's shame.[49] The explanation is simple: shame was an affront to honour. For there was nothing more precious to the king's person, nor more essential to the reputation of the kingdom, than honour. Thus, whenever the king was left prone to shame, e.g. when faced with military defeat, the chroniclers provided other emotions as an accompaniment (pain, anger) which pointed directly towards repairing the damage. Since shame was a genuinely unbearable emotion for a king, it had to be immediately commuted by gaining satisfaction for the offence, by a cry for vengeance: that is why it acted as a motor of political action. Conversely, one of the surest means of discrediting a prince was to trap him in his shame, and to deprive him of any escape route by which he might recapture his honour. This was the fate suffered by Emperor Otto IV (d. 1218) in July 1214 after the battle of Bouvines. According to the historian Primat (active in the second half of the thirteenth century), a monk of Saint-Denis and partisan of the Capetian cause, it was King Philip Augustus in person who proclaimed the shame of his adversary: 'Otto has fled: from this day forth, he will dare not show his face.'[50] The victory of Philip Augustus was complete, less because the emperor was defeated militarily than because Otto had placed himself in a dishonourable position before the eyes of all. That was the nature of the political coup the French monarch had achieved. It did not matter whether the emperor felt a sense of shame or not, since the charge was politically effective from the moment he 'showed his back' and ran away.

The only circumstance in which a monarch could use his own shame for political advantage was through the *amende honorable*. There are

173

many well-documented examples of this from the Carolingian age onward, the most famous being the public penance of Louis the Pious at Attigny in 822 and that of the Germanic emperor Henry IV (d. 1106) at Canossa in 1077. Given that the king's shame was meant to go unspoken, however, the emotions displayed in these events were rather those of sadness and suffering. But the fact that the feeling of shame was not made explicit does not mean that the emotion was unrelated to the political efficacy of the demonstration. For shame was implicit within these rites of self-inflicted humiliation. The religious origin of the *amende honorable* removes all uncertainty on this point, and *a fortiori* for the last centuries of the Middle Ages, by which time canon law had made the efficacy of penance dependent on the authentic feeling of shame. It was thus not only a matter of feigning repentance, but of offering every assurance that it was sincere. To give the appearance that the emotion was truly felt did not mean that this was actually the case, nor indeed, in the case of the royal *amende honorable*, that such was required. It sufficed that every guarantee was given in word and in deed. The fact that shame was contained within the ritual (through public appearance in a penitent's habit, bare feet, sometimes a rope around the neck, kneeling, supplication, tears, etc.) gave it an objective character without witnesses needing to make it explicit: that is what made it politically effective.

The ritual also made the emotion bearable for the guilty party, who was asked to display a depersonalized and restorative shame. The shame of the *amende honorable* did not destroy the honour of the man who submitted, but merely bent it so that it might be better restored. At least that is how the emotional mechanics were supposed to play out. This was the path Henry II took the day after the assassination of Thomas Becket. He retired to his room for three days, dressed in a penitent's habit, and made a display of his sadness. This penance in fact continued for almost four years, until 12 July 1274, when he walked through the city of Canterbury in just his shirt, barefoot, flaying himself all the way to the cathedral, where he prostrated himself for a whole day before the martyr's tomb. Witnesses insisted on the authenticity of his repentance, thus recognizing that penitential shame was an indispensable element for reconciliation.[51] Repentance, displayed through public rituals of sincere feeling, had produced the desired political effect. In the eyes of all who saw and reported it, the political and military successes of the king in the months that followed bore testament that the ritual had borne fruit. It was also the moment at which Henry II reconciled himself with his sons.

Thus this decade of Henry's reign, marked both by the conflict with Thomas Becket and by its resolution, can be divided into two phases, each characterized by a specific and well-adapted emotional schema. The first phase, from the Assizes of Clarendon in 1164 to the archbishop's assassination in 1170, was defined by anger. The second, from 1170 until his public penance in July 1174, was marked by sadness, repentance, and pain. Within each political context, these dominant emotions were well-adjusted to drive events.

Negotiating emotions

Sovereignty and the transformation of political emotion: the example of friendship

Political society in the Middle Ages was bound by emotional constraints. The ties that joined people together required friendship or love; hate and anger were unleased when they broke. It was why emotional rhetoric held such importance at every level of political communication. It was also why, in the later Middle Ages, political relationships were themselves understood in terms of affective categories, even if their truly emotional content had gradually ebbed away. Such was the case for friendship, for instance, which, as has been seen, acted throughout the Middle Ages as a defining tool of social stability due to its ability to create symbolic equality at the heart of hierarchical relationships. Until the eleventh and twelfth centuries, friendship was also a relationship of proximity, and sometimes even of intimacy. Among the aristocracy, friendship was at once a common language and a lived experience. Courtly literature, especially epic poetry, idealized the pacifying role of this chivalric and vassalic friendship in which the participants were in reach of each other's senses. Peace was an emotional embrace.

Little by little, however, political friendship grew more distant, under pressure from the ideology of sovereignty and the administrative practice of government: it increasingly became a universal contract of mutual understanding, and ever less a trading of bodies.[52] In the last two centuries of the Middle Ages, the political texts that took account of the value of friendship only became more numerous. This was largely due to the new interest in Cicero's *De amicitia* and Aristotle's *Nicomachean Ethics*, the latter translated into Latin in the second half of the twelfth century. In the thirteenth century, books VIII and IX of *Nicomachean Ethics* – those dealing with moral and political friendship – began to be commented upon within the universities. Several dozen commentaries of this sort were produced throughout Europe.[53] For scholastic authors, the contractual nature of friendship made it a fundamental value for society. Nevertheless, it was a sign of the times that the symbolic equality of friends, which was still at the heart of twelfth-century reflections on friendship, became a potential issue. While friendship was supposed to equalize social relationships, Thomas Aquinas reversed the proposition: equality was not the consequence, but the condition of friendship.[54] Friendship did not make people equal; rather, it could only exist between equals. Other commentators, such as Albert the Great, introduced a principle of proportionality: the degree of affection and proximity due was a function of the gap in social status. This idea was unthinkable only a century earlier: then true friendship was a singular concept, and demanded that friends gave all their love to each other. Friends might be unequal in rank, but not in affection, as the author of *Spiritual Friendship* would confirm in *c.* 1160:

> Moreover, thanks to the influence of friendship, the greater and the less become equal. Often persons of lower rank, station, dignity, or knowledge are accepted into friendship by their betters. Then it befits both parties to despise and consider as trifles and vanity everything extraneous to human nature and to focus at all times on the beauty of friendship.[55]

From then on, however, it became possible to conceive of an affection that was proportionate to social rank.

The universalization of friendship posed another problem, that of how and how often one's friends were to be frequented. According to the spirit of Cicero's *De amicitia*, physical presence was necessary for friendship. There was no greater suffering than to be deprived of the sight of one's friend. But amid a political environment in which friendship was becoming a social contract, the question of physical distance, like that of social distance, took on a different aspect. All this was resolved through the principle of 'proportionate conviviality': friendship remained, but familiarity evolved according to the respective positions of the friends. Thus Jean Buridan (*c.* 1360) asked a faintly absurd question: if Plato had been made pope, what would have happened to his friendship with Socrates? The two friends would no longer express their affection without one taking precedence over the other; rather, it would become proportionate. For Buridan, Socrates would doubtless have become the minister of Pope Plato. He would still have been his friend, but a serving friend. This proportionate friendship thus carried with it a governmental ideal in which friends became the best advisers, and good counsellors received the title of friends.[56]

And what of the king, could he have friends? University masters provided a variety of answers to this essential question. For Albert the Great, friendship was a solely personal affair, uniting two physical beings. Because it implied familiarity, it was a threat to royal majesty, a sacred value that imposed a symbolic distance between the king and others. The Dominican did not separate the personal experience of friendship from its political aspect: the king thus could not have true friends, lest he risk weakening the dignity and authority of his office.

This answer was quite different from that provided by Nicole Oresme (d. 1382) a century later.[57] This great scholar and precocious humanist was a familiar of Charles V, the 'wise king', who asked him to translate the *Nicomachean Ethics* for his famous library; Oresme in turn also produced a commentary on it. Unlike Albert the Great, Oresme, writing at the end of the fourteenth century, looked beyond the intimate obligations of friendship; rather, political friendship emerged from the ambiguity between personal affection and political ties. The king was not only allowed to cultivate friendship, but compelled to. For it was not aimed at individuals, but rather at the body politic; it acted for the common good of the state rather than being a private affair. Oresme also drew from ancient thought, especially that of Seneca. The prince, like the sage, did not need friends by necessity: he needed them in order to practise virtue and thus make clear the good will of his government.

At the end of this journey, later medieval political friendship had not been deprived of its emotional aspect. At least as far as it concerned the person of the king, however, it had taken on a new face.[58] The king was to pursue an emotional relationship with his subjects, but it was an affectivity without conviviality, founded on a novel approach to political friendship that allowed it to produce its effects at a distance. The more the exercise of the royal government asserted itself as the expression of a sovereign, universal good, the personal implications of affectivity diminished. A process of distancing had begun, mirrored in turn by the decline in rituals of bodily intimacy (for example, the political practice of sharing a bed became rarer).[59] If the ideology of majesty required increased staging and visibility for the king's person, it was the king 'in majesty' who was put on display and displayed himself, rather than the king as a friend.

Emotion as a political event

Emotions went hand-in-hand with princely communication due to their integration within the codes of political language. Is it too much to say that emotions *did* politics? A symbolic resource at the disposal of the powerful, the emotions they produced and perceived could also influence the course of events, or even determine them. The question here is not whether the emotions, more or less predictable in their expression, provided answers to political situations, but whether contemporaries thought and reported that this was really the case. There is no need to fall back on an essentialist understanding of emotions as unstable, spontaneous phenomena to see that they could arise and play out politically in ways that went off-script. Rather, it suffices to say that ritual did not define everything, that obligatory expressions did not preclude the possibility of feeling and thus that the very unpredictability of emotions was part and parcel of political negotiations.[60]

One need not look far for narratives that attest to the pacifying power of gestures and emotions when princes met face-to-face at the negotiating table. The negotiations that took place between the Burgundian and Armagnac factions prior to the peace of Auxerre in 1412 provide a good example.[61] In July that year, following the failure of royal troops to capture the city of Bourges by siege, the two sides met, with King Charles VI (d. 1422) and his ally John the Fearless, duke of Burgundy (d. 1419) on the one side, and John, duke of Berry (d. 1416), the uncle of the king, and the princes of Orléans on the other. The chronicler Michel Pintoin (d. 1421), a witness to the scene, recounted that the two enemy dukes were very moved when they met. Other chroniclers testified to an evolution that took place during the discussions: an initially cold atmosphere gradually thawed during the encounter, the duke of Berry shedding tears when he embraced his grand-nephew, the dauphin Louis (d. 1415). Witnessing this new understanding between the princes, their assistants also 'began to weep with pity'. Once the peace was accepted, the narratives describe only joy among the princes. When the treaty was ratified at Auxerre shortly afterwards – oaths were taken on 22 August – the representatives of the Paris Parlement, the University, and the bourgeois delegations of several cities (Rouen, Reims, and Tours) flooded the scene with their tears. The return of the princes to the capital of the realm would likewise be triumphant and joyous.

Classic in its manifestations, this emotional drama was of course merely the ritualized and obligatory expression of a successful negotiation. The fact that the civil war continued leaves little doubt as to the real political intentions of both sides. Nevertheless, the chroniclers, who were also witnesses, suggested that emotions had helped to convince the warring parties. Why not believe them? Here well-calculated interests and emotions were not opposed. It was neither a cold affair, nor a poignant scene where the outpouring of emotions suddenly swept all enmities aside. Rather, it was the final phase of a peace process in which emotion, gesture, and felt presence had played an active role. Several decades later, the Burgundian chronicler Georges Chastellain would likewise recount how Louis XI put an end to the quarrel between Louis of Luxembourg, the Count of Saint-Pol (d. 1475), and Antoine de Croÿ (d. 1475) by locking the two men in a room together to force them to come to terms. While both were at first rather displeased at having walked into this trap, they emerged joyfully, 'arm in arm, like two brothers',[62] a reversal that even surprised the chronicler himself.

In a context where emotional expression and physical contact were important ingredients in pronouncing and sealing agreements, it is easy to see how such demonstrations, however ritualized, could influence the course of events.

'To cry is to govern'[63]

Within such an environment, tears were among the most polysemic and effective emotional signals. They could express joy, sadness, anger, or shame in equal measure; above all, they eased the transition between these emotions.[64] For instance, Chastellain related the tearful bargaining of Charles, count of Charolais (later duke of Burgundy), before the Flemish Estates in 1463.[65] His relationship with his father had become very strained; the latter had cut him off from his incomes in one fell swoop. At that moment, Charles had no recourse but to beg the Flemish notables for new subsidies. He chose to tug at their heartstrings, assuring the assembly of his love without asking anything from it. Faced with such a demonstration of humility amid suffering, tears flowed freely down the cheeks of the notables, who assured the count of their support: 'Take joy in this adversity; for nothing is so hard that we would not suffer it for you.' Moved by such a proof of love, Charles wept in turn, stammering as he thanked them: 'Children, I thank you for your love [...] Now live and suffer; and I will suffer for you.'[66] What matters here is not whether they truly cried on that day, but that the Burgundian chronicler felt the need to script the episode as a tearful drama. But Chastellain's narrative rhetoric could only function if contemporaries recognized the persuasive power of tears and sincerely expressed feelings. The political effectiveness of the event was not in the reality of these tears, but arose from the fact that, within this theatrical setting, Charles had given the pledges expected of an agreement in good faith. Charles was sincere because he showed the expected signs of sincerity: he had cried.

Such efficacious tears were not confined to one sex alone. While medieval princes wept frequently, for princesses tears were often the only way they could influence the course of events: they usually deployed them to obtain a pardon or restore peace. In 1340, Joan of Valois (d. 1342) tearfully begged her brother, the king of France, to end his conflict with the English. On 17 January 1457, Isabelle of Bourbon (d. 1465) was so troubled by the fury of Philip the Good, duke of Burgundy, against his son Charles, who was her husband, that she wept profusely for their reconciliation. Twenty years later, during the crisis that followed the death of Charles the Bold at the siege of Nancy in 1477, his daughter Marie (d. 1482) streamed with tears during her vain attempt to avert the killing of her father's servants in the marketplace of Ghent.[67]

179

If such tearful mediation was often the preserve of princesses, this was not solely due to contemporary beliefs concerning the 'wet' complexion of women or the influence of literary models: it was also down to the fact that these princesses were not governing. Due to their respective complexions, men and women did not have the same emotional predispositions. In a political context, however, tears were primarily related to the language of mediation and intercession. Above all else, the economy of emotions and their effectiveness were determined by the standing of the intervening party in relation to the centre of power. When women governed, they took on sovereign emotions: the anger of princesses did not end with the early Middle Ages, as can be seen in the example of Countess Jacqueline of Bavaria (d. 1436), who Chastellain distinguished for her 'feminine fury', or the even more emblematic case of Countess Yolande of Flanders (d. 1395).[68] These princesses were nevertheless harshly judged by the chroniclers, who clearly preferred women to make political use of their emotions only within their traditional role, i.e. as a persuasive wife, mother, or daughter. Thus, even if political emotions were not gendered, aristocratic women certainly had a more restricted palette at their disposal than men: quite the irony within a society that thought of women as more emotional than men! Outside of their usual remit of gentleness and tearful persuasion, the political use of emotion was a risky business for a princess.

If emotions were at the heart of politics, it was because they were the tangible, bodily expressions of both persuasion and action. They were not only considered, but also experienced, serving as interfaces between verbal language, body language, and action. Emotions were more than a communication tool for the powerful among themselves: they marked discontinuities and drove political events. A prince's sadness or anger was seen as physical evidence that the course of events had changed, that an old order was crumbling and a new one was being prepared. Princely emotion signalled that action was imminent. Twenty years ago, Jacques Krynen concluded his great synthesis of later medieval political ideas and beliefs by emphasizing the importance of the value of love. For him, love was central to the French people's attachment to the monarchical state; he considered its role as a political virtue to be deserving of its own study.[69] Nourished by the studies of the affective dimension of power that have been written since 1990, this chapter has shown that part of this gap has now been filled; indeed, we have now gone far beyond the matter of love alone. Krynen's reflection remains most pertinent, however, since it opens up another question, immense and doubtless even more difficult to answer: how should we understand the use of emotions among broader social communities and anonymous populations?

— 8 —

THE MYSTICAL CONQUEST OF EMOTION (THIRTEENTH TO FIFTEENTH CENTURIES)

At the turn of the thirteenth century, the churches and public spaces of the West brimmed with bodies, with cries, and with a devotion which was expressed through the incarnation of emotion. Certain women, often drawn from the laity, laid bare a troubling piety before the eyes of all, intense and literal in its way of embodying the metaphors of Christian tradition. Modern historians call them mystics. The *vita* of the beguine Mary of Oignies (d. 1213), written by Jacques de Vitry (d. 1240) in the wake of her death, says that she drew 'so much grace of compunction and such an abundance of tears' from the Passion 'that her tears flowed so copiously on the floor that the ground in the Church became muddy with her footprints'.[1] The blood shed by Christ on the cross found its response in the inexhaustible flow of tears that bathed the faces of women in late medieval paintings (see Figure 7). Angela of Foligno (d. 1309) fell into ecstasy and let out piercing shrieks in the upper basilica of Assisi at the sight of a stained-glass window depicting the glorification of St Francis (d. 1226).[2] She thought of receiving communion as ingesting the body of Jesus and delighted in this 'symbolic cannibalism':[3] 'When she receives communion, the host lingers in her mouth. She said that it does not have the taste of any known bread or meat. It has most certainly a meat taste, but one very different and most savoury.'[4]

A few decades later, Clare of Rimini (d. 1324 or 1329), a penitent and recluse from Romagna and, like Angela, a fellow traveller of the Spiritual Franciscans, hired two men to brutalize her 'on Good Friday when Christ was crucified and endured such pain'. Her actions echoed an earlier feat of self-humiliation performed by St Francis of Assisi:[5]

> [Led by a rope around her neck and then attached] to a stone column, she remained there, tied up, until the hour of none on the following Saturday.

181

Then, once the offices were recited, they detached her from the column. Her hands still shackled, the halter still around her throat, and dressed only in her underwear, she asked each of them to beat her cruelly, striking blows with bundles of twigs and flails. Processing in this manner, she visited the churches of the city and boroughs [...] Finally, having been beaten in this way, she returned to her cell.[6]

At least in appearance, this demonstrative, sensual, and bodily religiosity was far removed from the ascetic silence of the monks and nuns of the eleventh and twelfth centuries. Closer in style to hermits, this emotionally charged body of female mystics followed a new 'order' of disorder and excess.[7] While the spiritual people and mystics of earlier centuries had tried to flee, suppress, and transcend their bodies, the bodies of these late medieval women became the privileged setting for an encounter with the divine: embodying emotion became a key tool for this devotion.

This transition from a self-contained and entirely spiritual monastic *discretio* towards bodily performances that were often transgressive and ecstatic raises many questions. What was the relationship between this mysticism – founded on hunger for the Eucharist, on amorous union and rapture in the arms of Christ, and on sharing in the bodily suffering of the Crucified Christ – and the ascetic tradition that preceded it? To what extent was this devotion a 'women's issue', as historiography has long framed it? If the experiences of Mary, Angela, and Clare transport us to a realm where natural laws were abrogated, should they be considered as marginal phenomena in the Church and society of their time? Finally, what was the significance of this emotional expressionism in religious and social terms? To answer these questions, we must grasp the deep ties that bind the various aspects of these phenomena together. Simultaneously, we must take account of the contributions of historical anthropology on male-female relationships, of the intellectual history of religious thought, and of the history of the social practices found at the confluence of these different movements. For, as disconcerting as it might appear to our modern sensibilities, this emotional effervescence possessed an anthropological and cultural coherence. It is beyond doubt that the turn of the thirteenth century heralded the dawn of a new era. Lay and religious cultures intermingled in many new ways. The sources, more abundant, more varied, and better preserved, allow access to a devotion that was now open to women and which derived from the lay diffusion of religious culture.[8] Women, barely visible in the preceding period, gained a hold on public and religious life: they represented more than half of the laity canonized between 1198 and 1431.[9] It thus appears that the 'feminization of religion', 'affective mysticism', and the bodily

182

performances associated with them were by no means marginal phenomena, nor solely a matter of women. Rather, they were deeply rooted in
the cultural, religious, and anthropological developments of their time.

The cultural roots of 'affective mysticism'

The Gregorian renewal of theology and the anthropology of religious practices

The success of this emotional religiosity marked a profound change and
stemmed from transformations within theology and anthropology. The
gradual progress towards the 'embodiment' of religious practice and
imagination, an expression of the new devotion to the humanity of
Christ, was closely linked to the establishment of the doctrine of transubstantiation. Indeed, the Gregorian reform of Eucharistic doctrine and
practice placed the body of Christ at the core of the institutional Church
and devotion.[10] The flowering of an ever more expressive emotional
spirituality from the eleventh century onwards – especially marked in
Cistercian and Victorine circles – ran parallel to the victory of 'real presence' dogma.[11] Incarnation and 'affectivization' intertwined within
anthropological representations: devotion to the humanity of Christ,
whether as a child or during his death, brought the emotions, senses,
and imagination into play. The theological anchoring of this new style
of mystical devotion could hardly have been more orthodox. First
invented and practised by vowed religious, this affective piety was then
introduced to those women for whom they acted as spiritual guides. The
traits of an emotional, embodying devotion were thus constructed in
light of new configurations of Christian anthropology and theology, long
before women and laypeople began to exert significant influence over
religious life. Indeed, it was only from the beginning of the thirteenth
century that men and women once deprived of power within the Church
began to appropriate these forms and to play with their possibilities in
a remarkable way.[12]

The theory and practical developments of the sacraments of penance
and of the Eucharist, both definitively elaborated in the twelfth century,
regularly impacted the lives of the faithful in the thirteenth century. In
1215, the Fourth Lateran Council made it compulsory to receive communion at least once a year: alongside the private confession that had
to precede it, the Eucharist became the principal tool for the religious
management of the laity. And while confession might have been the most
frequently received sacrament in the Middle Ages, the commemoration
of the Last Supper remained the sacred symbol to surpass all others.
It was *the* sacrament. Gradually, the consecrated host became the very

place in which God was present on earth, as Francis of Assisi evoked in his *Testament*: 'In this world, I see nothing corporally (*corporaliter*) of the most high Son of God except His most holy Body and Blood which they [priests] receive and they alone administer to others.'[13]

Against the grain of the very Gregorian reasoning that had established it, the doctrine of transubstantiation in fact allowed the faithful to establish personal communication with Christ during communion at mass: from then on, he could be perceived directly by the senses. Eucharistic realism went on to contribute to the emergence of innovative devotional practices. But at the same time as the Church prescribed annual communion to the laity, it gradually restricted their access to the chalice. Only the body of Christ was accessible to them, and usually by sight and sound alone. The elevation of the consecrated host, accompanied by the ringing of a bell during mass, thus became a special moment for contemplation and admiration, and one bathed in emotions and tears: 'never had so much of Christ's blood been spilled than at the moment where the chalice was withdrawn from the lips of the faithful'.[14] The emergence of devotion to the blood occurred at the same time as (or just a little before) the withdrawal of communion in both kinds from the laity. In the decades following the Fourth Lateran Council, pious women, barred from the clergy and thus from handling the sacraments by virtue of their female and lay status, flung themselves into Eucharistic devotion with an ever increasing fervour. At a time when meditation on the sufferings and love of Christ was gaining favour, spiritual communion – an interior and affective phenomenon which could take place outside the mass – represented a perfectly logical devotional development. The birth of the Eucharistic cult formed part of the same dynamic, aided too by the new practice of elevating the host during the consecration and subsequently by the institution of the feast of Corpus Christi in 1264: the latter in fact resulted from its promotion by Juliena of Mount-Cornillon (d. 1258), a mystic from the diocese of Liège. A perfect encounter between pastoral strategy and popular expectations provided the context for devotional investment in the sacraments, an investment that was at once imaginative, affective, and bodily.

Over the long term, the Gregorian dynamic gave rise to two evolutions that appear contradictory, but were in fact complementary. On the one hand, the gap between clerics and the laity was only becoming wider, due to the mediation and resultant reduction of the laity's access to the divine. On the other, the earthly life and sufferings of Christ received more and more attention as an increasing number of laypeople, both men and women, actively participated in acts aimed at increasing their chances of salvation. This twofold and fundamental evolution of the institutional Church – which itself held that the reform that looked towards the unification of Christendom with the Body of Christ required everyone's adherence – opened the way, in theological and practical terms, to the emergence of a piety of embodiment.

Religious fervour: a collective emotion

The emotional and bodily appropriation of the path of salvation rapidly took the form of collective religious movements and occasions. While they varied in scale, these convulsions became recurrent and striking phenomena in the last centuries of the Middle Ages. To understand them within the context of the emotional embodiment of devotion requires a departure from the most frequent characterization of those centuries – one which defines them as an important stage in the historical rise of individualism and, more precisely, in the birth of the Western and modern individual.[15] Every individual conversion, regardless of social context, of course implied an anxiety over individual salvation. Nevertheless, Gregorian reform broadly reinforced the concern for salvation among a *populus christianus* now conscious of its unity within the framework of Christendom (*Christianitas*) and which regularly made demonstrations of its collective march towards conversion.[16] The religious fervour that frequently shook the Western world in the second half of the Middle Ages always involved both body and soul: their total engagement was often signalled by strident emotions and gestures. It also suggests a qualitative leap from the individual quest for salvation to one that stirred entire crowds, the latter taking its place alongside traditional forms of conversion.[17]

It was a sense of shared conviction and feeling that, for example, stirred the population of a village when it accompanied a relic on procession and prayed for the saint's intercession in ending a drought or stopping a neighbouring lord's harassment. The crowds that came to listen to Pope Urban II (d. 1099) preach the crusade at Clermont in 1095 or to hear Bernard of Clairvaux do the same at Vézelay in 1146, and who were so enthused that they readied themselves to march, perhaps went a step further: by agreeing to leave for the Holy Land, the participants collectively converted to a life of penitence, at least temporarily. Listeners touched by the charisma of itinerant preachers, such as Robert of Arbrissel (d. about 1116–17), Vitalis of Savigny (d. 1122), and later Francis of Assisi and Anthony of Padua (d. 1231), sometimes entirely abandoned their old way of life. Such commitments might be short-lived, lasting as long as it took to participate in a ritual or a local or regional pilgrimage; or they might endure for many months, or even years when men left on crusade. The laity finally had the opportunity to change their lives definitively through religious conversion. In all these cases, the descriptions

185

reveal the same religious enthusiasm, one that tore them out of their daily lives in order to devote themselves, whether for a moment or for the rest of their lives, exclusively to their salvation. If these narratives reflected the *topos* of sudden conversion, the chroniclers devote no less attention to describing the events that had marked their memory. For instance, the biographer of Anthony of Padua eloquently depicted the saint's return to his city:

> Gathering in an impressive crowd, the people came from everywhere to listen to him, like the land that thirsts for rain. [Anthony] established daily stations through the churches of the city. And as soon the churches could not contain the growing throngs of men and women who had come to listen to him, he retired to the vast meadows [outside the city]. They came from the cities, castles, and villages surrounding Padua in an almost innumerable crowd. There were both men and women there, all united in the greatest devotion, thirsting for the word of life, hanging on his words for their salvation with a steadfast hope. Rising in the middle of the night – everyone wanted to get there first – they went out enthusiastically, in torchlight, to the place where he was going to preach. You would have seen knights and noble ladies rushing out into the darkness, warming exhausted limbs in soft blankets, who then, without any difficulty by all reports, spent a good part of the day wide-awake before the preacher. The old were there, the young hurried along: they were men and women of every age and condition. Casting off their ornaments and jewellery, each took on, if I may say so, the habit of religion. Even the venerable Bishop of Padua, along with his clergy, was a devoted follower of the preaching of Anthony, the servant of God: moved in his soul to become a model for his flock, through his humble example he showed the people that they should listen. Each and every one of them sought to grasp his words; they did this so avidly that, despite the size of the gathering, amounting to thirty thousand men according to some accounts, there were no loud voices nor murmuring to be heard. Rather, in continuous silence, they were as if one man, the ears of their body and those of their heart held in suspense: all looked to the orator.[18]

While this text dates from the thirteenth century, the West had experienced such phenomenal outpourings of religious enthusiasm for some time, as far back as the emergence of the *Pax Dei* (*c.* 975–80) and the popular religious movements of the beginning of the eleventh century. Some of these were promoted by the Church; others were born or ended up at its margins. Some found success through institutionalization; others mobilized men and women for a time and then disappeared, regardless of whether or not the adherents were persecuted. In each case, however, there was the thrill of shared emotion, a thrill that diverted people from their accustomed path, a thrill that could render them silent or make

186

them cry out in chorus, a thrill that made them give up their 'ornaments and jewellery' and much more besides, all to follow a preacher, a hermit, or a nascent community, re-enacting the gesture of the first apostles who had left everything to follow Christ.

The emotion of such conversions is well illustrated by an *exemplum* provided by Jacques de Vitry. He portrayed a man who wanted to go on crusade but whose wife had forbidden him to listen to a preacher's recruitment sermon, perhaps given by Jacques himself: as it happened, canon law recognized the right of wives to forbid their husbands to join a crusade. The man then heard the preaching from his lodgings and, unable to resist his urge, jumped out of the window to join the crowd: he would be the first to take up the cross.[19] Finally, in the wake of the scattered phenomena of the eleventh and twelfth centuries, it was St Francis who, according to Thomas of Celano (d. *c.* 1260), came up with the idea of perpetual conversion: from the early thirteenth century, one's whole life could be envisaged as a process of conversion, marked by regular events that repeated the act or its symbolic essentials.

Stirred up by the rhetoric of preachers, the ardent desire to go on crusade witnessed in Jacques de Vitry's *exemplum* provoked a similar fervour to that which, a little later, prompted many to join the flagellant movements that first arose in Northern Italy and then crossed the Alps. It was in Perugia – in Umbria, not far from Assisi – amid the atmosphere of crisis that followed the famine of 1258 and against the background of clashes between the Guelphs and Ghibellines, that the first group of flagellants appeared in the spring of 1260. This movement brought together two, perhaps even three, rituals of penance for the first time:[20] the collective procession; flagellation, a monastic penitential practice that had previously been individual; and finally, the penitential pilgrimage, prescribed to those who had committed grave sins. Sociologically heterogeneous and supported for a time by the Church, the movement was quickly abandoned by the bourgeoisie and clerics and became marginalized in Northern Europe. Nevertheless, it left a lasting impression on the memory of eyewitnesses and, more broadly, of the inhabitants of the towns through which it passed. For flagellant processions offered a dramatic and Christocentric spectacle of unprecedented sensorial and symbolic intensity. Men walked the streets bare-chested; later, when the movement reached Northern Europe, they went about dressed as penitents, their faces covered by hoods. Intoning doleful chants and whipping their shoulders – where Christ had borne the cross – until the blood flowed, they implored God's mercy. Aiming to ward off evil and restore peace, they stopped at church parvises, where they threw themselves onto the ground with their arms outstretched in the form of a cross. A reflection of an insatiable desire for penitence and peace, the movement re-emerged in contexts of great unrest, such as in the Rhineland at the end of the thirteenth century: it would likewise enjoy spectacular revival during the plague of 1348. It played a vital role in both the development of the penitential confraternity movement in Italian cities (from the last decades of the thirteenth century) and, closely related to that trend, the rise of religious theatre.[21] The practice of collective penitential flagellation would eventually become part and parcel of the regular demonstrations of Italian urban piety. It not only portrayed emotion, but also provoked it, as seen in a famous scene from Genoa described by Jacobus de Varagine (d. 1298):

> When the [processing flagellants] walked through the city, they were ridiculed as madmen ... But suddenly, the whole city was stirred by the power of God, so that those who led the way in mockery later led the way in self-flagellation. [...] They went as a group, two by two, whipping themselves all the way, preceded by religious and clerics carrying crosses and banners. Many had killed men: they went up to their enemies, put their unsheathed swords in their hands, and offered to accept whatever vengeance their foes wished to take. But these latter cast the swords on the ground, and fell at the feet of their enemies: all who saw it wept with devout joy and heartfelt exultation.[22]

In this description, the witnesses gradually move from mockery to conversion and personal penitence, strengthened by the sight of such humble remorse; by offering themselves up to righteous vengeance, the flagellants' behaviour thus came to promote the peace and cohesion of society. Is it right, then, to describe the flagellants in terms of cathartic, uncontrolled, and hysterical emotions, as historians so often have?[23] First-hand sources instead suggest controlled rituals – flagellation ended at first blood – full of dense Christocentric symbolism: they demonstrated the collective appropriation of religious models which, in the previous two centuries, had generally been considered the province of monastic figures and contexts. From pilgrimages to the crowds that thronged to popular preachers, from the *Caputiati* (the 'White Hoods') to Eucharistic devotional practices, from the Lombard 'Great Hallelujah' to the Shepherds' Crusade, there are numerous examples of collective emotion and devotion that attest to the same phenomenon. The events and their emotional mechanics naturally followed scripts not only governed by ritual and code but also by the unique perspective of each author. To understand them correctly, it is essential to isolate the scriptural, hagiographic, and narrative models that shaped these descriptions. Yet regardless of discursive form, these accounts all convey penitential or Eucharistic emotions that were in every case bound up with devotion to Christ and his imitation: such emotions were shared by men and women of all social ranks throughout Christian Europe. This shared religious emotion, which subsequently grew to a crescendo, was one of the major characteristics of the period: it created new communities of varying duration and new social bodies of converts, as well as reinforcing old ones.

Francis of Assisi and the revolution of embodied emotion

As a demonstration of the victory of embodied religious emotion in the West during the first third of the thirteenth century, no figure stands out quite like Francis of Assisi. It is with him that the reversal which transformed the use of the body and the emotions into means of salvation within the Church truly took shape. Products of a long evolution and closely related to Gregorian reform, the ingredients for this switch were firmly in place by the end of the twelfth century. Through his values and his actions, Francis inaugurated a new way of communicating the sacred and a new religious paradigm, in which the embodiment of emotion took centre stage. Once considered ambiguous or even dangerous expressions (albeit ones that were indispensable to human life), embodied emotions now became powerful instruments employed on the path towards salvation. Indeed, it was often through an emotional process that spiritual change took place, or through the presence of an emotion that a new inner state revealed itself.

Francis was an ascetic; as such, he followed in the footsteps of those athletes of God before him. Thomas of Celano's *vita prima* of Francis, written immediately after his death, provides numerous examples of his ascetic and penitential practices.[24] His decision not to possess anything in his own right, his rejection of good food, the privations he imposed upon himself, his desire to sleep 'naked against the bare ground', and his mortifications all recall the well-worn actions of eleventh- and twelfth-century hermits.[25] The scenes of the *vita prima* likewise refer back to a network of biblical citations that nourish the saint's experiences. And yet, Francis went much further than the hermits who preceded him. If his conversion can be understood as a radical and literal rejection of the life of the flesh and its concerns – symbolized by his father's wealth – he demonstrated his rejection of this flesh not by denying the material world but by his commitment to spiritualizing it, to infusing it with the soul. For Francis, any occasion served as a good opportunity to show and prove the Incarnation, the presence of the divine on earth. As Thomas of Celano said, 'He knew that the kingdom of heaven was established in every corner of the earth.'[26]

> There was in him such harmony of flesh with spirit and such obedience that, as the spirit strove to reach all holiness, the flesh did not resist but

even tried to run on ahead, according to the saying: 'For you my soul has thirsted; and my flesh in so many ways!' (Ps 63: 1)[27]

While transcending the age-old difficulty of flesh-spirit cohabitation in his own person, the Francis of the *vita prima* provided a new interpretation of the kingdom of heaven: it was present in all of God's creation. The result was an anthropology, a cosmology, and an eschatology that all possessed a new emotional tone, where enthusiasm, joy, and exultation drove away 'sorrow according to God' and the fear of judgement, where nature itself, as the work of God, stood as continual praise to the Creator, and where the present already embodied the future. It was this new vision of the world that created the constant joy which dwelt within the *poverello*.

For as ascetic as he was, and as much as his mission demanded a life of singular rigour and harshness, Francis was a happy saint. His message, personally received from heaven at the start of his vocation, was that of joy and love:

> One day, when he had invoked the Lord's mercy with his whole heart, the Lord showed him what he must do. He was filled with such great joy that, failing to restrain himself in the face of his happiness, he carelessly mentioned something to others. Even though he could not remain silent because of the greatness of the love inspired in him, he nevertheless spoke cautiously and in riddles.[28]

The loving joy that animated him is reminiscent of both the Cistercian commentaries on the Song of Songs and the tastes of courtly environments. Francis seems to have had some attachment to the latter, since he spoke, and indeed sang, in the language of the troubadours: 'a sweet melody of the spirit bubbling up inside him would become a French tune on the outside'.[29] The praise of creation so characteristic of his writings and his life would have been almost unthinkable without the intellectual rehabilitation of nature in the preceding century or without the mystical tradition of prayer bequeathed by monasticism. But alongside these, it also echoed the love of melody inherited from lay and courtly society.

This intimate and ever-present love of God left Francis wholly transfigured and guided him through his tribulations. As he set out to renounce the world and came into conflict with his father, Francis pitted his divinely inspired joy and enthusiasm against the rage and violence of his earthly parent. To escape his furious father, he hid in a pit, a sort of penitential tomb, where for a month he lived a life of prayers, fasts, and tears: 'There [...] he was imbued with an indescribable happiness never

190

before experienced. Then totally on fire, he abandoned the pit and openly exposed himself to the curses of his persecutors.'[30] Towards the end of his life, the *sortes biblicae* repeatedly touch on the Passion, revealing to him the sufferings to come and their significance: 'Thus he remained undisturbed and happy.'[31] Beyond their use as combative weapons, joy, gentleness, and enthusiasm – the visible expressions of the love of God that animated him – escorted him through many episodes of his life: they were the vehicles of his spiritual message.

Since he himself embodied the Word, Francis taught primarily through example. He made gestures to spell out his message in a style that at times recalls the Desert Fathers; for instance, in the best monastic tradition, he plunged himself into a pit full of ice to ward off the temptations of the flesh.[32] While remaining a simple deacon for the sake of humility, he created emotive and moving spectacles.[33] One can see this principle in action within the best-known episodes of his *vitae*. Indeed, his conversion can be read as a literal performance of austerity. Francis wanted to give the profits of his last sale to a small church, even though he was meant to take them back to his merchant father. But when the priest refused the gift, Francis threw the money out of a window, scattering it: in his eyes, it was worth nothing.[34] He publicly expressed his conversion from a secular life to a life consecrated to God by becoming nude. According to the *vita prima*, this gesture left nothing to the imagination: returning to his father everything that connected them, 'he did not even keep his trousers on and he was completely stripped bare before everyone'. Moved by the spectacle and admiring the constancy, fervour, and courage that had led Francis to cast aside shame, the Bishop of Assisi covered him with his cloak and symbolically gathered him into the bosom of the Church.[35] Disregard for shame was here a mark of his courage, but also of his self-contempt, of his adoption of a posture of absolute humility and penitence. Further on in the *vita prima*, Thomas of Celano recounted another spectacular episode, depicting a Francis who humbled himself without any fear of public shame:

> Once, because he was ill, he ate a little bit of chicken. When his physical strength returned, he entered the city of Assisi. When he reached the city gate, he commanded the brother who was with him to tie a cord around his neck and drag him through the whole city as if he were a thief, loudly crying out: 'Look! See this glutton who grew fat on the flesh of chickens that he ate without your knowledge.' Many people ran to see this grand spectacle and, groaning and weeping, they said: 'Woe to us! We are wretches and our life is steeped in blood! With excess and drunkenness we feed out hearts and bodies to overflowing!' They were touched in their hearts (Acts 2: 37) and were moved to a better way of life by such an example.[36]

The unusual spectacle of a holy man dressed as a public penitent and presenting himself as a criminal left many in awe and encouraged those who witnessed it to change their own lives. By repeatedly rescuing wild animals, sheep, and lambs, he performed another feat that encouraged conversion through emotion.[37] However, the best illustration of the *poverello's* *modus operandi* is the preparation of the manger at Greccio: here the very mystery of the Incarnation itself was staged in a manner far removed from the liturgical norms of Francis' time.[38] As Christmas approached, Francis announced:

> For I wish to enact the memory of that babe who was born in Bethlehem: to see as much as is possible with my own bodily eyes the discomfort of his infant needs, how he lay in a manger, and how, with an ox and an ass standing by, he rested on hay.

The crib scene he prepared at Greccio had a real ox and a real ass, but left the place of the child empty: it was this child that Francis truly hoped to see, and in the flesh if possible. The child would thus have to be miraculously incarnated. When the saint's 'brethren' and 'the men and women of that land' had gathered 'with exultant hearts', Francis came, 'and finding all things prepared, he saw them and was glad (Jn 8: 56)'. The scene, described in detail, moved the participants, who felt like they were taking part in the true birth of Christ: each experienced its joy, exultation, jubilation, and sweetness (see Figure 6): 'The holy man of God stands before the manger, filled with heartfelt sighs, contrite in his piety, and overcome with wondrous joy. Over the manger the solemnities of the mass are celebrated and the priest enjoys a new consolation.' Finally, the mystery revealed itself: 'A virtuous man sees a wondrous vision. For the man saw a little child lying lifeless in the manger and he saw the holy man of God approach the child and waken him from a deep sleep.' As Thomas commented:

> Nor is this vision unfitting, since in the hearts of many the child Jesus has been given over to oblivion. Now he is awakened and impressed on their loving memory by His own grace through His holy servant Francis. At length, the night's solemnities draw to a close and everyone went home with joy.

By focusing on the conditions of Jesus' birth as described by the Gospels – a historical first – Francis staged an authentic performance that was both mystical and participatory. In turn, it gave birth to a new emotional community. The novelty of the experiment is repeatedly underlined in the text. Its theatre enticed all the senses, rendering it accessible to all: the manger, animals, and hay could be seen, touched, and smelt by every parishioner, whether man, woman, or child. If most of them could only visualize the baby Jesus by way of Francis, the scene at Greccio allowed everyone access to the sacred, to the symbolic meaning that the event conveyed, leading to contagious joy and enthusiasm. As if he were the new 'Word made flesh', the *poverello* reconstructed the community of the primitive *ecclesia*, one united by affection and without any hierarchical distinctions. This episode, which imparted remembrance of the Christ Child, immediately precedes the appearance of Francis' stigmata in Thomas of Celano's *vita*. Through this startling shortcut, we are transported from one image to another – from the Incarnation to the Passion – thus uniting the Christ Child with the sacrificed Christ. It is indeed this unity between Incarnation and Passion – birth, sacrifice, and salvation – that the Christmas celebration portrayed: mass was said above the manger, which functioned as an altar, while the sanctified host represented Christ, barely born yet already sacrificed.[39]

The Greccio narrative allows us to sketch the twofold and paradoxical relationship between the doctrine of transubstantiation, by which the celebration of mass was transformed from a commemoration to a re-enactment of the Last Supper, and the manger scene of Christ's birth, spontaneously invented and prepared by and for Francis, which created an opportunity for everyone present to relive the birth of Jesus. They ran both in parallel and in opposition. On the one hand, from the first third of the thirteenth century, mass came to be characterized by the restriction of access to the sacred, a development entirely in line with the logic of the post-Gregorian Church. This was symbolized by the fact that lay communion not only remained rare but was thence reduced to a single species: communion in both kinds became a privilege reserved for clerics and a few exceptional laypeople. On the other hand, the collective preparation of the manger and common participation in the Christmas celebration cast aside all restrictions and offered broad sensory and emotional access to a community event. Finally, while the participatory re-enactment at Greccio extended joyous and pious affection to all its human witnesses, it also included animals. The famous scenes of Francis offering praises to the birds and of the swallows obeying his command suggest that he did not want to limit this affection to humanity. Rather, he was open to including all God's creatures within it, even plants:

> Whenever he found an abundance of flowers, he used to preach to them and invite them to praise the Lord, just as if they were endowed with reason. Fields and vineyards, rocks and woods, and all the beauties of the field, flowing springs and blooming gardens, earth and fire, air and wind: all these he urged to the love of God and to willing service.[40]

Here terrestrial matter itself is spiritually and emotionally transformed and a Church that embodied the sharing of emotions is recreated: the sacred seems to take flesh through emotion. Spiritualization through asceticism – a negative theology – thus gave way to the emotional embodiment of the spiritual in the flesh. The flesh could be transfigured in life, as the stigmata imprinted on Francis' body make clear: the way was cleared for many of the female experiences witnessed in the thirteenth and fourteenth centuries.[41] In keeping with the long-standing hagiographic doctrine of the 'odour of sanctity' – of which the description of Francis' post-mortem flesh provides an eloquent example – the flesh no longer obeyed the laws of generation and corruption.[42]

The experience of pious women

Like the new paths forged by Francis of Assisi, the affective devotion of thirteenth- and fourteenth-century women was also grounded in an anthropology and spirituality of Gregorian inspiration. To judge by hagiographical accounts, one of its distinctive features resided precisely in the bodily expression of emotion. Most of these displays can be understood within the same paradigmatic framework discerned with Francis, but it can hardly be considered his 'invention' alone. Indeed, at the exact same time, in Brabant and Hainaut, far from the Umbrian world of Francis, Mary of Oignies had experiences that were in many respects comparable. It is characteristic of these later medieval phenomena that they were not tied to any particular order or institutional framework: religious, beguines, laywomen, and third-order mendicants alike experienced spiritual phenomena that were both emotional and bodily. The textual references that run through the sources indeed suggest a very wide circulation of models, with various origins. The path taken by these women and the very way in which they made their journeys explain not only the success, but also the religious and social efficacy of a devotion that was both emotional and embodied.

Vision, imagination, and embodiment: paths towards union with the suffering of Christ

Imagination, a cognitive function halfway between rational intelligence and the bodily senses – especially that of sight – played a very important role in affective devotion.[43] Stirred by the sight of holy images, which were commonplace in the churches of the late Middle Ages, imagination acted as a powerful springboard for pious meditative practices, which relied on affectivity, bodily metaphors, or even the use of the body.[44]

194

Imaginative meditation made use of visualization, representation, and even re-enactment as props or 'scripts'.[45] Through them, the qualities of holy figures could be revived and appropriated, and compassion and empathy aroused. These emotions in turn engendered bodily experiences, and sometimes even experiences of incorporation, identification, and union with the body of Christ, the Virgin, or a saint. In fact, the medieval Christian anthropology that was consolidated between the patristic and scholastic ages had long recognized the capacity of imagination and sight to leave traces on the body. If the idea had its roots in the patristic exegesis of the Old Testament story of Laban and his sheep (Gen. 30: 25–43), in the thirteenth-century discussion had been revived by both the development of facultative psychology within university environments and religious and scientific attempts to explain miraculous phenomena such as Francis' stigmata. In his *Treatise on the Miracles of St Francis*, Thomas of Celano stated that the sight of the crucifix had imprinted the image of the crucified Christ's wounds so firmly in Francis' imagination following his conversion that, in time, the same wounds re-emerged on his own body through the work of visual memory:

> From the earliest days when he began his knightly service for the Crucified, various mysteries of the cross shone around him [...] Christ spoke to him from the wood of the Cross while he prayed. From the mouth of Christ's image, a voice declared: 'Francis, go, rebuild my house, which, as you see, it is all being destroyed.' From that moment the memory of the Lord's passion was stamped on his heart with a deep brand-mark [...] Just as, internally, his mind had put on the crucified Lord, so, externally, his whole body put on the cross of Christ.[46]

For the Dominican Jacobus de Varagine, it was not sight, but rather the imagination that had played the key role: 'In a vision he had received, St Francis imagined the crucified Seraph: his imagination was so powerful that it printed the wounds of the Passion on his flesh.' Jacobus de Varagine also cited the role of Francis' love for Christ: 'Since the love of the Lord's Passion burned so ardently within the heart of St Francis, it produced miraculous effects on his flesh.'[47] While the interpretations are slightly different, in both cases it was the interaction of sight, imagination, and emotion that, in cooperation with the divine, had produced physical effects on Francis' body.[48] Many other written and pictorial examples attest to this sort of reasoning. They illustrate both the workings and the impact of the embodied emotional phenomena that flourished under the influence of Eucharistic devotional practices, especially that of spiritual communion, which prolonged and multiplied the reception of communion for faithful men and women starved of the body of Christ.

195

A closer look at the interactions between vision, imagination, and embodied emotion witnessed in textual and iconographic sources points to the vital role that this mechanism played within late medieval devotion.[49] The Incarnation, the central object of devotion in the post-Gregorian Church, allowed for greater investment in the world of religious images. Since God had not only shown himself in signs and symbols but assumed human form to take his place in sacred history, it stood to reason that he wished to be depicted in this form. As seen in Francis' novel depiction of the manger at Greccio, images (whether described or illustrated) and their staging became imaginative, gestural, and emotional means of approaching the divine.

This approach is clearly visible in an image drawn from an Alsatian manuscript (1290–1320), and included in a treatise entitled *Tres Estaz de bones ames* (see Figure 8).[50] The text contains instructions on how nuns could progress through the 'three states of pious souls': fear, hope, and love. Each describes one of the three phases of the mystical path that began with penitential confession, proceeded through meditation or devotion, and led to a contemplative union with God. These states are represented on the page by four framed scenes, arranged on two levels. The first quadrant (top left), where the nun is depicted as a humble penitent in prayer, is a snapshot of confession, soon to be capped by the absolution of a Dominican brother. In the second quadrant (top right), which illustrates the devotional role of images, the nun prays before a depiction of the Coronation of the Virgin: she adopts the same bodily pose as the Virgin, whose likeness she becomes. While the upper two quadrants refer to concrete moments in the religious life of the faithful, the lower two take us to another plane: they serve to communicate two orders of reality, one gestural and terrestrial, the other visionary and celestial. In the first scene, on the lower left, the nun prostrates herself in prayer before the altar; on it sits a chalice, a prop for imaginative devotion which referenced the mystery of the Eucharist. But here the mystery takes flesh: above the altar, addressing the nun from a ring of clouds, the crucified Christ appears, having come back to life. Christ shows his wounds to her; blood drips from his chest and both of his hands into the chalice on the altar. He speaks to her through a phylactery: 'See what I have endured for the life of the people.' Unlike in the upper quadrants, no cleric is present here. Stirred by confession and contemplating the image of the Coronation of the Virgin (above) and that of the Eucharistic mystery (below), the contact between the nun praying before the altar and Christ becomes direct. In the lower right quadrant, the final scene likewise depicts the nun in prayer before the altar; several motifs from the previous image are repeated with variations. In this one, however, it is an apparition of the Trinity that descends from the same

196

type of cloud seen in the preceding quadrant. Blood flows from three wounds of the crucified Christ, whose image stands out, into the chalice placed below. This fourfold illustration shows how access to the sacraments, meditation on sacred history, and above all Eucharistic prayer might bring Christ to life before the eyes of the faithful. Just as Paul had said, the host was alive; in fact, by the end of the eleventh century, it had become the real body of Christ thanks to transubstantiation. It is thus hardly surprising that it could speak to the faithful, just as the cross could come to life in an image. In the *Memorial* of Angela of Foligno, Christ appears during mass at the moment of elevation: he speaks to her, filling her with great joy.[51] She experienced these apparitions so frequently that her confessor would habitually ask her what she had seen during communion.[52]

The interaction in the scenes studied here puts us in the presence of a Christ who entered the life of the faithful whenever they prayed or came to mass. In other cases, conversely, it was the faithful man or woman in devotion who entered the contemplated image. Just as in the scenes of incorporation with Christ (or with the Virgin or the saints) found in texts, the motif of 'entering the image' was frequently deployed in medieval devotional iconography. It can be seen, for instance, in a miniature from the Dominican *Lectionary* of the Heilig Kreuz convent in Regensburg: this manuscript dates from between 1267 and 1276 and was most likely produced by the nuns themselves.[53] The illustration is found at the beginning of the *Life of St Francis*: the saint is drawn with stigmata, praying before the Seraph. In the margins, outside the main image, is a small drawing of a Dominican sister of the monastery, along with her name: Hailwigis. She kneels behind Francis to pray, imitating his posture. Was she the artist or the copyist? If that much remains unknown, 'it is beyond doubt that Hailwigis had long gazed at this image in which she drew herself and wrote her name'.[54] While contemplating the image, Hailwigis, or indeed any other nun, could use her imagination to 'enter' it: first they identified with the sister, and then with St Francis, all the while deeply feeling the effects of prayer.

Another image of devotion depicts such an entry even more directly, by illustrating incorporation (see Figure 9). Attributed to a female monastic artist who worked in the fourteenth-century Rhineland, and preserved on a loose sheet (25.5 cm by 18 cm), it depicts the Eucharist – the body and blood of Jesus – in the form of a highly realistic crucifixion scene. The body of Christ floods the page with his crimson blood, which somehow leaves the two figures at his feet unstained: Bernard of Clairvaux stands on the right of the crucifix, a nun to its left. To modern observers with a knowledge of later medieval altarpieces, they seem to stand in for the figures of sacred history: the Virgin, St John, and the others usually depicted at the foot of the cross. At the centre of the image, the bloodied, crucified corpse is drawn at the same scale as the two living figures at its feet. 'Almost entirely covered with blood, he is presented as an enormous wound',[55] which Bernard and the nun embrace: their devotion to the body and blood of Christ, presented as if relics, is thus rendered an object of devotion in and of itself. Despite all this bright red blood, it is interesting to note the expressive sobriety of the image. Bernard and the nun remain immaculate, the blood of the crucified Christ dripping on the ground between their knees. The image, structured around an empathic, participatory devotion to the sufferings of Christ, brings together at least two or perhaps even three ages that nevertheless remain distinct: that of the Incarnation, on the one hand, and that of the Church on the other, in which Bernard and the sister are drawn together despite living two centuries apart. Like Hailwigis, the anonymous sister certainly belonged to the monastic community where the image was produced.

An important component of Eucharistic devotion, this devotion to the wounds of the crucified Christ brought together emotions that might appear contradictory to us: there were emotions of suffering and compassion on the one hand, and those of love and joy – products of a supernatural emotional communion – on the other. This devotion led directly to the wounds becoming pathways for a joining of bodies, a powerful lever for affective union and identification with the crucified Christ. The incorporation phenomena experienced by women were in turn directly linked to the emotional, imaginary, and symbolic implications of chewing and ingesting the host, the body of Christ. In keeping with the iconographic motifs seen above, incorporation involved, in emotional as well as visual terms, either the physical or spiritual insertion of all or part of the body of Christ or the instruments of his Passion into the body or soul of the mystic; or, conversely, the spiritual and symbolic insertion of the mystic themselves into the body of Christ.[56] The devotional experience of incorporation found its corollary in the emotions and intense physical sensations that one felt through identification with Christ's suffering or participating in divine beatitude.

Texts sometimes prove even more eloquent than images. For instance, when combined with the practices of affective devotion, the multiple meanings of the term *passio* – which could at once designate suffering and illness, Christ's Passion, and emotional passion – opened up an extraordinary field of possibilities for psychosomatic experience. Feeding off this versatility, the anonymous *vita* of Lukardis of Oberweimar (d. 1309) depicts her as an authentic 'woman of passion'.[57] In two stages, her body suffered (*patitur*) a transformation of heavenly origin. Two years after her arrival at the convent of Oberweimar in Thuringia, while still a very young girl of about fourteen years of age, she began to suffer

198

from *passiones* (constant illness), which deformed her body and left her unable to follow the 'normal' collective life. Alone, away from the others, she spent her life in bed. While cast aside due to her illness, heavenly care would compensate for the lack of earthly attention. The Virgin consoled her and soothed her sore limbs and wounds; Christ came to encourage her, to strengthen her in her calling to His service.[58] She received love and proofs of love; her suffering gained meaning as her own participation in the Passion. Lukardis was showered with love in her spiritual relationships. The reader is struck by the atmosphere of intimacy and affection in which these encounters with Christ and the Virgin unfolded, indicated by terms denoting sweetness (*dulcedo, dulcis,* and *affectuosus*) as well as those that suggest the sharing of emotions: com*passio*, con*solatio*, con*dolere*, con*fortare*. Even as Lukardis suffered in body and tensions arose with her convent sisters, the hagiographer focuses on the emotional delights she enjoyed in her spiritual relationships: it was these that gave her life meaning.

Heaven burst into the life of Lukardis – and it did not stop at conversations. She prayed that she might carry the memory of Christ's burden during the Passion in the most intimate regions of her heart. One scene from her *vita* provides an astonishing parallel with the images analysed above, which likewise had their origin in German women's convents:[59] Lukardis received a vision of Christ on the cross, still alive and bleeding, his arm hanging down as if begging her for help. She entered the image and tried, as best as she could, to hold onto the arm of Christ. The crucified Christ then asked her to press her hands into his hands, her feet against his feet, and her chest against his chest, in order to soothe him. Lukardis did just that and felt a violent pain in her hands, feet, and side, albeit without the appearance of any physical marks.[60] In this episode, a clear link is established between the Passion of Christ and the nun's bodily sufferings. Two very different senses of *passio* are placed side-by-side: while in the plural the term refers to Lukardis' bodily ailments, in the singular it denotes the Passion of Christ. The use of the same term serves to tie their two stories together, and thus to underline the profound significance of the saint's life. At the beginning of this vision, Lukardis prayed and desired; it is this which, through interior motion, moved her towards Christ. Thus, *in spiritu*, she could see herself passing through a doorway, behind which she found Christ in his death-throes. Entering another order of reality, she could interact with the crucified Christ, who came to life for her. Lukardis received Christ's stigmata: imprinted body-to-body, they formed a mirror image reminiscent of certain depictions of Francis of Assisi. What is more, she was granted the embrace of the crucified Christ.[61] This bodily contact brought about the internal transition of the nun towards conformity with the Redeemer. The stigmata of Lukardis were at first interior, without any visible sign: the traces of this incredible encounter remained intimate. But three chapters (and two years) later, the process continued. During the night on the feast of St Gregory,[62] Lukardis mentally envisaged a handsome young man. He was tender and delicate, and marked by five wounds. He approached her in a friendly manner, taking her right hand in his right hand; he squeezed it tightly and said to her: 'I want you to suffer with me' (*volo te pati mecum*). As the biographer comments, 'by this she understood that the passion she herself endured had long been foreseen by the will of God'.[63] Following this episode, stigmata of Christ's wounds gradually appeared on Lukardis' body; just like Francis, she long hid them from others.[64] The biographer explains these events in a passage reminiscent of Thomas of Celano's *Treatise on Miracles*:

> Thus it came to pass that Jesus Christ made a display of this servant of God – who had strived, in the depths of her soul, to conform herself to the image of Christ's Passion through perpetual remembrance – showing to all through her body that He had granted her conformity with his Passion. And the marks of Christ's Passion, which she had long carried secretly within her soul, the Lord then revealed, before the eyes of all, to be printed on her body.[65]

And to those who asked her how she could bear so many sufferings or passions (*in tanta passione*) with such a serene appearance, Lukardis said that the suffering of her body was tempered by the marvellous sweetness of divine consolation within her soul.[66]

At the other end of Christendom, in Umbria, a woman who died in the same year as Lukardis would take up an equally assiduous devotion to Christ's wounds, which gradually led her towards incorporation with the crucified Christ: her name was Angela of Foligno. Early on, a certain distance was maintained between Angela and Christ: she rejoiced in contemplating the marks left by the nails, but, according to her *Memorial*, longed for the physical contact that might transport her to another plane. It has already been noted how Eucharistic communion aroused joy and pleasure within her. Contact – visual and quasi-physical – generated the same emotions:

> Then he called me to place my mouth to the wound in his side. It seemed to me that I saw and drank the blood, which was freshly flowing from his side. His intention was to make me understand that by this blood he would cleanse me. And at this I began to experience a great joy...[67]

Further on in the *Memorial* and in line with these experiences, Angela received a wholly sanctifying embrace, highlighting both the

200

visual grounding and the emotional dimension of her experience of incorporation:

> And while I was thus gazing at the cross with the eyes of my body, suddenly my soul was set ablaze with love; and every member of my body felt it with the greatest joy. I saw and felt that Christ was within me, embracing my soul with the very arm with which he was crucified. [...] The joy that I experienced to be with him in this way and the sense of security that he gave me were far greater than I had ever been accustomed to. Henceforth my soul remained in a state of joy in which it understood what this man, namely Christ, is like in heaven, that is to say, how we will see that through him our flesh is made one with God. This was a source of delight for my soul beyond words and description, and it was a joy that was abiding.[68]

The imagination served as a powerful tool for identification: stirred by painted or written images, it aroused a piety driven by emotion. The metaphors of the Scriptures and the Fathers, as well as the images of the sacred history, were incarnated, both literally and figuratively, in the sensorial, affective, and bodily experiences of these holy women. When these elements are lined up and carefully studied, it also becomes possible to grasp the religious and social power that the turn to mystical devotion granted its practitioners. This exploration draws us back, once again, to the organic link between theology and sacramental practices, on the one hand, and affective and embodied devotion, on the other.

The sacramental 'emotive': the emotional navigation of mystics

The penitential purification of sins that had been thoroughly dissected by twelfth-century sacramental theology possessed an important emotional component: the feeling of repentance and the deep regret for sins committed, expressed by tears, played an active role in the process of purification. Beyond tears, there were other penitential gestures that choreographed the process, and these became increasingly numerous and scripted in the final centuries of the Middle Ages. In the *vita* of Mary of Oignies, Jacques de Vitry invited the reader to contemplate 'how wondrously she immolated her body for the Lord and with what great love and wondrous delight she was tortured in body by embracing the cross of Christ'.[69] Ancient metaphors for the religious life (especially its monastic forms) that had been common since Gregory the Great – the crucifixion of the flesh, the sacrifice of the monk's body for the love of God – were now applied to pious laywomen. Understood in the most literal manner, they were invested with a new power that was both gestural and emotional. The *vita* of Mary of Oignies offers an entirely literal understanding of such an image:

201

One day she brought back to her memory a time when she had been forced to eat meat and, from necessity since she had had a most grievous illness, had drunk a little watered wine. Then from a kind of horror at her previous delight, she did not have rest in her spirit and by a wondrous torture of the flesh she afflicted herself until she had made recompense for those delights she had had before. As if inebriated and from the fervour of her spirit, she began to loath her flesh in comparison with the sweetness of the Paschal Lamb and in her mistaken fervour, she cut out a large piece of her flesh with a knife which, because of her modesty, she buried in the earth. So inflamed had she been by an exceeding fire of love that she had risen above the pain of her wound and, in this ecstasy of mind, she had seen one of the seraphim standing close by her.[70]

Here we leave aside the question of how plausible this scene of penitential self-mutilation was: for as exceptional and particular as it might seem, the gesture recounted here was not uncommon in hagiography. An initial parallel can be drawn with Francis of Assisi's act of public penance seen above: while undertaken in a way that might seem equally excessive to modern eyes, that excess in fact served to illustrate his sanctity. As if the sacramental penance dispensed by clerics was not enough for her, Mary's emotions made her inflict exceptional penances upon herself. Contrition, recommended to all the faithful, was an integral (and active) part of her penance; sacramental emotivity served first to materialize, and perhaps even increase, the effectiveness of the sacrament. But she went further. The torture of sin, the love of Christ, and the exhilaration she felt in her fervour literally took hold of the beguine. Under their grip, she cut chunks of flesh off her body, as if to excise all trace of sin. Throughout this narrative, she appears governed and inwardly transformed by her emotions: they led her through an 'effective emotional navigation'.[71] The shame wrought by Mary's unusual actions was followed by ardent love, drawn from the grace of God. It enveloped her as if a reward for her sacrifice, leaving her unable to feel the pain she had inflicted upon herself. Finally, love whisked her away into ecstasy. In allegorical terms, the narrative of Mary of Oignies' self-mutilation outlines the journey from penance to the Eucharist. Through her passionate, compulsive, and exaggerated actions, she sought to purify her body. In this way, she appropriated the efficacy of the sacraments, destroying sin at the same time as imitating Christ: she literally crucified her flesh. The process described here resulted in a metamorphosis that was both spiritual and emotional. Her purification was accomplished, proved by the divine love that she felt in reward, as well as by her vision of an angel. While disheartened and tortured at the outset of the process, Mary of Oignies gained certainty over the divine favour that followed shame. As Jacques de Vitry remarked, she was saved because she sacrificed herself.

This phenomenon of transformation – at once spiritual and emotional – can be witnessed in the religious experiences of Mary of Oignies, Lukardis, and many others.[72] Such an experience constituted what might be called a 'sacramental emotive', to borrow William Reddy's notion of an 'emotive'.[73] As with Lukardis' passionate transformation, Mary's experience was one of 'emotional navigation', in the sense that the emotions she felt and expressed transformed each other, succeeded one another, and responded to each other and did so according to their own rationality, which the subject did not necessarily control. It was 'effective' in so far as this emotional odyssey provided the holy woman with palpable advancement on the road to salvation. Providing an infusion of grace without any ecclesiastical intervention, such emotional navigation worked in similar ways to the sacraments themselves. If Mary's approach was clearly penitential, the sacrificial aspect of her self-mutilation lent it a Eucharistic symbolism. In the *vita* of Lukardis, the penitential dimension of her sickness gradually gave way to a Eucharistic and uniting aspect, which reached its zenith in the stigmata she received. The meeting of the two sacraments on the path towards emotional, bodily, and spiritual transformation – a path which led from suffering to peace, joy, and ecstasy – was commonplace in the experiences and practices of holy women in this era. Here one finds a new version of the conversion path drawn from monastic tradition: within it, the role of emotions and the body was heightened, and at the end of the journey, a sensual foretaste of beatitude was in easy reach, even if such delights were never lasting.

Given that the embodied emotivity found in thirteenth- and fourteenth-century piety so often followed a similar pattern, this anthropological reading allows us to understand the fundamental reason why these women – and some men too, since there was nothing to stop them – sought to express their emotions in a body language that now seems overwrought. The masochism of affective mysticism – the self-transformation wrought through suffering to become the suffering Christ – provided major gains on the individual level, albeit that their institutional recognition would prove much more problematic. Emotional navigation imbued mystical experiences with both spiritual and social significance. The 'sacramental emotive' brought about the most important transformation imaginable in Christian anthropology, allowing one to pass from a state of sin to a state of purity and sanctity, and did so solely by way of intimate experiences. Furthermore, by joining bodies with Christ through this mystical route, the devout woman reaffirmed her place within the Church, itself the body of Christ: she gained a unique spiritual authority within it, given that she alone had brought about her spiritual transformation.

The emotional incarnation of the sacred: gender and society

While the bulk of the writings that attest to it were produced by men, affective piety is still often described as an 'invention' of late medieval women. Here one can see a rather paradoxical effect of giving women their due as an object of historical study. Mary of Oignies, Margaret of Cortona (d. 1297), Hadewijch of Antwerp (d. *c*. 1260), and Beatrice of Nazareth (d. 1268) are thus presented to us as those courageous enough to make the 'voice of the women' heard and fly the flag of a feminine sensibility in the religious and public sphere. Having made them visible by separating them from men, it is very tempting to see a 'gender identity' within them, which in fact breathes new life into old divisions. One might garner the impression that what they said and embodied in religious terms was, in essence, feminine; that women had a natural predisposition to affective and bodily mysticism; and thus that reason, reasoning, and rationality were male qualities.[74] To do so would be to forget that the aspects of spirituality most commonly identified with feminine piety – Eucharistic desire, devotion to Christ's wounds, the erotic expression of the love of Christ – had been thoroughly articulated in the preceding centuries by men who drew from patristic heritage, long before these qualities would be assigned to women.[75] For a long time, the deployment of gender dynamics within spiritual rhetoric barely had any relation to physical sex, and indeed transcended it. The spiritual use of the lovers of the Song of Songs is well known: the bride and bridegroom were respectively likened to the soul and to the Church. Elsewhere, within twelfth-century monastic and canonial communities, the figure of Jesus was presented as a mother in devotional terms.[76] In other words, it is as if those historians who worked to legitimize women's history appropriated, sometimes despite themselves, a medieval discourse on the feminine predisposition to all things emotional, bodily, sensual, and sexual. For while affective spirituality was developed in male monastic circles, it was also men who constructed the medieval cultural and ecclesiastical norms that assigned women an identity defined by affect and emotion. Drawing from St Paul (1 Tim. 2: 12), the twelfth-century masters of theology reinforced the exclusion of women from *ex officio* spiritual authority within the Church, but nevertheless granted them a potential *ex gratia* authority by way of paramystic experiences.[77] Furthermore, it was texts written by men that defined the spiritual experiences of women as being essentially expressed through their bodies and emotions.

A product of both assignment and appropriation, the female mysticism of the final centuries of the Middle Ages – which, from medieval times to the present day, has always been identified with intense emotions and the body – thus appears to be an avatar of the 'female nature' fashioned by male domination. It emerged in a triumphant era for the institutional authority of the Church, which had successfully imposed itself as the indispensable mediator between God and mankind; it was an age where clerical control over the laity was tighter than ever, and where the demand for access to the sacred was equally strong. It was within a Church that increasingly withdrew this access from the laity that mystical women came to grasp it directly, by bringing their emotions and their bodies into play. To do so, they appropriated ecclesiastical and scriptural language, and gave flesh to the images and metaphors of what was, for the most part, a traditional religious discourse. As with Francis of Assisi, their novelty resided in their manner of speaking, acting, and feeling, and in a complex narrative game where an access to the divine that bypassed clerical mediation paradoxically arose through the written mediation of men and clerics.

At least as they are described in the texts, such women seemed ready to assume the role assigned to them: as a result of the exclusions and diminutions that weighed against them – exclusion from the priesthood, relegation from learned culture – they simultaneously found authority, a space for resistance, and an escape route in an affective and embodying piety. Yet their path, always individual, was not without its dangers. For its part, the institutional Church preserved an ambiguous attitude towards the charismatic imitation of Christ by women, even if the female model of sanctity promoted by the papal Curia experienced an unprecedented boom within the West from the late twelfth century onward. Indeed, for a long time, the mystical path had been essentially reserved for men; all of a sudden, it was flooded with women. Despite this, with just a few exceptions, only the echoes of those women deemed worthy of a *vita* have come down to us.[78] Even with a figure as extraordinary as Hadewijch of Antwerp, we have no trace of historical background – not even a *vita* – to work from.

Starting from this fragile position, a single misstep was enough for such women to be deemed intolerable by the Church. Beguines had been both admired and suspected throughout the thirteenth century, prior to their condemnation at the Council of Vienna in 1311–12. Marguerite Porete (d. 1310), burnt at the stake in Paris shortly after the trial of the Templars, stated in her treatise that a 'simple and annihilated soul' that had approached God through the negative path of annihilation had no further need for works of virtue, no need for the usual gestures of piety, and hence, no need for institutional frameworks, in order to attain union with God.[79] Today, the 'quirks' of the trial of Marguerite are well known, not least the fact that the masters of theology who condemned statements drawn from her book had likely never even held it in their own hands.[80]

Be that as it may, the appropriation of theological authority by a woman – worse still, a woman who wrote! – was indeed enough to ensure her condemnation, driven by men who were sure of their own authoritative position within the institutional Church.

Historians who focus on issues of gender have attempted to understand the reasons why men constructed a mystical path marked by emotion and corporeity that was specifically for women. Such schemas have been explained by relationships drawn from social expectations that both created distinctions and defined value: between woman and food, and between woman and motherhood. One might also wonder whether clerics ascribed novelties to women that they themselves wouldn't dare take up due to their status. It is sufficient to compare the mystical writings of women and men in the thirteenth and fourteenth centuries to know that the latter had deliberately put the accent on female bodily dynamics. Thus, when the biographer of Beatrice of Nazareth summarized a treatise written by the saint (*The Seven Ways of Love*) in her *vita*, he transposed the spiritual experiences recounted by his heroine into bodily experiences.[81] As if in a sort of strange compensation for this, men imbued women with a power of social action, a religious efficacy and authority at the margins of the norm that they themselves had built, a space in which they nevertheless sought to confine them. But while more nuanced than earlier essentialist readings (woman = affect + body / man = reason + spirit), these 'gendered' analyses of the 'feminine' manner of emotionally embodying the sacred only partially account for the complexity of the sources.

At the beginning of the thirteenth century, Francis of Assisi and Mary of Oignies embodied, in their similarities and contemporaneity, a point of equilibrium: at that moment, a man and a woman, despite their very different places in the Church, could express religious sensibilities that were very much alike. The late thirteenth-century *Vie de sainte Douceline*, written in the vernacular and likely by a woman, shows that the hagiographical genre itself, such as it was practised at the time, privileged certain themes which could then pass easily from male to female authors.[82] Conversely, it is hardly surprising to find themes that might be labelled as 'feminine' – for instance, the physical and emotional manipulation of one's own body in compassion for Christ – in a man's *vita*, given that, from the early eleventh century, and perhaps since the beginning of Christianity itself, men had used emotions in devotional contexts and freely played with the symbolic qualities of gender. An example of this can be found in *The Life of the Servant*, a text most likely written in tandem by the mystical couple of Henry Suso (d. 1366) and his spiritual daughter Elsbeth Stagel (d. *c.* 1360), abbess of the convent of Töss near Constance, and often described as the *vita* of the former.[83] Here, Suso performed a feat comparable to Mary of Oignies' penitential self-sacrifice, engraving the name of Jesus on his chest:

> He set to work, and with his style he pierced the flesh over his heart, pricking backwards and forwards, up and down, till he had drawn the name IHS right over his heart. From the sharp stabs the blood flowed copiously out of the flesh and ran down over his body and down his chest. It was such a lovely sight that in the glow of his love he did not heed the pain much.[84]

Feats of this sort would come to enjoy a certain success in religious literature; fifteenth-century manuscript illuminations, for instance, depict the contemporary English hermit Richard Rolle with the same letters (IHS) on his chest.[85] The unanswerable question concerning their authenticity is not what is of interest here, but rather the model that such hagiographical legends offered to the men and women who read them. The act of self-engraving seen here, and indeed the spiritual joy it gave to its author and victim – a joy that transcended physical pain – clearly illustrate that 'philopassionism' (the search for salutary suffering)[86] and the religious manipulation of the body and the emotions belonged to a model of sanctity that was not exclusively feminine. Suso's severe ascetic practices, so pronounced within *The Life of the Servant*, were in line with a long tradition of penitential mortification which Western monasticism inherited from the Desert Fathers; indeed his *vita* also relates how Suso had a chapel decorated with scenes from the *Vitae Patrum* at the Dominican convent of Constance.[87] But within a text which contained courtly accents, his endurance of the widest range of self-inflicted mortifications for Christ also allowed Suso to become a spiritual knight, armed by an angel.[88] Finally, Suso's mortifications also had a compassionate meaning, recalling the example of St Francis, who had fashioned them into a sort of affective participation in the sufferings of Christ, a form of *imitatio Christi*: 'More than all the other exercises, he felt an ardent desire to bear on his body some sign of the sympathy he felt for the painful sufferings of his crucified Lord.'[89]

With Henry Suso, we enter the world of Rhineland mysticism, a mysticism usually thought of as philosophical rather than affective in its point of departure. Suso was a figure whose numerous writings brought together an intellectualized mystical discourse with an affective, ascetic, and Christocentric piety. A disciple of Meister Eckhart (d. 1328), the Dominican Suso in fact belonged to a world marked by significant contacts with beguine circles in the urban environments of Rhineland and Flanders, environments well-known for their devotional creativity, as well as their size and social importance. On closer inspection, the world

of the beguines probably contributed about as much to the reconfiguration of gender logics in the late medieval religious world as Francis of
Assisi had.[90]

Whatever the respective influence of men and women in the elaboration of the mystical discourses that have come down to us, the skilful
devotional and emotional handling of ideas and images that allowed
pious women not only to interact directly with Christ, but also to unite
with him or the Virgin is proof that they possessed a good knowledge
of the issues and possibilities of contemporary theology. Moreover, the
texts written by women themselves establish a close bond between
emotion and intelligence, sensation and understanding.[91] While for the
most part these female authors did not read Latin, they often had access
to both courtly culture and devotional literature, especially through oral
dissemination. Some were able to venture even further as a result of their
backgrounds. This is proved by the texts written in the vernacular by
two of the most striking figures of the Middle Ages, both of whom hailed
from the urban climes of Hainaut-Brabant: the poetess Hadewijch of
Antwerp, writing around 1240, and the 'vernacular theologian' Marguerite Porete.[92] Hadewijch's mystical poetry, like Marguerite's famous
work, *The Mirror of Simple Souls*, drew not only from a French courtly
culture that defined their language and expression, but also from a shared
religious culture that also left its mark on the works of Meister Eckhart,[93]
that great mystical philosopher of the early fourteenth century: recent
research has shown that he had read the *Mirror* and that he concurred
with some of its ideas.[94] Hadewijch and Marguerite very likely both
knew Latin, but wrote in the vernacular. This was also the language in
which Hadewijch, acting as a spiritual master, instructed a group of
religious women who lived to serve divine love. Marguerite, for her part,
would appear to have had less of a following, at least to judge by her
tragic fate.[95] Indeed her book, which offered a path of spiritual ascension
to God (and to love) through the progressive abandonment of formal
constraints, was primarily addressed to a spiritual elite, those 'reduced
to nothing by true love': they were distinguished both from those souls
merely touched by God (whether they were active – priests – or passive
– religious), and, most especially, from the 'common folk'.[96] In spite of
their different contexts, the writings of Hadewijch and Marguerite shared
a mystagogical aim in the etymological sense of the term: they sought to
provide a pedagogical initiation into the divine mysteries and mystical
life. Yet, like Beatrice of Nazareth, if both spoke of the love of God and
described the knowledge of God in terms of love, the language in which
their discourse was formulated did not follow the ascetico-mystical path
based on bodily commitment that can be observed in the largely Latin
hagiography of their contemporaries. Self-inflicted physical suffering, as

well as that compassionate suffering that became delight, are absent from their texts, which instructed their readers on the quest for union with the divine.

Greatly influenced by the commentaries on the Song of Songs by William of Saint-Thierry and Bernard of Clairvaux, as well as by Victorine spirituality, the writings of Hadewijch focus on the loving quest for the divine lover; they were expressed in a language that is by turns poetic, erotic, courtly, and discursive. For Hadewijch, the emotion of love (*minne*) was no simple sensation: rather it was an ontological principle. Her perspective here is reminiscent of courtly love: love was the profound attraction between two beings that enabled the transformation of the less perfect of the pair, who came to equal the qualities and perfection of their partner.[97] This spiritual love entered the intellect, the highest faculty of the soul, where God nurtured an unremitting desire for union between man and his Creator. This desire was the active principle of the mystical process: it enabled the human spirit to attain its divine perfection.[98] When framed within a mystagogical discourse in the *Book of Visions*, desire – the *orewoet*, as it is described – was not nurtured by bodily practices but by the author's spiritual and contemplative experiences. Nevertheless, her sensuality and eroticism clearly brought her close to experiencing the emotional incarnation of the sacred:

> On a certain Pentecost Sunday, I had a vision at dawn. Matins were being sung in the church, and I was present. My heart and my veins and all my limbs trembled and quivered with eager desire and, as often occurred with me, such madness and fear beset my mind that it seemed to me I did not content my Beloved and that my Beloved did not fulfil my desire, so that dying I must go mad, and going mad I must die. On that day my mind was beset so fearfully and so painfully by desirous love that all my separate limbs threatened to break, and all my separate veins were in travail. The longing in which I then was cannot be expressed by any language of any person I know; and everything I could say about it would be unheard-of to all those who never apprehended Love as something to work for with desire, and whom Love had never acknowledged as hers. I can say this about it: I desired to have full fruition of my Beloved and to understand and taste him to the full. I desired that his Humanity should to the fullest extent be one in fruition with my humanity, and that mine should hold its stand and be strong enough to enter into perfection until I content him who is perfection itself, by purity and unity, and in all things to content him fully in every virtue. To that end I wished he might content me interiorly with his Godhead, in one spirit, and that for me he should be all that he is, without withholding anything from me.[99]

The purpose of this desire was to bring God to fruition: it was Eucharistic, just like the emotions embodied by the women already encountered.

Hadewijch's ecstasies occurred at important liturgical feasts, for it was her desire for and expectation of the sacramental union that provoked them.

Hadewijch's collection of songs, however, has an entirely different tone. The relationship of mystical love between the soul and God is openly described in terms of courtly love, wherein the knight – the soul of the loving mystic – courted Lady Love, *Minne*, the most important allegorical figure (alongside her stood Desire [*Beherte*], Pleasure [*Geneuchte*], Reason [*Rede*], and others, almost always of feminine gender):[100]

> Alas, where is new love now
> With her new good things?
> For my distress brings me
> into many a new woe;
> My soul melts away
> In the madness of love[101]

Marguerite Porete likewise employed the same courtly style,[102] and used personalities to express the mystical experience: her *Mirror of Simple Souls* presents itself as a dialogue between the Soul, Lady Love, and Reason. The Soul and Lady Love, the real teachers of the piece, sought to convince Reason of their superiority when it came to approaching God: beyond the faculty of the same name, Reason embodied the narrowness of the religious conventions and scholasticism of Marguerite's time.[103] What the Soul and Lady Love advocated was a path of negation, the abandonment of one's own will and, more broadly, of all created forms. Marguerite's work thus makes no mention of visions or psycho-corporeal experiences.[104] More abstract and discursive than the poems of Hadewijch, it is nevertheless expressed in the language of love, nourished by Cistercian mysticism and courtly poetry. It employs paradoxical reasoning (by annihilating the will, the will is liberated; by annihilating itself, the soul becomes everything), and, as a direct result, offers a practical and finely judged critique of scholastic thought.[105] To reach and become God, Love called on the Soul to become detached from itself by no longer willing, to annihilate itself in all of those things it contained that were simply created: only by doing this could it reach the state of pre-Adamic freedom to which Love called it.[106]

This affectivity devoid of embodiment, combined with the call to 'take leave of the virtues' – which must be read in Marguerite, and earlier in Hadewijch, in a very concrete manner, as the entrance into an existence entirely devoted to the contemplative life[107] – suggested a very different mystical path from the one offered to the faithful by the

1 *Adam and Eve Chased from Paradise*, Masaccio, *c.* 1425
Masaccio made the most of the emotional register in portraying the catastrophe of original sin. Moral shame, bodily modesty, and pain are brought together to express the new-found consciousness of sin and its consequences. In a society subject to the imperatives of honour, the Christian acculturation of shame represented a major concern throughout the Middle Ages (see chapter 1, p. 28).

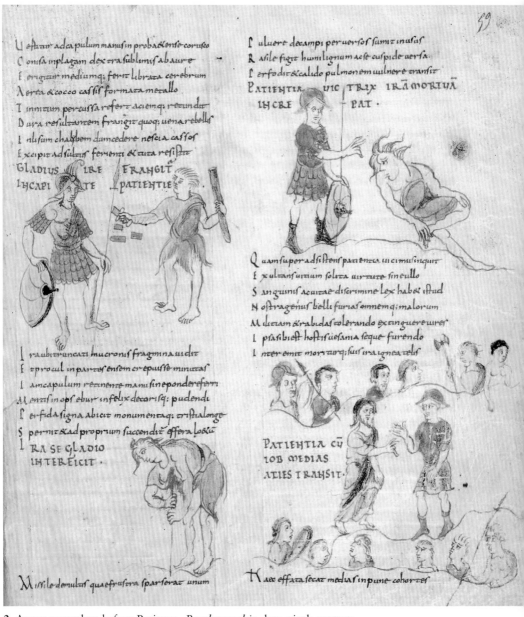

2 Anger powerless before Patience, *Psychomachia*, late ninth century
This confrontation between the personified figures of Patience and Anger is a classic portrayal of th
struggle between the vices and virtues in Carolingian monastic culture. Long-haired and shabby in appear
ance, Anger launches several assaults against a calm and heavily armed Patience, all of them in vair
Finally, in desperation, Anger commits suicide (see chapter 3, p. 45).

3 (opposite) John of Salisbury, Letter no. 305, *Ex insperato*, c. 1171–80
This, the earliest known representation of the assassination of Thomas Becket, depicts the two-stage
emotional scripting of the political event. The murderous act of the barons, dressed in dark colours, fulfi
the injunction of the *ira regis*. Meanwhile the shame of public humiliation, here represented by the ac
of prostration at the foot of Thomas' tomb, contributed to the reparation (see chapter 7, p. 172).

&ic inspato & in tŕistitī in di gŕa ppitiante nuŕ innotuit: qd ad uoŕ e rat lator pŕsentiū tūsni tur. Gauīsus q duium & munūtiaťā occasione śsbendi ad amicū eā gratū arripui: arbitrūs in longe calamitatis magnū da ṛt

solatiū qd in tuis auriṭ; liceat an gŕaŕi cumulū deplorare S; unde sumeŕ exordiū: Ña dicendi parīt inopia: mateia copiosa & exubant. & q̄ si tēpe ūo malicia excreuit set ad sūmū: fide excedit. Publicā angustiaŕ an domesticas deplora bo: S; gñales mūūo agnotur sua quēq; miseria puŋt acrī: ñ force

4 Lancelot and Guinevere's first kiss, *Lancelot-Graal*, with an interpolation of *Perlesvaus*, c. 1404–60
5 (**opposite**) Lancelot and Galahad depart from one another, *Lancelot-Graal*, c. 1470
Kissing on the lips and embracing were the principal gestures through which love was expressed in courtly
romance, with no distinction between the sexes. One should not, however, see any sexual open-minded-
ness in this similarity. Rather, it confirmed that true love was a bond that joined souls above all else
even if it was expressed by the body (see chapter 5, pp. 113–4).

6 (**overleaf**) *The Manger at Greccio*, Giotto, c. 1300
Giotto was one of the great masters of emotional expression who painted from the beginning of the
duecento. Here, he highlights the affective dimension of the scene at Greccio that Thomas of Celano
recounted by showing Francis of Assisi tenderly taking the infant Jesus in his arms. The audience, which
consists of readily identifiable groups, shares in the emotion and worship (see chapter 8, p. 192).

Et toute riens se trait plus a ioie quen
autre temps. En cellui terme lenu amut
i. iour aheure de midy quil aruueret
en loreille dune forueff deuant vne croiz
et virent yffir dela forueff i. cheualiez

7 *The Descent from the Cross* (detail), Rogier van Weyden, *c.* 1435
The emotional expressivity of saints and of depictions of the Passion increased markedly at the end of the Middle Ages. Tears and faces distorted in pain were no longer incompatible with the nobility of the soul. Emotion had to be seen, since its very representation could lead onlookers to become one with the suffering (see chapter 8, p. 181).

Penitence and Contemplation, *Livres de l'estat de l'ame, c.* 1290–1300
evotion to the crucifix and Eucharist was one of the preferred channels of lay piety at the end of the Middl
es, especially for women. It contributed to a very well-mastered use of the emotions in sacramental practices
e chapter 8, p. 196).

9 *Christ on the Cross* (*Vision des Heiligen Bernhard – sogennantes Blutkruzifixus*), fourteenth century
The adoration of the wounds of the crucifixion sometimes took a turn towards the extreme at the end of the Middle Ages, as can be seen in this sort of representation, where Christ is literally soaked in blood. In the same way, the emotions of suffering, love, and joy felt by the devotee reached fever-pitch, so as to signify the fullness of union with the tortured Christ (see chapter 8, p. 197).

10 The wedding of Fauvel and Vainglory, *Le Roman de Fauvel*, *c.* 1310–20
The joyful racket of the charivari, first described in the fourteenth century, was one of those rituals of
derision which cemented a community, in this case primarily that of young men. They came together to
denounce behaviour that was deemed immoral or destabilizing, such as an ill-matched union between a
widower and a young woman. The iconography seen here reminds us that open, emphatic laughter was
associated with folly, madness, and even demonic possession (see chapter 9, pp. 217–8).

11 Group of men in mourning. Tomb of Sancho Saiz de Carrillo, *c.* 1300

The ritualized expression of emotions was often related to processes of social definition. Such was the case with very demonstrative gestures of the grief of mourning, here seen making their mark within an aristocratic and lay culture. This culture differentiated itself from the prescriptions of the Church as well as those of certain urban communities, which required that pain was expressed with reserve and reverence during funerals (see chapter 9, p. 229).

12 Group of women in mourning. Tomb of Sancho Saiz de Carrillo, *c.* 1300

13 *Sermon* on the *Passion* of Jean Gerson, *c.* 1480

When led by a good speaker – or a good actor – the popular sermon was also an emotional spectacle. There were those emotions that were acted out or appealed to by the preacher, who knew all the tricks of the trade. But there were also those that were felt by the public, as can be seen in this example, where the men and women of the mixed audience each seem to react in their own way (see chapter 9, pp. 240–1).

reflections of female hagiography and, more broadly, by the institutional Church since the high Middle Ages. This path did not resort to suffering, works of virtue, or ecclesiastical mediation. Today it seems clear that the essence of Marguerite Porete's doctrine was in line with accepted mystical tradition and that her book was condemned for reasons that were institutional and contextual rather than doctrinal.[108] The solid association within medieval Christian anthropology between women, on the one hand, and embodiment, suffering, and Christ's passionate humanity, on the other, was cast aside in Marguerite's work. Meister Eckhart subsequently reprised this apophatic path when he expressed the retreat from the sensual world in Neo-Platonic language. 'By effacing the place of asceticism, paramystic phenomena and visionary experience in religious life, [Marguerite] Porete and Eckhart disrupted the main channels of authority and religious expression open to women' in the Church and the society of their time.[109] The condemnation of their works, and of Marguerite herself, makes clear that the alternative path they outlined was unacceptable to the institutional Church, and that it was even more so when expressed in a female voice. Contained within ever more normalized forms, the emotional incarnation of the sacred remained an honoured path of sanctification for women in the fourteenth century; there, they legitimized their access to ecstasy and divine joy through suffering.

Epilogue: the *devotio moderna* and the softening of affective piety

A few decades later in the same region – Flanders and the eastern Low Countries – a religious reform movement known as the *devotio moderna* took shape. Born from aspirations that were very different from those represented by Hadewijch, Ruusbroeck (d. 1381), Marguerite Porete or Eckhart and his disciples, their path was out of keeping with both the emotional and bodily effusiveness of mystical women and the quest for gradual detachment from the senses, if not an obvious reaction to them.[110] The initial difficulties that the movement endured steered the Sisters and Brothers of the Common Life towards forging strong clerical ties whilst still remaining open to the laity. It was then broadened to include a branch of tertiaries and regular canons (the congregation of Windesheim). Strongly influenced by the spirit of the Cistercians and the mendicant orders, the movement took up the simplicity of the *vita apostolica* and made a communal life of obedience, humility, and virtuous practice accessible to the faithful. At the same time, it promoted an internalized affectivity that did not require bodily expression. The aim of the 'new devout' was to attain the purity of the heart that had been so dear to John Cassian, as well as the love of God: that *caritas* defined by gentleness, delight, calmness, and a relationship with God founded on a confident tranquillity.[111] The same gentleness characterized their devotion to Christ, central to the practice of a day-to-day spirituality that involved deep meditation on the sufferings of the Passion.[112] This devotion to Jesus was defined neither by the imitation of his sufferings nor by mystical union, but rather by the desire to relive his virtuous life and his redeeming Passion, as well as by an affectionate piety. Entirely affective, the *devotio moderna* thus appears in keeping with monastic tradition; the excesses of embodied emotion were avoided. To its followers, it offered the values of simplicity, humility, and purity of heart, all far removed from scholarly debate. This can be seen in the following extract from perhaps the most popular book produced by the new devout, *The Imitation of Christ*, attributed to Thomas à Kempis (d. 1471), a canon of Windesheim:

> Of what use is it to discourse learnedly on the Trinity, if you lack humility and therefore displease the Trinity? Lofty words do not make a man just or holy; but a good life makes him dear to God. I would far rather feel contrition than be able to define it. If you knew the whole Bible by heart, and all the teachings of the philosophers, how would this help you without the grace and love of God?[113]

Within the communities of the Sisters and Brothers of the Common Life, the quest for heartfelt conversion was supported by a collective life in which everyone helped one another through counsel, fraternal correction, and even non-sacramental confession. On top of this, they formed groups for vernacular spiritual reading and held 'collations' (sermons) which allowed for the discussion of readings and spiritual teachings; these were open to the townspeople on Sundays. But in a spirit that was both monastic and Franciscan, the keystone remained the continual conversion of each devotee through a combination of emotional and moral effort. It was a form of 'spiritual carpentry' (*geestliker tymmeringe*), constructed through emotional and moral education: following an initial uprooting of vices, one was to progress through the virtues, controlling passions and transforming emotions along the way. This programme of affective reform favoured an inward-looking spiritual life. It was lived out in the privacy of rooms where the devout read and copied pious citations in the vernacular, prayed, meditated, and self-examined.[114] In a world that tended to visualize, the modern devout were neither producers nor consumers of images; in the way they thought out their way of life, they appear rather traditional and sober, attached to texts and mental images alone.[115] For at the heart of every solitary spiritual exercise lay the effort of meditating on the self, attending to every little stirring of the soul. This daily practice of the sisters and brothers unfolded like a form of 'self-care', and was the foundation of an authentic culture of the inner man.

When compared to the unbridled affectivity seen in emotional attempts to embody the sacred, this tendency towards deep introspection expressed a return of sorts to more conservative norms. It is best understood when the context of its birth is taken into account. This movement of life conversion emerged in the Low Countries in the 1380s,[116] amid a regional atmosphere that had witnessed successive condemnations of various semi-religious movements within the previous two centuries: the sad fate of Marguerite Porete, the condemnations of the Council of Vienna (1311–12) forbidding the beguines from making pronouncements on theological matters, and those of Pope John XXII (d. 1334) against Meister Eckhart's theses in 1329 can hardly be forgotten.[117] Taking root within this difficult context, the modern devout had to defend themselves constantly from the suspicions and accusations of urban magistrates and the Church, who likened them to beguines and beghards, and even to the 'heretics of the Free Spirit'.[118] Indeed, the very manner of their conversion, their communal life, and their pious vernacular reading circles were in keeping with the semi-religious tradition that had flourished in the region for two centuries.[119] Beyond the well-known changes in the attitude of the institutional Church, it was their own choice of both accessibility and humility, and of feeling rather than knowledge – a choice perhaps partly imposed by what was, in many respects, a rather delicate situation – that accounts for what can appear like a form of conservatism: the return to the interior affectivity of reformed monasticism.

More complex than it at first appears, the path of affective devotion that emphasized embodiment was riven by many tensions. This is obvious in the different choices and tones that it threw up, and in the varied answers it offered to challenges, whether religious or social. These tensions often make it possible to identify the 'dosages' of the various traditions that intersected within this new lay religious culture as it took shape. One can detect a spiritual culture of monastic origin, not always distinct from the learned culture of the schools and which more often than not reached the laity through preaching. But alongside this there was the culture of the beguines and other urban devotees, and the courtly culture of aristocratic origin, both of which expressed themselves in the vernacular. Finally, these tensions were related to the variety of reactions and relationships possible with an ecclesiastical hierarchy that gradually became closed to lay religious innovation as the latter took root and diversified in the thirteenth century. The path of emotionally incarnating the sacred was not without risk, in part because it was easily associated with doctrinal errors in a Church which, in the late Middle Ages, was increasingly preoccupied with the matter of orthodoxy. The individual path towards God found through embodying emotion – much like its opposite, the path that led to God through sensory withdrawal – became less and less feasible from the beginning of the fourteenth century onward. Just like language, the affective expression of piety needed to be channelled and standardized within religious institutions to survive in a gentler form. Otherwise, it was not without risk.

— 9 —

COMMON EMOTION (THIRTEENTH TO FIFTEENTH CENTURIES)

In a memorable scene from *The Name of the Rose* (1986), Jean-Jacques Arnaud's film adaptation of Umberto Eco's eponymous novel, a corpulent monk is startled by a mouse in the *scriptorium* of a great monastery. He lets out a shrill cry and climbs onto a chair: contagious laughter ensues. When the laughter spreads in waves and stirs almost every monk despite their serious surroundings, the venerable Jorge, in his cavernous voice, launches into an authoritarian condemnation of laughter. Following this scene, there is a rather scholarly discussion between Brother William and Jorge: the first represents the knowledge of the schools and the Franciscan position on laughter and joy, the second, the austere Benedictine tradition. For Jorge, the laughter in the *scriptorium*, whether in derision or merriment, had gone against what it meant to be a monk: that is, to devote oneself to a life of compunction. For men like him, laughter was related to sin and futility. The affective disposition of *gravitas* – a seriousness founded on the banishment of worldly values, repentance, and compunction, and undertaken to weep over sins, both one's own as those of others – was at the very heart of their collective identity, and perhaps even what defined monks within society. Besides joy and laughter, it excluded all spontaneous and sudden emotions, such as anger; the monk had to be serious and measured. Although the codes governing the emotional behaviour of lay elites were often palpably different, and in many respects less severe than those of the monks who formed the spiritual elite of Christian society, there were important parallels between these two circles: the importance of good measure and the need to maintain honour. The smile – spiritual, moderate, even modest – was promoted in the thirteenth century, while open laughter – provocative or otherwise crude, sexually charged, bound to the lower body and from there to the world of perdition found in the taverns – remained condemned.[1] The emotion shared by the monks who succumb to contagious laughter in the *scriptorium* creates an ephemeral emotional community, a revolt of sorts against the collective attitude required of their social group, whose norms they re-espouse when called to order.[2] At the same time, such gaiety could exclude. Here, it excludes the one laughed at (who had provoked laughter by his foolish reaction, his sudden, instinctive movement), and also those who failed to laugh because they did not share in the common emotion. The cry of rage of the old monk Jorge, who matched emotion with emotion, is in this sense a legitimate response.

This scene, drawn from late twentieth-century medieval fiction, opens the door on a commonly evoked *topos* concerning the Middle Ages. Since the time of Johan Huizinga, we have seen the end of this period as a time of shared and contagious emotion, which the Dutch scholar – and Norbert Elias after him – contrasted with modern Reason. Yet, perhaps precisely because of the influence exerted by *The Autumn of the Middle Ages*, the sharing of emotions has until now rarely attracted the attention of historians, who have too often been preoccupied with understanding the emotions of individuals. It is certainly not an easy subject. The first difficulty is evidential in nature. Beyond the sighs and tears of mystics, for whom we at least usually have a name and some scraps of biography, beyond the love songs of renowned poets and the philosophical and medical theories of great scholars, a gap emerges: what do we know of the emotions of the illiterate in the Middle Ages? The question forces us to interrogate the emotions of the anonymous crowds who accompanied relics during processions, who made up the audience of urban sermons, who attended royal entries into their cities and who were present at burials and weddings. The 'silent masses' of those distant times are especially silent about their emotions; if they sometimes come to life in the chronicles of the Middle Ages, it is only through the eyes of a social and cultural elite. Indeed, it is the distinctive characteristic of the emotions of the masses that they cannot be accessed through their own testimony: the veil of the sources is here at its most opaque.[3] Their emotions were always codified by others; they emerge suddenly around certain events or phenomena that attracted attention. The emotions of the people were the turbulent, sometimes troubling emotions of the mob or, conversely, the pathetic emotions of 'the good people' communing with their masters. The question thus arises of the role played by popular emotion in the narratives and visions of society of the chroniclers and their readerships.

It should not be forgotten that all descriptions of emotion were extremely codified, to the point where they say much more about the representation of emotional norms than they do about the feelings of the actors and the emotions expressed. Nevertheless, the emotional

216

exchanges that occurred made sense for those who experienced them and those who described them. Three major arguments prevail among the historians who have recently studied the semiotics of such emotional performances. For some, the staging of emotion has a solely communicative function, driving the performance. Others, on the contrary, believe that the descriptions of expressed emotions can tell us about feelings, both those they were intended to produce and the deep motivations behind the emotional gestures. Finally, there are those – including ourselves – who believe that while the expressed emotions do not allow access to the feelings experienced by the actors, they nevertheless played a fundamental role in the process of transformation that took place during the performance.[4]

Reflecting on the organization of early medieval societies, Barbara H. Rosenwein established a methodology for examining emotional sharing on a micro-historical scale, one that simultaneously allows the historian to escape the grand narrative of the 'civilizing process'.[5] We have already encountered that emotional component of being together which expressed the norms of social communities: one can indeed judge a social group by the way it values emotions. But the social sharing of emotions raises many questions which the idea of 'emotional community' on its own, at least as it has been elaborated thus far, does not necessarily answer. Experiencing an emotion can trigger a chain reaction: the affected individual shares their emotional experience with others, who in turn pass on the sensation. When members of a social group experience an emotional event together, they interact in an intense manner. These interactions can revitalize or confirm their sense of belonging to the group; conversely, they can also bring about new groupings.[6] Such emotions can thus serve both to order and exclude:[7] by creating or reaffirming the identity of a group, emotion also creates rejection, marginalization, exclusion, and opposition. In the well-known Sienese fresco depicting the effects of good government, emotion served as a political language, employed by a regime to create an identity in resistance or in opposition to another regime. Thus the fear and melancholy portrayed in the fresco referred to that felt by the members of the Commune of Siena before the menace of the *Signoria* and the risk of their communal institutions being usurped for the profit of one man alone.[8] Historically, it was this game of inclusion and exclusion through shared emotion that allowed one to become a member of a group, or to affirm or confirm the same. This can be seen in the phenomenon of charivari, popular from the Middle Ages through to the modern period. This ritual of derision characterized by pot-clanging and farce was organized by young people to mark various events; its most well-known version in France was performed on the occasion of marriages deemed inappropriate due to a wide gap in age and/or widowhood (see Figure 10).[9] Even today, are not some feelings of belonging forged precisely through the exclusion of others, creating hatred as much as love and solidarity? Looking deeper, one can wonder to what extent a community wrought through emotion might exclude by the very delineation of its characteristics. In the case of medieval preachers who made their audience laugh and cry, their work of educating through emotion was designed to convey certain values. In other cases, shared emotion functioned through its public aspect. As seen already, it could even possess a performative power in demonstrative acts: the 'emotive' thus played its part in social change.[10] Going further, those rituals and events where participation produced feelings of belonging raise questions over the formation and duration of emotional communities and, more generally, the ways in which emotions were shared.

The public sharing of performative emotions

Even if the most recent psychological and historical studies of emotion have often limited themselves to individual feelings, the affective power of emotions shared on the public stage remains no less startling. The narrative sources of the late Middle Ages put the emphasis on such public outpourings; they, in turn, have reinforced the image of an emotional Middle Ages. Froissart's (d. 1404/1410) account of the ritual humiliation faced by six townsmen of Calais during the surrender of the town to the English provides an eloquent example.[11] On 3 or 4 August 1347, the city of Calais capitulated, having been starved during eleven months of siege. King Edward III (d. 1377) then asked that the keys of the city be delivered to him by the 'six most notable townsmen'. He wanted them to come barefoot, dressed only in shirts, and with ropes around their necks; he would do whatever he pleased with these men in exchange for sparing the rest of the population. When the inhabitants of the city learned of these terms:

> They all began to cry out and weep so much and so bitterly that there is no heart so hard in the world who, if they had seen or heard their wailing, would not have felt pity. And for a while they could not speak or reply; and even Sir Jean de Vienne took such pity at the news that he too wept most tenderly.

When the first townsman, Eustache de Saint-Pierre, stepped forth, 'everyone of them was ready to worship him in pity, and many men and women flung themselves at his feet, weeping bitterly'. This collective weeping only intensified when the six bourgeois took the road to leave

218

the city: 'Those present saw men, women, and children weeping, wringing their hands and crying out most bitterly. There is no heart so hard in this world who would not have pitied them.' Finally, they arrived at their destination:

> The king stood silent and looked on them very cruelly, for he hated the inhabitants of Calais for the great losses and reverses they had inflicted on him at sea in the past. [...] The king gazed on them most angrily, for his heart was so hard and so overcome by wrath that he could not speak. And when he spoke he commanded that their heads be cut off.

It was only then that Queen Philippa (d. 1369), his wife, intervened to save the six men:

> The noble queen of England, then heavily pregnant, made a great show of humility, weeping so tenderly with pity that she could not support herself. Then she threw herself to her knees before the king, her lord, and said the following: 'Ah, gentle lord, since I crossed the sea in great peril, as you well know, I have asked nothing of you. But now I humbly beseech you and ask this gift from you, that for the sake of St Mary, and for my sake, you might have mercy on these six men.'
> The king paused a while before speaking, and looked at the good lady, his wife, who was weeping most tenderly on her knees. She had softened his heart, for he did not wish to distress her in the state she was in. Thus, he said: 'Ah my lady, I can only wish that you were anywhere else but here. You beseech me so seriously that I can hardly dare refuse you. And while I do so under duress, I will give them to you. Do with them as you please.'[12]

The famous scene has been analysed in depth by Jean-Marie Moeglin, who notes that the emotional elements within it were for the most part superimposed by Froissart on top of a more basic narrative, originally written by Jean le Bel (d. c. 1370).[13] The tears that flowed so profusely are thus literary flourishes above all else. Nevertheless, the chronicler, who prided himself on investigating the events he related, fashioned a believable scenario for his contemporaries, nourished by the norms of behaviour and emotional expression of his time and readership. The course of events, above all the reversal of the fortunes of the six townsmen, is governed by an emotional staging in which tears – of distress, pity, and compassion – played the leading role. From the outset, the inhabitants of the city of Calais are united by emotions and tears, first when they learn of the terms of surrender and then in standing by the relatives of the townsmen who were to sacrifice themselves. They weep in distress, which in turn moves Jean de Vienne, the Burgundian nobleman

219

sent as captain by the king of France, to tears. They weep in admiration and pity when the six townsmen volunteer themselves. The weeping of the people of Calais is loud: it is accompanied by yells, a monument to their grave misfortune. They are ritual tears that bring a defeated city together in communion. In the second scene, the king's decision to have the townsmen beheaded expresses his anger and hatred towards the city which, according to Froissart, had inflicted defeat upon him through their coastal piracy. He seems firm in his decision, but the 'tender' tears of his wife conquer his wrath. The actors not only communicate through emotions, but are literally moved by them. Emotion is indeed at work when Edward's heart, hardened by anger, is soothed by love and he delivers the townsmen to his wife who frees them. While collective stirrings appear as reactions to an event that has united the city emotionally, individual emotions, portrayed in a vocabulary we have seen before, lie at the root of what motivated action. The public staging of socially and politically effective emotions is a fundamental ingredient in the rhetoric that renders the six townsmen heroes.[14] For their 'twist of fate' is also a rhetorical effect: the ritual humiliation of ropes being tied around their necks foreshadows their pardoning as humble penitents, even while pointing loudly and strongly to the opposite outcome.[15]

Emotion and violence: popular movements

Taken as a whole, this scene portrays an anonymous mass of people being stirred by political emotions. Performative, effective, and collective, such emotions form part of the narrative in late medieval chronicles. The 'joyful entrance' rituals of princes when they came to towns also offered highly ritualized occasions for popular emotional expression: while the sovereign expected joy, the people could also choose to remain silent for political reasons.[16] When it was a matter not of urban harmony but of discord or even violence, the testimony offered by the chroniclers, representatives of the elites, often pours scorn over those anonymous masses moved by emotion. Emotion could serve as a political language to discredit the movements of the *populares*. The example of the Ciompi – Florentine wool workers who revolted in the summer of 1378 – provides an elegant illustration of this function. Defined as 'people of the lowest condition' at the bottom rung of the social ladder – their very name denoted 'nothing other than the crude, filthy, and ragged', since they performed the most dirty and repugnant tasks – the chroniclers used a variety of unflattering labels to describe them, e.g. 'brainless', 'riff-raff' (*popolazzo*).[17] In France too, well-to-do witnesses – lords, judges, chroniclers – often described rebels as 'hooligans' (*malefactores*), 'thieves and pillagers', or, worse still, '*maistres d'artillerie vineuse et bons biberons*, men who haunted the taverns rather than the churches'.[18] Their reports depict a people drawn together and united by emotion. But that emotion was a bad, senseless, unjust, and uncontrollable emotion, an expression of malice, ignorance, and perdition: in a word, it was an emotion which served to deprive popular demands of any legitimacy. Even worse are those medieval descriptions of peasants revolting in anger as wild animals.[19] These contemptuous narratives directed at the 'lesser people' were aimed at depoliticizing or even delegitimizing their anger – which, as has been seen, was an emotion reserved for God, the king, and the nobility.

A close look at the *wapeningen* or *wapenings* – those characteristically Flemish urban revolts of the late Middle Ages that brought together the men of the guilds when their interests were threatened or contested – provides a completely different perspective on the emotions of the masses.[20] These emotions were unleashed by events; for instance, the imprisonment of a craftsman in Ypres in March 1477, or an announcement, like that of 1451 which called for corrupt patricians who had long ignored the claims of the small guilds of Ghent to be tried. The craftsmen armed themselves with clubs and rushed to their guildhall, waiting for a sign from their leader to act. It was shared emotion that gripped the people, an emotion that mixed anger, disappointment, and fear. Armed to defend their collective interests, the men of the guilds rebelled against the notables of the city and its lord. The *wapening* proper – the revolt – occurred when this gathering of furious men occupied the marketplace of the city. At this moment, the emotional impulse had already been reigned in: it took on a more temperate form, aiming to attract the attention of the powerful and draw them into negotiation. Generally, the chroniclers described a people of low stock, mad with rage and violent. In fact, these armed gatherings of 'malicious villains' functioned in a ritualistic manner, as warnings to the local powerholders. The *wapeningen* expressed the anger of the people in a well-defined form, and they were generally led by middle-class ringleaders; they constituted a ritual specific to medieval Flemish towns. As the anger spread, the leaders of the rebellion roused the people by ringing the town's bells or, failing that, those of their guilds. A common practice throughout medieval Europe, the act of ringing a town's bells could unite communities in rituals of dissatisfaction as well as those of peace and joy.[21] The ritual performance of anger and collective discontent became a political instrument that paradoxically signalled a will to negotiate to the city authorities, and thus the possibility of restoring peace and order in the town. Far from being unbridled outbursts, these revolts in fact reveal a 'choreography of the masses', an emotional expression and performative gesture aimed at producing a political effect, whose meaning and purpose was obvious to every participant.[22] One might even wonder whether those craftsmen who rushed yelling to their guildhall, clubs in hand, were *really* angry. It is much more fruitful, however, to think of their anger as finding its correct expression in this political gesture.

In surviving testimonies, the popular emotions that received public expression generally follow a dynamic narrative scheme. The form and intensity of the emotions that mobilized the people were tied to the importance of the message: emotions activated or reactivated events.[23] Emotion thus became not only a tool of communication, but a powerful driver of political action.[24] The harnessing, staging, and ritualization of collective emotions were all the more crucial because, conversely, it was frightening when they broke free from predefined scenarios. The cry could be one of unity (an acclamation of joy and enthusiasm during a royal entrance) or one of social division (a cry of hatred that called for murder; a cry for revolt and popular agitation).[25] If the exorcism of the possessed, marked by inarticulate yelling, was a noisy spectacle, the 'ordering' envisaged was aimed at silencing the demon.[26] In the same circumstances where the expression of emotion was expected, expressions that transgressed the ritual framework caused concern and might be condemned.

Seigneurial disputes, urban conflicts, and popular revolts were all occasions in which emotions were at work.[27] The pronouncement of grievances and the anger and sadness that came with them served to gain satisfaction for demands or to justify vengeance. In everyday disputes, what was most often at stake in such emotional performances was honour, which affected the social standing and key interests of those concerned. In this respect, the deployment of shared emotion differed little, if at all, from that of individual emotion. In each case, the publicity of the emotion and action was indispensable. A personal insult was all the more insulting when it was expressed publicly: it called into question the integrity and thus the reputation of the person.[28] The same rule can be applied to collective emotions, whose meaning and efficacy depended on how public they were. By taking account of the 'social logic of the text',[29] these discourses – and through them, the practices and emotions they described – can be understood as an integral part of a negotiation aimed at creating or recreating social identities and relationships.[30]

Settling conflicts through the sharing of emotion

Whether they caused an event or responded to it, and whether they did so spontaneously or according to expected norms, emotions as they were expressed and grasped played a role in both the daily and exceptional negotiations of medieval public life. This was especially the case in the procedures for resolving conflicts and redressing faults. These rituals brought forth many emotions, from the shame of wounded honour to

222

the vengeful anger that called for violence (sometimes replaced by a symbolic reparation). The poignant surrender of the Calais townsmen – barefoot, dressed in just a shirt, with ropes around their necks – was not merely a gesture of public humiliation. It also formed part of a *deditio/receptio in misericordiam*, a ritual which, when accomplished, could implicitly assure the vanquished that the conqueror would refrain from vengeance and show mercy.[31] Emotion was expected and necessary within this: displayed publicly through appropriate gestures and words, it played a key role in the symbolic reparation. The shame inflicted redressed the scandalous offence. By subtly mixing religious (sin/redemption) and civil (fault or crime/punishment) dimensions, the ritual of public penance was transposed into lay justice to become the *amende honorable*, a ritual that restored damaged honour without recourse, in the Middle Ages at least, to physical punishment.[32]

In the thirteenth century, public penance – punishment though shame – was the sentence for those who had committed serious and public crimes. But it can also be found in the context of ecclesiastical mediation aimed at ending enmity and 'deadly hatred'. Asking for forgiveness, making a penitential procession, founding masses: there were various ways to appease the resentment of the victim's family. Religious and secular rituals thus functioned in a similar manner; even their remits became confused whenever the offence was deemed to have occurred not only against an individual, but against society, against the king, and thus against God. The ritual of penance became, by stages, the model for the lay ritual of reconciliation and peace.[33] Public emotion possessed a performative value at every level, both immediate and distant, that the offence impacted.

A relatively early description of public penance clearly explains the emotional interaction between the actors and witnesses, all of whom were involved in bringing the ritual transformation to fruition:

> For those whose sins are public, their own atonement will not suffice: the help of the Church is required. So let the sinner lie on the ground as if he were dead, let him proclaim in public that he is dead, let him show the fruits of his penance in public, so that the crowd may weep for him, and show their grief for the dead man [...] He who has offended many by his sins ought to atone for them publicly. Thus, the Christian community previously scandalized by his sins will yield in mercy upon seeing his conversion, and pray for the one over whom it wept when he was dead. Through this, God – He who first had mercy – will be inclined to forgive him.[34]

Drawn from *De vera et falsa poenitentia* – a pseudo-Augustinian treatise composed in the eleventh century and cited by Gratian's

Decretum and Peter Lombard's *Sentences* in the mid-twelfth – this extract shows that both social interaction and symbolic transformation were emotional in nature and dependent on the precise meaning of the emotions expressed. The penitent had first to become 'dead from shame' and show the 'fruits of his penance' – i.e. his tears, which indicated his genuine regret – in order to soften the hearts of the public, who would then suffer with him and weep over his fault. Next, he had to publicly atone in order to gain the prayers of the Christian community, who asked for God's forgiveness. If this ritual was the prototype for what was described at Calais, one can truly appreciate the ritual – rather than solely rhetorical – necessity of the people's tears at the sight of the townsmen roped at the neck.

The aforementioned flagellant processions, which first took place in Perugia in 1260 and then spread in several waves, first in Italy and then across many regions of the medieval West, can thus be seen as very specific extensions of this ritual of public penance. With their chests bare and their heads often hooded to avoid recognition, these men put the penitential act of self-flagellation at the heart of a cathartic display. It was conceived as a way of imitating the suffering Christ, and undertaken to beg divine mercy for both their sins and those of a city in need of peace. From this perspective, it is noteworthy that the Italian cities which did not experience flagellant movements in 1260 were those engaged in war, like Siena, or preparing for it, like some of the Guelph towns: for them, the time was not right for a public ritual of pacification.[35] The public nature of these feats made lay self-flagellation a political manifesto; whether the objective was to reconcile warring factions or to appease divine wrath, as it was during the plague of 1348–9, one form of suffering was always inflicted to ward off another. The once-private monastic practice of penitential discipline on which the lay flagellants drew became doubly visible; it not only entered the lay world, but was staged on city streets. Through this practice of self-abasement and bodily suffering, which contained an aspect of solidarity, the penitents sought both to prove their love for the community and redeem their sins in the process.[36]

A similar power can be witnessed in practices of peacemaking.[37] Peace brought with it a joy that united and reconciled, a joy that was no less compulsory and codified than the shame that followed humiliation. This stereotype can be applied to the behaviour of the actors as much as the narratives of the chroniclers; in both, we witness what Marcel Mauss would call an obligatory expression of feeling and what Gert Althoff has termed a codified, constraining language.[38] At the announcement of peace, bonfires were lit, bells were sounded, *Te Deum laudamus* was sung, and great feasts were organized, as seen in Paris on 12 July 1419, when news arrived of the peace signed a day earlier at Pouilly-le-Fort.[39] For poets and writers, joy and peace were so tightly linked as to be inseparable. For instance, in 1413, when describing the peace of Pontoise which brought the Cabochian revolt to an end, Christine de Pizan spoke of 'joy and peace' and 'joyous peace'.[40] Such peace was shared socially: it belonged as much to the princes who signed it as to the people who attended the festivities, even if some chroniclers wanted to distinguish between the three estates' expressions of joy in their narratives. Gladness responded to the announcement of peace: joy flowed through capillary motion from the good prince to his subjects. If one rejoiced *in* peace, one wept *for* peace. By virtue of their rare and occasional nature, tears were seen as more sincere than words. In negotiations, they took on precise meaning: they were the language of mediation. Just like their warrior forebears, princes easily succumbed to tears when they came to terms; their weeping acted both as a form of penance for past violence and as the requisite sign that communion had been restored. Holding hands and kissing, the two traditional gestures of affection witnessed in peacemaking rituals, demonstrated their forgiveness and sealed the friendship of the reconciled parties. Banquets likewise helped to cement the alliance. There, the parties could share convivial emotions as well as food. Drinking and eating together allowed them to feel united as companions: thus, one drank *'par bon amour'*.[41] Emotions thus participated in the newly restored social bond as much as they had in the acts that led up to it.

Emotions and social identities

Emotion is by nature ambiguous. As discussed earlier, the sharing of emotions might create order as much as exclude from it, unite as much as divide, and signal the presence of disorder as much as take account of it. More often than not, it does both simultaneously. In medieval societies, war and peace, 'bloodtaking and peacemaking',[42] seem to have been the twin faces of human coexistence; they were ceaselessly expressed by and with great emotion in relations between social groups just as between rival families and clans.

When emotions expressed communities

Festivals, weddings, hunts, business gatherings, and liturgical processions are just some of the essential moments that generate and regenerate shared beliefs and emotions. These in turn create or reinforce collective identities. Emotional events unite the people who participate in them, setting off processes of emotional communion and identity fusion.[43] The social sharing of emotions fulfils precisely this function of bringing collective identity to life.[44]

Affection within the family unit – between spouses, between parents and their children, between brothers and sisters – but also within wider circles of familiars, is a well-evidenced reality both today and throughout history: it was present at every level of medieval society.[45] The moment of non-violent death is, from this perspective, a particularly important rite of passage: it provides the occasion for an emotional union of the families and communities close to the deceased. Just as no one lives alone, no one dies alone. Medieval literature has a predilection for death scenes, and Cluniac customaries explicitly prescribed that a monk must die surrounded by his community.[46] In the Middle Ages, a 'good death' was defined by a period of calm, long enough for final arrangements and tender exchanges to be made. Many descriptions of the deaths of the great lay and ecclesiastical lords portray these last moments, which might even last for weeks.[47] The death of William Marshal provides an excellent example. 'The greatest knight in the world' took as much time as he needed to dispose of his responsibilities and possessions, to ensure the salvation of his soul, to organize his funeral, and to converse with his sons, daughters, and the poor; with his loved ones, he shared intense moments of affection.[48] Guarded day and night by his son, his friends, and his knights, who all shared the same love and the same pain, William was never alone during the long weeks of his agony. Reading his *History*, it seems that the responsibility to surround the dying man fell above all on the count's male *familia*, united by the emotion, even if his wife and his daughters appear on occasion, and clerics, never absent, intervened when necessary. In any case, crying and funeral lamentations, seen throughout the Middle Ages, can hardly be considered exclusively female gestures in the aristocratic world of the twelfth and thirteenth centuries. From songs of Homer through to the *Chanson de Roland* and indeed the *History of William Marshal*, the epic tradition, well known in aristocratic circles, assigned the most expressive gestures of mourning to male warriors.[49] Such ritualistic expressions of grief strengthened the bonds between those men on whom feudal society relied for order and authority.[50] Sons, retainers, servants, and knights all wept at the imminent departure of the aged nobleman:

> *E quant il out itels moz diz,/ Lors plora tendrement sis fiz,/ E tuit li chevalier qu'i érent/ Dolerosement en plorérent,/ E li valet et li servant/ Plorérent et firent duel grant ;/ E trestuit cil de la maison,/ Firent duel, et ce fu reison.*

> After he had spoken these words,/ his son wept pitifully,/ all the knights present/ wept tears of sorrow,/ the young retainers and servants/ cried and vented their great grief,/ and all in the household/ lamented, as was right.

It was in fact to lessen his suffering, that anguish which seized the dying man by the throat, that his relatives remained near him. But the text shows how they felt even more pain than the dying:

Idonques sis fils se leva/ A cui trop durement greva/ La grant angoisse e la dolor/ Qu'il vit souffrir a son seignor,/ E quant il s'ent fu issi fors/ Les chevaliers appela lors ;/ Si lor dist : Vez la grant dolor/ Qui trop engreige a mon seignor,/ Estre en devons por vérité/ Plus près que nos n'avons esté.

And then the son rose to his feet,/ deeply pained by the sight/ of the great torment and pain/ suffered by his lord./ And, once he had gone out of the room,/ he summoned the knights/ and said to them: 'You see the great pain/ by which my lord is so afflicted,/ In the very truth, we ought to be closer/ to him than we have been hitherto.'[51]

Finally, when he felt his time had come, William asked his family and his court to surround him:

Li filz et la contesse vindrent/ Et tuit li chevalier suvindrent/ A cui ainz ainz, a cel afeire/ Qui durement lor pot desplére/ E il lor dist a toz itant :/ Je me muir ; a Deu vos commant./ Ne me leist mès a vos attendre/ Ne me puis de la mort défendre./ Li filz s'adresse ; si s'assist/ La ou Johans d'Erlée sist ;/ En ses braz son père rechut ;/ Tendrement plora, comme il dut,/ Simplement et o basse voiz./ L'en li apporta une croiz,/ Devant lui, et il l'aora.

The son, the countess,/ and all the knights appeared,/ vying with one another to be first on a scene/ which sorely distressed them./ He spoke these words to all present:/ 'I am dying and commend you all to God./ I am no longer able to think of your needs,/ for I cannot fight against death.'/ The son came up, sat/ where John of Earley was sitting,/ and took his father in his arms./ He wept tears of pity, as was natural,/ quietly and openly./ The Marshal was brought a cross,/ to which he gave his adoration.[52]

The description of the 'good death' of William Marshal has a tempo commensurate with the gravity of the moment. Tender and orderly, the scene is full of emotion. Aware that they were experiencing a unique event, everyone duly accomplished what was required of them: the count bade farewell, while his son 'wept tears of pity, as was natural'. The long-expected death of the elderly lord, who was able to prepare himself for this moment, was a demonstration of his status and honour. Here too, we can sense an obligatory expression of feelings, rendered purposeful precisely through its ritual qualities. One can also sense a problem characteristic of the methodological difficulties of the history of emotions, one which Jeroen Deploige has called the problem of '*représentation au carré*' ('representation squared'): not only did the world of William

227

Marshal have its own codes of emotional behaviour; the author of his *History* also chose themes, values, and narrative strategies appropriate to his genre, which dictated how the emotions were represented.[53] To better understand all of the motifs within the *History*'s portrayal, it is interesting to compare William's death to that of a saint or a great abbot dying among his monastic family. In those scenes, likewise standardized by their Christian outlook, we can see how death was meant to unfold and which emotions were invited to play a role in the process. In both types of portrayal, there is no emotional excess to be seen. Medieval iconography highlights the same sombre gestures of affection. Those involved are depicted with their heads lowered and held in their hands, their bodies often hunched; all bear witness to a pensive and sad atmosphere.[54]

Iconographic evidence also provides the best access to the fault lines that existed between the mourners. The exceptional miniatures of the *Sacramentary* of Bishop Warmundus of Ivrea (Northern Italy, eleventh century) provide a ten-stage illustration of the actions that surrounded someone's death.[55] These images underline the contrast between the lively gestures of the woman present (most likely the wife or mother of the deceased layman, albeit she could also be a professional mourner), which seem to reflect intense suffering, and the sober gestures of the men, especially the clergy who provide the last rites for the subject both during and after death. It is a contrast that reflects the same tension between grief and pacification that can also be detected in the long death scene of the *History of William Marshal*. The mourning scenes of the lay world found in medieval documents thus contrast not two, but three groups of participants – clerics, laymen, and women – to whom we can assign three different conceptions of mourning and three models of behaviour and emotional expression. The theoretical position and attitudes of the Church are well-known and well-studied. Despite legislative efforts in late antiquity and the early Middle Ages, the Christian and clerical conception of death – which defined it as a solemn moment, critical to the soul's salvation – was never able to erase or even limit post-mortem expressions of the grief by relatives; at best, the Church sought to promote acceptance and consolation.[56] Among the laity, on the other hand, the mourning gestures of the inconsolable woman of the Ivrea *Sacramentary* belong to a totally different emotional register from those of the familiars surrounding William Marshal: the former are defined by excess, the latter by moderation. The female figure of the liturgical codex, who reveals her pain by unknotting and plucking her hair, alludes to images of pagan mourning rituals: these were critiqued by the Church since its inception not only because they failed to show faith in the Resurrection but also on the pretext that women who lost control of their actions made an erotic spectacle of themselves.[57] In gender terms, an opposition seems apparent: an excessive, feminine emotion, one of heart-break, which offered an image of death that sheared the bonds between the living; and a well-tamed, uniting male emotion which remained contained among one's nearest and dearest, whose community or *familia* was strengthened by the shared emotional experience. If these two models were clearly codified, allowing medieval people to give meaning to suf-fering and to soothe it by externalizing it,[58] such a 'gendered' divide in the expression of grief – dignified/undignified, controlled/excessive – was far from fixed during the Middle Ages. While in some regions throughout the period female mourners were hired to ritually perform the most intense gestures of grief, elsewhere men and women participated together in these rituals.

In Orvieto, in 1295, Signore Muntanari groaned loudly in front of his house over the passing of his son Pietro; he did so in the company of at least sixteen other noble and notable townsmen. They wept and wailed in a loud voice, launching into a *corrotto*, a song of mourning in memory of Pietro. A few years earlier, in 1288, after the death of young Lotto Morichelli, at least 129 men went out into the streets to take part in mourning him. Among them were distinguished noblemen, city officials, even ex-ambassadors of the pontifical court, as well as craftsmen, a tavern-keeper, a butcher, and Lotto's nephew, a young knight. Removing their hats, several of them not only wept and groaned loudly, but pulled out their hair or tore off their beards to demonstrate their pain.[59] Were these tears so different from those of the sons and loved ones of William Marshal? Were they more like those of the wildly gesturing woman in the *Sacramentary* of Warmundus of Ivrea? The paintings adorning the tomb of the Castilian knight Sancho Saiz de Carrillo (d. *c.* 1300), which portray the mourning rituals of a group of men and a group of women, as well as that of a child, suggest that members of both sexes could behave almost identically during the ritual, regardless of their age (see Figures 11 and 12). The gestures established here as exemplary behaviour were, in Orvieto and other Italian cities, at the same time condemned and monitored by agents of the Commune specially charged with denouncing the guilty. Heartbreaking sorrow and communal action were far from opposites in Italy or Spain at the end of the thirteenth century: one group's emotional sharing might be perceived by others as an emo-tional gathering liable to provoke public disorder.

It might seem surprising that the condemnation in Orvieto did not come from the Church, but from the lay authorities of the city, and even more so that the overwhelming majority of those condemned were men (218 out of 220), even though the laws sought to restrict such passionate displays on account of their 'femininity'.[60] Judging by the facts, the type of mourning that was condemned can hardly be identified with feminine grief. Rather, the behaviour seems closer to that which had been openly accepted at seigneurial courts, whether Italian or English. If there was condemnation and prosecution of ritual mourning in Italian cities, it was because sensibilities were changing at the end of the thirteenth century. As seen earlier, emotional ostentation and coming together in affection remained noble and chivalrous virtues.[61] Such behaviours were characteristic of feudal society: they had been experienced so many times during the conflicts of clans and factions that had divided Italy in the communal era of the twelfth century – a time when hatred and love, hostility and friendship were but two facets of the same relationship, albeit that hatred seemed more determining and inescapable, perhaps even more believable and more frequent.[62] The strident emotional expressionism of the funerals described in the documentary evidence draw the eye back to noble emotional culture, to the Charlemagne who wept and pulled out his white beard in the *Chanson de Roland*, and to the tears shared by the knights of William Marshal. It was this aristocratic culture that was condemned by the new popular regime in Orvieto at the end of the thirteenth century. The legislators – who represented a cross-section of social classes in which knights and nobles mingled with the leaders of the *popolo* who had recently come to power – no longer aspired to adopt aristocratic manners and values. The mix of this new urban elite is well represented by the sample of men gathered at the funeral of the young Lotto Morichelli. They wanted to build social order on new foundations, more inclusive and more solid, that would be based on other values and driving forces. The new sumptuary laws provide a good representation of these foundations. They aimed to regulate both excessive sorrow and public anger; also targeted were blasphemy, prostitution, and even displays of wealth during weddings and funerals. In an age where cities preferred to promote the judicial settlement of conflicts, emotion as a social privilege of the noble and chivalric classes seems to have had its day.

If this should not necessarily be seen as evidence of a 'civilizing process', the period does seem to have favoured what was, in contemporary eyes, a channelling of emotion with a view to making it acceptable. The presence of such an evolution within an increasingly emancipated lay world can be better understood in light of late medieval evaluations of emotion and passion within the Church, discussed in the previous chapter. Elsewhere in Europe, outside of the Italian city-states, the evolution was certainly less clear. Royal courts hardly obeyed the same social imperatives, even if, there too, the legal settlement of conflicts was also gaining ground. Surprisingly, the increasing use of courts did not mean that the structures of enmity and hatred disappeared, but rather that their expression was transformed: due to the very length of trials, court action in fact helped to perpetuate them.[63] The expression of emotion, for so long the privilege of an elite, seems to have become accessible to all and accentuated, even if it remained just as strictly codified. The restriction of loud and ostentatious emotional expressions indeed also took place within the Church, as seen with the flagellants and the weeping of the mystics. The danger – or at least the ambiguity – of collective emotional expressions was recognized by all: if they could bring people together and express communities, by the same token they could stigmatize, exclude, and foment hatred.

Excluding through emotion: fomenting hatred

While conflict resolution had evolved greatly in urban societies by the late Middle Ages, the age-old pairing of *inimicitia* and *amicitia* could still be found in martial circles. Discord and hatred did not need to disappear for later medieval societies to function smoothly. On the contrary, they formed part of the social structure and can even be seen as something of an institution in societies founded on honour.[64] Hatred announced one's social status: every self-respecting man had to have one or two enemies. In Marseille, at the end of the fourteenth century, it was common for both men and women from all rungs of the social ladder to foster and display hatred. Hence, the handling of hatred in a peace-loving society reveals as much about social negotiations as social change. In vernacular communication, love, friendship, and hatred were like clothes: not only were they on full display, they could also be changed easily.[65] For instance, two people or two families could evoke or publicize their hatred when seeking to force a compromise. In negotiating peace, hatred could be used to obtain greater concessions. When reconciliation was desired, a 'hardened' or 'mortal' anger could be downplayed and discursively redefined as a 'hot anger', a fleeting passion that motivated violent action. An emotional motivation for a crime could thus be presented as a mitigating circumstance before the courts. All of this seems to suggest that while the increasingly judicial approach to conflict resolution was a sign of the evolution of social structures, it did not eliminate this emotional horse-trading, but simply gave it a different content. Trials allowed the Marseillais who made their hatred public to avail themselves of it before the courts; giving voice to hatred helped them to gain emotional, rather than material, satisfaction.[66] Thus, in 1413, when Matieu Vital said to a court official that '*Vous manez mala voluntat et sapias que yeu vos ay por ennemie mortal*' ('You show malevolence, know that I have made you my mortal enemy'), he knew that he would have to pay a fine. Nevertheless, by publicizing his hatred, he not only cautioned the official, but let everyone at the doors of the Notre-Dame-des-Accoules church at the time of his declaration know that he had done so.[67] Emotional vocabulary (love/

hate, friendship/enmity, *benevolentia/malevolentia*) made it possible to publicly draw out the structures and networks of solidarity as well as the social divisions that motivated accusations and prosecutions. What took place in the courts was emotionally trying: more often than not, the parties found themselves humiliated by both the accusation and the testimony. The shoemaker Antoni d'Ays, whose reputation was previously spotless, found himself accused of being a pimp, and his concubine Dousa of being a prostitute; his accuser was a neighbour, the respectable Guilhem de Podio, also a shoemaker and a married man. Antoni was ready to spend an enormous sum and a considerable amount of time on clearing his name of this bad *fama*.[68] Far from representing a rationalization of ties, the legal settlement of conflicts suggests that the centre of gravity within social relationships had shifted towards the emotional sphere, and towards public emotional satisfaction; in the past, it had been possible to put a price on crime and punishment and thus render them more material.

This type of structural hatred, an organic part of the networks of friendship and solidarity within societies founded on honour, was not the only kind encouraged and regulated within what has been described as the 'persecuting society' of post-Gregorian Western Christendom.[69] In the course of defining its identity, the Gregorian Church propounded the ideal of an inclusive Christian love in order to build cohesion among the faithful. But the same affirmation engendered exclusion, violence, and hatred of others. Heretics, Jews, and Muslims became the immediate enemies of the community of the faithful and paid the price for the Church's awareness of this new power.

While Christian anti-Judaism stemmed from the religion's earliest days – the Jews were held responsible for the murder of Christ – Christians and Jews coexisted rather peacefully for the first few centuries. Nevertheless, the Church Fathers left behind an ambiguous discussion of the place of Jews within Christian society, by turns evoking notions of protection, service, conversion, and pollution. This explosive legacy created a lasting difficulty for ecclesiastical and lay powers when it came to establishing a coherent Christian policy towards them; they found themselves torn between economic and political motivations, on the one hand, and ideological motivations, on the other.[70] During the early Middle Ages, Jewish communities – which posed no threat and whose members practised professions that were useful but prohibited for Christians – lived in relative security throughout most of the West (with the well-known exception of Visigothic Spain).

The hatred of the Jews that was stirred up from the end of the eleventh century onwards was the result of an ongoing 'cultural revolution'.[71] As a consequence of both the message of the Gregorian reform and the anti-Jewish polemics of the Church militant, latent hostility towards the Jews was thrust into broad daylight, allowing for endless suspicion and endemic eruptions of violence. It was nourished by economic as well as religious rationales. During the spectacular growth of Western cities in the eleventh and twelfth centuries, Jews occupied economically enviable positions as entrepreneurs, merchants, doctors, scholars and, above all, as 'usurers', i.e. pawnbrokers. They represented an economically successful social group, at a time when others found themselves exposed to a new poverty, and when, most significantly, the Church promoted voluntary poverty and developed a militant moral discourse concerning money 'that multiplied' in an 'unnatural' manner.[72] On the religious front, the preaching of the crusade translated a Gregorian outlook that demanded the unity of society and Church into concrete action: all of a sudden, the Jews no longer appeared as slightly unusual neighbours but as non-Christians and outsiders above all else. In the eyes of the Christian warrior who took up arms through personal fervour to defend his faith in Christ, the Other could be found even before reaching the Holy Land in the person of the Western Jew, as Guibert of Nogent (d. 1125) made clear in his description of the events which took place in Rouen at the start of the First Crusade.[73] The Jews found themselves accused of having crucified the body in which God took flesh, a body that Christians not only worshipped with ever greater devotion from the eleventh century onward, but which they collectively formed part of as the body of the Church.[74] The authorities certainly sought to contain the violence; on their way to the Holy Land, the crusaders were more likely to lash out at the Jews if they were poorly organized or starving. However, the testimony of the Hebrew chronicles shows that massacres and forced conversions became part of the Christian agenda during the First Crusade. The extreme violence of these pogroms is suggested by the fact that they were sometimes followed by acts of self-sacrifice: survivors preferred to kill their children and set themselves on fire, as in the case of Rachel and Isaac ben David in Mainz, rather than give themselves up to the Christians. Such actions were poorly received, however: if the Jews were capable of killing their own children, would they not be even more likely to slaughter the children of Christians?[75] In this way, anti-Jewish hatred rapidly took shape around stereotyped accusations – the ritual murder of Christian children, the desecration of the host, the poisoning of wells at the time of the Great Plague – and Jews became victims of aggression that would grow ever more frequent and serious. But above all else, on occasions where divine wrath was perceived, they represented the sinfulness that unleashed it. The regular outbursts of popular violence could go as far as anti-Jewish riots and massacres, such as those which followed in the wake of the flagellant processions across

Europe (a fact not without significance), or which regularly accompanied Holy Week in the Iberian peninsula. All, however, represented ritual but unforeseeable responses to accusations: the causes behind them were always circumstantial.

Hatred of the Jews was a collective emotion that took violent forms and spread throughout the entirety of Western Christendom; it is a prime example of a contagious emotion. Historians often explain it in political, religious, and social terms. An outlet for the frustrations of a late medieval community of the faithful faced with hard times, the hatred of this 'other' certainly allowed for bonds of identity to be re-established within a Christian society deeply affected by socio-economic changes that had increased social inequalities.[76]

It might nevertheless seem surprising that this hatred has hitherto rarely been considered as an emotion, the corollary of which would be the fear felt by the Jews themselves.[77] Yet the hatred of the Jews arose as an emotional event on specific occasions, such as the ritual violence that occurred during Holy Week in the kingdom of Aragon. To what extent did collective emotion transcend the ritual framework? Or was the latter its result? What was the relationship between a ritual, a tool for the maintenance of order, and the emotional violence that was its exact opposite? The study of the various elements of the celebration of Holy Week allows for a precise examination of the source of violence and how this hatred was fashioned.[78] Indeed, the liturgical plays used during the Easter celebrations in Girona and Palma in Majorca re-enacted the suffering of Jesus and his followers as well as the visitation of the tomb, a scene that emphasized the incredulity of the Jews: the latter was a well-worn theme illustrating the theological confrontation between the two communities. In the *Planctus*, a poetic lament expressed the feelings of those present during the crucifixion, those of the Son in his death throes, as well as those of the Virgin and the other witnesses with her. Its vernacular lyrics described acts that, at every stage, evoked not only sorrow but a whole range of emotions: they had the potential to provoke an emotional reaction among the audience, be it one of sorrow or anger, towards those responsible for the crucifixion. In these liturgical plays, the use of the Catalan language during those scenes that played most heavily on the emotions allowed the public to become more fully involved in the events. The faithful would have heard about the same events in the Holy Week sermons, which might in turn arouse the same emotions. Simultaneously, the obligation to receive communion at Easter provided the faithful with a third reminder of Christ's sacrifice.

All this suggests that shared outrage created an emotional communion and eased the way towards violent action, always described as impulsive. And yet this violent action appears just as ritualized as what preceded it, even if its forms remained unspoken and the level of violence could vary. The acts perpetrated against the Jews were always the same: stonings (of goods, but also of persons) were the most common. As far as the authorities were concerned, such gestures could not exceed what was permitted by the ritual framework.[79] When this was breached, as happened in Girona in 1293 when the Christians 'broke into the houses of the Jews, set them on fire, caused destruction, and [...] injured other Jews',[80] the king's reaction was immediate. Forty years later, when, as in 1293, the Jewish Passover and the Christian Easter fell in the same week, the violence was much worse; the king intervened, both to condemn what had happened and impose preventative sanctions and to warn the Jews. He did not, however, seek to suppress the violence, but to restrain it within the usual limits tacitly foreseen by Christian ritual. On a broader level, whether anti-Jewish violence was of the usual variety or more catastrophic, it acted, paradoxically, as one of the mechanisms 'by which the Christian majority laid out the terms of coexistence and made it possible'; such actions would thus have been 'intended as much to strengthen the social order of this multi-faith community as to destroy it'.[81] As members of an urban religious minority, Jews became props in a ritual performance that served as a reminder of their otherness and promoted the social bond between Christians, whom it brought together in emotional communion. The Jews found themselves by turns protected, exploited, and rejected by kings, and attacked by Church-promoted polemics that spread through preaching. They entered the later medieval Christian imagination by way of the popular stories and accusations that circulated about them, which assigned them very specific roles and left them less and less room to defend themselves. All the while, they remained neighbours in the flesh, just as they had always been.

The 'pastoral of emotions'

Hatred, fear, and cruelty on the one side, love on the other: such were the human passions that animated the masses. They are the same passions that Lucien Febvre identified as the principal subjects for the history of the emotions long before this historiographical field had even been named.[82] More than thirty years later, Jean Delumeau wrote a series of works proposing the idea of a 'pastoral of fear' (pastorale de la peur), a Church-led 'culpabilization' of the West that took place between the Fourth Lateran Council (1215) and the modern era.[83] For him, the history of the institutional Church between the thirteenth and eighteenth centuries was defined by fearful rhetoric, the imposition of guilt on the faithful, and, last but not least, a constructed sense of security that was only accessible under the protective mantle of the Virgin. The Church sought to make its flock fear hell and be frightened and ashamed of sin by way of a strategy that would, in the long run, allow it to 'reassure and protect' the faithful within its bosom. Moralizing humanity by shaping its imagination and inner life, it thus contributed to the 'civilizing process' within the West.

Today there are serious reservations over this notion of a behavioural civilizing process (led by Catholicism in this instance), as well as the idea of a 'pastoral of fear'. Nevertheless, it can hardly be ignored that, towards the end of the Middle Ages, the Church became particularly concerned with the emotional education of the faithful as part of its plan to re-evangelize a Western society that had fallen prey to heresies. As Carla Casagrande has suggested, however, this activity might be better termed a 'pastoral of emotions',[84] an idea that finds ample support in sermons, *exempla*, confession and preaching manuals, vernacular devotional literature, and iconography. Since the apostolic age, the emotions had in fact always been the Church's best teaching materials and they went on to play several roles in pastoral practice. The importance of sincere emotion – of true religious feeling – within practices of individual prayer had long been emphasized; this was still the case at the end of the Middle Ages, when attention turned to the prayers of 'ordinary people'.[85] The development of this 'pastoral of emotions' gathered pace from the twelfth century onward, a time when the Church stepped up its fight against heresy and its efforts to convert the West from within. A part of spiritual discourse by virtue of its moral connotations, it took root in both nascent scholastic psychology and sacramental theology. This pastoral strategy took in the full range of emotions: those to be avoided at all costs, those to be promoted, and finally – the largest category – those whose origins and motivations had first to be examined. Building on developments within sacramental theology, and, more precisely, its detailed descriptions of how the sacrament of penance operated, the priest tried first to stir up and then guide the penitent's emotions so that they would ease the remission of sins and make the sacrament 'effective'.[86] Finally, the emergence of a vernacular approach to preaching at the beginning of the thirteenth century meant that emotional conversion and pedagogy became matters of significant importance. The art of educating through the emotions became critical: if it made its mark in academic treatments of the theory of pastoral care, it became no less of a concern for the ordinary priest in his daily practice of *cura animarum*. Aimed at moralizing the life of the faithful, preaching could make use of emotions far removed from fear and shame as means of persuasion. Joy and laughter were not uncommon, albeit that this shared laughter was often derisive, in turn provoking shame. Here, the emotions took on a multifaceted role that formed a counterpart to the public sharing of emotion for political purposes. In addition, the 'pastoral of emotions' promoted a culture within the late medieval Church that knew no social distinctions: it targeted Western society from top to bottom, aiming to bind all together in a virtuous march towards salvation.

The scholastic theory of emotional education

From their patristic beginnings, the rules of Christian preaching followed those of ancient rhetoric. It was thus expected that, in order to teach and transmit doctrines (*docere*) most effectively, the preacher's words had also to move his audience (*movere*).[87] This idea was very common within *artes praedicandi* manuals, even if the role their authors gave to emotional pedagogy was more variable. For those who viewed rhetoric as an instrument of morality, politics, or theology, the capacity of their speeches to provoke emotions (*movere affectum*) became crucial; whereas those who regarded rhetoric as an instrument of logic and, ultimately, of the search for truth, considered it inferior to rational persuasion.[88] While the speaker's ability to move his audience would thus be valued in religious rhetoric, two opposing traditions came to govern the use of emotions in preaching. Augustine defined the aims of preaching in his *De doctrina christiana*: to teach, to please, and to sway the souls of the listeners (*docere, delectare, flectere*). For him, the last objective took priority when it came to sparking the emotional conversion of the public. In his *City of God*, Augustine also defined the passions as instruments essential to man's hopes of salvation. Like Christ, the highest possible model for the proper use of emotions, the preacher himself had to feel – or at least display – the emotions that he sought to provoke in his audience.[89] In keeping with the principle of *docere verbo et exemplo*, he had to use his own emotions and present himself as an example in order to affect the emotions of others. Gregory the Great, on the other hand, drew more from the age-old Stoic mistrust of the emotions: he recommended a heightened attention to the emotional state of the audience, to how the passions were playing out among them, as well as a very moderate use of emotions within the sermon itself. As seen earlier, the monastic tradition that inspired him viewed emotions as disturbances of the soul; some were even vices. The preacher had to use emotions discerningly so that they served the aim of purifying his audience.[90] From the late twelfth century, these two attitudes were often interwoven within the new tools of practice and learning that defined how emotions should be used within evangelizing rhetoric. From preaching manuals to collections of *exempla*, there were now both models and precise directions for priests and mendicant brothers.

Thomas of Chobham (d. 1233/36) – an English cleric trained by Peter the Chanter in Paris, who became a master of theology there in the 1220s after a career in England – defined what made a good sermon in his *Summa de arte praedicandi*: it had to combine the love and the fear of God. Thus, 'on the one hand, it should always arouse the fear of God among its audience, on account of infernal damnation; and on the other, it should always invite them to the love of God, on account of the glorious reward'.[91] Thomas devoted several pages to this essential aim of preaching, attempting to define which remarks – i.e. speaking of merciful acts or of the fires of the hell – worked best to incite the love and fear that led to salvation.[92] A little later, the Dominican Humbert of Romans (d. 1277) produced a collection of *exempla* devoted to the 'gift of fear', a text that would become very influential among preachers.[93] The aim of preaching was to arouse contrasting emotions simultaneously, e.g. the hatred of sin and the love of virtue; the fear of divine justice and the hope of mercy.[94] The preacher also had to avoid emotions that endangered salvation, particularly those associated with worldly desires. Thomas of Chobham, like most of his contemporaries, sought a balance between two contrasting attitudes towards the emotions: on the one hand, the imperative of arousing them, and on the other, that of repressing and moderating them, depending on whether they were deemed conducive or harmful to salvation. At the same time, he sought a happy medium between the *inflammatio affectus* and the *illuminatio intellectus*.

Some authors recommended the use of *sermo affectuosus* – speech capable of 'ravishing the soul of the listener to lead him, without his perceiving it, to love the good and flee the bad'.[95] They were suspicious of preaching that was too intellectual and refined: the sort that asked useless questions, the sort that would only 'stimulate intellectual curiosity rather than raise the affections',[96] the sort that would sooner make one fall asleep than provoke grief and life conversion. Bonaventure's *Legenda maior* exalts the emotional preaching of Francis of Assisi, associating heartfelt speech with the breath of the Holy Spirit:

> For his word was like burning fire penetrating the innermost depths of the heart; and it filled the minds of all with admiration, since it made no pretence at the elegance of human composition but exuded the perfume of divine revelation.[97]

In the hands of Bonaventure – and elsewhere in the *vitae* of Francis – true preaching was most definitely emotional: it was barely related to any technique but rather derived from divine inspiration. According to an anecdote reported by Bonaventure, Francis, preaching before the

Pope, had 'memorized a sermon which he had carefully composed'. Standing before the multitude who had come to hear him, however, he forgot the words:

> This he admitted to them in true humility and directed himself to invoke the grace of the Holy Spirit. Suddenly he began to overflow with such effective eloquence and to move the minds of those high-ranking men to compunction with such force and power that it was clearly evident it was not he, but the *Spirit* of the Lord who *was speaking* (Acts 6: 10).[98]

This emotive remit of preaching was likewise supported by a great line of preachers, most of them Franciscans. In the writings of the English Franciscan Roger Bacon (d. 1294) and in a treatise attributed to William of Auvergne,[99] it is stated that the true aim of preaching is to sway the soul by provoking those emotions that would make the audience change their lives. This *sermo affectuosus* had to make use of poetic techniques and arguments capable of rousing affections and tears, as well as gestures and a rhythm appropriate to the content of sermon.[100] Thus, emotional effectiveness was not only a matter of technique, but also of spontaneity: together, they were capable of moving the soul towards salutary sentiments. For many of his contemporaries, the good preacher was embodied by another Franciscan, Berthold of Regensburg (d. 1272), at least to judge from the testimony of Roger Bacon and Salimbene di Adam (d. 1290). According to Roger Bacon, the preaching of Berthold alone was more effective than all the brothers of the two mendicant orders put together.[101] Speaking in the vernacular, Berthold called the laity to the virtue of charity as follows:

> The eighth virtue is charity [...] On the Day of Judgement, Our Lord will ask what happened to our charity. Let those who have nothing to give with the hand, give with the heart, with their good will. Thus says St John: 'Feed the hungry.' And if you don't give whenever you can help, you have committed a crime against the less fortunate. Shame on you, greedy people! How many people have you committed crimes against? They die by your fault because you'd rather let the wheat rot than sell it honestly![102]

Through such images, as lively as they are brutal, images which play on several emotions at once and which have been constructed to place vices and virtues in diametric opposition, the sermon makes its point with ease. Failing to give to the poor is tantamount to letting them die of hunger, and similar to leaving nutritious wheat to rot. It is thus not only a breach of the virtue of charity, but a vicious act, a proof of greed. In this rhetoric, sharpening the sense of guilt ('they die by *your* fault') and sharpening the sense of shame (of having done wrong by failing to do good) go hand-in-hand. On the rise throughout the thirteenth century, emotional rhetoric was not solely a Franciscan preserve, however. If Francis of Assisi was making use of it at the beginning of the century, the secular priest Jacques de Vitry was also becoming famous for his preaching at the very same time. According to Étienne de Bourbon (d. 1261), he 'moved and inflamed the whole of France as no one had done before and as no one could do after him', and did so by way of striking and amusing *exempla*.[103] Such fiery rhetoric can also be found among Dominicans. For example, the young and turbulent Robert of Uzès (d. 1296) must have cast terror among his audience – probably in Avignon, a city in social turmoil in the early 1290s – when he preached the following:

> Come, my servant, enter the city of Avignon. Preach there and speak to it: 'To arms, to arms, for it [the city] burns when chilled and is frozen by fire. And its people, spreading out like water, will burn. Alas, how painful it is! The successors of those who received the Holy Spirit in the form of fire are now frozen solid.[104]

Emotional rhetoric: the manufacture of laughter and shame

If the preachers loved to paint medieval cities as centres of heresy and sites of all manner of depravity, contemporary historians have seen them as places where 'values descended from heaven to earth';[105] their life was far removed from the monastic *contemptus mundi* idealism that had shaped the Gregorian reform. To evangelize this society and safeguard ecclesiastical authority over it, the Church had to find new tools; the birth of the mendicant orders provided an answer to this imperative. This urgent need – combined with the difficulty of addressing an often tired and distracted public not necessarily given to moralistic discourse – undoubtedly explains the increased preoccupation with the rhetorical art among thirteenth-century preachers and, more precisely, the enthusiasm for emotional rhetoric as part of their 'new way of speaking'.[106] If authors were more or less happy to acknowledge the benefit of the rhetorical manipulation of emotions, preachers invariably made use of them, and with great inventiveness. To command attention, the sermon had to be brief and the preacher had to subtly mix moving rhetorical elements with those that brought the audience back to salutary reflection. This set of elements can be witnessed in an illustration that accompanies Jean Gerson's (d. 1429) *Sermon on the Passion* (see Figure 13). Here, one can see the preacher using his body by leaning towards his audience, as well as the diversity of the emotional reactions among the listeners. Some adopt a posture of devotion, while another group, heads in hands, make a display of repentance; others look away or lower their eyes, perhaps in shame. The feelings that saved a person could be quite varied, a topic taken up in a sermon of Anthony of Padua, who provided an eloquent evocation of penance:

> The Book of Esther tells how she, 'with a rosy colour in her face, and with gracious and bright eyes, hid a mind full of anguish and a heart seized by great fear. So going in she passed through all the doors in order, and stood before the king' (Esther 15: 8–9). Esther is the penitent soul, whose face in confession should be suffused with the rosy colour of shame. Shame (*verecundia*) blushes at the truth, and whoever fears the true judgements of God undoubtedly has the shame which, in confession, leads to glory. Whoever does not blush, does not fear. Jeremiah says: 'Thou hast a harlot's forehead, thou wouldst not blush' (Jer. 3: 3). But Esther had a mind that was sorrowful and constrained by fear, because the penitent is worn down with sorrow in contrition, and constrained with fear in confession. Her gracious eyes are bright with the tears she has shed, and she enters through all the doors in order, numbering all her sins just as she has committed them, the sins which like doors bar us from the entrance to eternal life.[107]

A sermon designed to provoke penance thus summoned up those emotions which characterized by turns the stages of the emotional progression brought about by penance: sadness, embarrassment, fear, and finally tears of relief and joy as sins were washed away. The listener would have been struck by Jeremiah's reprimand as well as by the wondrous verses from the book of Esther; he might also identify with the emotions evoked at one or other of the stages, depending on his own disposition and state of mind.

Speaking in the vernacular to a lay audience, thirteenth-century preachers sometimes went even further in their deployment of emotional rhetoric. The use of humour in sermons went hand-in-hand with how they were adapted *ad status*, i.e. to the social status of listeners.[108] In an environment that had little time for theoretical complexities and where people preferred the pursuit of pleasure, laughter and humour seem to have been the most effective tools for winning over an audience and thus for temporarily creating a real emotional community, wherein the faithful would adopt the preacher's line and make his objective of conversion their own. Some *exempla* that mocked the weakest – for example, targeting the poor and the simple-minded – seem designed to cause contagious laughter, a laughter that would have been both exclusive (of its object) and inclusive by creating a sense of collusion among those who shared in it.[109] While the preacher and his lay audience might not have much in common at the outset, complicity in emotional sharing engendered a situation that could push the audience in the direction he desired. Thus, the use of humour was not only a pastoral matter, but part of a much larger 'operational strategy' within the Church, a strategy that valued effective communication as much as infusing hearts and minds with apostolic ideals.[110]

As it happened, a far from insignificant portion of these humorous *exempla* conveyed an element of social critique that was very often aimed at the Church, which found itself accused of luxuriance, ignorance, and depravity. The story of the Parisian priest Maugrin, told by Jacques de Vitry, depicts a parish vicar who could not understand Latin. When the Bishop of Paris learned of it,

> [He] feigned an illness, and called for the priest, and said to him: 'Maugrin, sir, you are a learned man and one of discretion; that is why I have sent for you to hear my confession and to ask you for absolution.' The priest tried to excuse himself, but the bishop would not listen, and began to speak to him in Latin of dialectics and other learned matters, pretending that he was confessing. At each sentence, Maugrin responded: 'God will forgive you!' At last the bishop, unable to back his laughter any longer, assured [Maugrin] that even if God pardoned him, he himself was less inclined towards mercy. He was even planning to take his parish away from him, until Maugrin paid a fine of 100 *livres*.[111]

This story of a learned bishop toying with an ignorant parish priest offers a fine example of double-edged mockery, which decried both of its protagonists and portrayed a secular Church that was simultaneously incompetent and corrupt from top to bottom: the bishop, as learned as he was, revealed himself to be just as corrupt – in his case, through greed – as the priest he wanted to punish. While pointing out the major evils of contemporary society, the *exemplum* is free from any explicit moralizing. Something similar can be seen in another *exemplum*, once again penned by Jacques de Vitry, that portrays a simple woman and a corrupt judge:

> I once heard of a certain corrupt and unjust judge, who left a poor woman unable to assert her rights. A certain other woman told her, 'This judge is the kind from whom no one gets justice unless they've greased his palm.' The poor woman was simple, however, and understood these words literally. So she took some pork lard, went to the judge, and in front of everybody began to smear his hand.
>
> – 'What are you doing, woman?,' the judge demanded.
>
> – 'My lord,' she replied, 'I was assured that unless I greased your palm, I would never obtain justice from you.'[112]

Whereas in these two narratives all the protagonists are subjected to mockery, some tales took up the cause of the poor and the weak, thus helping the sermon gain the approval of the crowd:

The Bishop of Würzburg was travelling on horseback one day, accompanied by a large cohort of horsemen, when he saw a peasant leave his plough and sit himself down on the roadside: there he lent on his stick, his mouth gaping, hoping to get a better look at this fine procession. 'Blessed are the poor in spirit!', thought the bishop. He approached him and said:

– 'Friend, tell me the truth, what do you think of seeing me ride with my escort?'
– 'Bishop, Monseigneur,' replied the peasant, 'I wonder if Saint Kilian of Würzburg ever rode with such a great following of horses.'
– 'You forget,' said the bishop, 'that I am not only a bishop. I am also a temporal prince, and it is he whom you see today. If you want to see the spiritual prince, you have only to come to Würzburg on the feast of Our Lady.'

The peasant then fell about laughing.

– 'Why are you laughing?,' asked the bishop.
– 'Because,' said the man, 'I think of the fatal moment when the devil will run off with the temporal prince. Who, then, will be the spiritual prince?'
– The bishop ran his hand over his mouth, rejoined his escort, and did not breathe a word of it.[113]

In this *exemplum*, written by Johannes Pauli (late fifteenth/early sixteenth century), it is the peasant who is closer to evangelical poverty than the prince-bishop, which is hardly surprising given its Franciscan author. Taking cues from numerous biblical *exempla* (Matt. 19: 24, Luke 16: 19–26, etc.), its message is essentially that simple men had much more chance of entering paradise than the rich and the powerful. This truculent little story, whose moral lesson is more explicit than those of the preceding examples, brings to life what was, in fact, an emotional rhetoric of significant technical skill. By using neat contemporary tales to evoke the actions, ways of life, and feelings that led to salvation alternately with those that led to perdition, the preacher could manipulate the emotions of his audience in a most subtle manner. What made some listeners laugh made others feel ashamed; some would be brought together by the shared laughter and others tormented by the same. In a sense, this technique split the foundations of the preacher's position of superiority in two: on the one side, there was his ecclesiastical status, on the other, his ability to make people laugh. It is indeed this rhetoric that governs the numerous *exempla* concerning usurers, the favourite targets of the Church's invective in the thirteenth century, as well as those – no

243

less abundant – that mock the vanity of women who liked to buy themselves lots of beautiful clothes and then struggled to get them on. Far from simply serving to entertain and keep the audience awake, 'humour in the pulpit' appears to have been a powerful tool of persuasion to judge by such examples: laughter amused some and humbled others. It united the former to divide them from the latter, in line with the needs of salvation. If such mockery could be caustic, it was also a powerful corrective.[114]

The scripting of emotional persuasion

A preacher's means of persuasion were not limited to the tales he narrated. Pastoral literature provides numerous reports of the real theatrical staging that preachers made pedagogical use of in bringing their words to life. Étienne de Bourbon recounted the following *exemplum* concerning Bernard of Clairvaux. While Bernard had managed to get all his blood brothers to join the monastic profession, his father resists, firmly set in the ways of the world. Bernard comes to his village to preach before him, and, seeing his stubbornness, he asks his men to bring dry wood to light a great fire:

> Then the saint began to speak of the pains of hell and told his father that he was like a tree trunk: he could neither be inflamed by divine fire, nor weep for his sins, nor desire God. But in hell, unless he did penance, he would burn for eternity, weep and emit a fetid smoke. At these words, the shaken father was seized by compunction and became a monk.[115]

Doubtless it is not only the words of his son, but also the sight of the fire that converts the father. It was a matter of putting the objects of preaching on stage: the fire of hell and the hardened father, who, like a dry trunk, was difficult to set fire to. Taking a step forward in time to the end of the Middle Ages, one witnesses the lighting of bonfires onto which men and women would throw their 'vanities' to avoid being burnt themselves at the Last Judgement, their devotion having been stoked by the preacher's fiery tongue. The account given by the Bourgeois of Paris (1405–49) sets the scene:

> [Brother Richard] preached on St. Mark's day at Boulogne-la-Petite, and there were great crowds there [...] Indeed when they came away from the sermon that day, the people of Paris were so moved and so stirred up to devotion that in less than three or four hours' time you would have seen over a hundred fires alight in which men were burning chess and backgammon boards, dice, cards, balls and sticks, *mirelis*, and every kind of covetous game that can give rise to anger and swearing. The women, too, this

244

day and the next, burned in public all their fine headgear. [...] Indeed the ten sermons he preached at Paris and one at Boulogne did more to turn people towards piety than all the preachers who had preached in Paris for the past hundred years. [...] And indeed, on that Tuesday when Brother Richard finished his last sermon, the tenth, because he had not got permission to preach in Paris any more, when he said goodbye and commended the people of Paris to God and that they should pray for him and he would pray to God for them, everyone, great and small, cried and wept as bitterly and as feelingly as if they had been watching their dearest friends be buried, and so did he too.[116]

Such scenes were not far removed from religious theatre, which used exactly the same tools at exactly the same time. Even at the end of the thirteenth century, amid the new religious paradigm that Francis of Assisi inaugurated, the Dominican Robert of Uzès turned his sermons into genuine theatrical productions when he attacked the powerful Church and defended the people by castigating the riches and abuses of the clergy. At Pentecost in 1294 or 1295, before preaching to a group of prelates, he appeared with handcuffs around his wrists and an iron chain around his neck to mimic the slavery of the common people, 'children of the beloved Church of the Lord'. Elsewhere, he sprinkled himself with blood that dripped onto his face to represent the sufferings of the people. On another occasion, in order to portray the tribulations of the Lamb – the persecuted Christ – he sacrificed and butchered a lamb before his audience.[117] These theatrical performances have come down to us by way of Robert's own personal notes; they are all the more precious since such improvisations of preachers have largely left no trace, unless a cultivated listener took note of them. If they probably made him popular, the words and methods of Robert of Uzès, who died at the age of thirty-three, did not enjoy the unanimous support of his Dominican province; it is unlikely that he fared much better in the eyes of the Church hierarchy of the Midi. Indeed, he would experience many tribulations during his brief life. Nevertheless, emotional preaching, ever more theatrical, proved very successful at the end of the Middle Ages, as the Church became interested in popular audiences and, conversely, as growing portions of society began to worry for their salvation. Robert's sort of passionate preaching had every chance of stirring the passions of the public. A ritual experience at a time when contemporaries were quite used to the spectacle of emotional preaching as an expression of the Church militant, a sermon delivered by an itinerant preacher like Robert, who crisscrossed the Uzès-Orange-Avignon triangle in the first half of the 1290s, could provoke passion through dramaturgical representation; it served to create a moment of shared religious emotion, a cathartic experience in the true sense of the term.

Preaching to the laity and religious theatre drew ever closer in the final centuries of the Middle Ages. Sermons were enriched by dialogue scenes inspired by liturgical drama to render them more colourful and striking, and even by *tableaux vivants* with narrators, in the style of mystery plays; the latter themselves could also include long homilies. The Passion play of Jean Michel (d. 1501), a rewrite of an earlier work by Arnoul Gréban (d. 1471/85), opens with a long sermon on the theme of penitence.[118] From the end of the fifteenth century, mendicant brothers themselves directed mystery plays: Brother Pierre Odilon, the Dominican prior of Châlons-en-Champagne, was so absorbed with his production of the Passion for the Easter of 1486 that he gave up preaching during Lent.[119] At the turn of the century, Jacobins and Cordeliers employed *tableaux vivants* to give figurative representation 'to sermons, preaching and the Passion by way of characters' ('*figurativement [l]es sermons et preschement, La Passion par personnaiges*').[120] This kind of innovation, deploying emotional rhetoric to combine edification and entertainment in the best way possible, at first provoked resistance from the Church hierarchy but soon spread. Following an earlier example at Laval in 1507, in 1515 Metz witnessed a staging of the Passion to support the sermon of an Observant Cordelier. Philippe de Vigneulles (d. 1527/28) described it in minute detail:

> For near him he had a tabernacle erected, enclosed by tapestry in the manner of a chapel. Within it was the *Corpus Domini* in a silver vessel with a lamp, just like the Blessed Sacrament. Also enclosed within it were two or three people, along with a wooden crucifix, although no one could see any of this. And with this done, during his sermon, one of his brothers repeatedly and loudly cried out to the people: 'Mercy!' Then, when he came to describe how our sweet Jesus was nailed to the cross, one of the people enclosed in the tabernacle took a large hammer and struck an anvil three times, as if he were nailing the hands and feet of the Redeemer. Thereby, accompanied by the most pious and grief-stricken words, which brought tears to the hearts of all those who heard and saw, with another cry of 'Mercy!' the crucifix was raised on high. With this complete he then showed them the true body of Jesus and the lamp through the light of a torch. And then you would have heard the people cry and shout in such clear voice – 'Mercy!' – that it was moving to hear them. In this way, he brought the mystery to life before all.[121]

Historiography has long maligned emotions that were collective and popular and has even used them to discredit mass movements. Here, however, we have sought to make sense of them as much as the sources allow. While our own age prefers to think of emotions as solely individual, or even psychological, this chapter, perhaps more than any of the others, has attempted to show the extent to which emotion was found at the core of social ties, at the core of what makes a society, and how all kinds of gatherings, at all levels of society, were conducive to arousing emotion and putting it to use. We have seen how shared emotion could reinforce the bonds of identity and feeling within groups – or even create new ephemeral communities, such as those born during a sermon or a theatrical performance. In doing so, it served to mark the boundaries of a community: it excluded outsiders at the same time as it embraced those who shared in it. There was nothing quite as powerful as shared emotion to assert the identity of a community, whether it came through love or through hatred, two emotions that indeed often went hand-in-hand. The effectiveness of shared emotion could transform it into a real manifesto, be it social, religious, or political. The ritualization of emotion, 'the obligatory expression of feelings', made use of this power to create, join, or divide communities and society. The rituals were there both to provoke emotion and to channel it. One can thus rightly speak of a genuine 'affective contract' that joined the people to those who governed them. Found at the heart of communication and ritual, emotion was a major political issue.

CONCLUSION

The history of the emotions forces us to recognize the infinite cultural malleability of the strange, affective material from which we are made. The Middle Ages do nothing to disprove that analysis: medieval emotions, so often public, demonstrative, and full of gestural value, were an accepted and ever-present part of the social fabric and cultural identities. They even formed the basis for man's relationship with God. If today we primarily think of and live out our emotions as intimate occurrences, we can only understand those of the Middle Ages by going beyond the dichotomy of the intimate and the shared, of what is private and what is public. It is only by refusing to separate the psychological and the social, and instead drawing them together, that affectivity will find its place within the broader historical narrative. We have sought to shed light on just some of the myriad ways in which emotion shaped the course of medieval lives. If the history of emotions has become a field of its own in recent years, its autonomy only matters in so far as it is taken fully into account, in so far as it achieves its aim of counterbalancing a long historiographical tradition in which affectivity has been either absent or disparaged, and where emotion has all too often been reduced to an ersatz of history, a decoration, or a 'natural' bedrock, set aside from culture, which is mastered by man and subjected to change.

The emotions affect history on many levels. Their cognitive and moral dimensions are a subject of fascination; so too is their relationship with the body that bears them. They both make and sometimes break strong bonds and solidarity. They can underline individuality but also efface it, depending on whether they conform to expectations or ignore them. The 'emotional navigation' which William Reddy speaks of describes well their quality of both putting things into motion and affecting the course of action. Whether felt, pondered, spoken, shown, or acted out, emotions

248

impact both the individual and the group. They can symbolize relationships at the same time as modifying them; they play their role both in defining the contours of society and in effecting the social developments so dear to historians. From the anger of a powerful leader to the indignation of the masses, from the demonstrative shame of a saint to the nobleman's fear of embarrassment, from the enthusiasm of a crusading band to the fear of a town threatened by the approach of war or plague, the examples are many: emotions are no mere expression of mental confusion or social upheaval. Far from it. While they are expressions common to all humanity, all of these outbursts of joy and pain have meanings which can only be understood within their own context. While the rise of the cognitive sciences in recent decades has made it easier for emotion to be understood as a mode of social communication, the idea of approaching emotions as forms of rationality owes nothing to them. Aristotle, the 'Philosopher' of the scholastic age, broached it long ago; the idea was ever-present throughout the Middle Ages and lay at the heart of Christian anthropology. The new questions posed by the cognitive sciences have certainly given energy to the rethinking of emotional power, which had for so long seemed lifeless within historiography. Nevertheless, they do not offer an analytical framework for the historian, whose only guides are the systems of thought and representations of the men and women of the past.

The path taken in this book has shed light on some of the affective characteristics of medieval societies and their capacity to define hierarchies. In a general sense, emotion played a role in creating social distinctions. Unfortunately, the emotions of the humble and illiterate have left no direct witnesses, and the few who rose out of this class hardly spoke in their name. Usually, it was only the members of the elite who were socially permitted to feel emotions; this was even more the case when it came to displaying and 'owning' them. Eloquent examples of this fact can be found in the emotion of anger, and especially that of 'ennobling love' (to borrow C. Stephen Jaeger's phrase): the latter shaped friendships between nobles and holy men, as well as the culture of courtly love. By contrast, the emotions of peasants, the common people, the anonymous masses were most often deemed excessive and degrading. Of course, these social judgements were shaken in the last centuries of the Middle Ages by the emotional excesses of mysticism, sometimes accepted, sometimes attacked: the evolution of the ecclesiastical attitude here – which went from admiring and rarely criticizing such practices to suspecting and even condemning them – shows that society had trouble accepting emotion when it felt it lacked a point of reference. As much in this era as in others, emotions that were framed, ordered, and contained were preferred.

249

It is thus difficult to escape the question of emotional intensity. Was the period, either as a whole or in part, characterized by an emotional hyperactivity, as Johan Huizinga or Elias' Freudian thesis of the 'civilizing process' would have it? Is it helpful to envisage an emotional ebb and flow within history? Did a particularly emotive late Middle Ages lead to a retrenchment during the Renaissance? Such an ebbing of emotions into the private corridors of the intimate self might even seem to pave the way for the emergence of that calmer setting of the 'French spirit', so proud of its Cartesian rationalism, that would follow a little later. But how can one read the Merovingian authors alongside the works of Gregory the Great and Alcuin, the *vita* of Marie of Oignies, or the spiritual writings of John of Fécamp and Aelred of Rievaulx, without concluding that the comparative quantification of affection is doomed to fail? The historian must renounce such linear narratives from the very start. From the beginning of the period and throughout the feudal age, the values and affective behaviour of male friendship were maintained by monks, clerics, and laymen alike, even if they remained distinctive features of the upper levels of society. At the same time, the written evidence suggests considerable diversity in how emotions were used. In some circumstances they were legitimate, in others they were mistrusted. They differed according to social groups, genders, age, and situations. And, last but not least, they varied according to the textual genres in which they were expressed, some of which – devotional literature, miracle stories, sermons, vernacular narratives, and poetry – clearly favoured the resort to emotional rhetoric. Moreover, the supposed birth of a premodern humanist sentiment does not explain the emotional saturation of the last centuries of the Middle Ages. Each medieval 'renaissance' – the Carolingian renaissance, the twelfth-century renaissance – contributed its share of emotional figures: Alcuin, Anselm of Canterbury, Heloise, and others besides. Nevertheless, the sources of the last centuries of the Middle Ages are marked by a pointed attention to emotion, ever-present across the widest variety of discourse. This was doubtless due to the influence of Christianity, which represented a true social structure in the Middle Ages, with its powerful portrayal of the Incarnation and the Passion. For medieval Christian anthropology, the love of God and the suffering of Christ were the two prototypical emotions: to medieval eyes, their combined action had saved mankind, and thus changed history. In addition, the key moments of the Incarnation and the Passion presented the emotions involved as evocations of a truth that words alone could not express. The necessity of emotional conversion was pressed with increasing vigour by the Church from the eleventh century onward; it did so at the very moment when the ecclesiastical edifice was gaining an unrivalled political power and, before long, an ability to impose a

250

tight framework of social expectations, of the sort that no secular power would attain for a long time to come. Hence, it was in proportion to deepening Christianization that the importance of emotion increased, defining one's relationship with God – and, therefore, with oneself – as well as one's ties to others. The Christian model of affectivity was ever-growing and ever-spreading, penetrating every aspect of medieval society. All the while it interacted with other models of affective evaluation, both those that were already present and those constructed in parallel. It remains, nevertheless, the most visible model within the sources, hardly surprising given the nature of what survives: largely clerical or para-clerical in origin, the texts privilege the ecclesiastical outlook, even if this was itself multifaceted and evolving. For all that the period was marked by a growing number of dissonant voices, the theme of Christ's suffering and loving humanity became the primary 'myth' of Christianity in the later centuries of the period.

This emotional amplification, strongly related to the Christian anthropology of the Incarnation and the Passion, was neither without tension nor without competition in the period. While this book has sought to underline the grip of this model in its different forms and evolutions, it has also defined its limits. When one examines the emotions, how they were perceived, and the norms that governed them in the Middle Ages, it is clear that this plan for Christian society first arose on a small scale in the monastic laboratories of the patristic era, where a new anthropology, psychology, and sociability were experimented with. This is where the moral and practical methodology of conversion, which made the transformation of men and societies possible, first took shape. Its implementation on a broader societal level as a collective outlook on salvation came only through the efforts of Charlemagne and, *a fortiori*, of Gregorian reform. It is in these monastic microcosms, which exerted enormous long-term influence, that one first meets the emotional narratives which later spread throughout the medieval West. Both Testaments contain many figures and episodes that provided normative models for medieval emotional behaviour. Beyond the most important model of Christ, there were also those of the Virgin Mary, Mary Magdalene, the apostles, and others, such as Job or the Old Testament kings. On top of these, there were the saints, their stories becoming more numerous over time, and the protagonists of vernacular literature. The Psalms, which the monks knew by heart, and the Song of Songs functioned alongside prayers and spiritual and devotional texts as guides for the faithful to follow in their devotional moments. Finally, iconography, ever more abundant during the later Middle Ages, presented its own visual cues from biblical, hagiographic, and literary narratives. All this goes to show the immense weight of Christian normativity within the medieval

251

emotional domain. These norms ran alongside and sometimes clashed with other structuring logics, particularly those that governed solidarity and shaped the culture of the secular elites, which was very deeply marked by the demands of honour.

However one looks at it, medieval emotions created meaning and provided the lifeblood for social relationships; they could be interpreted in many different ways and enjoyed an impressive cultural vitality. Why, then, have so many modern observers long seen in those emotions only psychological disturbance and social immaturity? There are many reasons for this misapprehension. But perhaps it is no less pertinent to question the paradox of our emotional lives today. Our imaginations binge on emotions, and yet socially we distrust them: is that not symptomatic of our partial renunciation of something we once relied on to build political community? If the study of medieval emotion delivers no lessons for the present, we can at least hope that it helps us to better understand our own world, and, perhaps, provides food for thought as we gaze upon ourselves.

ABBREVIATIONS

AASS   *Acta Sanctorum*, Antwerp-Brussels, Société des bollandistes, 1643–1940
BA   *Bibliothèque augustinienne*, Paris, Institut d'études augustiniennes, 1933–
BHL   *Bibliotheca hagiographica latina antiquae et mediae aetatis*, éditée par la Société des bollandistes, Subsidia hagiographica 6 (3 vols), Brussels, Société des bollandistes, 1898–1901
BUCEMA   Bulletin du centre d'études médiévales d'Auxerre
CCCM   *Corpus Christianorum continuatio mediaevalis*, Turnhout, Brepols, 1951–
CCSL   *Corpus Christianorum series latina*, Turnhout, Brepols, 1951–
MGH   Monumenta Germaniae Historica, Munich, 1819–
PG   *Patrologia Graeca*, Paris, J.-P. Migne, 1857–66
PL   *Patrologia Latina*, Paris, J.-P. Migne, 1841–55
SC   *Sources chrétiennes*, Paris, Cerf, 1942–

NOTES

INTRODUCTION

1 Febvre, 'Pour l'histoire d'un sentiment', p. 247.
2 See Rosenwein, 'Worrying about Emotions in History'; Boquet and Nagy, 'Pour une histoire des émotions'.
3 Matthew Paris, *Chronica majora*, 6: 465, cited in *Les Propos de Saint Louis*, ed. O'Connell, p. 102; see also Le Goff, *Saint Louis*, pp. 872–3.
4 See Boucheron, *The Power of Images*, p. 107.
5 Humbert of Romans, *De Dono Timoris*, p. 67 [4].
6 Ibid., p. 68 [4]. This verse is attributed to God by Humbert. In Proverbs, however, it is said by the character of Wisdom.
7 Plamper, *Geschichte und Gefühl*, pp. 56–61; id., 'L'histoire des émotions'; Deluermoz et al., 'Écrire l'histoire des émotions'; Mazurel, 'De la psychologie des profondeurs à l'histoire des sensibilités'; Ambroise-Rendu et al. (eds), *Émotions contemporaines. XIXe-XXIe siècle*.
8 Ansart, *La Gestion des passions politiques*; Braud, *L'Émotion en politique*; Ansart and Haroche (eds), *Les Sentiments et le Politique*; Marcus, *Le Citoyen sentimental*; Prochasson, *L'Empire des émotions*; Boquet and Nagy, 'L'historien et les émotions en politiques'; Lordon, *La Société des affects*.
9 Within a flourishing field of study, see especially Frijda, *The Emotions*; Harré (ed.), *The Social Construction of Emotions*; Damasio, *L'Erreur de Descartes*; id., *Le Sentiment même de soi*; id., *Spinoza avait raison*; Solomon, *The Passions*; de Sousa, *The Rationality of Emotions*; Elster, *Alchemies of the Mind*; Nussbaum, *Upheavals of Thought*; Livet, *Émotions et rationalité morale*.

254

10 Illouz, *Les Sentiments du capitalisme.*
11 Lane, *Comment la psychiatrie et l'industrie pharmaceutique ont médicalisé nos émotions.*
12 Rosaldo, *Knowledge and Passion*; Lutz, *Unnatural Emotions*; Abu-Lughod, *Veiled Sentiments.*
13 Reddy, 'Against Constructionism. The Historical Ethnography of Emotions'.
14 Febvre, 'La sensibilité et l'histoire. Comment reconstituer la vie affective d'autrefois?'.
15 Huizinga, *The Autumn of the Middle Ages*, p. 128.
16 Michelet, *Histoire de France. Le Moyen Âge*, p. 22.
17 The original German work of Elias, *Über den Prozess der Zivilisation* (1939) was translated into English first in two volumes: *The History of Manners* (1978) and *State Formation and Civilization* (1982). The most recent revised translation was published in a single volume, *The Civilizing Process.*
18 Elias, *The Civilizing Process*, p. 169.
19 See Boquet, 'Des émotions très rationnelles'.
20 Bloch, *Strange Defeat*, pp. 147–8.
21 See the very mixed assessment of Mandrou, 'Pour une histoire de la sensibilité'.
22 See the introduction of Delumeau, *La Peur en Occident.*
23 See Boquet and Nagy, 'Émotions historiques, émotions historiennes'; id., 'Une histoire des émotions incarnées'.
24 Stearns and Stearns, 'Emotionology'; Stearns, *American Cool*; Le Goff, 'Le rire au Moyen Âge'; Frandon et al. (eds), 'Pour une histoire de la souffrance'; Cairns, *Aidos.*
25 Rosenwein, *Emotional Communities in the Early Middle Ages*; id., *Generations of Feeling*; see also Nagy, 'Les émotions et l'historien'; Boquet, 'Le concept de communauté émotionnelle selon B. H. Rosenwein'; and Nagy, 'Faire l'histoire des émotions à l'heure des sciences de l'émotion'.
26 Reddy, *The Navigation of Feeling.*
27 Jaeger, 'L'amour des rois: structure sociale d'une forme de sensibilité aristocratique'; id., *Ennobling Love.*
28 Deploige, 'Studying Emotions'.
29 See Rosenwein, 'Thinking Historically about Medieval Emotions'; id., 'Eros and Clio'; Benthin and Kasten (eds), *Emotionalität*; and Jaeger and Kasten (eds), *Codierungen von Emotionen im Mittelalter.*
30 Mandressi, 'Le temps profond et le temps perdu'.
31 See Dixon, *From Passions to Emotions*; Gross, *The Secret History of Emotion.*

32 See Hochner, 'L'invention du terme émotion'.
33 On Bloch, see Schmitt, '"Façons de sentir et de penser"'. For a contemporary example, see Mandrou, *Introduction à la France moderne 1500–1640*.
34 Mauss, 'Les techniques du corps'. On the notion of 'emotional scenarios', see Kaster, *Emotion, Restraint, and Community in Ancient Rome*, p. 29; and Pancer, 'Les hontes mérovingiennes'.

CHAPTER 1

1 On the emotional vocabulary of the Bible, see Rosenwein, 'Emotion Words', esp. p. 103.
2 The Biblical references are taken from the Vulgate. The translation used – and sometimes modified – is the Douay-Rheims version.
3 See the references provided by Ingremeau in Lactantius, *La Colère de Dieu*, p. 15.
4 On this issue, see for instance this fourteenth-century example: Bevegnati, *Legenda de vita et miraculis beatae Margaritae de Cortona*, p. 328 [chap. VII, § 15].
5 See Nygren, *Erôs et agapè*.
6 See Pétré, *Caritas*, p. 45.
7 On the Christianization of 'affect' (*affectus-affectio*), see Boquet, *L'Ordre de l'affect au Moyen Âge*, pp. 51–91. From a broader perspective, see Sorabji, *Emotion and Peace of Mind*.
8 See Spanneut, *Le Stoïcisme des Pères de l'Église*.
9 Spanneut, 'L'impact de l'apatheia stoïcienne sur la pensée chrétienne jusqu'à saint Augustin', esp. p. 46; see also, id., 'Apatheia ancienne, apatheia chrétiennne'.
10 Origen, *On First Principles*, p. 94 [2.4.4]; cited by Ingremeau in the translator's preface to Lactantius, *La Colère de Dieu*, p. 22, n. 5.
11 Novatian, *De Trinitate 5*, cited by Ingremeau in the translator's preface to Lactantius, *La Colère de Dieu*, p. 21, n. 6.
12 For broader context, see the classic work by Brown, *The Body and Society*.
13 See Perrin, *L'Homme antique et chrétien*.
14 See Lactantius, *The Wrath of God*, in *The Minor Works*.
15 Ibid., p. 66.
16 There is a considerable body of literature on the theological, social, and political importance of the bond of 'love'. Among the most stimulating works, see the differing perspectives of, Nygren, *Erôs et agapè*; Arendt, *Le Concept d'amour chez Augustin*; and Guerreau-Jalabert, 'Caritas y don en la sociedad medieval occidental'.

17 Augustine, *The Happy Life*, in *Selected Writings*.
18 Augustine, *The Trinity*, p. 266 [VIII.X.14].
19 The historian of theology Gunnar Hultgren spoke of 'the psychological-ontological order'; see *Le Commandement d'amour chez saint Augustin*, p. 121.
20 See Coccia, 'Citoyen par amour'.
21 On this tradition, see Imbach and Atucha (eds), *Amours plurielles*.
22 Pseudo-Dionysius, 'The Divine Names', p. 82 [712 A], cited in Javelet, *Image et ressemblance au douzième siècle*, 2, p. 24.
23 The phrase is borrowed from de Libera, *La Mystique rhénane d'Albert le Grand à Maître Eckhart*, p. 33.
24 'Gospel of Peter', in *The Apocryphal New Testament*, p. 155. There is a key ambivalence in the Greek text, reflected in the James/Elliott translation provided here. The text could be read 'as if he felt no pain', thus supporting the notion that Jesus did feel pain but mastered it.
25 'Acts of John', in *The Apocryphal New Testament*, p. 319.
26 Tertullian, *Treatise on the Incarnation*, pp. 19–21.
27 This discussion is directly inspired by Emanuele Coccia's 'Il canone delle passioni. La passione di Cristo dall'antichità al medioevo'.
28 Origen, *Homilies 1–14 on Ezekiel*, VI, 6, cited in Coccia, 'Il canone delle passioni', p. 150.
29 On this terminology, see Boquet, *L'Ordre de l'affect au Moyen Âge*, pp. 33–49.
30 On the change of persepective introduced by Lacatantius, see Ibid., pp. 59–62.
31 See Lactantius, *Divine Institutes: Books I–VII*, pp. 433–9 [VII.14–16].
32 Ibid., p. 434 [VI.15].
33 Ibid., p. 435 [VI.15].
34 Ibid., p. 435 [VI.15].
35 Ibid., p. 446 [VI.18].
36 Ibid., p. 440 [VI.17].
37 Lactantius, *Epitome of the Divine Institutes*, p. 108 [61].
38 Lactantius, *Divine Institutes*, p. 438 [VI.16].
39 Ibid., p. 435 [VI.15].
40 Brown, *Augustine of Hippo: A Biography*.
41 On the Augustinian theory of the emotions, see Thonnard, 'La vie affective de l'âme selon saint Augustin'; O'Daly and Zumkeller, 'Affectus (passio, perturbatio)'; Bermon, 'La théorie des passions chez saint Augustin'; Knuuttila, *Emotions*, pp. 152–76; Casagrande,

'Agostino, i medievali e il buon uso delle passioni', pp. 65–75; id., 'Per una storia delle passioni in Occidente'; Boquet, *L'Ordre de l'affect au Moyen Âge*, pp. 77–91.

42 Augustine, *The City of God*, pp. 361–2 [IX.IV.1].

43 On these 'first movements' in Augustine, see Sorabji, *Emotion and Peace of Mind*, pp. 372–84; Byers, 'Augustine and the Cognitive Cause of Stoic "Preliminary Passions"'.

44 Aulus Gellius, *Attic Nights*, 3, pp. 349–55 [XIX.1]; and Augustine, *The City of God*, pp. 362–4 [IX.IV.2].

45 Jerome, *Commentary on Matthew*, p. 81 [I.5.28].

46 Augustine, *De Sermone domini in monte*, p. 37 [I, § 12, 34].

47 Augustine, *The City of God*, pp. 598–9 [XIV.IX.1].

48 Ibid., p. 590 [XIV.VI].

49 Ibid., p. 365 [IX.V].

50 Ibid., p. 606 [XIV.XI.2].

51 Ibid., p. 612 [XIV.XV.1].

52 Ibid., p. 603 [XIV.X].

53 Ibid., p. 365 [IX.V].

54 Ibid., p. 618 [XIV.XVII]. See Wu, 'Shame in the Context of Sin'.

55 Galen, *On the Passions and Errors of the Soul*, p. 45 [5].

56 See Burrus, *Saving Shame*.

57 Bernard of Clairvaux, *On Grace and Free Choice*, p. 79 [§ 21].

CHAPTER 2

1 Brown, *The Body and Society*, pp. 214–40.

2 Palladius, *The Lausiac History*, p. 33.

3 *The Sayings of the Desert Fathers*, p. 177 [Poemon 72].

4 Ibid., p. 173 [Poemon 50].

5 *The Anonymous Sayings of the Desert Fathers*, p. 401 [N.591.1].

6 Palladius, *The Lausiac History*, p. 17 [Foreword].

7 Ibid., p. 28 [Prologue, 14].

8 Ibid., pp. 27–8 [Prologue, 13].

9 See, for example, Evagrius of Pontus, *The Monk*, pp. 69–70, 76–7, 107.

10 On Evagrius, see Sinkewicz' introduction to *The Greek Ascetic Corpus*; see also A. and C. Guillaumont, 'Introduction' in Evagrius of Pontus, *Traité pratique*; A. and C. Guillaumont, 'Évagre le Pontique', in *Dictionnaire de spiritualité*; A. Guillaumont, 'Un philosophe au désert'; Driscoll, *The 'Ad Monachos of Evagrius Ponticus'*. Finally, on Evagrius and the emotions, see Sorabji, *Emotion and Peace of Mind*, pp. 357–71.

11 Sinkewicz, 'Introduction' in Evagrius of Pontus, *The Greek Ascetic Corpus*, pp. xviii–xxii; A. Guillaumont, 'Étude historique et doctrinale', in Evagrius of Pontus, *Traité pratique*, 1, p. 28.

12 See Sheridan, 'The Controversy over Apatheia'; Somos, 'Origen, Evagrius Ponticus and the Ideal of Impassibility'; see more broadly, Clark, *The Origenist Controversy*, pp. 43–84. On transmission, see A. Guillaumont, 'Étude historique et doctrinale', 1, pp. 30–1. From the 380s, Evagrius produced a systematic reflection on the problems of the ascetic life which he related to a mystical anthropology and a cosmogony. Condemned for Origenism in 553, his works circulated under other names, most notably that of St Nilus, before being reconstructed by contemporary scholarship.

13 Evagrius of Pontus, *Sur les pensées*, p. 11.

14 Evagrius of Pontus, *The Monk*, p. 109 [84].

15 See Driscroll, *The Ad Monachos of Evagrius Ponticus*, introduction, pp. 8 ff.

16 Evagrius of Pontus, *The Monk*, p. 107 [52].

17 Gregory the Great, *Moralia in Job*, 31, 45: PL 76:621A. On the deadly sins in the Middle Ages, see Casagrande and Vecchio, *Histoire des péchés capitaux au Moyen Âge*; Newhauser (ed.), *The Seven Deadly Sins*. For John Cassian, the number remained eight: *Conferences*, p. 183 [V.II].

18 Evagrius of Pontus, *The Monk*, pp. 97–8 [6]; Sorabji interprets the doctrine of Evagrius in the same way: see *Emotion and Peace of Mind*, pp. 359–60.

19 Evagrius of Pontus, *The Monk*, p. 104 [38].

20 Ibid. [37].

21 Ibid., p. 99 [10].

22 Ibid., p. 100 [11].

23 Ibid., pp. 101–2 [23].

24 Ibid., p. 100 [15].

25 Ibid., p. 101 [20].

26 Ibid., pp. 96, 110 [Prologue 8, 81].

27 See also Rosenwein, *Emotional Communities*, pp. 47–8.

28 John Cassian, *The Institutes*, pp. 97–8 [IV.35].

29 John Cassian, *Conferences*, p. 183 [V.III].

30 Ibid., chapter VII especially, but also the reflections in chapters I, IX, X, XXIV.

31 John Cassian, *The Institutes*, p. 93 [IV.27.3].

32 On this subject, see Nagy, *Le Don des larmes au Moyen Âge*.

33 John Cassian, *Conferences*, p. 327 [IX.XVIII].

34 On this Conference and the theme of friendship in Cassian, see White, *Christian Friendship in the Fourth Century*, pp. 174–84;

McGuire, *Friendship and Community*, pp. 78–83; Fiske, 'Cassian and Monastic Friendship'; Neuhausen, 'Zu Cassians Traktat De amicitia'.

35 Pichery, 'Introduction', p. 39.
36 From both the analogous nature of his schema and the allusions in the text, it is clear that Cassian was very familiar with Cicero's *De amicitia*, even if he did not explicitly cite it.
37 John Cassian, *Conferences*, p. 558 [XVI.III].
38 Ibid., p. 559 [XVI.V].
39 Pichery, 'Introduction', pp. 45–9.
40 John Cassian, *Conferences*, p. 562 [XVI.VII].
41 Ibid., p. 571 [XVI.XXII].
42 Ibid.
43 Ibid., pp. 564–5 [XVI.XIV].
44 Ibid., p. 565 [XVI.XIV]
45 Ibid.
46 On this aspect of monasticism, beyond the suggestions of Brown in *Body and Society*, see Helvétius and Kaplan, 'Asceticism and its Institutions', pp. 275–98 and 703–12.
47 J. Biarne, 'Moines et rigoristes en Occident'; Helvétius and Kaplan, 'Asceticism', pp. 276–7.
48 Helvétius and Kaplan, 'Asceticism', p. 277.
49 Biarne, 'Moines et rigoristes', p. 761. The *Ordo monasterii* was written around 395 within the circle of Augustine and with his approval: the Bishop Alypius represents a probable author. The *Praeceptum*, written by Augustine himself, dates from 397–400. See the introduction to these texts by Desprez and de Vogüé in *Règles monastiques d'Occident IVe–VIe siècle: D'Augustin à Ferréol*, pp. 64–6; and de Vogüé, *Le Monachisme en Occident avant saint Benoît*, p. 29.
50 See the texts collected in *Règles monastiques d'Occident*.
51 Augustine, *The Monastic Rules*, p. 114 [4.4].
52 Caesarius of Arles, *Regula Sanctarum Virginum*, pp. 9–10 [23].
53 Augustine, *The Monastic Rules*, p. 147 [6.3].
54 See Nagy, *Le Don des larmes*, pp. 139–44. The equivalent passages are as follows: Rule of the Master 6.3 = Rule of St Benedict, VIII.33; Rule of the Master, 9.3; Rule of the Master, 10.80 = Rule of St Benedict, VII.60.
55 Le Goff, 'Le rire dans les règles monastiques du haut Moyen Âge'.
56 'Règle orientale', in *Les Règles des Saints Pères*, 2, p. 137; *Règles des moines*, pp. 90–1; *The Rule of St Benedict*, pp. 96–7 [22].
57 Caesarius of Arles, *Regula Sanctarum Virginum*, pp. 7, 20 [10, 61].

58 Caesarius of Arles, 'Règle des moines', in *Œuvres monastiques*, 2, pp. 210–11 [13].

59 *The Rule of St Benedict*, pp. 22–5 [22.22, 22.24].

60 Ibid. pp. 8–9 [Prologue 49].

61 Colombanus, *Sancti Columbani Opera*, Introduction, pp. xi, xiii; Bullough, 'The Career of Columbanus'.

62 Colombanus, *Regula monachorum*, in *Sancti Columbani Opera*, p. 128 [VI].

63 Ibid., pp. 134–6 [VIII].

64 Ibid., p. 126 [IV].

65 Ibid., p. 124 [I].

66 Rosenwein, *Emotional Communities*, pp. 157–61.

67 Ibid., pp. 142–3 [X].

68 Colombanus, *Regula coenobialis*, in *Sancti Columbani Opera*, p. 144.

69 *Règles monastiques d'Occident*, Introduction, p. 55.

70 On Gregory's thought on the emotions, see Rosenwein, *Emotional Communities*, p. 79–99. On Gregory more broadly, see Markus, *Gregory the Great and his World*; Straw, *Gregory the Great*. Finally, for the affective anthropology of Gregory, see Nagy, *Le Don des larmes*, pp. 124–34.

71 See Gregory the Great, *Moralia in Job*; and the commentary of Rosenwein, *Emotional Communities*, pp. 82–3.

72 See Straw, *Gregory the Great*, esp. p. 54.

73 See Penco, 'Eucaristia, ascesi e martirio spirituale'.

74 See Straw, *Gregory the Great*, pp. 179 ff., esp. p. 188.

75 Jos 15: 18–19 and Jg 1: 14–15.

76 Gregory the Great, *Dialogues*, p. 174 [34.3–5]. One finds the same passage in other works of Gregory: *Ep.* 7.23; *Ep.* 7.26; *Moralia*, XXIV.10; *Hom. Ez.*, II.10, 20–1; *In I Reg.* 5.148.

77 For the idea of 'emotional navigation', see Reddy, *Navigation of Feeling*.

78 To take the full measure of this highly nuanced and multiform vision of affectivity in the works of Gregory, see the chapter and numerous passages on this subject in Rosenwein, *Emotional Communities*, chap. 4, pp. 100–29.

79 A new edition and French translation is in preparation: Valère du Bierzo (viie siècle), *Œuvres autobiographiques et récits de vision*. See more broadly, Henriet, 'Origines du christianisme ibérique et communauté de parfaits'; id., 'Les démons de Valère du Bierzo'.

80 Sot, 'Héritages et innovations sous les rois francs', p. 64.

CHAPTER 3

1 In this regard, see also Le Jan, *La Société du haut Moyen Âge*, pp. 3, 28.
2 See also, Pancer, *Sans peur et sans vergogne*.
3 See Rosenwein, *Emotional Communities*, pp. 63–4, 77.
4 Ibid., pp. 72–7.
5 Jaeger, *Ennobling Love*. See also Le Jan, 'Entre haine et amour du roi'.
6 Pancer, 'Violence domestique ou conflits politiques?'.
7 See *Pactus Legis Salicae, MGH, Leges nationum germanicarum, IV, 1* (Hanover, 1962), v. LX, p. 225, v. LIX, p. 222; a commentary is provided by Le Jan, *Famille et pouvoir*, p. 77.
8 Le Jan, *Famille et pouvoir*, p. 232, and n. 41.
9 Dhuoda, *Handbook for William*, p. 21 [III, 1].
10 Ibid., pp. 77–9; see Lynch, *Godparents and Kinship in Early Medieval Europe*; and Jussen, *Patenschaft und Adoption im frühen Mittelalter*.
11 Duby, 'Les jeunes dans la société aristocratique de la France du Nord-Ouest au xiie siècle'; Le Jan, *Famille et pouvoir*, p. 80.
12 Le Jan, *Famille et pouvoir*, p. 83.
13 This is the thesis of Jaeger, *Ennobling Love*.
14 See Althoff, *Family, Friends and Followers*, pp. 67–8.
15 Ibid., p. 66.
16 Le Jan, *La Société*, p. 247.
17 Althoff, *Family, Friends*, pp. 70–1.
18 Venantius Fortunatus, *Opera Poetica*, p. 75 [III.XXVI].
19 Jaeger, *Ennobling Love*, pp. 33–4; V. Epp, 'Männerfreundschaft und Frauendienst bei Venantius Fortunatus', pp. 14–16.
20 Venantius Fortunatus, *Opera Poetica*, p. 260 [XI.VI].
21 See Rosenwein, *Emotional Communities*, pp. 112–4; Le Jan, *La Société*, p. 247.
22 *Vita Bertae abbatissae Blangiacensis*, p. 50; Le Jan, *La Société*, p. 240; *Bibliotheca Sanctorum*, vol. III, p. 90.
23 Le Jan, *La Société*, p. 240.
24 Ibid.
25 See Epp, *Amicitia*.
26 *Epistolae Austrasicae* n. 12, p. 127. Le Jan, *La Société*, p. 247.
27 See Wallach, ' "Amicus amicis, inimicus inimicis" '; Cl. Garnier, *Amicus amicis, inimicus inimicis*.
28 Althoff, *Family, Friends*, p. 70; Rosenwein, 'Les émotions de la vengeance'; Le Jan, 'Timor, amicitia, odium'.

29 Pancer, *Sans peur et sans vergogne*.
30 Gregory of Tours, *Libri historiarum X*, p. 92 [II.42]. See Pancer, *Sans peur et sans vergogne*, p. 113. The date of this event (possibly *c.* 510) has been debated by historians.
31 Pancer, *Sans peur et sans vergogne*, p. 114. On this matter, see also, by the same author, 'Les hontes mérovingiennes'.
32 Auerbach, *Mimésis*, pp. 88–105. On the project, see Heinzelmann, *Gregory of Tours*, chapter 3: 'Ten Books of History: Genre, Structure and Plan'. See also the many studies in Barthélemy et al. (eds), *La Vengeance, 400–1200*.
33 Gregory of Tours, *Libri historiarum X*, p. 456 [IX.35]; Pancer, *Sans peur et sans vergogne*, p. 123.
34 On violence, see also the account of Le Jan, *La Société*, pp. 267 ff., esp. pp. 277–81.
35 See Depreux, 'Une faide exemplaire? À propos des aventures de Sichaire', and Geary, 'Gabriel Monod, Fustel de Coulanges et les "aventures de Sichaire"'.
36 Gregory of Tours, *Libri historiarum X*, p. 366 [VII.47].
37 Gregory of Tours, *Libri historiarum X*, pp. 432–3 [IX.19]; Pancer, *Sans peur et sans vergogne*, pp. 124–5.
38 See Rosenwein, *Emotional Communities*, p. 111.
39 See the Council of Paris (614), 4, in *Concilia Galliae a. 511–a. 695*, p. 276.
40 See Rosenwein, *Emotional Communities*, p. 156.
41 See Augustine, *Confessions*, 5.8.15; but above all, see the examples and analysis of Rosenwein, *Emotional Communities*, pp. 149–55.
42 Gregory of Tours, *Libri historiarum X*, p. 268 [VI.4]. Emphasis added by the authors.
43 Gregory of Tours, *Libri historiarum X*, pp. 101–2 [III.6]; White, 'Clotild's Revenge: Politics, Kinship, and Ideology in the Merovingian Blood Feud'.
44 This is one of the central arguments of Pancer, *Sans peur et sans vergogne*.
45 See Nelson, 'Les reines carolingiennes', esp. p. 132.
46 Joye, 'Grégoire de Tours et les femmes', p. 77; Réal, *Vies des saints, vie de famille*, pp. 130 ff.
47 Pancer, *Sans peur et sans vergogne*, p. 244.
48 Ibid., pp. 246–7. On the same matter, see, Joye, 'Grégoire de Tours et les femmes', p. 90.
49 Gregory of Tours, *Libri historiarum X*, pp. 302–2 [VI, 32]; Pancer, *Sans peur et sans vergogne*, p. 248–1.
50 On this question, see also Pezé, 'Les émotions et le moi chez quelques théologiens du haut Moyen Âge'.

51 See Rosenwein, *Emotional Communities*, chap. 2.
52 Ibid., pp. 131–4.
53 Ibid., pp. 131–49.
54 Ibid., p. 156.
55 Ibid., pp. 157–9.
56 Columbanus, *Sancti Columbani Opera*, p. 31; see also Rosenwein, *Emotional Communities*, p. 160.
57 Rosenwein, *Emotional Communities*, p. 161.
58 Deshusses, *Le Sacramentaire grégorien*, nos 111 and 112, *Missa pro petitione lacrimarum*, pp. 128–30. The second mass focused on tears [no. 112] is also found among the masses of Alcuin edited by Jean Deshusses [no. 9], 'Les messes d'Alcuin', the text is found at p. 23.
59 See respectively nos 109–10 and 113–14.
60 Alcuin, *Ep.* 250, MGH, *Epist.*, v. IV, pp. 404–6.
61 Driscoll, *Alcuin et la pénitence à l'époque carolingienne*, p. 130, and n. 156–60.
62 See Palazzo, *Les Sacramentaires de Fulda*, pp. 187–92.
63 Paris, BNF, MS Lat. 816 (eighth–ninth centuries), *Le Sacramentaire gélasien d'Angoulême*; and Rom. Cod. Ross. lat. 204 (mid–ninth century), *Sacramentarium Rossianum*. For the Roman missal, see Bruylants, *Les Oraisons du Missel romain*, vol. I, pp. 193–4, and vol. II, prayers nos 574, 600, 752.
64 See Bouhot, 'Des livres pour prier', pp. 23–9; and *Precum libelli quattuor aevi karolini, nunc primum publici iuris facti cum aliorum indicibus*.
65 Cottier, 'Psautiers abrégés et prières privées durant le haut Moyen Âge'.
66 See especially, *Precum libelli quattuor*.
67 Cited by Bouhot, 'Des livres pour prier', p. 26. It derives from collection conserved among the manuscripts of Orléans, BM 184 [161], ff. 240–55, and of Munich, Bayern Staatsbibl., Clm14392 (first half of the ninth century).
68 Bouhot, 'Des livres pour prier', pp. 26–7.
69 Edited in *Precum libelli quattuor*, p. 54, along with the rest of Cologne, Diözesanbibliothek MS 106 (805); cited by Bouhot, 'Des livres pour prier', p. 28. See also Driscoll, *Alcuin et la pénitence*, pp. 118–19.
70 See Cottier, 'Psautiers abrégés et prières privées durant le haut Moyen Âge'.
71 See the exposition of Dubreucq, 'Autour du De virtutibus et vitiis d'Alcuin'; on its dating, see pp. 269–70.
72 Alcuin, *De virtutibus et vitiis liber*, PL 101, col. 613–38, see chap. 1, col. 613; and chap. 36, col. 638.

73 Ibid., col. 638.
74 Dubreucq, 'Autour du De virtutibus et vitiis d'Alcuin', p. 271.
75 No less than twenty-two manuscripts have survived from the eleventh and tenth centuries. See Wallach, *Alcuin and Charlemagne*, p. 247.
76 Veyrard-Cosme, 'Introduction' in *L'Œuvre hagiographique en prose d'Alcuin*, p. LIX.
77 See Banniard, 'Niveaux de compétence langagière chez les élites carolingiennes', pp. 39–62.
78 See Bullough, *Alcuin: Achievement and Reputation*.
79 Douglas, *Purity and Danger*, p. 99.
80 Garrison, 'Les correspondants d'Alcuin', pp. 325–6.
81 Alcuin, Ep. 39, in MGH, *Epistolae Karolini Aevi II*, p. 82.
82 Garrison, 'Les correspondants d'Alcuin', p. 327.
83 Alcuin, *Carmen 55*, in MGH, *Poetae Latini Aevi Carolini* I, p. 266.
84 See Bullough, 'Amicitia and Sexual Orientation' in *Alcuin: Achievement and Reputation*, pp. 110–17; beyond this, see McGuire, *Friendship and Community*, pp. 117–27.
85 Jaeger, *Ennobling Love*, p. 37.
86 Ibid., pp. 40–1.
87 Alcuin, Ep. 148, MGH, *Epist.*, 4, p. 241; Veyrard-Cosme, 'Littérature latine du haut Moyen Âge et idéologie politique', pp. 193–4. Our italics.
88 See Alcuin, Ep. 229, MGH, *Epist.* 4, pp. 372–3, cited by Veyrard-Cosme, 'Littérature latine du haut Moyen Âge', p. 195, n. 12.
89 de Jong, 'Sacrum palatium et ecclesia', esp. pp. 1255–6.
90 Garrison, 'Les correspondants d'Alcuin', pp. 329–30.
91 Nagy, 'La notion de christianitas et la spatialisation du sacré au xe siècle', pp. 121–40.

CHAPTER 4

1 The expression derives from Peter Damian's description of his master: 'Adeo ut putaretur totum mundum in heremum velle convertere'. It is found in Peter Damian, *Vita beati Romualdi* (BHL 7324), p. 78 [chap. 37]; Caby, 'Faire du monde un ermitage'; and Henriet, 'L'érémitisme hors de la société ou dans la société'.
2 Tabacco, 'Romualdo di Ravenna e gli inizi dell'eremitismo camaldolese', pp. 73–4; Leclercq, *Saint Pierre Damien*, p. 33; G. Fornasari, 'Pater rationabilium eremitarum'; Longo, 'La conversione di Romualdo di Ravenna come manifesto programmatico della riforma eremitica'.

3 On this matter, see Caby, 'Faire du monde un ermitage'.
4 Peter Damian, *Vita beati Romualdi*, pp. 23–25 [chap. 5]; pp. 32–33 [chap. 11]; pp. 47–8 [chap. 22]; pp. 106–8 [chap. 65].
5 The monastery was that of St Michael of Verghereto, in Bagno di Romagna (Italy, Emilia-Romagna).
6 Peter Damian, *Vita beati Romualdi*, pp. 43–4.
7 Henriet, *La Parole et la Prière au Moyen Âge*, p. 229 (and more generally, pp. 228–35). See also Lohmer, 'Multae sunt viae quibus itur ad Deum'.
8 Peter Damian, *Vita beati Romualdi*, p. 40 [chap. 16].
9 Peter Damian, *Vita beati Romualdi*, pp. 67–8 [chap. 31]. On this episode, see Nagy, *Le Don des larmes*, pp. 177–8.
10 Romuald was born *c.* 952; this episode took place between 1001 and 1003, according to Fornaciari, 'Romualdo di Ravenna, i suoi discepoli Benedetto di Benevento e Giovanni e il monachesmimo missionaria dell'età ottoniana', pp. 237–8.
11 The term comes from Bruno of Querfurt, *Vita quinque fratrum eremitarum seu Vita uel passio Benedicti et Iohannis sociorumque suorum*, chap. 2. See also Tabacco, ' "Privilegium amoris": aspetti della spiritualità romualdina'.
12 The *Vita Romualdi* dates from 1042, while Bruno of Querfert died in 1009.
13 See Peter Damian, *Vita beati Romualdi*, chap. 27.
14 Bruno of Querfurt, *Vita quinque fratrum*, p. 35 [II].
15 Ibid., pp. 31–6 [II].
16 Ibid., p. 32 [II].
17 Ibid., p. 38 [III]. For Horace, see Carm. I.3.8: 'animae dimidium meae'.
18 Bruno of Querfurt, *Vita quinque fratrum*, p. 39–40 [IV–V].
19 Peter Damian, *Vita beati Romualdi*, chap. 49. See also Henriet, *La Parole et la Prière*, p. 230.
20 Tabacco, ' "Privilegium amoris" ', p. 171; see Peter Damian, *Vita beati Romualdi*, chapters 6, 11, and 15. See also Fornaciari, 'Romualdo di Ravenna, i suoi discepoli'.
21 On the penitential asceticism promoted by Peter Damian, see Longo, 'L'esperienza di riforma avellanita e i rapporti con il mondo monastico'.
22 On how the two fit together, see Longo, 'O *utinam anima mea esset in corpore tuo!*'
23 Another reflection of this tension can be found in the growing distance between the ecclesiology of Peter Damian and that of the papacy. See Longo, 'L'esperienza di riforma avellanita'.

24 Peter Damian, *Vita beati Romualdi*, pp. 47–9 [chapters 22–3]. Romuald only reluctantly accepted the abbacy of St Apollonius and abandoned it rapidly. Bruno of Querfurt, *Vita quinque fratrum*, p. 36 [II]. Benedict refused the abbacy which Romuald entrusted him with, with the result that the community was left adrift.

25 This penitential style is embodied within Peter Damian's hagiographic corpus by the strange figure of Dominic Loricatus: Peter Damian, *Vita Dominici loricati* = Ep. 109 in *Die Briefe des Petrus Damiani*, v. III, pp. 207–23. On the place of this *vita* within his hagiographic efforts, see Henriet, *La Parole et la Prière*, pp. 153–7.

26 For further depth on the topic of this section, see Lauren Elisabeth Mancia's unpublished doctoral thesis: 'Affective Devotion and Emotional Reform in the Eleventh-Century Monastery of John of Fécamp', Yale University, December 2013.

27 Gazeau, 'Guillaume de Volpiano en Normandie: état des questions'; Gazeau and Goullet, *Guillaume de Volpiano, un réformateur en son temps*.

28 See the excellent article by Falconieri on 'Giovanni di Fécamp', in *Dizionario Biografico degli Italiani*.

29 This is the heading used by Wilmart, who published the text in *Auteurs spirituels et textes dévots du Moyen Âge latin*, pp. 126–37.

30 Ibid., p. 131.

31 'Heu homo, heu homo, heu te miser homo/ [...]/ Miserere Christe, miserere pie,/ Tu miseris tuis semper miserere.' Ibid., pp. 131–4.

32 See, for example, Peter Damian, Ep. 32 and Ep. 40, *Die Briefe*, v. I, pp. 333–31 and pp. 384–509; For a bibliography on this matter, see Longo, 'L'attesa della fine: Monaci e eremiti'.

33 John of Fécamp, *Confessio theologica*, pp. 109–82. John of Fécamp never stopped re-editing the material of this work, which comes down to us in two other redactions, the *Libellus scripturis et verbis patrum*, or *The Little Book of Writings and Words of the Fathers*, and the *Confessio fidei*, PL 101, col. 1027–98. Likely dating from between 1030 and 1050 and addressed to Empress Agnes (d. 1077), the widow of the Emperor Henry III (d. 1056), the *Libellus* is found in its complete version in an MS of the Metz municipal library (MS. 245, ff. 12–35). See Leclercq, *Un maître de la vie spirituelle du XIe siècle*, pp. 39–40, for the connection of the *Theological Confession* with this text and the Pseudo-Augustinian *Meditations* published in the PL 40, col. 901–42. De Vial, 'Introduction' in Jean of Fécamp, *Confession théologique*, pp. 17–8, treats the relationships between the two texts again. On the dating of work, see Wilmart, 'Deux préfaces spirituelles de

Jean de Fécamp', esp. p. 44; an analysis of the text can be found in Leclercq, *Un maître de la vie spirituelle du XIe siècle*, pp. 41–4.

34 John of Fécamp, *Confessio Theologica*, prologue, p. 121 [II].

35 Ibid., p. 142 [II–III].

36 See Nagy, *Le Don des larmes*.

37 John of Fécamp, *Confessio Theologica*, pp. 155–6 [III, XII]

38 Ibid., p. 128 [II.6]

39 Paradoxically, the texts of John of Fécamp have long been integrated within the Pseudo-Augustinian *Meditationes*.

40 John of Fécamp, *Confessio Theologica*, pp. 147–9 [II.12]

41 See also Nagy, 'Larmes et Eucharistie'.

42 Peter Damian, Letter to the hermit Leo de Sitria, formerly entitled *Dominus vobiscum* (c. 1048–55), *Die Briefe*, Ep. 28, vol. I, pp. 248–78, esp. pp. 255–7, 259–60; English translation, *Letters 1–30*, p. 262.

43 An English translation is found in *The Complete Philosophical and Theological Treatises of Anselm of Canterbury*, pp. 295–389. Latin text edited by Schmitt, *L'Œuvre d'Anselme de Cantorbéry*, v. III.

44 Anselm of Canterbury, *The Harmony of the Foreknowledge*.

45 For an analysis, see Boquet, *L'Ordre de l'affect au Moyen Âge*, pp. 103–8.

46 On this transformation of affect into a force of the soul in the twelfth century, see *infra* Chapter 6.

47 Anselm of Canterbury, Prayer 19, in *The Prayers and Meditations of Anselm of Canterbury*, p. 328.

48 Ibid., Prayer 4, p. 124.

49 Ibid., Prayer 16, pp. 304–5.

50 Ibid., Prayer 15, p. 294.

51 Ibid., Meditation 1, p. 332.

52 Ibid., Prayer 18, p. 318.

53 Ibid., p. 319.

54 Ibid., p. 321.

55 Anselm of Canterbury, Letter 4, in *The Letters of Anselm of Canterbury*, 1, p. 81. This passage is quoted in Cottier, 'Saint Anselme et la conversion des émotions', pp. 292–3, n. 76. See also pp. 291–5 for a stylistic study of the passage.

56 Anselm sent several letters on the same subject to Gundulf, confirming the idea that his old cloistral companion felt grief over his absence; see Letters 16 and 59 in *The Letters of Anselm of Canterbury*. The collection of letters from Anselm's Bec era contains no less than twelve letters to Gundulf, who became Bishop of Rochester in 1077. The *vita* of Gundulf confirms the closeness

of the two men; see McGuire, *Friendship and Community*, pp. 224–5.

57 See Boswell, *Christianity, Social Tolerance, and Homosexuality*, pp. 280–2. On the relationship between homo-affective rhetoric and homosexuality in the eleventh and twelfth centuries, see *infra* Chapter 5.

58 See McGuire, 'Love, Friendship and Sex in the Eleventh Century'; Southern, *Saint Anselm: A Portrait in a Landscape*, pp. 148–53; and above all, Cottier, 'Ganymède médiéval?'

59 See Southern, *Saint Anselm*, p. 141.

60 See Robinson, 'The Friendship Network of Gregory VII'; Longo, '*O utinam anima mea esset in corpore tuo!*' On the change of tone within twelfth-century spiritual friendship, see McGuire, *Friendship and Community*, pp. 194–230.

61 This question has quite rightly been raised by Haseldine, 'Love, Separation and Male Friendship', esp. p. 246.

62 See Southern, *Saint Anselm*, p. 163.

63 Anselm of Canterbury, Letter 4, in *The Letters of Anselm of Canterbury*, 1, p. 82.

64 See Cottier, 'Saint Anselme et la conversion des émotions', p. 294. In addition, Cottier has used the episode of Osbern's death as narrated by Eadmer, author of the *vita* of St Anselm (cf. 1109–15), to show that the abbatial government of Anselm – or at least of Eadmer's idealized Anselm – applied this ideal of emotional conversion to life within the cloister.

65 See Fiske, 'Saint Anselm and Friendship'.

66 Anselm of Canterbury, Letter 84, in *The Letters of Anselm of Canterbury*, 1, p. 219.

67 See Haseldine, 'Love, Separation and Male Friendship', p. 251.

68 Anselm of Canterbury, Letter 16, in *The Letters of Anselm of Canterbury*, 1, 103–4.

69 For a stimulating discussion of the paths of exploration offered by monastic sources, see Tock, 'Les émotions dans le monde régulier au Moyen Âge'.

70 For general context, see Vauchez, *La Spiritualité du Moyen Âge occidental*, pp. 77 ff., even if it now seems appropriate to shift the emergence of this 'religion des temps nouveaux' back by a century (to the end of the tenth century, rather than the end of the eleventh as A. Vauchez had suggested). See also the classic Bultot, *La Doctrine du mépris du monde en Occident de saint Ambroise à Innocent III*.

71 Guerreau-Jalabert, 'Occident médiéval et pensée analogique'. We are grateful to the author for giving us access to a draft of this

article prior to publication. Another, briefer version is also available: Guerreau-Jalabert, '*Spiritus et caro*. Une matrice d'analogie générale'.

72 Guerreau-Jalabert, 'Occident médiéval et pensée analogique'.

73 There is a considerable bibliography on love mysticism and ordered charity in the monastic writings of the twelfth century: see above all McGinn, *The Growth of Mysticism*, pp. 149–418; Leclercq, *L'Amour vu par les moines au XIIe siècle*; Javelet, *Image et ressemblance au douzième siècle de saint Anselme à Alain de Lille*, v. 1, pp. 409–50. For a compilation of the essential texts (in Latin and French), see Imbach and Atucha, *Amours plurielles*.

74 Imbach and Atucha, *Amours plurielles*, p. 17.

75 The efforts of Bernard were continued by Gilbert of Hoyland (d. 1172) and completed by John of Ford (d. *c.* 1214). Together they form an exceptional body of 253 sermons commenting on the entirety of the Song of Songs.

76 Bernard of Clairvaux, *On the Song of Songs I*, pp. 38–39 [7.2].

77 Bernard of Clairvaux, *On Loving God*; William of Saint-Thierry, *Deux traités sur l'amour de Dieu*; Aelred of Rievaulx, *The Mirror of Charity*; Richard of Saint-Victor, *On the Four Degrees of Violent Love*.

78 See Aelred of Rievaulx, *The Mirror of Charity*, pp. 221–34 [III.1–19]. On the role of the monks in the formation of twelfth-century learned anthropology, see *infra* Chapter 6.

79 Bernard of Clairvaux, Sermon 10, in *Monastic Sermons*, pp. 63–6. William of Saint-Thierry proposed a similar outlook in his *The Nature and Dignity of Love*, pp. 74–85 [§18–25].

80 Aelred of Rievaulx, *The Mirror of Charity*, p. 270 [III.72]. For an analysis, see Boquet, *L'Ordre de l'affect*, pp. 226–41.

81 These three levels are found frequently in such discussions of the love of God. They formed the very structure of the long ascetic work of William of Saint-Thierry, *Lettre aux frères du Mont-Dieu (Lettre d'or)*.

82 Aelred of Rievaulx, Sermon 136 in *Sermones LXXXXV–CLXXXII: collectio Radigensis*, p. 326.

83 Richard of Saint-Victor, *On the Four Degrees of Violent Love*, p. 275 [2].

84 Ibid., p. 275 [4].

85 See the analysis by Dumeige in Richard of Saint-Victor, *Les Quatre Degrés de la violente charité*. For another discussion of the structure of this work, see Nagy, *Le Don des larmes*, pp. 351–4. See also Châtillon, 'Les quatre degrés de la charité d'après Richard

de Saint-Victor'; and Dumeige, *Richard de Saint-Victor et l'idée chrétienne de l'amour.*

86 Richard of Saint-Victor, *On the Four Degrees of Violent Love,* p. 282 [17].

87 This trend was accurately identified by Baladier, *Érôs au Moyen Âge,* p. 35.

88 Richard of Saint-Victor, *On the Four Degrees of Violent Love,* p. 285 [24].

89 Bernard of Clairvaux, *On Loving God,* p. 3.

90 See, for example, William of Saint-Thierry, *Exposé sur le Cantique des Cantiques,* pp. 152, 188 [§ 57, § 76]. The formula was inspired by Gregory the Great, for whom the love of God was a knowledge of God (*amor ipse notitia est*). See Déchanet, 'Amor ipse intellectus est', pp. 349–74. More broadly, see Javelet, 'Intelligence et amour chez les auteurs spirituels du xiie siècle'.

91 Richard of Saint-Victor, *On the Four Degrees of Violent* Love, p. 294 [45].

92 Ibid., p. 292 [39]. See Boureau, 'Incandescences médiévales'.

93 Bernard of Clairvaux, *Monastic Sermons,* p. 248 [50.2].

94 Bernard of Clairvaux, *On Grace and Free Choice,* § 17. For a later example of the ordering of the emotions in spiritual literature, see Carla Casagrande's analysis of the *Specchio di croce,* written in the vernacular by Domenico Cavalca (d. *c.* 1342) for a lay audience, which confirms the lasting Cistercian influence on this matter. Casagrande, 'Specchio di croce'.

95 Richard of Saint-Victor, *The Twelve Patriarchs, the Mystical Ark, Book Three of the Trinity.*

96 Ibid., p. 57 [IV]; see Nardini, 'Affectio e ratio nell'itinerario mistico del Beniamin Minor di Ricardo di San Vittore'.

97 See the synthesis by McGinn, *The Growth of Mysticism,* p. 402.

98 The number and order of the base emotions vary in the writings of Richard, as with the majority of the authors of the age, confirming that these nomenclatures had a value that was more relational and analogical than descriptive.

99 Richard of Saint-Victor, *The Twelve Patriarchs,* p. 60 [VII].

100 Ibid., p. 61 [IX].

101 On same in the *Benjamin Minor,* see Vecchio, 'La honte et la faute', esp, pp. 106–11.

102 See Tisseron, *La Honte;* and Cyrulnik, *Mourir de dire la honte.* For a more controversial contemporary perspective, see, for example, Williams, *Shame and Necessity.*

103 See Bologne, *Histoire de la pudeur;* Habib (ed.), *La Pudeur.*

104 See Baladier, 'La honte et l'honneur dans les langues d'Europe occidentale'; Boquet, 'La vergogne historique'; Thomas, *Déshonneur et honte en latin*; and Alexandre et al., *Rubor et pudor*.

105 See *supra*, Chapter 1.

106 See Cairns, *Aidos*; and Kaster, *Emotion, Restraint, and Community*. From a broader philosophical and historical perspective, see Nussbaum, *Hiding from Humanity*.

107 See Casagrande, 'Le emozioni e il sacramento della penitenza'.

108 See Sère, 'Penser la honte comme sanction dans la scolastique des xiiie-xive siècles', in Sère and J. Wettlaufer (eds), *Shame Between Punishment and Penance*. This volume as a whole offers a very complete reflection on the conceptions and uses of shame in the Middle Ages.

109 Baldwin of Ford, 'Sermon 13 sur l'annonciation (traité VII)'.

110 See Bologne, *Pudeurs féminines*.

111 See Richard of Saint-Victor, *The Twelve Patriarchs*, p. 108 [LI].

112 Ibid., p. 102 [XLVI].

113 For a good introduction to these themes, see Châtillon et al. 'Cor et cordis affectus'.

114 *Dulcis Jesu memoria, poème anonyme* (Aelred de Rievaulx?), p. 239.

115 See Bynum, *Jesus as Mother*.

116 Aelred of Rievaulx, *On Jesus at Twelve Years Old*.

117 Aelred de Rievaulx, *La Vie de recluse*, p. 120 [§ 29].

118 On this development, see Boquet, 'Le sexe des émotions'.

119 Aelred de Rievaulx, *La Vie de recluse*, p. 124 [§ 31].

120 Ibid., pp. 134–8 [§ 31].

121 See Lauwers, *Naissance du cimetière*; and Iogna-Prat, *La Maison Dieu*.

122 Henriet speaks of the 'déspatialisation idéelle du sacré'; see 'La recluse, le corps, le lieu'.

123 See Guerreau-Jalabert, 'Caritas y don en la sociedad medieval occidental'.

124 See Haseldine, 'Understanding the Language of *amicitia*'; id., 'Friends, Friendship and Networks'; id., 'Friendship, Intimacy and Corporate Networking in the Twelfth Century'; id., 'Affectionate Terms of Address in Twelfth Century Latin Epistolography'.

125 *The Letters of Peter the Venerable*, I, pp. 130–1 [letter 38]; Haseldine, 'Friendship, Intimacy and Corporate Networking', p. 258.

126 See Rosenwein, 'The Political Uses of an Emotional Community', and id., *To Be Neighbor of Saint Peter*. On the abbacy of Aymard, we follow here period defined by Rosenwein, 'The Political Uses of an Emotional Community', p. 205, n. 1.

127 Iogna-Prat, *Ordonner et exclure*, p. 99.

128 See Guerreau-Jalabert, 'Spiritus et caritas'.

129 On the place of charity in spiritual (and blood) kinship for Peter the Venerable, see Henriet, 'Pro se ipsa'.

130 This statement is applicable to ecclesiastical networks in general, see Moulinier, 'Jean de Salisbury, un réseau d'amitiés continentales'.

131 See McGuire, *Brother and Lover*.

132 Aelred of Rievaulx, *De spirituali amicitia*.

133 Mews, 'Cicero and the Boundaries of Friendship in the Twelfth Century'. For broader background, see Hyatte, *The Arts of Friendship*; Haseldine (ed.), *Friendship in Medieval Europe*; Fontes Baratto (ed.), *Écritures et pratiques de l'amitié dans l'Italie médiévale*. On the literary, intellectual, and political implications of friendship in the later Middle Ages, see *infra* Chapters 5 and 7.

134 See White, *Christian Friendship in the Fourth Century*; see also *supra* Chapters 2 and 3.

135 See Boquet, *L'Ordre de l'affect au Moyen Âge*, pp. 275–323.

136 Aelred of Rievaulx, *De spirituali amicitia*, p. 317; *Spiritual Friendship*, pp. 91–2 [III, 2–3].

137 Davy (ed.), *Un traité de l'amour au XIIe siècle*. The *De amicitia christiana* of Peter of Blois is in fact largely a rewriting of the works of Aelred of Rievaulx: see Vansteenberghe, 'Deux théoriciens de l'amitié au xiie siècle'; and Delhaye, 'Deux adaptations du De amicitia de Cicéron au xiie siècle'. On the manuscript diffusion and dispersal of *De spiritali amicitia* and its *compendia*, see Hoste, *Bibliotheca Aelrediana*, pp. 63–73.

138 Aelred of Rievaulx, *De spirituali amicitia*, pp. 348–9; *Spiritual Friendship*, p. 126 [III, 131–4].

139 Ibid., p. 301; *Spiritual Friendship*, p. 69 [I, 69].

140 Ibid., p. 301; *Spiritual Friendship*, p. 69 [I, 70].

141 See *infra* Chapter 7.

CHAPTER 5

1 Le Goff, 'Le rituel symbolique de la vassalité'.

2 de Lorris and de Meun, *Le Roman de la rose*.

3 Augustine, *Confessions*, 49–50 [X], *The Works of Saint Augustine* I:1, p. 270.

4 Boethius, *Traité de la musique*, p. 22.

5 William of Auvergne, *De universo*, in *Opera omnia*, 1, p. 1057 [III.3.20]; cited and discussed by Boccadoro, 'La musique, les passions, l'âme et le corps', esp. pp. 79–80.

6 Le Vot, 'Réalités et figures'.
7 See Cullin, *Brève histoire de la musique médiévale*, p. 35.
8 Thomas of England, *Le Roman de Tristan*, pp. 48–9.
9 Le Vot, 'Réalités et figures', p. 380.
10 See the classic de Rougemont, *L'Amour et l'Occident*.
11 On pre-courtly romantic literature, see Jaeger, *Ennobling Love*, pp. 54–81.
12 Numerous works deserve to be cited here, but in recent decades the influence of Georges Duby has been critical in placing these themes at the heart of social history. See especially his celebrated essay collection *Mâle Moyen Âge*.
13 Régnier-Bohler, 'Amour courtois'.
14 Peire Rogiers, *Canso* in *Les Troubadours*, pp. 86–7 [strophe 1].
15 On this notion, see Huchet, *L'Amour discourtois*, pp. 203–16; on the controversial etymology of the word, see pp. 218–9, n. 27.
16 Guiraut Riquier, *Sérénade*, in *Les Troubadours*, p. 158 [strophe 2].
17 Baladier, *Erôs au Moyen Âge*; id., *Aventure et discours dans l'amour courtois*.
18 For an excellent synthesis of the emotional states associated with sexual desire, see Baldwin, *Les Langages de l'amour dans la France de Philippe Auguste*, pp. 181–256.
19 Bernart Marti, cited in Huchet, *L'Amour discourtois*, p. 17.
20 Bernart de Ventadorn, *Canso*, in *Les Troubadours*, p. 72 [strophe 6].
21 Jaufre Rudel, *Canso*, in *Les Troubadours*, p. 50 [strophe 4].
22 See Corbellari, 'Retour sur l'amour courtois'.
23 Andrew the Chaplain, *The Art of Courtly Love*, p. 28 [1].
24 Duby, 'Que sait-on de l'amour en France au xiie siècle?', p. 4.
25 Thomas of England, *Le Roman de Tristan*, Sneyd fragment 1, v. 522–5, pp. 362–3. On the literary interplay which the dialogue between *dilectio* and carnal passion could engender, see the correspondence (sadly damaged) of Heloise and Abelard at the time of their liaison, which represents the pinnacle of the genre: *Lettres des deux amants attribuées à Héloïse et Abélard*.
26 On this confrontation between the ecclesiastical and aristocratic models of love, see the evocative work of Reddy, *The Making of Romantic Love*.
27 See Boquet, 'L'amitié comme problème au Moyen Âge'.
28 Boswell, *Christianity, Social Tolerance, and Homosexuality*, pp. 370–1.
29 On such couples within the *chansons de geste*, see Legros, *L'Amitié dans les chansons de geste à l'époque romane*, pp. 255–99; and Ailes, 'The Medieval Male Couple and the Language of Homosociability'.

30 This is the case for Aude, Roland's fiancé, who is only present in twenty-nine of the 4002 verses that make up the poem: less than 1 per cent of the text. See Tin, *L'Invention de la culture hétérosexuelle*, p. 17.

31 *Ami et Amile: Chanson de geste*, pp. 6–7 [v. 175–81].

32 *Ami and Amile: A Medieval Tale of Friendship*, p. 36.

33 See Bray, *The Friend*, pp. 13–41; and Boquet, 'Faire l'amitié au Moyen Âge'.

34 To name but one exemplary study, see Carré, *Le Baiser sur la bouche au Moyen Âge*.

35 *Gesta regis Henricis Secundi Benedicti abbatis*, 2, p. 7, cited in Boswell, *Christianity, Social Tolerance, and Homosexuality*, p. 231.

36 See Jaeger, *Ennobling Love*, pp. 128–33.

37 This is Tin's argument in *L'Invention de la culture hétérosexuelle*. This view is contested by Lett in his review of the work, 'Compte rendu de l'ouvrage de L.-G. Tin, L'Invention de la culture hétérosexuelle'. See also Lett, *Hommes et femmes au Moyen Âge*.

38 Chrétien de Troyes, *Yvain ou le Chevalier au lion*, ed. K. D. Uitti and Ph. Walter, in *Œuvres complètes*, p. 503; *Yvain: the Knight of the Lion*, p. 203.

39 See Jordan, *The Invention of Sodomy*, pp. 45–66.

40 See Théry, 'Atrocitas/enormitas'; Chiffoleau, 'Dire l'indicible'; Cottier, '*Vitium contra naturam*: Sexualité et exclusion dans le Liber Gomorrhianus de Pierre Damien'.

41 Kuefler, 'Male Friendship and the Suspicion of Sodomy in Twelfth-Century France'.

42 *Le Roman d'Énéas*, pp. 524–7 [v. 8621–30 and 8649–65]; *Eneas: A Twelfth-Century French Romance*, pp. 226–7.

43 Andrew the Chaplain, *The Art of Courtly Love*, p. 30 [2].

44 See Lett, *Famille et parenté dans l'Occident médiéval*, pp. 178–80.

45 Leclercq, *Le Mariage vu par les moines au XIIe siècle*, pp. 22–3.

46 See Elliott, *Spiritual Marriage*, pp. 266–96.

47 Alain of Lille, *De fide*, PL 210, col. 366; for the evolution of this tendency, see Lett, *Famille et parenté*, pp. 181–4.

48 See Sère, *Penser l'amitié au Moyen Âge*, pp. 153–209. See also *infra* Chapter 7.

49 Ménard, *Le Rire et le sourire dans le roman courtois en France au Moyen Âge*; Levron, 'Naissance de la mélancolie dans la littérature des xiie et xiiie siècles', and id., 'Mélancolie, émotion et vocabulaire'.

50 Debailly and Dumora (eds), *Peur et littérature du Moyen Âge au XVIIe siècle*.

51 Köhler, 'Les troubadours et la jalousie'.

52 See, for example, Bolens, *Le Style des gestes*, and Balgradean, 'The Poet's Grasp at Emotion'.

53 See Madelénat, *L'Épopée*.

54 See, for example, Ribémont, 'La "peur épique"'; Flori, 'Le héros épique et sa peur, du Couronnement de Louis à Aliscans'; Méniel, 'La colère dans la poésie épique, du Moyen Âge à la fin du xvie siècle'.

55 See Ribémont, 'La "peur épique"'.

56 *Jourdain de Blaye*, p. 120 [v. 3697]; cited in Ribémont, 'La "peur épique"', pp. 566–7. Ribémont provides a useful representation of the types of fear in epic (social fear, fear linked to weather events, fear of the miraculous, and the metaphysical fear of divine justice) and the subjects concerned (individual and collective fears, masculine and feminine fears, knightly and bourgeois fears, etc.).

57 Ribémont, 'La "peur épique"', p. 585.

58 *Le Charroi de Nîmes*, pp. 50–1 [v. 81–2].

59 On this subject, see Micha, 'Le mari jaloux dans la littérature romanesque des xiie et xiiie siècles'; Köhler, 'Les troubadours et la jalousie'; J. de Caluwé, 'La jalousie, signe d'exclusion dans la littérature médiévale en langue occitane'; Luce-Dudemaine, 'La sanction de la jalousie dans les "novas" du xiiie siècle'; Rieger, 'Le motif de la jalousie dans le roman arthurien; Lazzerni, 'Une jalousie particulière'.

60 See Vincent-Cassy, 'L'envie au Moyen Âge'; Casagrande and Vecchio, *Histoire des péchés capitaux au Moyen Âge*, pp. 67–92.

61 'Le Roman de Flamenca', in *Les Troubadours*, pp. 698–9 [v. 1037–41]; *The Romance of Flamenca*, p. 57.

62 Ch. Baladier, 'La honte et l'honneur dans les langues d'Europe occidentale', pp. 19–26.

63 Thomas, *Le Roman de Tristan*, pp. 362–3 [v. 504].

64 Chrétien de Troyes, *Lancelot ou le Chevalier à la charrette*, p. 516 [v. 360–77]; *Lancelot: The Knight of the Cart*, pp. 12–13.

65 See Jacquart, 'La maladie et le remède d'amour', and the discussion in Balgradean, 'The Poet's Grasp at Emotion', pp. 42–9.

CHAPTER 6

1 For a synthesis of ancient and medieval philosophical theories of the emotions, see Besnier et al. (eds), *Les Passions antiques et médiévales*; Sorabji, *Emotion and Peace of Mind*; Knuuttila, *Emotions*. For the Middle Ages, see the remarkable synthesis by Imbach,

'Les passions médiévales (perspectives philosophiques)', and Casagrande and Vecchio, *Passioni dell'anima.*

2   See Le Goff, 'Du ciel sur la terre'.

3   See Wéber, *La Personne humaine au XIIIe siècle.*

4   This is the title which Boureau gave to the first chapter of his
book *De vagues individus*: 'Les puissances de l'âme. L'invention
de l'anthropologie au xiie siècle', pp. 19–54.

5   This expression is drawn from Boureau, 'Un sujet agité', p. 187.

6   See Chapter 1 and Boquet, 'Des racines de l'émotion'.

7   Gregory the Great, *Moralia in Job* [XXX, XVIII, 61], cited in
Vecchio, 'Il piacere di Abelardo a Tommaso', p. 68, n. 6.

8   See Lottin, 'Les mouvements premiers de l'appétit sensitif'; Knuuttila, *Emotions*, pp. 185–95; and Vecchio, 'Il piacere da Abelardo
a Tommaso', pp. 67–86.

9   Peter Abelard, 'Know Yourself', p. 11 [I:49].

10 Ibid., pp. 1–2 [I:4–5].

11 On this affair and its chronology, see Zerbi, 'Les différends doctrinaux'. See also Mews, *Abelard and Heloise*, pp. 233–43.

12 Bernard of Clairvaux, 'Sententia 107. Series tertia', in *Sancti Bernardi Opera*, VI-2, p. 173.

13 See Aelred of Rievaulx, *Mirror of Charity*, p. 250 [III.38]. The
English abbot distinguished carnal pleasure and delectation, which
was inevitable, from consent which was truly a matter of moral
responsibility. See, 'Sermon XXII, pour la Purification de Marie',
in *Aelredi Rievallensis*, p. 263 [17–18].

14 For the continuation of the debate in the later Middle Ages and
beyond, see Couture, *L'Imputabilité morale des premiers mouvements de sensualité.*

15 For an introduction to medical science in the Middle Ages, see
Grmek (ed.), *Histoire de la pensée médicale en Occident, 1. Antiquité et Moyen Âge*; and Jacquart, *La Science médicale entre deux
renaissances.*

16 On Constantine the African and his translation efforts, see Burnett
and Jacquart, *Constantine the African and 'Ali ibn al-'Abbas al-
Magusi.* An impressive number of translations have been attributed to Constantine. Today, specialists believe that certain Arab
texts were already circulating in Sicily and in Southern Italy, and
that translations developed gradually over the course of the tenth
century: on this idea, see Burnett, 'Physics Before the Physics',
esp. pp. 78–9.

17 See Moulinier, 'Magie, médecine et maux de l'âme dans l'œuvre
scientifique de Hildegarde de Bingen', esp. p. 551.

18 See Constantine the African, *Pantegni, Theorica*, [VI.109; IV.7], cited in Knuuttila, *Emotions*, p. 214.

19 For example, see *infra*, Chapter 7 for the influence of medical thought on the emotions within chronicles and political theory at the end of the Middle Ages.

20 The treatise of Avicenna, *Kitab al-nafs*, was translated *c.* 1160–70 by Domingo Gundisalvo; it contains a general classification of the emotions. See Avicenna (Latin), *Liber de anima seu Sextus de naturalibus*, pp. 54–62 [IV.IV]

21 See Haase, *Avicenna's* De anima *in the Latin West*, p. 139.

22 See Avicenna, *Kitab al-nafs*, I, 5, discussed in Sebti, *Avicenne*, p. 66.

23 See Andretta and Nicoud (eds), *Être médecin à la cour*.

24 For an introduction to this 'rule of health' genre, see Gil-Sotres, 'Les régimes de santé', and Nicoud, *Les Régimes de santé au Moyen Âge*. On the genre of *consilia*, see Agrimi and Crisciani, *Les Consilia médicaux*.

25 See Arnold of Villanova, *Regimen sanitatis ad regem aragonum*. The monumental introduction by Gil-Sotres (pp. 471–885), offers an accomplished synthesis on the emotions in the 'rules of health', pp. 803–27. See also Gil-Sotres, 'Modelo teórico y observación clínica'; and Ziegler, *Medicine and Religion c. 1300*.

26 See Arnold of Villanova, *Speculum medicine*, ff. 27r–28v; discussed in Gil-Sotres, introduction to Arnold of Villanova, *Regimen sanitatis*, pp. 811–14.

27 Maino de Mainieri, *Regimen sanitatis*, p. 21 [II, *c.* 9]; cited in Gil-Sotres, introduction to Arnold of Villanova, *Regimen sanitatis*, p. 827.

28 See Cohen-Hanegbi, 'Accidents of the Soul', p. 211. The identification of the writer has been questioned: see Nicoud, *Les Régimes de santé*, 1:100–14.

29 Gil-Sotres, introduction to Arnold of Villanova, *Regimen sanitatis*, p. 819.

30 Gentile de Foligno, *Consilia* (Pavia, 1488), cited in Cohen-Hanegbi, 'Accidents of the Soul', p. 212.

31 Barnabas de Reggio, *Regimen sanitatis*, Ms. Paris, B.N., Lat., 16189 (XIV), fol. 10rb, cited in Gil-Sotres, introduction to Arnold of Villanova, *Regimen sanitatis*, p. 827. On the writings of Barnabas and his place in spreading the practice of medicine within lay society at the end of the Middle Ages, see Nicoud, 'L'adaptation du discours diététique aux pratiques alimentaires'.

32 William of Auvergne, *De universo*, p. 1057 [*Opera omnia*, II.3.20]; cited in Boccadoro, 'La musique, les passions, l'âme et le corps', p. 79. See Boethius, *Traité de la musique*, p. 26.

33 See Boethius, *Traité de la musique*, p. 28.
34 See Ziegler, *Medicine and Religion*, pp. 252–4, and id., '*Ut dicunt medici*'; Berlivet et al. (eds), *Médecine et religion*.
35 See Klibansky et al., *Saturne et la mélancolie*.
36 See Jacquart, 'La scolastique médicale'.
37 See Pigeaud, *Maladie de l'âme*; id., *De la mélancolie*.
38 See Moulinier, 'Magie, médecine et maux de l'âme', p. 554.
39 On the place of melancholy and the passions in this text, see the rich index created by Moulinier in Hildegard of Bingen, *Cause et cure*, and its introduction, pp. xciii, ciii–cx; and id., 'Magie, médecine et maux de l'âme', pp. 555–6.
40 Taddeo Alderotti and Michele Giuseppe Nardi, *I Consilia, trascritti dai codici lat. n. 2418 e Malatestiano D. XXIV*, pp. 52–6, cited in Cohen-Hanegbi, 'The Emotional Body of Women', p. 471.
41 See Cohen-Hanegbi, 'The Emotional Body of Women', pp. 465–82.
42 In his commentary on Aristotle's *Problems* (Padoue, 1482) [prol. XXX.1], Pietro d'Abano (d. 1316) reported the case of an illiterate woman, who, in a state of melancholy, spoke Latin, and then forgot it once healed; cited in Jacquart, *La Médecine médiévale dans le cadre parisien*, p. 314, n. 233.
43 On this subject, see Levron, 'Mélancolie, émotion et vocabulaire'.
44 *Le Roman de Tristan en prose*, 3:153–154 [chap. 852]; cited in Levron, 'Mélancolie, émotion et vocabulaire', p. 235.
45 Arnold of Villanova, *De amore heroico*, pp. 43–54. For analysis, see the introduction of the editor, pp. 11–39, and Jacquart and Thomasset, 'L'amour "héroïque" à travers le traité d'Arnaud de Villeneuve'.
46 See Aristotle, *Problems*, pp. 155–69 [XXX.1]
47 For a revisionist intellectual history of the twelfth century, see Giraud, *Per verba magistri*.
48 This progression has been brought to light by Boureau, *De vagues individus*, pp. 45–54.
49 Isaac of Stella, *Epistola de anima*, PL 194, col. 1877 B.
50 Ibid., col. 1878 D.
51 Isaac of Stella, 'Sermon 17' in *Sermons*, I, pp. 320–8 [§ 14–26] and *Epistola de anima*, col. 1879B.
52 See Boquet, *L'Ordre de l'affect au Moyen Âge*, pp. 169–70, n. 111.
53 Pseudo-Alcher of Clairvaux, *De spiritu et anima*, PL 40, col. 829–30.
54 William of Saint-Thierry, *The Nature of the Body and the Soul*, p. 143.
55 The thought of the canons of Saint-Victor is very similar to that elaborated by the Cistercians in the same period: see

Hugh of Saint-Victor, *De sacramentis christianae fidei*, PL 176, col. 331B.

56 Isaac of Stella 'Sermon 19', in *Sermons*, II, pp. 176–7 [§ 13].
57 Aelred of Rievaulx, *Mirror of Charity*, p. 241 [III.31].
58 Aelred of Rievaulx, 'Sermon LI', in *Sermones XLVII–LXXXIV*, p. 41 [§ 5].
59 Aelred of Rievaulx, *Mirror of Charity*, p. 200 [II.53].
60 Ibid., p. 152 [I.105].
61 Ibid., p. 254 [III.48].
62 See Bernard of Clairvaux, *On Loving God*, pp. 31–2 [§ 30].
63 Ibid., p. 32.
64 Hugh of Saint-Victor, *De unione corporis et spiritus*, col. 285–94.
65 Isaac of Stella, *Epistola ad quemdam familiarem suum de anima*, col. 1881C, 1882C.
66 Aelred of Rievaulx, *Dialogus de anima*, in *Aelredi Rievallensis Opera Omnia. 1, Opera ascetica*, p. 701 [I.52].
67 William of Saint-Thierry, *The Nature of the Body and the Soul*. For an analysis, see Boquet, 'Un nouvel ordre anthropologique au xiie siècle'; McGinn, *Three Treatises on Man*, pp. 27–47; Gröne, 'Le premier écrit scientifique cistercien'.
68 On William's sources, see Lemoine, 'Les ambiguïtés de l'héritage médiéval'.
69 See William of Saint-Thierry, 'Lettre sur les erreurs de Guillaume de Conches'; and Lemoine, 'Guillaume de Saint-Thierry et Guillaume de Conches'; Jacquart, *La Médecine médiévale dans le cadre parisien*, pp. 34–6.
70 See the note on the uses of *passio* of Lemoine, in his edition of William of Saint-Thierry, *La Nature du corps et de l'âme*, p. 129, n. 91. See also Boquet, *L'Ordre de l'affect*, pp. 146–7; and Boureau, 'Un sujet agité', pp. 190–1.
71 William of Saint-Thierry, *The Nature of the Body and the Soul*, pp. 126, 123.
72 Ibid., p. 125.
73 Ibid., p. 134.
74 Ibid.
75 Ibid., pp. 138–9.
76 Casagrande and Vecchio, 'Les théories des passions dans la culture médiévale'.
77 See King, 'Emotions in Medieval Thought'.
78 See John Blund, *Tractatus de anima*, pp. 18–21 [§ 62–73]; commented on by Knuuttila, *Emotions*, pp. 226–30, and King, 'Emotions in Medieval Thought', p. 175.
79 See Bejczy, '*De origine virtutum et vitiorum*'.

80 Ibid., pp. 127–8; and Bejczy's commentary, p. 107.
81 Ibid., p. 140.
82 On the philosophical anthropology of William of Auvergne, see Wéber, *La Personne humaine*, pp. 76–84, and above all Morenzoni and Tilliette (eds), *Autour de Guillaume d'Auvergne*. On the passions, see the following essential articles collected in the latter volume: Vecchio, 'Passio, affectus, virtus', pp. 173–87, and Casagrande, 'Guglielmo d'Auvergne e il buon uso delle passioni nella penitenza', pp. 189–201.
83 See Vecchio, 'Passio, affectus, virtus', p. 176.
84 See William of Auvergne, *De virtutibus*, in *Opera omnia*, 1, p. 119. The passage is discussed in Vecchio, 'Passio, affectus, virtus', p. 178.
85 See William of Auvergne, *De virtutibus*, in *Opera omnia*, 1, p. 122.
86 See Anciaux, 'Le sacrement de pénitence chez Guillaume d'Auvergne'.
87 William of Auvergne, *De Sacramentis*, in *Opera omnia*, 1, p. 465, cited in Casagrande, 'Guglielmo d'Auvergne', p. 194.
88 See the analysis of Casagrande, 'Guglielmo d'Auvergne', pp. 196–7.
89 Morenzoni, 'La bonne et la mauvaise honte'.
90 John of La Rochelle, *Summa de anima*. On the anthropology of John of La Rochelle, see Boureau, *De vagues individus*, pp. 93–129. See also Lottin, 'Les traités sur l'âme et les vertus de Jean de la Rochelle'.
91 John of La Rochelle, *Summa de anima*, pp. 263–5 [chap. 108].
92 Ibid., p. 254 [chap. 105]
93 Ibid., pp. 256–62 [chap. 107]. See the description by Vecchio, 'Passions de l'âme et péchés capitaux', p. 58, n. 35.
94 See John of La Rochelle, *Summa de anima*, pp. 147–50 [chap. 46]; analysed by Boureau, *De vagues individus*, p. 128.
95 See John of La Rochelle, *Summa de anima*, p. 150 [chap. 46].
96 See Michaud-Quantin, 'Le traité des passions chez Albert le Grand', and id., *La Psychologie de l'activité chez Albert le Grand*, pp. 91–113.
97 Albert the Great, *Super Ethica*, pp. 113–4 [II.5]. Cited in Vecchio, 'Il discorso sulle passioni nei commenti all'Etica Nicomachea', p. 95. Albert gives other definitions of passion in the *Summa De Bono* [III, 5, 1]: see Michaud-Quantin, *La Psychologie de l'activité chez Albert le Grand*, pp. 92–3.
98 Vecchio, 'Il discorso sulle passioni nei commenti all'Etica Nicomachea'.
99 See Thomas Aquinas, *Summa theologiae*, Ia–IIae, q. 22–48. The theologian also addressed the passions in his *Commentary on the*

Sentences and in his *Commentary on the Nicomachean Ethics*. A large number of publications have discussed Aquinas' treatment of the passions of the soul. See the introduction by Vecchio to his translation of the 'treatise on the passions' in *Tommaso d'Aquino, Le Passioni dell'anima*, pp. 5–18, and King, 'Aquinas on the Emotions'. See also Gondreau, *The Passions of Christ's Soul in the Theology of Saint Thomas Aquinas*; and Imbach, 'Physique ou métaphysique des passions?'.

100 On this issue, see especially Aquinas, *Summa theologiae*, Ia–IIae, q. 37, a. 4 and the commentary by Knuuttila, *Emotions*, p. 241.

101 Aquinas, *Summa theologiae*, Ia–IIae, q. 24, a. 1.

102 Ibid., Ia–IIae, q. 46–8.

103 Ibid. Ia–IIae, q. 47, a. 6.

104 The list of passions provided by Thomas went beyond the eleven base passions that he defined. Rosenwein has identified a large number of passions only found in the *Summa theologiae*: see 'Emotion Words', pp. 104–5.

105 Aquinas, *Summa theologiae*, Ia–IIae, q. 48, a. 1.

106 For the scholastic theories of the passions that followed Aquinas, see above all Perler, *Transformationen der Gefühle*.

107 Boulnois, 'Duns Scot: existe-t-il des passions de la volonté?', esp. p. 285; Knuuttila, *Emotions*, pp. 265–72.

108 Duns Scotus, *Opus Oxoniense*, III, d. 33, q. 1, § 3; cited in Boulnois, 'Duns Scot', p. 282.

109 For example, in the debate over whether interjections could directly express the affects in language. See Rosier-Catach, 'Discussions médiévales sur l'expression des affects'; and Lucken, 'Éclats de la voix, langage des affects et séduction du chant'.

110 Boureau, *De vagues individus*, p. 26.

CHAPTER 7

1 See Hochner, 'Machiavelli: Love and the Economy of Emotions'.

2 Machiavelli, *The Prince*, p. 58.

3 On the articulation of this dialectic of love and fear in Christian political culture, see Sassier, 'Inspirer l'amour, inspirer la crainte?', pp. 27–43.

4 As testament to this development, see Andenmatten et al. (eds), *Passions et pulsions à la cour*.

5 The pages that follow are greatly indebted to the work of Smagghe, *Les Émotions du prince*.

6   On the place of emotions in the political theory of John of Salisbury, see especially books III and IV of *Policraticus*, and the remarks of Sassier in 'Inspirer l'amour, inspirer la crainte?', pp. 35–8.

7   On this critical relationship, see Courtine and Haroche, *Histoire du visage*.

8   Georges Chastellain, *Œuvres*, 7, p. 219; cited in Smagghe, *Les Émotions du prince*, p. 133.

9   Christine de Pizan, *Le Livre des fais du sage roy Charles*, p. 222, cited in Smagghe, *Les Émotions du prince*, p. 147.

10 On self-government and the passions, see Lachaud, *L'Éthique du pouvoir au Moyen Âge*, pp. 93 ff.; and Boquet, 'Le gouvernement de soi et des autres selon Bernard de Clairvaux'.

11 See Buc, *L'Ambiguïté du Livre*, pp. 71–122.

12 Gregory the Great, *Moralia in Job*, XXI, 15, 24, cited in Vincent of Beauvais, *De morali principis institutione*, p. 55 [X].

13 Vincent of Beauvais, *De morali principis institutione*, p. 56 [X].

14 See Krynen, *L'Empire du roi*, pp. 179–87.

15 See Marmo, '*Hoc autem etsi potest tollerari*'.

16 Giles of Rome, *Livres du gouvernement des rois*, pp. 94–121.

17 Ibid., p. 98.

18 See Giles of Rome, *Expositio super Libros Rhetoricorum Aristotelis*, 49rb–51ra; and Knuuttila, *Emotions*, pp. 254–5.

19 For a synthetic analysis of love in *De regimine principum*, see Scordia, 'Concepts et registres de l'amour du roi'.

20 Joinville, *Vie de Saint Louis*, p. 578.

21 *Essais sur les mœurs*, cited by Le Goff, *Saint Louis*, p. 11.

22 Matthew Paris, *English History*, 3, p. 96.

23 Michelet, *Le Moyen Âge*, p. 389.

24 Geoffrey of Beaulieu, *Life and Saintly Comportment of Louis*, p. 97.

25 Joinville, *The Life of St Louis*, pp. 26–7.

26 Ibid., p. 135.

27 Ibid., p. 126.

28 This episode is discussed in Le Goff, *Saint Louis*, p. 490.

29 Joinville, *The Life of St Louis*, p. 64.

30 Matthew Paris, *English History*, 2, p. 269; cited in O'Connell, *Les Propos de Saint Louis*, p. 159.

31 Joinville, *The Life of St Louis*, p. 152.

32 See Le Goff, *Saint Louis*, pp. 487–9.

33 Joinville, *The Life of St Louis*, p. 153.

34 Ibid., p. 168.

35 See Verdon, 'La course des amants adultères'.

36 By way of introduction, see Althoff, 'Ira Regis'.

37 See Jolliffe, *Angevin Kingship*, p. 96.

38 See Smagghe, 'Sur paine d'encourir nostre indignation'.

39 See Zimmermann, 'Le vocabulaire latin de la malédiction du ixe au xiie siècle'.

40 Casagrande and Vecchio, *Histoire des péchés capitaux*, pp. 93–125.

41 See Sère, 'Le roi peut-il avoir honte?', pp. 65–6.

42 See M. Aurell, *L'Empire Plantagenêt* (Paris, Perrin, 2004), p. 120.

43 See, for example, Smagghe's study of Molinet's vocabulary in *Les Émotions du prince*, pp. 232–3; see also the study of Froissart's terminology in Raynaud, 'Le courroux et la haine dans les Chroniques de Jean Froissart'.

44 Macé, *Les Comtes de Toulouse et leur entourage*, pp. 261–8; and Grassotti, 'La ira regia en León y Castilla'. On the *ira regis* of the English royalty, see Jolliffe, *Angevin Kingship*; and Hyams, 'What Did Henry III of England Think in Bed and in French about Kingship and Anger?'.

45 See, for example, Giles of Rome's analysis of anger in his commentary on Aristotle's *Rhetoric*, discussed in Sère, 'Déshonneur, outrage et infamie'.

46 Smagghe has presented a detailed study of the bodily manifestations of princely anger among the dukes of Burgundy: *Les Émotions du prince*, pp. 167–292.

47 See, for example, William of Newburgh, *Historia*, 1, p. 142 [II.16], cited in Aurell, *L'Empire Plantagenêt*, pp. 267–8; as well as the examples cited in Hyams, 'What Did Henry III of England Think', pp. 102–3. More generally, see Duggan, *Thomas Becket*, and Staunton, *Thomas Becket and his Biographers*.

48 William of Newburgh, *Historia*, 1, p. 142 [II.16], cited in Aurell, *L'Empire Plantagenêt*, p. 268.

49 This section is greatly influenced by the analysis of Sère, 'Le roi peut-il avoir honte?'

50 Duby, *Le Dimanche de Bouvines*, p. 82.

51 See Moeglin, *Les Bourgeois de Calais*, pp. 338–40.

52 On this evolution, see Offenstadt, *Faire la paix au Moyen Âge*, pp. 186–7.

53 The paragraphs which follow take account of the fine work of Sère, *Penser l'amitié au Moyen Âge*.

54 Ibid., p. 104.

55 Aelred of Rievaulx, *Spiritual Friendship*, p. 110 [§ 90].

56 See Sère, *Penser l'amitié*, pp. 134–5.

57 On royal friendship in Oresme, see ibid., pp. 170–88.

58 On political friendship among the later medieval aristocracy, see Oschema, *Freundschaft und Nähe im spätmittelalterlichen Burgund*.

59 See Offenstadt, *Faire la paix*, p. 223.

60 See Buc, *Dangereux rituel,* and Moeglin, ' "Performative Turn" '.

61 See Offenstadt, *Faire la paix,* pp. 204–6.

62 This episode has been treated from this aspect by Oschema, 'Toucher et être touché', p. 155. In this article, Oschema shows that the obligation of adversaries in fourteenth-century judicial duels to jointly pronounce an oath while holding hands represented a final attempt at reconciliation through physical contact.

63 This is the title of an article by M. Colonna in *L'Histoire.*

64 See Offenstadt, *Faire la paix,* pp. 201–3.

65 This episode has been analysed by Smagghe, *Les Émotions du prince,* pp. 388–90.

66 Georges Chastellain, *Œuvres,* 4, p. 336; cited in Smagghe, *Les Émotions du prince,* p. 389.

67 See Smagghe, *Les Émotions du prince,* pp. 358–61.

68 Ibid., p. 254. See Bubenicek, 'Femme, pouvoir, violence', and Bousmar, 'Jacqueline de Bavière, trois comtés, quatre maris'.

69 Krynen, *L'Empire du roi,* p. 458.

CHAPTER 8

1 Jacques de Vitry, *The Life of Marie d'Oignies,* p. 17.

2 Angela of Foligno, *Memorial,* in *The Complete Works,* p. 141 [III]; see also the critical edition of Thier and Calufetti (eds), *Il libro della Beata Angela da Foligno,* Grottaferrata. For background, see Menestò (ed.), *Il 'Liber' della Beata Angela da Foligno.*

3 Bynum, *Fragmentation and Redemption,* p. 185

4 Angela of Foligno, *Memorial,* in *The Complete Works,* p. 186 [VII].

5 Thomas of Celano, *The First Life of St Francis,* 1, pp. 227–8 [52, chap. XIX].

6 Dalarun, *Claire de Rimini,* p. 113 (commentary on pp. 112–15), and id., 'Lapsus linguae', pp. 305–9, 324–6. The same penitential flagellation can also be witnessed with Margaret of Cortona (d. 1297) in the last quarter of the thirteenth century, but her saintly model was Mary Magdelene.

7 Dalarun, 'Le corps monastique entre *opus Dei* et modernité', p. 21 and n. 16, where it is noted that Max Weber and Michel Foucault had proposed a similar idea.

8 Dalarun, *'Dieu changea de sexe, pour ainsi dire'.*

9 Vauchez, *La Sainteté en Occident,* p. 317.

10 Rubin, *Corpus Christi.*

11 See *supra* Chapter 4.

12 On this, see Dalarun, *François d'Assise, un passage*.
13 Francis of Assisi, *Testament*, in *Francis of Assisi: Early Documents*, 1, p. 125.
14 Dalarun, 'Lapsus linguae', p. 388. On the question of the end of communion in both kinds and its relationship to the devotion to the blood of Christ, see Boquet, 'Corps et genre des émotions'.
15 See Bedos-Rezak et al. (eds), *L'Individu au Moyen Âge*.
16 Dickson, *Religious Enthusiasm in the Medieval West*, provides an excellent guide to these movements.
17 Ibid., p. 231.
18 *Vita prima di san Antonio o Assidua*, pp. 338–43 [13].
19 Dickson, *Religious Enthusiasm*, p. 18; *Ad cruce signatos*, 2, pp. 421–30 [no. 48].
20 Förstemann, *Die christlichen Geisslergesellschaften*, pp. 16–7; Dickson, *Religious Enthusiasm*, p. 231.
21 Ibid.
22 Jacobus da Varagine, *Cronaca di Genova*, 2, pp. 389–90.
23 See Dickson, *Religious Enthusiasm*, pp. 227–9, 238–9.
24 See most recently, Thomas of Celano, *Vita beati patris nostri Francisci*. The evidence provided by this very short text, an intermediary between the *vita prima* and the *Memorial*, does not alter the analysis provided here.
25 Thomas of Celano, *The First Life*, 1, pp. 221–2 [44, I, chap. XVI], 1, p. 228 [53, I, chap. XIX]; 1, p. 219 [40, I, chap. XV]; 1, pp. 220–1 [42, I, chap. XVI].
26 Ibid., 1, pp. 275 [106, II, chap. VII].
27 Ibid., 1, pp. 266 [97, II, chap. IV], citing Ps 62 (63): 2.
28 Ibid., 1, pp. 188 [7, I, chap. III], citing Ps 125 (126): 2.
29 Thomas of Celano, *The Remembrance of the Desire of a Soul*, 2, p. 331 [127, II, chap. XC]. See also Thomas de Celano, *First Life* [16, I, chap. VII]. On this subject see Dalarun, 'François d'Assise et la quête du Graal'; Battais, 'La courtoisie de François d'Assise'; Dessì, 'Prière, chant et prédication', p. 250; Le Goff, 'Une musique de jubilation', p. 16.
30 Thomas of Celano, *First Life*, 1, p. 191 [10, I, chap. V].
31 Ibid., 1, p. 263 [93, II. chap. II].
32 Ibid., 1, p. 221 [42, I. chap. XVI].
33 See Johnson (ed.), *Franciscans and Preaching*, especially the chapters by M. W. Blastic, 'Preaching in the Early Franciscan Movement', pp. 15–40, and J. A. Wayne Hellmann, 'A Theology of Preaching – a Theology of Transformation', pp. 61–9. For further depth, see Manselli, 'Il gesto come predicazione per san Francesco d'Assisi'.

34 Thomas of Celano, *First Life*, 1, pp. 189–90 [9, I, chap. IV].

35 Ibid., 1, p. 192 [15, I, chap. VI]; see Boquet, 'Écrire et représenter la dénudation'.

36 Thomas of Celano, *First Life*, 1, p. 228 [52, I, chap. XIX].

37 Ibid., 1, pp. 248–9 [77–8, I, XVIII]; and also 1, pp. 234–6 [58–61, I, XXI].

38 Ibid., 1, pp. 254–6 [84–6, I, chap. XXX], for the entirety of the scene cited below. On the liturgical representation of Christmas before Francis, see Frugoni, 'Sui vari significati del Natale di Greccio', esp. pp. 37–9; see also Young, *The Drama of the Medieval Church*, 2, pp. 3–198; Gougaud, 'La crèche de Noël avant saint François d'Assise'.

39 Frugoni, 'Sui vari significati del Natale di Greccio'.

40 Thomas of Celano, *First Life*, 1, p. 251 [81, I, chap. XXIX]. For the birds and the swallows, see ibid., 1, pp. 234–5 [58–9, I, chap. XXI].

41 For a historical study of stigmata and those affected, see Klaniczay (ed.), *Discorsi sulle stimmate dal medioevo all'età contemporanea*.

42 Thomas of Celano, *First Life*, 1, pp. 279–81 [112–3, II, chap. IX].

43 See above all Schmitt, 'L'imagination efficace', esp. p. 346.

44 On this visual emotional culture in Gothic art, see D. Borlée, ' "Sculpter les mouvements de l'âme" '.

45 See McNamer, *Affective Meditation*; the notion of emotional 'scripts' derives from Kaster, *Emotion, Restraint and Community*.

46 Thomas of Celano, *The Treatise on the Miracles of St Francis*, 2, p. 401 [2, chap. II]; see Schmitt, 'L'imagination efficace', p. 353.

47 Jacobus de Varagine, *Sermo III de stigmatibus s. Francisci*, pp. 113 and ff.

48 See also the analysis of Boureau, *Satan hérétique*, pp. 233–4.

49 London, British Library, MS Yates Thompson 11, fo. 28. See, above all, Belting, *L'Image et son public au Moyen Âge*; id., *Image et culte: une histoire de l'image avant l'époque de l'art*; see also Ringbom, 'Images de dévotion et dévotions imaginatives'; Hamburger, *Peindre au couvent*; id., *The Visual and the Visionary*, chap. 2, pp. 111–48. A recent interrogation of the question from the emotional perspective provides a long bibliography at n. 5: d'Hainaut-Zveny, 'L'ivresse sobre'.

50 This image has been analysed by Hamburger, *The Visual and the Visionary*, pp. 131–4, and by Belting, *Image et culte*, pp. 558–9 (the image – no. 247 – is on p. 558). For its dating, Belting suggests 1290–1300, while Hamburger suggests 1310–20 in his article 'The Use of Images in the Pastoral Care of Nuns', p. 22.

51 Angela of Foligno, *Memorial*, in *The Complete Works*, pp. 157–8, 169–70 [IV], pp. 169–70 [VI]; p. 215 [IX].
52 Ibid., p. 158 [IV], p. 185–9 [VII].
53 See Schmitt, 'L'imagination efficace', p. 355, whose analysis is followed here; *Lectionary* of Heilig Kreuz, Oxford, Keble College, MS 49, 308 ff, 402–305 mm.
54 Schmitt, 'L'imagination efficace', p. 355; the image is reproduced on p. 356.
55 Hamburger, *Peindre au couvent*, p. 5; the image is found on the cover: Christ on the cross, isolated drawing, folio conserved at the Schnütgen Museum in Cologne.
56 On what follows, see Boquet, 'Incorporation mystique et subjectivité féminine'.
57 *Vita venerabilis Lukardis monialis O.C. in superiore Wimaria.*
58 Ibid., XXVII, p. 323.
59 Above all, see Hamburger, *Peindre au couvent*.
60 *Vita venerabilis Lukardis*, VII, p. 314.
61 By way of comparison, see Giotto's *La Stigmatisation de saint François* from the altarpiece of the church of St Francis in Pisa (today found at the Louvre); Frugoni, *François d'Assise*, p. 170, and above all, id., *Francesco e l'invenzione delle stimmate*.
62 The appearance of the stigmatized Christ draws close to the iconographic themes of the *Mass of St Gregory*, the origin of the legend on the same topic. While Jacobus did not know this legend, it does seem to have been born in fourteenth-century Italy. For an introduction to the topic, see Réau, 'Saint Grégoire'.
63 *Vita venerabilis Lukardis*, X, p. 315.
64 Ibid., X, pp. 315–16.
65 Ibid., XI, p. 316.
66 Ibid., XII, p. 316.
67 Angela of Foligno, *Memorial*, in *The Complete Works*, p. 128 [I].
68 Ibid., p. 175 [VI].
69 Jacques de Vitry, *Life of Marie d'Oignies*, VII, p. 21.
70 Ibid., VII, p. 22.
71 Reddy, *The Navigation of Feeling*, p. 129.
72 On Angela of Foligno, see Boquet and Nagy, 'L'efficacité religieuse de l'affectivité', pp. 171–201.
73 'An "emotive" is a type of speech act different from both performative and constative utterances, which both describes (like constative utterances) and changes (like performatives) the world, because emotional expression has an exploratory and a self-altering effect on the activated thought material of emotion.' Reddy, *The Navigation of Feeling*, p. 128. For a close reading of Reddy,

see Nagy, 'Les émotions et l'historien', pp. 10–22, and Boquet and Nagy, 'L'historien et les émotions en politique', pp. 5–30.

74 In a recent book that deserves discussion, Sarah McNamer even suggests that the emergence and success of compassionate spirituality – and affective piety more broadly – in the later Middle Ages was entirely the work of women: McNamer, *Affective Meditation*.

75 See Boquet, 'Le sexe des émotions'; see also the unpublished thesis by Mancia, 'Affective Devotion and Emotional Reform'.

76 See Bynum, *Jesus as Mother*.

77 De Gier and Fraeters, 'Introduction', in *eidem, Mulieres religiosae*, pp. 1–16; see, for instance, Henri of Ghent, *Summa questionum ordinarium*, fol. 78r [I, art. XI, q. 11], cited by McGinn, *The Flowering of Mysticism*, p. 21. More broadly, see L'Hermite-Leclercq, *L'Église et les Femmes*.

78 Fraeters, ' "Ô amour, sois tout à moi!" ', p. 355, n. 6.

79 Marguerite Porete, *The Mirror of Simple Souls*.

80 See above all the article by Field, 'William of Paris's Inquisitions Against Marguerite Porete'.

81 For the suggestions described above, see, in succession, Bynum, 'Women Mystics and Eucharistic Devotion in the Thirteenth Century', in *Fragmentation and Redemption*, pp. 119–50; de Libera, 'Angèle de Foligno et la mystique "féminine" '; Hollywood, *The Soul as Virgin Wife*, pp. 33–5.

82 *La Vie de sainte Douceline, texte provençal du XIVe siècle*, chapters IX–XI.

83 See Beyer de Ryke, 'Une souffrance christiforme', esp. p. 300; Hamburger, 'The Use of Images in the Pastoral Care of Nuns', p. 23.

84 Henry Suso, *The Life of the Servant*, p. 25 [chap. 4]. See also the critical edition, *Deutsche Schriften im Auftrag der Württembergischen Kommission für Landesgeschichte*, p. 16; Beyer de Ryke, 'Une souffrance christiforme', p. 314.

85 Hamburger, 'The Use of Images in the Pastoral Care of Nuns', p. 43.

86 Cohen, 'Towards a History of European Physical Sensibility'; and id., *The Modulated Scream*.

87 Ibid.

88 Beyer de Ryke, 'Une souffrance christiforme', p. 302.

89 Henry Suso, *The Life of the Servant*, p. 47 [chap. XVI]; *Deutsche Schriften*, p. 4 [chap. XVI]; Beyer de Ryke, 'Une souffrance christiforme', p. 310.

90 Woods, 'Conclusion: Women and Men in the Development of Late Medieval Mysticism'.

91 See Fraeters, ' "Ô amour, sois tout à moi!" ', p. 356.

92 The notion of a vernacular theology that ran alongside monastic and scholastic theology has been proposed by McGinn, 'Introduction: Meister Eckhart and the Beguines in the Context of Vernacular Theology', in *Meister Eckhart and the Beguine Mystics*, pp. 1–16. See the critical analysis by Piron, 'Marguerite, entre les béguines et les maîtres', pp. 77–80.

93 Beyond Hollywood's *The Soul as Virgin Wife*, see also McGinn (ed.), *Meister Eckhart and the Beguine Mystics*.

94 On this subject, see the articles by Lichtmann and Sells, in McGinn (ed.), *Meister Eckhart and the Beguine Mystics*, pp. 65–86, pp. 114–46.

95 Fraeters, ' "Ô amour, sois tout à moi!" ', p. 356; Piron, 'Marguerite, entre les béguines et les maîtres', p. 70.

96 For Marguerite's teaching and a comparison with the *Lettre aux frères du Mon Dieu*, see Boulnois, 'Qu'est-ce que la liberté de l'esprit?'; Van Engen, 'Marguerite (Porete) of Hainaut and the Medieval Low Countries'.

97 Fraeters, ' "Ô amour, sois tout à moi!" ', p. 356.

98 Ibid., p. 357.

99 *Hadewijch: The Complete Works*, p. 280. Discussed in Fraeters, ' "Ô amour, sois tout à moi!" ', p. 362.

100 Fraeters, ' "Ô amour, sois tout à moi!" ', pp. 366–7.

101 *Hadewijch: The Complete Works*, p. 145 [Poems in stanzas 7].

102 See Valette, 'Marguerite Porete et le discours courtois'.

103 Van Engen, 'Marguerite (Porete) of Hainaut and the Medieval Low Countries', esp. p. 42.

104 See Hollywood, *The Soul as Virgin Wife*.

105 See Boulnois, 'Qu'est-ce que la liberté de l'esprit?', and Van Engen, 'Marguerite (Porete) of Hainaut and the Medieval Low Countries', p. 44.

106 See Hollywood, 'Suffering Transformed', p. 99; Marguerite Porete, *The Mirror of Simple Souls*, chap. 90 and those that follow.

107 Piron, 'Marguerite, entre les béguines et les maîtres', pp. 74–5; Marguerite Porete, *The Mirror of Simple Souls*, chap. 66, p. 142.

108 See the articles by Piron and Boulnois in Field et al. (eds), *Marguerite Porete et le Miroir des simples âmes*.

109 Hollywood, 'Suffering Transformed', p. 112.

110 Our presentation of the spirituality of the brothers and sisters of the common life is indebted to Van Engen's *Sisters and Brothers of the Common Life*, above all chapters 7 and 8, pp. 238–304; see also Oberman and Van Engen (eds), Introduction to *Devotio Moderna*, pp. 25–35, esp. p. 26. On the *devotio moderna* more

broadly, see Post, *The Modern Devotion*; and Deploige, 'United or Bound by Death?' For an introduction to the mysticism of the *devotio moderna*, see McGinn, *The Varieties of Vernacular Mysticism*, chapters 1–4.

111 On this subject, see Salomé Sticken, *A Way of Life for Sisters*, pp. 176–86; the original text is edited by Kühler, *Johannes Brinckerinck en zijn klooster te Diepenveen*, pp. 360–80.

112 See *On the Life and Passion of Our Lord Jesus Christ, and Other Devotional Exercices*, in Oberman and Van Engen (eds), *Devotio Moderna*, pp. 187–204; and the original, *Epistola de vita et passione domini nostri*, p. 89–110.

113 Thomas à Kempis, *The Imitation of Christ*, p. 27.

114 Van Engen, *Sisters and Brothers of the Common Life*, pp. 277–8.

115 See Blommestijn et al. (eds), *Spirituality Renewed*, especially the articles by van Dijk, 'Toward Imageless Contemplation – Gerard Zerbolt of Zutphen as Guide for Lectio Divina', pp. 3–28, and by Waaijman, 'Image and Imagelessness – A Challenge to [the Modern] Devotion', pp. 29–40. In opposition to these, see Scheel, *Das altniederländische Stifterbild*, which we have not yet consulted.

116 Van Engen, *Sisters and Brothers of the Common Life*, p. 44 [chap. 1].

117 Twenty-six theses of Meister Eckhart were condemned by John XXII in the bull *In agro dominico*, promulgated 27 March 1329. This followed a long inquisition which had still not finished its work when Eckhart died in 1328.

118 Van Engen, *Sisters and Brothers of the Common Life*, pp. 84–118 [chap. 3].

119 Ibid., pp. 28–37 [chap. 1].

CHAPTER 9

1 Le Goff, 'Rire au Moyen Âge', p. 10.

2 See now, on the scholastic corpus, Delaurenti, *La Contagion des émotions*.

3 See Verdon, *La Voix des dominés*, p. 172.

4 See Boquet and Nagy, 'L'historien et les émotions en politique', pp. 5–30, esp. pp. 21–5.

5 On this subject, see Boquet, 'Le concept de communauté émotionnelle selon Rosenwein'.

6 Paez and Rimé, 'L'empathie dans le partage social de l'émotion'.

7 This is a reference to the title of the Iogna-Prat's book *Ordonner et exclure*.

8   Boucheron, *The Power of Images*.
9   See Le Goff and Schmitt (eds), *Le Charivari*; Davis, *Society and Culture in Early Modern France*, pp. 98–123 and 296–309; Thompson, 'Rough Music: Le Charivari Anglais' and 'Rough Music Reconsidered'.
10 Reddy, *The Navigation of Feeling*.
11 See Moeglin, *Les Bourgeois de Calais*.
12 Jean Froissart, *Chroniques*, livre I, chap. 121, vol. II, pp. 462–71. The text used here is the second version of the Chronicle, dating from *c*. 1390–1400. See Moeglin, *Les Bourgeois de Calais*, p. 38.
13 Moeglin, *Les Bourgeois de Calais*, pp. 39–48.
14 Ibid., pp. 93–7.
15 Ibid., p. 326.
16 Challet, ' "Moyran, los traidors, moyran", p. 83.
17 Cited by Stella, *La Révolte des Ciompi*, p. 61.
18 Gonthier, 'Acteurs et témoins des Rebeynes lyonnaises à la fin du Moyen Âge', p. 40; and for the last citation, see Champier, *L'Antiquité de la Cité de Lyon*, p. 53.
19 Freedman, 'Peasant Anger in the Late Middle Ages'.
20 On what follows, see Haemers, 'A Moody Community?'.
21 Offenstadt, 'Cris et cloches'. See also Challet, ' "Moyran, los traidors, moyran" ', pp. 83–5.
22 See Moscovici, *L'Âge des foules*, part III, chap. V, III.
23 Farge, 'Affecter les sciences humaines', p. 47.
24 See Verdon, *La Voix des dominés*, p. 172; White, 'Politics of Anger'; finally, see also Althoff, 'Empörung, Tränen, Zerknirschung. "Emotionen" in der öffentlichen Kommunikation des Mittelalters', pp. 60–79.
25 Challet, ' "Moyran, los traidors, moyran" ', p. 91.
26 See Chave-Mahir, 'Les cris du démoniaque', pp. 131–40.
27 See again Verdon, *La Voix des dominés*, p. 172 ff.; id., 'Expressions et usages des comportements affectifs', pp. 255–74.
28 Gauvard, '*De grace especial*', 2, p. 734.
29 Spiegel, 'History, Historicism and the Social Logic of the Text', pp. 3–28, 213–20.
30 Deploige, 'Meurtre politique, guerre civile et catharsis littéraire', p. 229. See also Hyams, *Rancor and Reconciliation in Medieval England*, pp. 35–9.
31 Moeglin, *Les Bourgeois de Calais*, p. 324.
32 See Mansfield, *The Humiliation of Sinners*, above all chap. 8. On the subject of scandal, see no. 25 in the *Cahiers de recherches médiévales et humanistes* (2013), entitled 'Le droit et son écriture: La médiatisation du fait judiciaire dans la littérature médiévale',

above all Lecuppre, 'Le scandale: de l'exemple pervers à l'outil politique', pp. 181–91, which comes with a rich bibliography.

33 Moeglin, *Les Bourgeois de Calais*, pp. 352–3.

34 *De vera et falsa poenitentia*, PL 40, col. 1123; Moeglin, *Les Bourgeois de Calais*, p. 336.

35 Vallerani, 'Mouvements de paix dans une commune de popolo', esp. p. 314.

36 Beyond the article by Vallerani, a good place to begin exploring what is now a flourishing bibliography is Vincent, 'Discipline du corps et de l'esprit chez les flagellants au Moyen Âge', pp. 593–614; and Martignoni, 'Entre textes et images', pp. 211–27.

37 For what follows, see Offenstadt, 'De la joie et des larmes', pp. 349–68, reprised in id., *Faire la paix*, pp. 196–213.

38 See the classic article by M. Mauss, 'L'expression obligatoire des sentiments'.

39 Clément de Fauquembergue, *Journal*, vol. 1, 12 juillet 1419, p. 306.

40 Christine de Pizan, The '*Livre de la Paix*', pp. 60, 91.

41 Gauvard, 'Violence et rituels', p. 199.

42 Miller, *Bloodtaking and Peacemaking*.

43 Durkheim, *Les Formes élémentaires de la vie religieuse*, book III, chap. IV, III, II, pp. 359 ff.

44 See Paez and Rimé, 'Collective Emotional Gatherings'. The two authors speak of the shared *flow* of emotions at these occassions, taking their lead from Csíkszentmihályi, *Vivre: la psychologie du bonheur*.

45 See Lett, *Famille et parenté*, pp. 189–212, and id., *L'Enfant des miracles*. For a synthetic study of the emotions between couples and within families in the later Middle Ages, occasionally discussed in our book (see *supra* Chapters 3 and 5), see Lett, 'Familles et relations émotionnelles (xiie-xve siècle)'.

46 See Henriet, 'Chronique de quelques morts annoncées', p. 101 and n. 47.

47 The death scene of an abbot is discussed by Henriet, *La Parole et la Prière*, pp. 287–386.

48 Duby, *Guillaume le Maréchal ou le Meilleur Chevalier du monde*, p. 7–30; *History of William Marshal*.

49 ' "Si grant doel ai que je ne vuldreie estre!" Sa barbe blanche cumencet a detraire...', *La Chanson de Roland*, v. 2929–2930. Lansing, *Passion and Order*, p. 79.

50 Lansing, *Passion and Order*, p. 76–81.

51 *History of William Marshal*, 2, pp. 415–17 [v. 18261–18278].

52 Ibid., 2, p. 447 [v. 18865–18879].

53 Deploige, 'Meurtre politique, guerre civile et catharsis littéraire', pp. 228–31, and id., 'Studying Emotions', esp. pp. 20–1; Rosenwein, *Emotional Communities*, pp. 26–9 and pp. 195–6.
54 Alexandre-Bidon, 'Gestes et expressions du deuil', p. 124.
55 Capitular library of Ivrea, MS. 86. Facsimile: *Sacramentario del Vescovo Warmondo di Ivrea*; *Le Miniature del Sacramentario d'Ivrea e altri codici Warmondiani*, ff. 191–206v, pl. XXXV–XL. Reproduced and analysed by Schmitt, *La Raison des gestes dans l'Occident médiéval*, pp. 211–24.
56 Treffort, *L'Église carolingienne et la Mort*, pp. 81–4; Lansing, *Passion and Order*, p. 83; Alexandre-Bidon, 'Gestes et expressions du deuil'.
57 Lansing, *Passion and Order*, p. 109 and pp. 117–21.
58 Alexandre-Bidon, 'Gestes et expressions du deuil', p. 122.
59 Lansing, *Passion and Order*, p. 12, and n. 1; p. 13, and n. 2–3.
60 Ibid., pp. 13 and 47.
61 Jaeger, *Ennobling Love*, and *supra* Chapter 5.
62 Maire-Vigueur, *Cavaliers et citoyens*, pp. 307–21, esp. p. 320.
63 Smail, 'Hatred as a Social Institution in Late-Medieval Society', and id., *The Consumption of Justice*.
64 Maire-Vigueur, *Cavaliers et citoyens*; Bartlett, ' "Mortal Enmities" '; Smail, 'Hatred', p. 94.
65 Smail, *The Consumption of Justice*, p. 93.
66 Smail, 'Hatred', pp. 100–1, 124.
67 Smail, *The Consumption of Justice*, p. 93.
68 Ibid., pp. 1–2.
69 By Moore, *The Formation of a Persecuting Society*. See also Iogna-Prat, *Ordonner et exclure*; Sapir Abulafia, *Christians and Jews in the Twelfth-Century Renaissance*; id., *Christians and Jews in Dispute*; id., *Christian–Jewish Relations, 1000–1300*; for opposing suggestions, see Laursen and Nederman (eds), *Beyond the Persecuting Society*; Elukin, *Living Together, Living Apart*.
70 Sapir Abulafia, *Christian–Jewish Relations*, pp. 30–1.
71 See Mazel, *Féodalités (888–1180)*, chap. 4: 'La rupture "grégorienne", une révolution culturelle'.
72 See Le Goff, *La Bourse et la vie*.
73 Guibert of Nogent, *The Autobiography of Guibert*, II, chap. V.
74 Sapir Abulafia, 'Bodies in the Jewish–Christian Debate', pp. 123–34, esp. p. 131; id. *Christian–Jewish Relations*, pp. 137 ff.; Rubin, *Corpus Christi*.
75 See Sapir Abulafia, *Christian–Jewish Relations*, chap. 7: 'Jewish Experience of the Crusades', pp. 135–66; Eidelberg (ed.), *The Jews and the Crusaders*.

76 Amid an enormous bibliography, two titles stand out for having proposed classic interpretations: Kriegel, 'Mobilisation politique et modernisation organique'; Richez, 'Émeutes antisémites et révolution en Alsace', pp. 114–21.

77 On this matter, much research still needs to be done, above all a comparison of normative and Christian theoretical sources with descriptions of actions from both sides. This is exactly what has been proposed by Sapir Abulafia, *Christian–Jewish Relations*.

78 We reprise here the conclusion of Soussen-Max, 'Violence rituelle ou émotion populaire?'

79 This is the analysis of Nirenberg, *Violence et minorités au Moyen Âge*, chap. VII.

80 Cited in Soussen-Max, 'Violence rituelle', p. 161, n. 45.

81 Nirenberg, *Violence et minorités*, p. 302.

82 Febvre, 'La sensibilité et l'histoire'.

83 Delumeau, *La Peur en Occident*; id., *Le Péché et la peur*; id., *Rassurer et protéger*.

84 Casagrande, 'Sermo affectuosus', p. 520.

85 See, for example, Nagy, 'Au-delà du verbe'; for the later Middle Ages, see the exposition of Carthusian explanation of prayer for ordinary people (ms. Charleville, 58: 1490), in Bériou et al. (eds), *Prier au Moyen Âge*, pp. 222–5.

86 Casagrande and Vecchio, 'Les théories des passions dans la culture médiévale', p. 116; Casagrande, 'Guglielmo d'Auvergne e il buon uso delle passioni nella penitenza'; id., ' "Motions of the Heart" and Sins'.

87 For what follows in this passage, see especially Casagrande, 'Sermo affectuosus', pp. 519–32; Casagrande and Vecchio, 'La théorie des passions dans la culture médiévale', p. 116, and n. 22 for the references to the texts of Augustine and Gregory the Great.

88 Casagrande, 'Sermo affectuosus', pp. 520–1. See also, von Moos, 'La retorica medievale', pp. 293–326.

89 Augustine, *De doctrina christiana* IV, XII.27–XVI33, XXV.55; *De civitate Dei*, IX.4–5 and XIV.5–9; see Casagrande, 'Sermo affectuosus', pp. 521–3.

90 See Gregory the Great, *Règle pastorale*, pp. 262–6 [II.III.I]; pp. 272–4 [III.III]; pp. 522–4 [III, XXXVII]; and Casagrande, 'Sermo affectuosus', pp. 524–5.

91 Thomas of Chobham, *Summa de arte praedicandi*, p. 28 [II.2], l. 335–7. This division drew from Gregory the Great's celebrated exegesis of Judges 1: 14–15, cited in Chapter 2.

92 Thomas of Chobham, *Summa de arte praedicandi*, pp. 28–52 [II.2.1–2].

93 Humbert of Romans, *De dono timoris*.
94 Casagrande, 'Sermo affectuosus', p. 519.
95 Roger Bacon, *Opus tertium*, pp. 304–5; see Rosier-Catach, 'Roger Bacon, Al-Farabi et Augustin'.
96 Roger Bacon, *Opus tertium*, pp. 309–10.
97 Bonaventure, *The Life of St Francis* (Legenda Maior), in *Bonaventure: The Soul's Journey into God; The Tree of Life; The Life of St Francis*, p. 297 [XII.7]
98 Ibid.
99 See de Poorter, 'Un manuel de prédication médiévale'; for its attribution, see Casagrande, 'Sermo affectuosus', p. 519.
100 Roger Bacon, *Moralis philosophia*, pp. 255–8, and *Opus tertium*, pp. 306–9, esp. p. 307; cited by Casagrande, 'Sermo affectuosus', p. 531.
101 Roger Bacon, *Opus tertium*, p. 310, cited by Casagrande, 'Sermo affectuosus', p. 532.
102 Berthold of Regensburg, *Péchés et vertus*, p. 63.
103 Horowitz and Menache, *L'Humour en chaire*, p. 65; the citation is drawn from Daunou, *Histoire littéraire de la France*, vol. 18, p. 213 (Étienne de Bourbon, *Traité des sept dons du Saint-Esprit*).
104 See Amargier, 'Robert d'Uzès, prédicateur', esp. p. 160, who cites the French translation of Robert's *Livre des Paroles: La Parole rêvée*, p. 101; for the Latin original (from which this translation is drawn), see Robert of Uzès, *Liber visionum et liber sermonum Dei*, p. 288.
105 Among others, see Le Goff, *Le Moyen Âge et l'Argent*, p. 118.
106 Horowitz and Menache, *L'Humour en chaire*, p. 65.
107 Anthony of Padua, *Sermons for Sundays and Festivals II*, pp. 387–8.
108 Horowitz and Menache, *L'Humour en chaire*, p. 73.
109 Ibid., p. 152; the distinction of these two aspects of laughter stems from E. Dupréel, 'Le problème sociologique du rire', pp. 253–5.
110 Horowitz and Menache, *L'Humour en chaire*, pp. 75–6.
111 Jacques de Vitry, *Die Exempla des Jacob von Vitry*, p. 146.
112 Jacques de Vitry, *The Exempla or Illustrative Stories*, p. 15 [no. 38].
113 Johannes Pauli, *Schimpf und Ernst*, in E. Reiber, *Propos de table de la vieille Alsace* (Strasbourg, Engelmann, 1886), pp. 118–19.
114 Horowitz and Menache, *L'Humour en chaire*, p. 163.
115 Étienne de Bourbon, *Tractatus de diversis materiis predicabilibus*, vol. I, p. 133 [I, IV].
116 *A Parisian Journal*, pp. 231–2.

117 Amargier, 'Robert d'Uzès, prédicateur', p. 169; Robert d'Uzès, *La Parole rêvée*, 24–6, pp. 118–19.

118 Martin, *Le Métier de prédicateur*, p. 581, n. 67. See Accarie, *Le Théâtre sacré à la fin du Moyen Âge*.

119 Martin, *Le Métier de prédicateur*, pp. 582–3, esp. n. 69, citing AC Châlons-sur-Marne, BB 6, f. 52.

120 Martin, *Le Métier de prédicateur*, p. 584; the quotation refers to an event at Laval in 1507.

121 Philippe de Vigneulles, *Les Cent Nouvelles nouvelles*, pp. 189–90 [IV]; cited by Martin, *Le Métier de prédicateur*, p. 584, n. 75.

BIBLIOGRAPHY

Sources

Ad cruce signatos, ed. J.-B. Pitra, in *Analecta Novissima Spicilegii Solesmensis*, 2 vols (Paris, Roger et Chernowitz, 1888), 2: 421–30 [no. 48].

Aelred of Rievaulx, *On Jesus at Twelve Years Old*, trans. G. Webb and A. Walker (London, A. R. Mobray and Co., Ltd., 1955).

— *La Vie de recluse*, ed. C. Dumont (Paris, Cerf, 1961).

— *De spirituali amicitia*, in *Aelredi Rievallensis Opera omnia*, ed. A. Hoste and C. H. Talbot (Turnhout, Brepols, 1971).

— *Sermones I–XLVI*, ed. G. Raciti (Turnhout, Brepols, 1989).

— *The Mirror of Charity*, trans. E. Connor (Kalamazoo, Cistercian Publications, 1990).

— *Sermones XLVII–LXXXIV*, ed. G. Raciti (Turnhout, Brepols, 2001).

— *Spiritual Friendship*, trans. L. C. Braceland, ed. M. L. Dutton (Collegeville, Liturgical Press/Cistercian Publications, 2010).

Alan of Lille, *De fide catholica*, PL 210, col. 305–430.

Albert the Great, *Super Ethica. Commentum et quæstiones*, in *Opera omnia*, ed. W. W. Kübel, vol. XIV (Münster, Aschendorff, 1987).

Ps.-Alcher de Clairvaux, *De spiritu et anima*, PL 40, col. 779–831.

Alcuin, *De virtutibus et vitiis liber*, PL 101, col. 613–38.

— *Carmina*, ed. E. Dümmel, in MGH, *Poetae Latini Aevi Carolini* I (Berlin, Weidmann, 1881), pp. 160–351.

— *Epistolae*, ed. E. Dümmler, MGH Epistolae IV.2 (Berlin, Weidmann, 1895), pp. 1–493.

Ami and Amile: A Medieval Tale of Friendship, trans. S. N. Rosenberg and S. Danon (Ann Arbor, University of Michigan Press, 1996).

Ami et Amile: Chanson de geste, ed. P. F. Dembowski (Paris, Champion, 1987).

Andrew the Chaplain, *The Art of Courtly Love*, trans. J. J. Parry (New York, Columbia University Press, 1941).

Angela of Foligno, *Il libro della Beata Angela da Foligno*, ed. L. Thier and A. Calufetti (Grottaferrata, Editiones Collegii S. Bonaventurae ad Claras Aquas, 1985).

— *The Complete Works*, ed. P. Lachance (New York, Paulist Press, 1994).

— *Il «Liber» della Beata Angela da Foligno, edizione in facsimile e trascrizione del ms. 342 della Biblioteca Comunale di Assisi, con quattro studi*, ed. E. Menestò (Spoleto, Centro Italiano di Studi sull'Alto Medioevo, 2009).

The Anonymous Sayings of the Desert Fathers, trans. J. Wortley (Cambridge, Cambridge University Press, 2013).

Anselm of Canterbury, *The Prayers and Meditations*, trans. B. Ward (London, Penguin Books, 1972).

— *The Letters of Anselm of Canterbury*, ed. W. Fröhlich, 3 vols (Kalamazoo, Cistercian Publications, 1990); Latin text edited by F.-S. Schmitt, *L'Œuvre d'Anselme de Cantorbéry*, vol. VI (Paris, Cerf, 2004).

— *The Harmony of the Foreknowledge, the Predestination, and the Grace of God with Free Will*, in *The Complete Philosophical and Theological Treatises*, ed. and trans. J. Hopkins and H. Richardson (Minneapolis, Arthur J. Banning Press, 2000), pp. 531–74; Latin text edited by F.-S. Schmitt, *L'Œuvre d'Anselme de Cantorbéry*, vol. V (Paris, Cerf, 1988).

— *Why God Became a Man* in *The Complete Philosophical and Theological Treatises*, ed. and trans. J. Hopkins and H. Richardson (Minneapolis, Arthur J. Banning Press, 2000), pp. 295–389; Latin text edited by F.-S. Schmitt, *L'Œuvre d'Anselme de Cantorbéry*, vol. III (Paris, Cerf, 1988).

Anthony of Padua, *Sermons for Sundays and Festivals II. From the first Sunday after Pentecost to the sixteenth Sunday after Pentecost*, ed. and trans. P. Spilsbury (Padua, Edizioni Messaggero Padova, 2015).

Aristotle, *Problems*, trans. W. S. Hett, 2 vols (Cambridge, MA, Harvard University Press, 1936–7).

Arnold of Villanova, *Speculum medicine*, in *Hec sunt Opera* … , ed. T. Murchi (Lyon, Fradin, 1509), fols. 1–55.

— *De amore heroico*, in *Arnaldi de Villanova Opera Medica Omnia*, vol. 3, ed. M. R. McVaugh (Barcelona, University of Barcelona, 1985), pp. 43–54.

— *Regimen sanitatis ad regem aragonum*, in *Arnaldi de Villanova Opera Medica Omnia*, vol. 10, 1, ed. L. García-Ballester and M. R. McVaugh (Barcelona, University of Barcelona, 1996).

Augustine, *The Trinity*, trans. S. McKenna (Washington DC, Catholic University of America, 'Fathers of the Church' series 45, 1963).

— *De Sermone domini in monte*, ed. A. Mutzenbecher (Turnhout, Brepols, 1967).

— *The Happy Life*, in *Selected Writings*, trans. M. T. Clark (New Jersey, Paulist Press, 'Classics of Western Spirituality' series, 1984), pp. 163–93.

— *De doctrina Christiana*, ed. and trans. R. P. H. Green (Oxford, Clarendon Press, 1995).

— *Confessions*, trans. M. Boulding, in *The Works of Saint Augustine* I:1 (New York, New City Press, 1997).

— *The City of God against the Pagans*, trans. R. W. Dyson (Cambridge, Cambridge University Press, 1998).

— *The Monastic Rules*, trans. G. Bonner, ed. B. Ramsey (Hyde Park, NY, New City Press, 2004).

Aulus Gellius, *Attic Nights*, trans. J. C. Rolfe, 3 vols (Cambridge, MA, Harvard University Press, 1927).

Avicenna (Latin), *Liber de anima seu Sextus de naturalibus*, ed. S. Van Riet (Louvain-Leiden, Brill, 1968).

Baldwin of Ford, 'Sermon 13 sur l'annonciation (traité VII)', in CCCM 99, ed. D. N. Bell (Turnhout, Brepols, 1991).

Barnabas da Reggio, *Regimen sanitatis*, Paris, BN, MS Lat. 16189 (fourteenth century).

Bernard of Clairvaux, *On the Song of Songs I*, trans. K. Walsh (Kalamazoo, Cistercian Publications, 1971).

—*Sententiae*, in *Sancti Bernardi Opera*, ed. J. Leclercq, H.-M. Rochais, and C. H. Talbot (Rome, Editiones Cistercienses, 1972), VI-2.

— *On Grace and Free Choice*, trans. D. O'Donovan (Kalamazoo, Cistercian Publications, 1988).

— *On Loving God*, ed. E. Steigman (Kalamazoo, Cistercian Publications, 1995).

— *Monastic Sermons*, trans. D. Griggs, ed. M. Casy (Collegeville, Cistercian Publications, 2016).

Berthold of Regensburg, *Péchés et vertus. Scènes de la vie du XIIIe siècle*, ed. C. Lecouteux and P. Marcq (Paris, Éditions Desjonquères, 1991).

Boethius, *Traité de la musique*, ed. C. Meyer (Turnhout, Brepols, 2004).

Bonaventure, *The Life of St Francis* (Legenda Maior), in *Bonaventure: The Soul's Journey into God; The Tree of Life; The Life of St. Francis*, ed. E. Cousins (New York, Paulist Press, 1978), pp. 177–327.

Bruno of Querfurt, *Vita quinque fratrum eremitarum seu Vita uel passio Benedicti et Iohannis sociorumque suorum, auctore Brunone Querfurtensi*, ed. H. Karwasinska (Warsaw, Panstwowe Wydawn, 1973).

Caesarius of Arles, *Regula Sanctarum Virginum aliaque opuscula ad sanctimoniales directa*, ed. G. Morin (Bonn, Petri Hanstein, 1933).

— 'Règle des moines', in *Œuvres monastiques*, ed. and trans. J. Courreau and A. de Vogüé, 3 vols (Paris, Cerf, 1988).

Le Charroi de Nîmes, ed. C. Lachet (Paris, Gallimard, 1999).

Chrétien de Troyes, *Yvain: The Knight of the Lion*, trans. R. Burton (New Haven, CT, Yale University Press, 1987).

— *Lancelot ou le Chevalier à la charrette*, ed. D. Poirion (Paris, Gallimard, 1994).

— *Œuvres complètes*, ed. D. Poirion (Paris, Gallimard, 1994).

— *Lancelot: The Knight of the Cart*, trans. B. Raffel (New Haven, CT, Yale University Press, 1997).

Christine de Pizan, *Le Livre des fais du sage roy Charles* (Paris, Renouard, 1841).

— *The 'Livre de la Paix'. A Critical Edition with Introduction and Notes*, ed. C. C. Willard (La Haye, Mouton, 1958).

Clément de Fauquembergue, *Journal*, ed. A. Tuetey (Paris, Renouard, 1903).

Colombanus, *Sancti Columbani Opera*, ed. G. S. M. Walker (Dublin, Institute for Advanced Studies, 1957).

Concilia Galliae a. 511–a. 695, ed. Charles de Clercq (Turnhout, Brepols, 1963).

Constantine the African, *Pantegni*, in *Opera omnia Ysaac*, II (Lyon, Johannes de Platea, 1515).

300

De vera et falsa poenitentia, PL 40, col. 1113–30.

Dhuoda, *Handbook for William: A Carolingian Woman's Counsel for Her Son*, ed. and trans. C. Neel (Lincoln, University of Nebraska Press, 1991).

Dulcis Jesu memoria, poème anonyme (Aelred de Rievaulx?), trans. M. Coune, in *Collectanea cisterciensia*, 55 (1993), p. 239.

Duns Scotus, *Opus Oxoniense* (Lyon, 1639, reprint Hildesheim, 1968).

Eneas: A Twelfth-Century French Romance, ed. J. A. Yunck (New York, Columbia University Press, 1974).

Epistola de vita et passione domini nostri. Der lateinische Text mit Einleitung und Kommentar, ed. M. Hedlund (Leiden, Brill, 1975).

Epistolae Austrasicae n. 12, MGH, *Epistolae Merowingici et Karolini aevi (I)* (Berlin, 1892).

Étienne de Bourbon, *Tractatus de diversis materiis predicabilibus*, vol. I, ed. J. Berlioz and J.-L. Eichenlaub (Turnhout, Brepols, 2002).

Evagrius of Pontus, *Sur les pensées*, ed. P. Géhin, C. Guillaumont, and A. Guillaumont (Paris, Cerf, 1998).

— *The Monk: A Treatise on the Practical Life*, in *Evagrius of Pontus: The Greek Ascetic Corpus*, ed. R. E. Sinkewicz (Oxford, Oxford University Press, 2003).

Francis of Assisi: Early Documents, ed. R. J. Armstrong, J. A. Wayne Hellman, and W. J. Short, 3 vols (New York, New City Press, 1999).

Galen, *On the Passions and Errors of the Soul*, trans. P. W. Harkins (Columbus, OH, 1995).

Gentile da Foligno, *Consilia* (Pavia, 1488).

Geoffrey of Beaulieu, *Life and Saintly Comportment of Louis, Former King of the Franks, of Pious Memory*, in *The Sanctity of Louis IX: Early Lives of Saint Louis by Geoffrey of Beaulieu and William of Chartres*, trans. L. F. Field, ed. M. C. Gaposchkin and S. L. Field (Ithaca, Cornell University Press, 2013).

Georges Chastellain, *Œuvres*, ed. K. de Lettenhove, 8 vols (Brussels, Heussner, 1863–6).

Gesta regis Henricis Secundi Benedicti abbatis, ed. W. Stubbs, 2 vols (London, Longman, 1867).

Giles of Rome, *Expositio super Libros Rhetoricorum Aristotelis* (Venice, 1515).

— *Livres du gouvernement des rois*, ed. S. P. Molenaer (New York, Columbia University Press, 1899).

Giunta Bevegnati, *Legenda de vita et miraculis beatae Margaritae de Cortona*, ed. F. Iozelli (Rome, Quaracchi, 1997).

'Gospel of Peter', in *The Apocryphal New Testament: A Collection of Apocryphal Christian Literature in an English Translation Based on M. R. James*, ed. J. K. Elliott (Oxford, Oxford University Press, 1993).

Gregory the Great, *Moralia in Job*, PL 75–6.

— *Dialogues* (Washington DC, Catholic University of America Press, 1959).

— *Règle pastorale*, ed. B. Judic, F. Rommel and C. Morel (Paris, Cerf, 1992).

Gregory of Tours, *Gregorii Turonensis Libri historiarum X*, ed. B. Krusch, MGH, *Scriptores Rerum Merovingicarum* (Hanover, 1951).

Guibert of Nogent, *The Autobiography of Guibert*, trans. C. C. Swinton Bland (London, George Routledge, 1925).

Guillaume de Lorris and Jean de Meun, *Le Roman de la rose*, ed. A. Strubel (Paris, Le Livre de Poche, 1992).

Hadewijch, *The Complete Works*, ed. and trans. C. Hart (Mahwah, NJ, Paulist Press, 1980).

Henry of Ghent, *Summa questionum ordinarium* (Paris, 1520); reprinted, 2 vols (New York, St Bonaventure, Franciscan Institute Publications, 1953).

Henry Suso, *The Life of the Servant*, trans. J. M. Clark (Cambridge, The Lutterworth Press, 1952); critical edition, *Deutsche Schriften im Auftrag der Württembergischen Kommission für Landesgeschichte*, ed. K. Bihlmeyer (Stuttgart, Kohlhammer, 1907).

Hildegard of Bingen, *Cause et cure*, ed. L. Moulinier (Munich, Akademie Verlag, 2003).

History of William Marshal, ed. A. J. Holden, trans. S. Gregory, 3 vols (London, Anglo-Norman Text Society, 2004).

Hugh of Saint-Victor, *De sacramentis christianae fidei*, PL 176, col. 173–617.

— *De unione corporis et spiritus*, PL 177, col. 285–94.

Humbert of Romans, *De dono timoris*, ed. C. Boyer (Turnhout, Brepols, 2008).

Isaac of Stella, *Epistola ad quemdam familiarem suum de anima*, PL 194, col. 1875–89.

— *Sermons*, ed. A. Hoste and G. Raciti, trans. G. Salet and G. Raciti, 2 vols (Paris, Cerf, 1967, 1974).

Jacobus de Varagine, *Sermo III de stigmatibus s. Francisci*, in L. Lemmens, *Testimonia minora saeculi XIII de s. Francisco Assisiensi collecta* (Ad Claras Aquas, Ex typ. Collegii S. Bonaventurae, 1926).

— *Cronaca di Genova*, ed. G. Monleone, 2 vols (Rome, Istituto storico italiano per il Medio Evo, 1941).

Jacques de Vitry, *Die Exempla des Jacob von Vitry*, ed. G. Frenken, *Quellen und Untersuchungen zur lateinischen Philologie des Mittelalters*, vol. 1 (Munich, Beck, 1914).

— *The Exempla or Illustrative Stories from the Sermones Vulgares of Jacques de Vitry*, ed. T. F. Crane (New York, Burt Franklin, 1971/1890).

— *The Life of Marie d'Oignies*, trans. M. H. King (Saskatoon, Canada, Peregrina Publishing, 1986).

Jean Froissart, *Chroniques* (Paris, A. Desrez, 1824).

Jerome, *Commentary on Matthew*, trans. T. P. Scheck (Washington DC, Catholic University of America Press, 2008).

Johannes Brinckerinck, *Johannes Brinckerinck en zijn klooster te Diepenveen*, ed. W. J. Kühler (Amsterdam, W. Nevens, 1908).

Johannes Pauli, *Schimpf und Ernst*, in E. Reiber, *Propos de table de la vieille Alsace* (Strasbourg, Engelmann, 1886).

John Blund, *Tractatus de anima*, ed. D. Callus and R. Hunt (London, British Academy, 1970).

John Cassian, *Conferences*, trans. B. Ramsey (New York, Paulist Press, 1997).

— *The Institutes*, trans. B. Ramsay (New York, Paulist Press, 2000)

John of Fécamp, *Confessio fidei*, PL 101, col. 1027–98.

— *Libellus de scripturis et verbis patrum*, PL 40, col. 897–942 (under the title of *Meditationes*).

— *Confessio theologica*, ed. J-P. Bonnes and J. Leclercq, in *Un Maître de la vie spirituelle du XIe siècle, Jean de Fécamp* (Paris, Vrin, 1946), pp. 109–82.

John of La Rochelle, *Summa de anima*, ed. J.-G. Bougerol (Paris, Vrin, 1995).

John of Salisbury, *Policraticus*, ed. K. S. B. Keats-Rohan (Turnhout, Brepols, 1993).

Joinville, *The Life of St Louis*, trans. R. Hague (London, Sheed and Ward, 1955).

— *Vie de Saint Louis*, ed. J. Monfrin (Paris, Classiques Garnier, 1995).

Jourdain de Blaye, ed. P. F. Dembowski (Paris, Champion, 1991).

Lactantius, *Epitome of the Divine Institutes*, trans. E. H. Blakeney (London, SPCK, 1950).

— *Divine Institutes: Books I–VII*, trans. M. F. McDonald (Washington DC, Catholic University of America Press, 1964).

— *The Wrath of God*, in *The Minor Works*, trans. M. F. McDonald (Washington DC, Catholic University of America, 1965), pp. 57–116.

— *La Colère de Dieu*, trans. C. Ingremeau (Paris, Cerf, 1982).

Lectionary of Heilig Kreuz, Oxford, Keble College, MS 49, 308 ff.

Lettres des deux amants attribuées à Héloïse et Abélard, ed. and trans. S. Piron (Paris, Gallimard, 2005).

The Life of Saint Douceline, a Beguine of Provence, ed. and trans. K. Garay, M. Jeay (Cambridge, D. S. Brewer, 2001).

Machiavelli, *The Prince*, trans. P. Bondanella (Oxford, Oxford University Press, 2005).

Maino de Mainieri, *Regimen sanitatis*, in *Praxis Medicinalis* (Lyon, Tardif, 1586), fols 1–61.

Marguerite Porete, *The Mirror of Simple Souls*, trans. E. Babinsky (Mahwah, NJ, Paulist Press, 1993).

Matthew Paris, *English History*, trans. J. A. Giles, 3 vols (London, 1852–4).

— *Chronica majora*, ed. H. R. Luard, 6 vols (London, Rolls Series, 1872–80).

Origen, *On First Principles*, trans. G. W. Butterworth (New York, Harper & Row, 1966).

— *Homilies 1–14 on Ezekiel*, trans. T. Scheck (New Jersey, Paulist Press, 2010).

Palladius, *The Lausiac History*, trans. R. T. Meyer (New Jersey, Paulist Press, 1965).

A Parisian Journal, ed. J. Shirley (Oxford, Clarendon Press, 1968).

Peter Abelard, 'Know Yourself', in *Ethical Writings*, trans. P. V. Spade, ed. M. McCord Adam (Indianapolis, Hackett Publishing, 1995), pp. 1–58.

Peter Damian, *Vita beati Romualdi* (BHL 7324), ed. G. Tabacco (Rome, Istituto storico italiano per il Medioevo, 1957).

— *Die Briefe des Petrus Damiani* (MGH, Die Briefe der Kaiserzeit), ed. K. Reindel, 4 vols (Munich, 1983–93).

— *Letters 1–30*, trans. O. J. Blum (Washington DC, Catholic University Press, 1989).

Peter the Venerable, *The Letters of Peter the Venerable*, ed. G. Constable, 2 vols (Cambridge, MA, Harvard University Press, 1967).

Philippe de Vigneulles, *Les Cent Nouvelles nouvelles*, ed. C. H. Livingston (Geneva, Droz, 1972).

Precum libelli quattuor aevi karolini, nunc primum publici iuris facti cum aliorum indicibus, ed. A. Wilmart (Rome, Ephemerides Liturgicae, 1940).

Les Propos de Saint Louis, ed. D. O'Connell, intro. J. Le Goff (Paris, Gallimard, 1974).

Pseudo-Dionysius, 'The Divine Names', in *The Complete Works*, trans. C. Luibheid (New Jersey, Paulist Press, 'Classics of Western Spirituality' series, 1987).

'Règle orientale', in *Les Règles des Saints Pères*, ed. A. de Vogüé, 3 vols (Paris, Cerf, 1982), 2: 298–482.

Règles des moines, ed. J.-P. Lapierre (Paris, Seuil, 1982).

Règles monastiques d'Occident IVe–VIe siècle: D'Augustin à Ferréol, trans. V. Desprez, ed. A. de Vogüé (Bégrolles-en-Mauges, Abbaye de Bellefontaine, 1980).

Richard of Saint-Victor, *Les Quatre Degrés de la violente charité*, ed. G. Dumeige (Paris, Vrin, 1955).

— *The Twelve Patriarchs, the Mystical Ark, Book Three of the Trinity*, trans. G. Zinn (New York, Paulist Press, 1979), pp. 51–147.

— *On the Four Degrees of Violent Love*, trans. A. Kraebel, in H. Feiss (ed.), *On Love: A Selection of Works of Hugh, Adam, Achard, Richard and Godfrey of St Victor* (Turnhout, Brepols, 2011), pp. 275–300.

Robert of Uzès, *Liber visionum et liber sermonum Dei*, ed. J. Bignami-Odier, in 'Les visions de Robert d'Uzès O. P. (1296)', *Archivum Fratrum Praedicatorum*, 25 (1955), pp. 258–310.

— *La Parole rêvée*, trans. P. Amargier (Aix-en-Provence, Centre d'études des sociétés méditerranéennes, 1982).

Roger Bacon, *Moralis philosophia*, ed. F. Delorme and E. Massa (Zurich, Thesaurus Mundi, 1953).

— *Opus tertium*, ed. J. S. Brewer, *Opera quaedam hactenus inedita Rogeri Baconi*, vol. I (Cambridge, Cambridge University Press, 1964/1859).

Le Roman d'Énéas, ed. A. Petit (Paris, Le Livre de Poche, 1997).

Le Roman de Tristan en prose, ed. R. L. Curtis (Cambridge, Brewer, 1985).

The Romance of Flamenca, ed. and trans. E. D. Blodgett (New York, Garland Publishing, 1995).

The Rule of St Benedict, ed. B. L. Venarde (Cambridge, MA, Harvard University Press, 2011).

Le Sacramentaire gélasien d'Angoulême, ed. P. Cagin (Angoulême, Société historique et archéologique de la Charente, 1919).

Sacramentario del Vescovo Warmondo di Ivrea (Ivrea Pavone Canavese, 1990), ed. L. Magnani, *Le Miniature del Sacramentario d'Ivrea e altri codici Warmondiani* (Vatican, Biblioteca apostolica vaticana, 1934).

Sacramentarium Rossianum. Cod. Ross. Lat. 204., Römische Quartalschrift für christliche Altertumskunde, ed. J. Brinktrine (Freiburg im Briesgau, Herder, 1930).

Salomé Sticken, *A Way of Life for Sisters*, trans. J. Van Engen, in J. Van Engen and H. A. Oberman (eds), *Devotio Moderna: Basic Writings* (New York, Crossroad, 1988).

The Sayings of the Desert Fathers: The Alphabetical Collection, trans. B. Ward (Kalamazoo, Cistercian Publications, 1984).

The Song of Roland, trans. J. J. Duggan and A. C. Rejhorn (Turnhout, Brepols, 2012).

Taddeo Alderotti and Michele Giuseppe Nardi, *I Consilia, trascritti dai codici lat. n. 2418 e Malatestiano D. XXIV. 3 con 4 tavole di reproduzione parziale in facsimile dei testi e pubblicati* (Turin, Minerva medica, 1937).

Tertullian, *Treatise on the Incarnation*, ed. E. Evans (London, SPCK, 1956).

Thomas à Kempis, *The Imitation of Christ*, trans. L. Shirley-Price (Harmondsworth, Penguin, 1952).

Thomas Aquinas, *Summa theologiae*, in *Sancti Thomae Aquinatis Opera omnia iussu Leonis XIII edita*, vols IV–XII (Ex Typographia Polyglotta S. C. de Propaganda Fide, 1888–1906).

— *Le Passioni dell'anima*, trans. S. Vecchio (Florence, Le Lettere, 2007).

Thomas of Celano, *The First Life of St Francis*, in *Francis of Assisi: Early Documents*, ed. R. J. Armstrong, J. A. Wayne Hellman, and W. J. Short, 3 vols (New York, New City Press, 1999), 1: 180–308.

— *The Remembrance of the Desire of a Soul*, in *Francis of Assisi: Early Documents*, 2: 239–393.

— *The Treatise on the Miracles of St Francis*, in *Francis of Assisi: Early Documents*, 2: 397–468.

— *Vita beati patris nostri Francisci (Vita brevior)*, ed. J. Dalarun, *Analecta Bollandiana*, 133 (2015), pp. 23–86.

Thomas of Chobham, *Summa de arte praedicandi*, ed. F. Morenzoni (Turnhout, Brepols, 1988).

Thomas of England, *Le Roman de Tristan*, in *Early French Tristan Poems II*, ed. and trans. N. J. Lacy (Cambridge, D. S. Brewer, 1998).

Les Troubadours. L'œuvre poétique, ed. and trans. R. Lavaud and R. Nelli (Paris, Desclée de Brouwer, 2000).

Valerio of Bierzo, *Œuvres autobiographiques et récits de vision. Édition, traduction et commentaire*, ed. P. Henriet (forthcoming).

Venantius Fortunatus, *Opera Poetica* (Berlin, 1881).

La Vie de sainte Douceline, texte provençal du XIVe siècle, ed. and trans. R. Gout (Paris, Bloud et Gay, 1927).

Vincent of Beauvais, *De morali principis institutione*, ed. R. J. Schneider (Turnhout, Brepols, 1995).

Vita Bertae abbatissae Blangiacensis, AASS. Jul. II (Venice, 1747), pp. 49–54.

Vita prima di san Antonio o Assidua, ed. V. Gamboso (Padua, 1981).

Vita venerabilis Lukardis monialis O.C. in superiore Wimaria, ed. J. De Backer, *Analecta Bollandiana*, 18 (1899), pp. 305–67.

William of Auvergne, *Opera omnia*, 2 vols (Orléans-Paris, F. Hotot, 1674).

William of Newburgh, *Historia*, in *Chronicles of the Reigns of Stephen, Henry II, and Richard I*, ed. R. Howlett, 4 vols (London, 1884), 1: 11–408.

William of Saint-Thierry, *De erroribus Guillelmi de Conchi*, PL 180, col. 333–40.

— *Deux traités sur l'amour de Dieu. De la contemplation de Dieu. De la nature et de la dignité de l'amour*, ed. M.-M. Davy (Paris, Vrin, 1953).

— *Exposition on the Song of Songs*, trans. C. Hart, ed. J. M. Déchanet (Shannon, Irish University Press, 1969).
— *On Contemplating God*, trans. P. Lawson (Kalamazoo, Cistercian Publications, 1970).
— *The Golden Epistle: A Letter to the Brethren at Mont Dieu*, trans. T. Berkeley, ed. J. M. Déchanet (Kalamazoo, Cistercian Publications, 1976).
— *The Nature of the Body and the Soul* in *Three Treatises on Man: A Cistercian Anthropology*, ed. B. McGinn (Kalamazoo, Cistercian Publications, 1977).
— *The Nature and Dignity of Love*, trans. T. X. Davis, ed. D. N. Bell (Kalamazoo, Cistercian Publications, 1981).
— *Lettre aux frères du Mont-Dieu (Lettre d'or)*, ed. J. M. Déchanet (Paris, Cerf, 1985).
— *La Nature du corps et de l'âme (De natura corporis et animae)*, ed. and trans. M. Lemoine (Paris, Les Belles Lettres, 1988).
— *Exposé sur le Cantique des Cantiques*, ed. J.-M. Déchanet, trans. M. Dumontier (Paris, Cerf, 1998).
— 'Lettre sur les erreurs de Guillaume de Conches', in M. Lemoine and C. Picard-Parra, *Théologie et cosmologie au XIIe siècle* (Paris, Les Belles Lettres, 2004), pp. 183–97.

Secondary Literature

Abu-Lughod, L., *Veiled Sentiments: Honor and Poetry in a Bedouin Society* (Berkeley and Los Angeles, University of California Press, 1999).
Accarie, M., *Le Théâtre sacré à la fin du Moyen Âge. Étude sur le sens moral de la Passion de Jean Michel* (Geneva, Droz, 1979).
Agrimi, J. and Crisciani, C., *Les Consilia médicaux* (Turnhout, Brepols, 1994).
Ailes, M. J., 'The Medieval Male Couple and the Language of Homosociality', in D. M. Hadley (ed.), *Masculinity in Medieval Europe* (London, Longman, 1999), pp. 214–37.
Alexandre, R., Guérin, C., and Jacotot, M., *Rubor et pudor. Vivre et penser la honte dans la Rome ancienne* (Paris, Rue d'Ulm, 2012).
Alexandre-Bidon, D., 'Gestes et expressions du deuil', in D. Alexandre-Bidon et C. Treffort (eds), *À réveiller les morts. La mort au quotidien dans l'Occident médiéval* (Lyon, Presses Universitaires de Lyon, 1993), pp. 121–33.
Alfonsi, D. and Vedova, M. (eds), *Il Liber di Angela da Foligno: temi spirituali e mistici, Atti del Convegno internazionale di studio (Foligno, 13–14 novembre 2009)* (Spoleto, CISAM, 2010).
Althoff, G., 'Empörung, Tränen, Zerknirschung. "Emotionen" in der öffentlichen Kommunikation des Mittelalters', in G. Althoff (ed.), *Spielregeln der Politik im Mittelalter. Kommunikation in Frieden und Fehde* (Darmstadt, Primus Verlag, 1996), pp. 258–81.
— 'Ira Regis: Prolegomena to a History of Royal Anger', in B. H. Rosenwein (ed.), *Anger's Past: The Social Uses of an Emotion in the Middle Ages* (Ithaca, Cornell University Press, 1998), pp. 59–74.

— *Family, Friends and Followers: Political and Social Bonds in Early Medieval Europe* (Cambridge, Cambridge University Press, 2004).

Amargier, P., 'Robert d'Uzès, prédicateur', in *La Prédication en pays d'Oc, Cahiers de Fanjeaux*, 32 (1997), pp. 159–70.

Ambroise-Rendu, A.-C., Demartini, A.-E., Eck, H., and Edelman, N. (eds), *Émotions contemporaines, XIXe–XXIe siècles* (Paris, Armand Colin, 2014).

Anciaux, P., 'Le sacrement de pénitence chez Guillaume d'Auvergne', *Ephemerides theologicae lovanienses*, 24 (1948), pp. 95–118.

Andenmatten, B., Jamme, A., Moulinier-Brogi, L., and Nicoud, M. (eds), *Passions et Pulsions à la cour (Moyen Âge–Temps modernes)* (Florence, SISMEL/Galluzzo, 2015).

Andretta, E. and Nicoud, M. (eds), *Être médecin à la cour, Italie, France, Espagne (XIIIe–XVIIIe siècle)* (Florence, SISMEL/Galluzzo, 2013).

Ansart, P., *La Gestion des passions politiques* (Lausanne, L'Âge d'Homme, 1983).

— and Haroche, C. (eds), *Les Sentiments et le Politique* (Paris, L'Harmattan, 2007).

Arendt, H., *Le Concept d'amour chez Augustin* (Paris, Rivages, 1999/1929).

Atsma, H. and Burguière, A. (eds), *Marc Bloch aujourd'hui. Histoire comparée et sciences sociales* (Paris, EHESS, 1990).

Attigui, P. and Cukier, A. (eds), *Les Paradoxes de l'empathie. Entre émotion et cognition sociale* (Paris, CNRS éditions, 2012).

Auerbach, E., *Mimésis. La Représentation de la réalité dans la littérature occidentale* (Paris, Gallimard, 1998/1968).

Aurell, M. (eds), *Culture politique des Plantagenêts (1154–1204)* (Poitiers, CESCM, 2003).

— *L'Empire Plantagenêt* (Paris, Perrin, 2004).

Baladier, C., *Érôs au Moyen Âge. Amour, désir et 'delectatio morosa'* (Paris, Cerf, 1999).

— 'La honte et l'honneur dans les langues d'Europe occidentale', *Sigila*, 14 (2004), pp. 19–28.

— *Aventure et discours dans l'amour courtois* (Paris, Hermann, 2010).

Baldwin, J. W., *Les Langages de l'amour dans la France de Philippe Auguste* (Paris, Fayard, 1997).

Balgradean, I., 'The Poet's Grasp at Emotion: Medieval Configuration of Sloth', doctoral thesis, Geneva, University of Geneva, 2011, unpublished.

Banniard, M., 'Niveaux de compétence langagière chez les élites carolingiennes: du latin quotidien au latin d'apparat', in F. Bougard, R. Le Jan, and R. McKitterick (eds), *La Culture du haut Moyen Âge: une question d'élites?* (Turnhout, Brepols, 2009), pp. 39–62.

Barbier, J., Cottret, M., and Scordia, L. (eds), *Amour et désamour du prince du haut Moyen Âge à la Révolution française* (Paris, Kimé, 2011).

Barone, G. and Dalarun, J. (eds), *Angèle de Foligno. Le dossier* (Rome, École française de Rome, 1999).

Barralis, C., Foronda, F., and Sère, B. (eds), *Violences souveraines au Moyen Âge. Travaux d'une école historique* (Paris, PUF, 2010).

Barthélemy, D., Bougard, F., and Le Jan, R. (eds), *La Vengeance, 400–1200* (Rome, École française de Rome, 2006).

Barthélemy, D. and Grosse, R. (eds), *Moines et démons. Autobiographie et individualité au Moyen Âge (VIIe–XIIe siècle)* (Geneva, Droz, 2014).

Bartlett, R. J., 'tal Enmities": The Legal Aspect of Hostility in the Middle Ages', in T. L. Billado and B. S. Tuten (eds), *Feud, Violence and Practice: Essays in Medieval Studies in Honor of Stephen D. White* (Burlington, Ashgate, 2010), pp. 197–212.

Battais, L., 'La courtoisie de François d'Assise. Influence de la littérature épique et courtoise sur la première génération franciscaine', *Mélanges de l'École française de Rome*, 109/1 (1997), pp. 131–60.

Bedos-Rezak, B., Iogna-Prat, D., and Anheim, É. (eds), *L'Individu au Moyen Âge: individuation et individualisation avant la modernité* (Paris, Aubier, 2005).

Bejczy, I. P., '*De origine virtutum et vitiorum*: An Anonymous Treatise of Moral Psychology (*c.* 1200–1230)', *Archives d'histoire doctrinale et littéraire du Moyen Âge*, 72 (2005), pp. 105–45.

Belting, H., *Image et culte: une histoire de l'image avant l'époque de l'art* (Paris, Cerf, 1998).

— *L'Image et son public au Moyen Âge* (Paris, Gérard Monfort, 1998/1981).

Benthin, C., Fleig, A., and Kasten, I. (eds), *Emotionalität. Zur Geschichte des Gefühle* (Cologne/Weimar/Vienna, Böhlau Verlag, 2000).

Bériou, N., Berlioz, J., and Longère, J. (eds), *Prier au Moyen Âge. Pratiques et expériences (Ve–XVe siècles)* (Turnhout, Brepols, 1991).

Bériou, N. and Caseau, B. (eds), *Pratiques de l'Eucharistie dans les Églises d'Orient et d'Occident*, 2 vols (Paris, Études Augustiniennes, 2009).

Berlivet, L., Cabibbo, S., Donato, M. P., Michetti, R., and Nicoud, M. (eds), *Médecine et religion: compétitions, collaborations, conflits (XIIe–XXe siècles)* (Rome, École française de Rome, 2012).

Bermon, E., 'La théorie des passions chez saint Augustin', in B. Besnier, P.-F. Moreau, and L. Renault (eds), *Les Passions antiques et médiévales* (Paris, PUF, 2003), pp. 173–97.

Besnier, B., Moreau, P.-F., and Renault, L. (eds), *Les Passions antiques et médiévales* (Paris, PUF, 2003).

Bernard de Clairvaux, Histoire, mentalités, spiritualité. Introduction aux œuvres complètes (colloque de Lyon-Cîteaux-Dijon) (Paris, Cerf, 1992).

Beyer de Ryke, B., 'Une souffrance christiforme. Émotions et déification dans Le Livre qui se nomme Suso', in D. Boquet and P. Nagy (eds), *Le Sujet des émotions au Moyen Âge* (Paris, Beauchesne, 2009), pp. 297–322.

Biarne, J., 'Moines et rigoristes en Occident', in A. Vauchez (ed.), *Histoire du christianisme, vol. II: Naissance d'une chrétienté* (Paris, Desclée, 1995), pp. 755–8.

Bibliotheca Sanctorum, 15 vols (Rome, Istituto Giovanni XXIII nella Pontificia Università Lateranense, 1963–88).

Bienert, W. A. and Kühneweg, U. (eds), *Origeniana Septima. Origenes in der Auseinandersetzungen des 4. Jahrhunderts* (Louvain, Peeters, 1999).

Billado, T. L. and Tuten, B. S. (eds), *Feud, Violence and Practice: Essays in Medieval Studies in Honor of Stephen D. White* (Burlington, Ashgate, 2010).

Bloch, M., *Strange Defeat*, trans. G. Hopkins (Oxford, Oxford University Press, 1949).

Blommestijn, H., Caspers, C., and Hofman, R. (eds), *Spirituality Renewed: Studies on Significant Representatives of the Modern Devotion* (Louvain-Paris, Peeters, 2003).

Boccadoro, B., 'La musique, les passions, l'âme et le corps', in F. Morenzoni and J.-Y. Tilliette (eds), *Autour de Guillaume d'Auvergne (1249)* (Turnhout, Brepols, 2005), pp. 75–93.

Boehm, I., Ferrary, J-F., and Franchet d'Espèrey, S. (eds), *L'Homme et ses Passions. Actes du XVII e Congrès international de l'Association Guillaume Budé organisé à Lyon du 26 au 29 août 2013* (Paris, Les Belles Lettres, 2016)

Boisson, D. and Pinto-Mathieu, É. (eds), *La Conversion: textes et réalités* (Rennes, Presses Universitaires de Rennes, 2014).

Bolens, G., *Le Style des gestes. Corporéité et kinésie dans le récit littéraire* (Lausanne, BHMS, 2008).

Bologne, J.-C., *Histoire de la pudeur* (Paris, Olivier Orban, 1986).

— *Pudeurs féminines. Voilées, dévoilées, révélées* (Paris, Seuil, 2010).

Boquet, D., 'Le sexe des émotions. Principe féminin et identité affective chez Guerric d'Igny et Aelred de Rievaulx', in P. Henriet and A.-M. Legras (eds), *Au cloître et dans le monde. Femmes, hommes et sociétés (IXe–XVe siècle). Mélanges en l'honneur de Paulette L'Hermite-Leclercq* (Paris, Presses de l'Université de Paris-Sorbonne, 2000), pp. 367–78.

— 'Un nouvel ordre anthropologique au xiie siècle: réflexions autour de la physique du corps de Guillaume de Saint-Thierry', *Cîteaux*, 55 (2004), pp. 5–20.

— 'Le gouvernement de soi et des autres selon Bernard de Clairvaux', in H. Taviani-Carozzi and C. Carozzi (eds), *Le Pouvoir au Moyen Âge* (Aix-en-Provence, Publications de l'Université de Provence, 2005), pp. 298–316.

— *L'Ordre de l'affect au Moyen Âge. Autour de l'anthropologie affective d'Aelred de Rievaulx* (Caen, Publications du CRAHM, 2005).

— 'Faire l'amitié au Moyen Âge', *Émotions médiévales, Critique*, 716–17 (2007), pp. 102–13.

— 'Incorporation mystique et subjectivité féminine d'après le Livre d'Angèle de Foligno (1309)', *Clio, Histoire, femmes et sociétés*, 26 (2007), pp. 189–208.

— 'Écrire et représenter la dénudation de François d'Assise au xiiie siècle', *Rives nord-méditerranéennes*, 30 (2008), pp. 39–64.

— 'Introduction. La vergogne historique: éthique d'une émotion sociale', *Rives nord-méditerranéennes*, 31 (2008), pp. 7–16.

— 'Des racines de l'émotion. Les préaffects et le tournant anthropologique du xiie siècle', in D. Boquet and P. Nagy (eds), *Le Sujet des émotions au Moyen Âge* (Paris, Beauchesne, 2009), pp. 163–86.

— 'L'amitié comme problème au Moyen Âge', in D. Boquet, B. Dufal, and P. Labey (eds), *Une histoire au présent. Les historiens et Michel Foucault* (Paris, CNRS éditions, 2013), pp. 59–81.

— 'Le concept de communauté émotionnelle selon B. H. Rosenwein', *BUCEMA*, hors-série no. 5 (2013), http://cem.revues.org/12535.

— 'Corps et genre des émotions dans l'hagiographie féminine au xiiie siècle', *Cahiers d'études du religieux. Recherches interdisciplinaires*, 13 (2014), http://cerri.revues.org/1335.

— 'Des émotions très rationnelles', *L'Histoire*, 409 (2015), pp. 46–53.

— and Nagy, P., 'Émotions historiques, émotions historiennes', *Écrire l'histoire*, 2 (2008), pp. 15–26.

— and Nagy, P., 'Pour une histoire des émotions. L'historien face aux questions contemporaines', in D. Boquet and P. Nagy (eds), *Le Sujet des émotions au Moyen Âge* (Paris, Beauchesne, 2009), pp. 15–51.

— and Nagy, P., 'L'historien et les émotions en politiques: entre science et citoyenneté', in D. Boquet and P. Nagy (eds), *Politiques des émotions au Moyen Âge* (Florence, SISMEL/Galluzzo, 2010), pp. 5–30.

— and Nagy, P., 'L'efficacité religieuse de l'affectivité dans le Liber (passus priores) d'Angèle de Foligno', in D. Alfonsi and M. Vedova (eds), *Il Liber di Angela da Foligno: temi spirituali e mistici, Atti del Convegno internazionale di studio (Foligno, 13–14 novembre 2009)* (Spoleto, CISAM, 2010), pp. 171–201.

— and Nagy, P. (eds), *Le Sujet des émotions au Moyen Âge* (Paris, Beauchesne, 2009).

— and Nagy, P. (eds), *Politiques des émotions au Moyen Âge* (Florence, SISMEL/Galluzzo, 2010).

— and Nagy, P., 'Une histoire des émotions incarnées', *Médiévales*, 61 (2011), pp. 5–24.

— and Nagy, P. (eds), *Histoire intellectuelle des émotions de l'Antiquité à nos jours. Ateliers du Centre de recherches historiques* (2015), http://acrh.revues.org.

Borlée, D., ' "Sculpter les mouvements de l'âme": traduction des affects et émotions dans la sculpture du xiiie siècle', *Source(s). Cahiers de l'équipe de recherche Arts, Civilisation et Histoire de l'Europe*, 5 (2014), pp. 29–45.

Boswell, J., *Christianity, Social Tolerance, and Homosexuality: Gay People in Western Europe from the Beginning of the Christian Era to the Fourteenth Century* (Chicago, University of Chicago Press, 1980/2015).

Boucher, N. (ed.), *Signy l'abbaye et Guillaume de Saint-Thierry, Actes du colloque international d'études cisterciennes, 9–11 septembre 1998* (Signy l'Abbaye, Association des amis de l'abbaye de Signy, 2000).

Boucheron, P., *The Power of Images: Siena, 1338*, trans. A. Brown (Cambridge, Polity, 2018).

Boudet, J.-P., Guerreau-Jalabert, A., and Sot, M. (eds), *Histoire culturelle de la France*, vol. 1: *Le Moyen Âge* (Paris, Seuil, 1997).

Bougard, F., Le an, R., and McKitterick, R. (eds), *La Culture du haut Moyen Âge: une question d'élites?* (Turnhout, Brepols, 2009).

J.-P. Bouhot, 'Des livres pour prier', in N. Bériou, J. Berlioz, and J. Longère (eds), *Prier au Moyen Âge. Pratiques et expériences (Ve–XVe siècles)* (Turnhout, Brepols, 1991), pp. 23–9.

Boulnois, O., 'Duns Scot: existe-t-il des passions de la volonté?', in B. Besnier, P.-F. Moreau, and L. Renault (eds), *Les Passions antiques et médiévales* (Paris, PUF, 2003), pp. 281–95.

— 'Qu'est-ce que la liberté de l'esprit? La parole de Marguerite et la raison du théologien', in S. L. Field, R. E. Lerner, and S. Piron (eds), *Marguerite Porete et le Miroir des simples âmes. Perspectives historiques, philosophiques et littéraires* (Paris, Vrin, 2013), pp. 139–50.

Boureau, A., 'Incandescences médiévales. La fusion du fer entre technique et spiritualité (xiie–xiiie siècle)', *Le Feu. Terrain*, 19 (1992), pp. 103–14.

— *Satan hérétique. La Naissance de la démonologie dans l'Europe médiévale (1260–1350)* (Paris, Odile Jacob, 2004).

— *De vagues individus. La condition humaine dans la pensée scolastique* (Paris, Les Belles Lettres, 2008).

— 'Un sujet agité. Le statut nouveau des passions de l'âme au xiiie siècle', in D. Boquet and P. Nagy, *Le Sujet des émotions au Moyen Âge* (Paris, Beauchesne, 2009), pp. 187–200.

Bousmar, E., 'Jacqueline de Bavière, trois comtés, quatre maris (1401–1436): l'inévitable excès d'une femme au pouvoir?', in E. Bousmar, J. Dumont, A. Marchandisse, and B. Schnerb (eds), *Femmes de pouvoir, femmes politiques durant les derniers siècles du Moyen Âge et au cours de la première Renaissance* (Brussels, De Boeck, 2012), pp. 385–456.

Braud, P., *L'Émotion en politique* (Paris, Presses de la Fondation nationale des sciences politiques, 1996).

Bray, A., *The Friend* (Chicago, Chicago University Press, 2003).

Brown, P., *The Body and Society: Men, Women, and Sexual Renunciation in Early Christianity* (New York, Columbia University Press, 1988).

— *Augustine of Hippo: A Biography* (Berkeley and Los Angeles, University of California Press, 2000/1967).

Bruylants, P., *Les Oraisons du Missel romain*, 2 vols (Louvain, Abbaye du Mont-César, 1952).

Bubenicek, M., 'Femme, pouvoir, violence: une adéquation? Quelques pistes de réflexion autour de Yolande de Flandre', in A. Nayt-Dubois and E. Santinelli-Foltz (eds), *Femmes de pouvoir et pouvoir des femmes dans l'Occident médiéval et moderne* (Valenciennes, PUV, 2009), pp. 259–72.

Buc, P., *L'Ambiguïté du Livre. Prince, pouvoir et peuple et dans les commentaires de la Bible au Moyen Âge* (Paris, Beauchesne, 1994).

— *Dangereux rituel. De l'histoire médiévale aux sciences sociales* (Paris, PUF, 2003).

Buckley, A. and Billy, D. (eds), *Études de langue et de littérature médiévales offertes à Peter T. Ricketts à l'occasion de son 70e anniversaire* (Turnhout, Brepols, 2005).

Bullough, D. A., 'The Career of Columbanus', in M. Lapidge (ed.), *Columbanus: Studies on the Latin Writings* (Woodbridge, Boydell & Brewer, 1997), pp. 1–28.

— *Alcuin: Achievement and Reputation* (Leiden and Boston, Brill, 2004).

Bultot, R., *La Doctrine du mépris du monde en Occident de saint Ambroise à Innocent III*, tome IV 'Le xie siècle', vol. 2: 'Jean de Fécamp, Hermann Contract, Roger de Caen, Anselme de Canterbury' (Louvain-Paris, Nauwelaerts, 1964).

311

Burnett, C., 'Physics Before the Physics: Early Translations from Arabic Texts Concerning Nature in Mss British Library, Additional 22719 and Cotton Galba E IV', in, *Arabic into Latin in the Middle Ages: The Translators and their Intellectual and Social Context* (Farnham, Ashgate, 2009), pp. 53–109.

— and Jacquart, D., *Constantine the African and 'Al ibn al-'Abbas al-Mas: The Pantegni and Related Texts* (Leiden, Brill, 1994).

Burrus, V., *Saving Shame: Martyrs, Saints and Other Abject Subjects* (Philadelphia, University of Pennsylvania Press, 2008).

Buschinger, D. and Crépin, A. (eds), *Amour, mariage et transgression au Moyen Âge* (Göppingen, Kümmerle Verlag, 1984).

Byers, S. C., 'Augustine and the Cognitive Cause of Stoic "Preliminary Passions"', *Journal of the History of Philosophy*, 41/4 (2003), pp. 433–48.

Bynum, C., *Jesus as Mother: Studies in the Spirituality of the High Middle Ages* (Berkeley, University of California Press, 1982).

— *Fragmentation and Redemption: Essays on Gender and the Human Body in Medieval Religion* (New York, Zone Books, 1992).

Caby, C., 'Faire du monde un ermitage: Pietro Orseolo, doge et ermite', in M. Lauwers (ed.), *Guerriers et moines. Conversion et sainteté aristocratiques dans l'Occident médiéval* (Antibes, APDCA, 2002), pp. 349–68.

— and Melville, G. (ed.), *Paradoxien der Legitimation. Ergebnisse einer deutsch-italienisch-französischen Villa Vigoni-Konferenz zur Macht im Mittelalter* (Florence, SISMEL/Galluzzo, 2010).

Cairns, D., *Aidos: The Psychology and Ethics of Honour and Shame in Ancient Greek Literature* (Oxford, Oxford University Press, 1993).

Caluwé, J. de, 'La jalousie, signe d'exclusion dans la littérature médiévale en langue occitane', *Senefiance*, 5 (1978), pp. 163–77.

Carozzi, C. and Taviani-Carozzi, H. (eds), *Le Pouvoir au Moyen Âge* (Aix-en-Provence, Publications de l'Université de Provence, 2005).

Carré, Y., *Le Baiser sur la bouche au Moyen Âge* (Paris, Le Léopard d'or, 1992).

Casagrande, C., 'Specchio di croce. Domenico Cavalca e l'ordine degli affetti', *Communicazioni sociali*, 25 (2003), pp. 221–30.

— 'Agostino, i medievali e il buon uso delle passioni', in E. Marini (eds), *Agostino d'Ippona. Presenza e pensiero. La scoperta dell'interiorità* (Milan, Franco Angeli, 2004), pp. 65–75.

— 'Guglielmo d'Auvergne e il buon uso delle passioni nella penitenza', in F. Morenzoni and J-Y. Tilliette (eds), *Autour de Guillaume d'Auvergne* (Turnhout, Brepols, 2005), pp. 189–201.

— '"Motions of the Heart" and Sins: The Specchio de' peccati by Domenico Cavalca OP', in R. G. Newhauser (ed.), *In the Garden of Evil: The Vices and Culture in the Middle Ages* (Toronto, Pontifical Institute of Mediaeval Studies, 2005), pp. 128–44.

— 'Per una storia delle passioni in Occidente. Il Medioevo cristiano (De civ. Dei, IX, 4–5; XIV, 5–9)', *Península. Revista de Estudos Ibéricos*, 3 (2006), pp. 11–18.

— 'Sermo affectuosus. Passions et éloquence chrétienne', in P. von Moos (ed.), *Zwischen Babel und Pfingsten. Sprachdifferenzen und Gesprächsverständigung in der Vormoderne (8.–16. Jh.) / Entre Babel et Pentecôte. Différences linguistiques et communication orale avant la modernité (VIIe–XVIe siècle)* (Münster, LIT, 2008), pp. 509–32.

— 'Le emozioni e il sacramento della penitenza', in M. Sodi and R. Salvarani (eds), *La Penitenza tra I e II millennio. Per una comprensione delle origini della Penitenzieria Apostolica* (Vatican City, Libreria Editrice Vaticana, 2012), pp. 213–31.

— and Vecchio, S., *Histoire des péchés capitaux au Moyen Âge* (Paris, Aubier, 2003).

— and Vecchio, S., 'Les théories des passions dans la culture médiévale', in D. Boquet and P. Nagy (eds), *Le Sujet des émotions au Moyen Âge* (Paris, Beauchesne, 2009), pp. 107–22.

— and Vecchio, S. (eds), *Piacere e dolore. Materiali per una storia delle passioni nel Medioevo* (Florence, SISMEL/Galluzzo, 2009).

— and Vecchio, S., *Passioni dell'anima. Teorie e usi degli affetti nella cultura medieval* (Florence, SISMEL/Galluzzo, 2015).

Céard, J., Naurin, P., and Simonin, M. (eds), *La Folie et le Corps* (Paris, PENS, 1985).

Challet, V., ' "Moyran, los traidors, moyran": cris de haine et sentiments d'abandon dans les villes languedociennes à la fin du xive siècle', in É. Lecuppre-Desjardin and A.-L. Van Bruaene (eds), *Emotions in the Heart of the City (14th–16th Century) / Les Émotions au cœur de la ville (XIVe–XVIe siècle)* (Turnhout, Brepols, 2005).

Champier, S., *L'Antiquité de la Cité de Lyon, ensemble la Rebeine ou rébellion du Populaire contre les conseillers de la cité en 1529* (Lyon, H. Georg, 1884).

Châtillon, J., 'Les quatre degrés de la charité d'après Richard de SaintVictor', *Revue d'ascétique et de mystique*, 20 (1939), pp. 3–30.

—, Guillaumont, J., and Lefèvre, A., 'Cor et cordis affectus', *Dictionnaire de spiritualité*, vol. II (Paris, 1952), col. 2278–307.

Chave-Mahir, F., 'Les cris du démoniaque. Exorciser les possédés dans les récits hagiographiques des xiie et xiiie siècles', in D. Lett and N. Offenstadt (eds), *Haro! Noël! Oyé! Pratiques du cri au Moyen Âge* (Paris, Grasset, 2003), pp. 131–40.

Chiffoleau, J., 'Dire l'indicible. Remarques sur la catégorie du nefandum du xiie au xve siècle', *Annales ESC*, 45 (1990), pp. 289–314.

Clark, E. A., *The Origenist Controversy: The Cultural Construction of an Early Christian Debate* (Princeton, Princeton University Press, 1992).

Coccia, E., 'Il canone delle passioni. La passione di Cristo dall'antichità al medioevo', in D. Boquet and P. Nagy (eds), *Le Sujet des émotions au Moyen Âge* (Paris, Beauchesne, 2009), pp. 123–62.

— 'Citoyen par amour. Émotions et institutions', in D. Boquet and P. Nagy, *Histoire intellectuelle des émotions de l'Antiquité à nos jours. Ateliers du Centre de recherches historiques* (2016), https://acrh.revues.org/6720.

Cohen, E., 'Towards a History of European Physical Sensibility. Pain in the Later Middle Ages', *Science in Context*, 81 (1995), pp. 47–74.

— *The Modulated Scream: Pain in Late Medieval Culture* (Chicago, Chicago University Press, 2010).

Cohen-Hanegbi, N., 'The Emotional Body of Women: Medical Practice between the 13th and 15th Centuries', in D. Boquet and P. Nagy (eds), *Le Sujet des émotions au Moyen Âge* (Paris, Beauchesne, 2009), pp. 465–84.

— 'Accidents of the Soul: Physicians and Confessors on the Conception and Treatment of Emotions in Italy and Spain, Late 12th–15th Centuries', PhD, Jerusalem, Hebrew University, 2011, unpublished.

Cohn Jr, S. K. and Epstein, S. A. (eds), *Portraits of Medieval and Renaissance Living: Essays in Memory of David Herlihy* (Ann Arbor, University of Michigan Press, 1996).

Colonna, M., 'Gouverner, c'est pleurer!', *L'Histoire*, 277 (2003), pp. 22–3.

Comprendre et maîtriser la nature au Moyen Âge. Mélanges d'histoire des sciences offerts à Guy Beaujouan (Paris and Geneva, Droz, 1994).

Copet-Rougier, É. and Héritier-Augé, F., *La Parenté spirituelle* (Paris and Basel, Éditions des Archives contemporaines, 1995).

Corbellari, A., 'Retour sur l'amour courtois', *Cahiers de recherches médiévales*, 17 (2009), pp. 375–85.

Corbin, A., Courtine, J.-J., and Vigarello, G. (eds), *Histoire des émotions*, 3 vols (Paris, Seuil, 2016–17, third volume forthcoming).

Cottier, J.-F., 'Ganymède médiéval? Quelques remarques sur la correspondance d'Anselme de Cantorbéry et la poésie de Baudri de Bourgueil', in P. Mauriès (ed.), *Les Gays Savoirs* (Paris, Gallimard, 1998), pp. 159–76.

— 'Psautiers abrégés et prières privées durant le haut Moyen Âge', *Recherches Augustiniennes*, 33 (2003), pp. 215–30.

— *La Prière en latin, de l'Antiquité au XVIe siècle. Formes, évolutions, significations* (Turnhout, Brepols, 2006).

— 'Vitium contra naturam. Sexualité et exclusion dans le Liber Gomorrhianus de Pierre Damien', in *L'Exclusion au Moyen Âge* (Lyon, Cahiers du Centre d'histoire médiévale, no. 4, 2007), pp. 127–44.

— 'Saint Anselme et la conversion des émotions. L'épisode de la mort d'Osberne', in D. Boquet and P. Nagy (eds), *Le Sujet des émotions au Moyen Âge* (Paris, Beauchesne, 2009), pp. 273–95.

Courtine, J.-J. and Haroche, C., *Histoire du visage. Exprimer et taire ses émotions (XVIe–début XIXe siècle)* (Paris, Payot & Rivages, 2007/1988).

Couture, R. A., *L'Imputabilité morale des premiers mouvements de sensualité, de saint Thomas aux Salmanticenses* (Rome, Presses de l'Université grégorienne, 1962).

Cruz Palma, O. de la, Ferrero Hernández, C., and Martínez Gazquez, J. (eds), *Estudios de latín medieval hispánico. Actas del V Congreso* (Florence, SISMEL/ Galluzzo, 2012).

Csíkszentmihályi, M., *Vivre: la psychologie du bonheur* (Paris, Laffont, 2004).

Cullin, O., *Brève Histoire de la musique médiévale* (Paris, Fayard, 2002).

Cyrulnik, B., *Mourir de dire la honte* (Paris, Odile Jacob, 2010).

Dalarun, J., 'Lapsus linguae', in *La légende de Claire de Rimini* (Spoleto, Centro italiano di studi sull'alto medioevo, 1994).

— *François d'Assise, un passage. Femmes et féminité dans les écrits et les légendes franciscaines* (Arles, Actes Sud, 1997).

— *Claire de Rimini. Entre sainteté et hérésie* (Paris, Payot, 1999).

— *'Dieu changea de sexe, pour ainsi dire.' La religion faite femme, XIe–XVe siècle* (Paris, Fayard, 2009).

— 'François d'Assise et la quête du Graal', *Romania*, 127 (2009), pp. 147–67.

— 'Le corps monastique entre Opus dei et modernité', in G. Melville, B. Schneidmüller, and S. Weinfurter (eds), *Innovationen durch Deuten und Gestalten. Klöster im Mittelalter zwischen Jenseits und Welt* (Regensburg, Schnell und Steiner, 2014), pp. 19–36.

Damasio, A., *L'Erreur de Descartes. La raison des émotions* (Paris, Odile Jacob, 1995).

— *Le Sentiment même de soi: corps, émotions, conscience* (Paris, Odile Jacob, 1999).

— *Spinoza avait raison. Joie et tristesse: le cerveau des émotions* (Paris, Odile Jacob, 2003).

Daunou, P., *Histoire littéraire de la France* (Paris, Firmin Didot, 1835).

Davies, B. and Stump, E. (eds), *The Oxford Handbook to Aquinas* (Oxford, Oxford University Press, 2012).

Davis, N. Z., *Society and Culture in Early Modern France* (Stanford, Stanford University Press, 1975).

Davy M.-M. (ed.), *Un traité de l'amour au XIIe siècle: Pierre de Blois* (Paris, de Boccard, 1932).

De Gier, I. and Fraeters, V. (eds), *Mulieres religiosae: Shaping Female Spiritual Authority in the Medieval and Early Modern Periods* (Turnhout, Brepols, 2014).

De Poorter, A., 'Un manuel de prédication médiévale. Le ms. 97 de Bruges', *Revue néoscolastique de philosophie*, 25 (1963), pp. 192–209.

Debailly, P. and Dumora, Fl. (eds), *Peur et littérature du Moyen Âge au XVIIe siècle, Textuel*, 51 (2007).

Déchanet, J.-M., 'Amor ipse intellectus est: la doctrine de l'amour-intellection chez Guillaume de Saint-Thierry', *Revue du Moyen Âge latin*, 1 (1945), pp. 349–74.

Delaurenti, B., *La Contagion des émotions. Compassio, une énigme médiévale* (Paris, Les Belles Lettres, 2015).

Delhaye, P., 'Deux adaptations du De amicitia de Cicéron au xiie siècle', *Recherches de théologie ancienne et médiévale*, 15 (1948), pp. 304–31.

Deluermoz, Q., Fureix, E., Mazurel, H., and Oualdi, M., 'Écrire l'histoire des émotions: de l'objet à la catégorie d'analyse', *Revue d'histoire du XIXe siècle*, 47 (2013), pp. 155–89.

Delumeau, J., *La Peur en Occident, XVIe–XVIIIe siècle* (Paris, Fayard, 1978).

— *Le Péché et la peur. La culpabilisation en Occident (XIIIe–XVIIIe siècle)* (Paris, Fayard, 1984).

— *Rassurer et protéger. Le sentiment de sécurité dans l'Occident d'autrefois* (Paris, Fayard, 1989).

Deploige, J., 'Studying Emotions. The Medievalist as Human Scientist?', in É. Lecuppre-Desjardin and A.-L. Van Bruaene (eds), *Emotions in the Heart of the City (14th–16th Century) / Les Émotions au cœur de la ville (XIVe–XVIe siècle)* (Turnhout, Brepols, 2005), pp. 3–26.

— 'Meurtre politique, guerre civile et catharsis littéraire au xiie siècle. Les émotions dans l'œuvre de Guibert de Nogent et de Galbert de Bruges', in D. Boquet and P. Nagy (eds), *Politiques des émotions au Moyen Âge* (Florence, SISMEL/ Galluzo, 2010), pp. 225–54.

— 'United or Bound by Death? A Case-Study on Group Identity and Textual Communities within the Devotio Moderna', *Revue d'histoire ecclésiastique*, 105/2 (2010), pp. 346–80.

Depreux, P., 'Une faide exemplaire? À propos des aventures de Sichaire. Vengeance et pacification aux temps mérovingiens', in D. Barthélémy, F. Bougard, and R. Le Jan, *La Vengeance, 400–1200* (Rome, École française de Rome, 2006), pp. 65–85.

— and Judic, B. (eds), *Alcuin de York à Tours. Écriture, pouvoir et réseaux dans l'Europe du haut Moyen Âge (Annales de Bretagne et des Pays de l'Ouest, t. 111)* (Rennes, Presses Universitaires de Rennes, 2004).

Deshusses, J., 'Les messes d'Alcuin', *Archiv für Liturgienwissenschaft*, 14 (1972), pp. 7–41.

— *Le Sacramentaire grégorien. Ses principales formes d'après les plus anciens manuscrits. Édition comparative, t. II: Textes complémentaires pour la messe* (Fribourg, Éditions Universitaires, 1979).

Dessì, R. M. (eds), *Prêcher la paix et discipliner la société. Italie, France, Angleterre (XIIIe–XVe siècle)* (Turnhout, Brepols, 2005).

— 'Prière, chant et prédication. À propos de la lauda: de François d'Assise à Machiavel', in J.-F. Cottier (eds), *La Prière en latin, de l'Antiquité au XVIe siècle. Formes, évolutions, significations* (Turnhout, Brepols, 2006), pp. 245–72.

D'Hainaut-Zveny, B., 'L'ivresse sobre. Pratiques de "rejeu" empathiques des images religieuses médiévales', in D. Boquet and P. Nagy (eds), *Le Sujet des émotions au Moyen Âge* (Paris, Beauchesne, 2009), pp. 393–413.

Di Carpegna Falconieri, T., 'Giovanni di Fécamp', in *Dizionario biografico degli Italiani*, vol. 56 (2001), http://www.treccani.it/enciclopedia/giovanni-di-fecamp_%28Dizionario-Biografico%29.

Dickson, G., *Religious Enthusiasm in the Medieval West: Revivals, Crusades, Saints* (Aldershot, Variorum, 2000).

Dierkens, A., Lebecq, S., Le Jan, R., and Sansterre, J.-M. (eds), *Femmes et pouvoirs des femmes à Byzance et en Occident (VIe–XIe siècle)* (Villeneuve d'Ascq, Centre de recherches sur l'histoire de l'Europe du Nord-Ouest, Université Lille III, 1999).

Dixon, T., *From Passions to Emotions: The Creation of a Secular Psychological Category* (Cambridge, Cambridge University Press, 2003).

Douglas, M., *Purity and Danger: An Analysis of Concepts of Pollution and Taboo* (New York, Praeger, 1966).

Driscoll, J., *The 'Ad Monachos of Evagrius Ponticus'. Greek Text and English Translation. Its Structure and a Select Commentary* (Rome, Pontifico Ateneo S. Anselmo, 1991).

Driscoll, M. S., *Alcuin et la pénitence à l'époque carolingienne* (Münster, Aschendorff, 1999).

Dubreucq, A., 'Autour du De virtutibus et vitiis d'Alcuin', in P. Depreux and B. Judic (eds), *Alcuin de York à Tours. Écriture, pouvoir et réseaux dans l'Europe du haut Moyen Âge*, Annales de Bretagne et des Pays de l'Ouest, vol. 111 (Rennes, Presses Universitaires de Rennes, 2004), pp. 269–87.

Duby, G., 'Les jeunes dans la société aristocratique de la France du Nord-Ouest au xiie siècle', *Annales ESC*, 19 (1964), pp. 835–46.

— *Guillaume le Maréchal ou le Meilleur Chevalier du monde* (Paris, Fayard, 1984).

— *Le Dimanche de Bouvines* (Paris, Gallimard, 1985/1973).

— *Mâle Moyen Âge. De l'amour et autres essais* (Paris, Flammarion, 1988).

— 'Que sait-on de l'amour en France au xiie siècle?', in *Mâle Moyen Âge. De l'amour et autres essais* (Paris, Flammarion, 1988), pp. 34–49.

Duggan, A., *Thomas Becket* (London, Arnold, 2004).

Duhamel-Amado, C. and Lobrichon, G. (eds), *Georges Duby. L'écriture de l'histoire* (Bruxelles, De Boeck, 1996).

Dumeige, G., *Richard de Saint-Victor et l'idée chrétienne de l'amour* (Paris, PUF, 1952).

Dupréel, E., 'Le problème sociologique du rire', *Revue philosophique*, 106 (1928), pp. 253–5.

Durkheim, É., *Les Formes élémentaires de la vie religieuse. Le système totémique en Australie* (Paris, PUF, 1968/1912).

Eidelberg, S. (ed.), *The Jews and the Crusaders: The Hebrew Chronicles of the First and Second Crusades* (Madison, University of Wisconsin Press, 1977).

El Kenz, D., Frandon, V., Grässlin, M., and Zombory-Nagy, P., 'Pour une histoire de la souffrance: expressions, représentations, usages', *Du bon usage de la souffrance, Médiévales*, 27 (1994), pp. 5–14.

Elias, N., *The Civilizing Process* (New York and Oxford, Basil Blackwell, 2000).

— *La Dynamique de l'Occident* (Paris, Calmann-Lévy, 1973/1939).

Elliott, D., *Spiritual Marriage: Sexual Abstinence in Medieval Wedlock* (Princeton, Princeton University Press, 1993).

Elster, J., *Alchemies of the Mind: Rationality and the Emotions* (Cambridge, Cambridge University Press, 1999).

Elukin, J., *Living Together, Living Apart: Rethinking Jewish–Christian Relations in the Middle Ages* (Princeton/Oxford, Princeton University Press, 2007).

Epp, V., 'Männerfreundschaft und Frauendienst bei Venantius Fortunatus', in T. Kornbichler and W. Maaz (eds), *Variationen der Liebe: Historische Psychologie der Geschlechterbeziehung* (Tübingen, Diskord, 1995), pp. 9–26.

— *Amicitia: Zur Geschichte personaler, sozialer, politischer und geistlicher Beziehungen im frühen Mittelalter* (Stuttgart, Hiersemann, 1999).

L'Eremitismo in Occidente nei secoli XI e XII. Atti della seconda settimana internazionale di studio, Mendola, 30 agosto–6 settembre 1962 (Milano, Vita e Pensiero, 1965).

Farge, A., 'Affecter les sciences humaines', in C. Gautier and O. Lecour Grandmaison (eds), *Passions et sciences humaines* (Paris, PUF, 2002), pp. 45–50.

Farmer, S. and Braun Pasternack, C. (eds), *Gender and Difference in the Middle Ages* (Minneapolis, University of Minnesota Press, 2003).

Febvre, L., 'La sensibilité et l'histoire. Comment reconstituer la vie affective d'autrefois?', *Annales d'histoire économique et sociale*, 3 (1941), pp. 5–20.

— 'Pour l'histoire d'un sentiment: le besoin de sécurité', *Annales ESC*, 11 (1956), pp. 244–7.

Field, S. L., 'William of Paris's Inquisitions Against Marguerite Porete and her Book', in S. L. Field, R. E. Lerner, and S. Piron (eds), *Marguerite Porete et le Miroir des simples âmes. Perspectives historiques, philosophiques et littéraires* (Paris, Vrin, 2013), pp. 233–47.

Field, S. L.– Lerner, R. E., and Pirson, S. (eds), *Marguerite Porete et le Miroir des simples âmes. Perspectives historiques, philosophiques et littéraires* (Paris, Vrin, 2013).

Fiske, A., 'Cassian and Monastic Friendship', *American Benedictine Review*, 12 (1961), pp. 190–205.

— 'Saint Anselm and Friendship', *Studia Monastica*, 3 (1961), pp. 259–80.

Flori, J., 'Le héros épique et sa peur, du Couronnement de Louis à Aliscans', *PRIS-MA*, 10 (1994), pp. 27–44.

Flüeler, C. and Rohde, M. (ed.), *Laster im Mittelalter* (Berlin/New York, de Gruyter, 2009).

Fontes Baratto, A. (ed.), *Écritures et pratiques de l'amitié dans l'Italie médiévale*, *Arzanà. Cahiers de littérature médiévale italienne*, 13 (2010).

Fornaciari, R., 'Romualdo di Ravenna, i suoi discepoli Benedetto di Benevento e Giovanni e il monachesmimo missionaria dell'età ottoniana', in *Ottone III e Romualdo di Ravenna. Imperio, monasteri e santi asceti, Atti del XXIV Convegno del Centro Studi Avellaniti, Fonte Avellana 2002* (Negarine, Il Segno dei Gabrielli editori, 2003), pp. 237–66.

Fornasari, G., 'Pater rationabilium eremitarum: tradizione agiografiaca e attualizzazione eremitica nella Vita beati Romualdi', in *Medioevo riformato del secolo XI* (Naples, Liguori, 1997), pp. 203–69.

Förstemann, E. G., *Die christlichen Geisslergesellschaften* (Halle, Renger, 1828).

Fraeters, V., ' "Ô Amour, sois tout à moi!" Le désir comme agent de déification chez Hadewijch de Brabant', in D. Boquet and P. Nagy (eds), *Le Sujet des émotions au Moyen Âge* (Paris, Beauchesne, 2009), pp. 353–74.

Freedman, P., 'Peasant Anger in the Late Middle Ages', in B. H. Rosenwein (ed.), *Anger's Past: The Social Uses of an Emotion in the Middle Ages* (Ithaca, Cornell University Press, 1998), pp. 171–9.

Frijda, N., *The Emotions* (Cambridge, Cambridge University Press, 1986).

Frugoni, C., *Francesco e l'invenzione delle stimmate. Una storia per parole e immagini fino a Bonaventura e Giotto* (Turin, Einaudi, 1993).

— *François d'Assise. La vie d'un homme* (Paris, Cerf, 1997).

— 'Sui vari significati del Natale di Greccio, nei testi e nelle immagini', *Frate Francesco*, 70 (2004), pp. 35–147.

Gambrelle, F. and Trebitsch, M. (eds), *Révolte et société. Actes du IVe colloque d'histoire au présent (Paris, mai 1988)*, 2 vols (Paris, Publications de la Sorbonne, 1989).

Garnier, C., *Amicus amicis, inimicus inimicis: Politische Freundschaft und fürstliche Netzwerke im 13. Jahrhundert* (Stuttgart, A. Hiersemann, 2000).

Garrison, M., 'Les correspondants d'Alcuin', in P. Depreux and B. Judic (eds), *Alcuin de York à Tours, Écriture, pouvoir et réseaux dans l'Europe du haut Moyen Âge* (Rennes, PUR, 2004), pp. 319–32.

Gautier, C. and Lecour Grandmaison, O. (eds), *Passions et sciences humaines* (Paris, PUF, 2002).

Gauvard, C., *'De grace especial'. Crime, État et société en France à la fin du Moyen Âge*, 2 vols (Paris, Publications de la Sorbonne, 1991).

— 'Violence et rituels', in *Violence et ordre public au Moyen Âge* (Paris, Picard, 2005), pp. 194–213.

Gazeau, V., 'Guillaume de Volpiano en Normandie: état des questions' (2003), http://www.unicaen.fr/mrsh/craham/revue/tabularia/print.php?dossier=dossier 2&file=04gazeau.xml.

— and Goullet, M., *Guillaume de Volpiano, un réformateur en son temps, 962–1031: Vita domni Willelmi de Raoul Glaber* (Caen, Publications du CRAHM, 2008).

Geary, P. J., 'Gabriel Monod, Fustel de Coulanges et les "aventures de Sichaire". La naissance de l'histoire scientifique au xixe siècle', in D. Barthélémy, F. Bougard, and R. Le Jan, *La Vengeance, 400–1200* (Rome, École française de Rome, 2006), pp. 87–99.

Genet, P. (ed.), *La légitimité implicite*, 2 vols (Paris/Rome, Éditions de la Sorbonne/École française de Rome, 2015).

Gil-Sotres, P., 'Modelo teórico y observación clínica: las pasiones del alma en la psicología medical medieval', in *Comprendre et maîtriser la nature au Moyen Âge. Mélanges d'histoire des sciences offerts à Guy Beaujouan* (Paris and Geneva, Droz, 1994), pp. 181–204.

— 'Les régimes de santé', in M. D. Grmek, *Histoire de la pensée médicale en Occident, 1. Antiquité et Moyen Âge* (Paris, Seuil, 1995), pp. 257–81.

Giraud, C., *Per verba magistri. Anselme de Laon et son école au XIIe siècle* (Turnhout, Brepols, 2010).

Gnilka, C. and Schetter, W. (ed.), *Studien zur Literatur der Spätantike* (Bonn, Habelt, 1975).

Goetz, H.-W. and Jarnut, J. (eds), *Mediävistik im 21. Jahrhundert, Stand und Perspektiven der internationalen und interdisziplinären Mittelalterforschung* (Munich, Wihelm Fink Verlag, 2003).

Goldie, P., *Oxford Handbook of Philosophy of Emotion* (Oxford, Oxford University Press, 2010).

Gondreau, P., *The Passions of Christ's Soul in the Theology of St. Thomas Aquinas* (Münster, Aschendorff, 2002).

Gonthier, N., 'Acteurs et témoins des Rebeynes lyonnaises à la fin du Moyen Âge', in *Révolte et société. Actes du IVe colloque d'histoire au présent* (Paris, Publications de la Sorbonne, 1989), pp. 34–43.

González Blanco, A. and Blázquez artínez, J.-M. (eds), *Cristianismo y aculturación en tiempos del Imperio Romano* (Murcia, Universidad de Murcia, 1990).

Gougaud, L., 'La crèche de Noël avant saint François d'Assise', *Revue des sciences religieuses*, 2 (1922), pp. 26–34.

Granger, C. (eds), *À quoi pensent les historiens? Faire de l'histoire au XXI e siècle* (Paris, Autrement, 2013).

Grassotti, M., 'La ira regia en León y Castilla', *Cuadernos de historia de España*, 41–2 (1965), pp. 5–135.

Grmek, M. D. (eds), *Histoire de la pensée médicale en Occident, 1. Antiquité et Moyen Âge* (Paris, Seuil, 1995).

Gröne, S., 'Le premier écrit scientifique cistercien: le De natura corporis de Guillaume de Saint-Thierry († 1148)', *Rives nord-méditerranéennes*, 31 (2008), pp. 115–30.

Gross, D. M., *The Secret History of Emotion: From Aristotle's Rhetoric to Modern Brain Science* (Chicago, Chicago University Press, 2006).

Guerreau-Jalabert, A., 'Spiritus et caritas. Le baptême dans la société médiévale', in É. Copet-Rougier and F. Héritier-Augé (eds), *La Parenté spirituelle* (Paris/Basel, Éditions des archives contemporaines, 1995), pp. 133–203.

— 'Caritas y don en la sociedad medieval occidental', *Hispania*, 60 (2000), pp. 27–62.

— '*Spiritus et caro*. Une matrice d'analogie générale', in T. Le Deschault de Monredon, F. Elsig, P.-A. Mariaux, B. Roux, and L. Terrier (eds), *L'Image en question. Pour Jean Wirth* (Geneva, Droz, 2013), pp. 290–5.

— 'Occident médiéval et pensée analogique: le sens de spiritus et caro', in P. Genet, *La légitimité implicite*, 2 vols (Paris/Rome, Éditions de la Sorbonne/École française de Rome, 2015), 1: 455–76.

Guillaumont, A., 'Étude historique et doctrinale', in Evagrius of Pontus, *Traité pratique ou le Moine*, ed. A. and C. Guillaumont, 2 vols (Paris, Cerf, 1971).

— 'Un philosophe au désert: Évagre le Pontique', *Revue de l'histoire des religions*, 91 (1972), pp. 28–56.

— and C. Guillaumont, 'Évagre le Pontique', *Dictionnaire de spiritualité*, vol. IV/2 (Paris, 1961), col. 1731–44.

— and C. Guillaumont, 'Introduction', in Evagrius of Pontus, *Traité pratique ou le Moine*, ed. A. and C. Guillaumont, 2 vols (Paris, Cerf, 1971).

Gvozdeva, K. and Velten, H. R. (eds), *Médialité de la procession: performance du mouvement rituel en textes et en images à l'époque prémoderne* (Heidelberg, Winter, 2011).

Haase, D. N., *Avicenna's De anima in the Latin West: the Formation of a Peripatetic Philosophy of the Soul 1160–1300* (London, Warburg Institute, 2000).

Habib, C. (ed.), *La Pudeur. La réserve et le trouble* (Paris, Autrement, 1992).

Hadley, D. M. (ed.), *Masculinity in Medieval Europe* (London, Longman, 1999).

Haemers, J., 'A Moody Community? Emotion and Ritual in Late Medieval Urban Revolts', in É. Lecuppre-Desjardin and A.-L. Van Bruaene (eds), *Les Émotions au cœur de la ville (XIVe–XVIe siècle)* (Turnhout, Brepols, 2005), pp. 63–81.

Hamburger, J. F., 'The Use of Images in the Pastoral Care of Nuns: the Case of Heinrich Suso and the Dominicans', *The Art Bulletin*, 71 (1989/1), pp. 20–46.

— *The Visual and the Visionary: Art and Female Spirituality in Late Medieval Germany* (New York, Zone Books, 1998).

— *Peindre au couvent: la culture visuelle d'un couvent médiéval* (Paris, Gérard Monfort, 2000).

Harré, R. (ed.), *The Social Construction of Emotions* (Oxford, Basil Blackwell, 1986).

Haseldine, J., 'Understanding the Language of *amicitia*. The Friendship Circle of Peter of Celle (*c*. 1115–1183)', *Journal of Medieval History*, 20 (1994), pp. 237–60.

— (ed.), *Friendship in Medieval Europe* (Stroud, Sutton, 1999).

— 'Love, Separation and Male Friendship: Words and Actions in Saint Anselm's Letters to his Friends', in D. M. Hadley (ed.), *Masculinity in Medieval Europe* (London, Longman, 1999), pp. 238–55.

— 'Friends, Friendship and Networks in the Letters of Bernard of Clairvaux', *Cîteaux*, 57 (2006), pp. 243–80.

— 'Friendship, Intimacy and Corporate Networking in the Twelfth Century: The Politics of Friendship in the Letters of Peter the Venerable', *The English Historical Review*, 126 (2011), pp. 251–80.

— 'Affectionate Terms of Address in Twelfth-Century Latin Epistolography: A Comparative Study of the Letters of Bernard of Clairvaux, Peter the Venerable, and Peter of Celle', *The Journal of Medieval Latin*, 23 (2013), pp. 201–54.

Heinzelmann, M., *Gregory of Tours. History and Society in the Sixth Century* (Cambridge, Cambridge University Press, 2001).

Helvétius, A-M. and Kaplan, M., 'Asceticism and its Institutions', in T. Noble and J. Smith (eds), *The Cambridge History of Christianity, 3: Early Medieval Christianities (c. 600–c. 1100)* (Cambridge, Cambridge University Press, 2008), pp. 275–98 and 703–12.

Henriet, P., 'Chronique de quelques morts annoncées: les saints abbés clunisiens', in *La Mort des grands. Médiévales*, 31 (1996), pp. 93–108.

— *La Parole et la prière au Moyen Âge* (Brussels, De Boeck, 2000).

— 'La recluse, le corps, le lieu. À propos d'Alpais de Cudot († 1211)', in C. Caby and G. Melville (eds), *Paradoxien der Legitimation. Ergebnisse einer deutsch-italienisch-französischen Villa Vigoni-Konferenz zur Macht im Mittelalter* (Florence, SISMEL/Galluzzo, 2010), pp. 403–24.

— 'Origines du christianisme ibérique et communauté de parfaits. Valère du Bierzo (viie siècle)', in O. de la Cruz Palma, C. Ferrero Hernández, and J. Martínez Gazquez (eds), *Estudios de latín medieval hispánico. Actas del V Congreso* (Florence, SISMEL/Galluzzo, 2012), pp. 367–76.

— 'Les démons de Valère du Bierzo', in D. Barthélemy and R. Grosse (eds), *Moines et démons. Autobiographie et individualité au Moyen Age (VIIeXIIe siècle)* (Geneva, Droz, 2014), pp. 13–25.

— 'Pro se ipsa. Raingarde de Montboissier († 1135) ou la conversion entre tradition et modernité (Pierre le Vénérable, Ep. 53)', in D. Boisson and É. Pinto-Mathieu (eds), *La Conversion: textes et réalités* (Rennes, Presses Universitaires de Rennes, 2014), pp. 179–89.

— 'L'érémitisme hors de la société ou dans la société. Des origines au xiie siècle', forthcoming.

— and Legras, A.-M. (eds), *Au cloître et dans le monde. Femmes, hommes et sociétés (IXe–XVe siècle). Mélanges en l'honneur de Paulette L'Hermite-Leclercq* (Paris, Presses de l'Université de Paris-Sorbonne, 2000).

Hochner, N., 'Machiavelli: Love and the Economy of Emotions', *Italian Culture*, 22/2 (2014), pp. 122–37.

— 'L'invention du terme émotion. Métamorphoses du corps social', in D. Boquet and P. Nagy (eds), *Histoire intellectuelle des émotions de l'Antiquité à nos jours. Ateliers du Centre de recherches historiques* (2016), https://acrh.revues.org/6720.

Hollywood, A., 'Suffering Transformed: Marguerite Porete, Meister Eckhart, and the Problem of Women's Spirituality', in B. McGinn (ed.), *Meister Eckhart and the Beguine Mystics, Hadewijch of Brabant, Mechthild of Magdeburg, and Marguerite Porete* (New York, Crossroad, 1994), pp. 87–113.

— *The Soul as Virgin Wife: Mechtild of Magdeburg, Marguerite Porete and Meister Eckhart* (Notre Dame, University of Notre Dame Press, 1995).

Horowitz, J. and Menache, S., *L'Humour en chaire. Le rire dans l'Église médiévale* (Geneva, Labor, 1994).

Hoste, A., *Bibliotheca Aelrediana. A Survey of Manuscripts, Old Catalogues, Editions and Studies Concerning St. Aelred of Rievaulx* (La Haye, Nijhoff, 1962).

Huchet, J.-C., *L'Amour discourtois. La 'fin'amor' chez les premiers troubadours* (Toulouse, Privat, 1987).

Huizinga, J., *The Autumn of the Middle Ages*, trans. R. J. Payton and U. Mammitzch (Chicago, University of Chicago Press, 1997).

Hultgren, G., *Le Commandement d'amour chez saint Augustin. Interprétation philosophique et théologique d'après les écrits de la période 386–400* (Paris, Vrin, 1939).

Hyams, P., 'What Did Henry III of England Think in Bed and in French about Kingship and Anger?', in B. H. Rosenwein (ed.), *Anger's Past: The Social Uses of an Emotion in the Middle Ages* (Ithaca, Cornell University Press, 1998), pp. 92–124.

— *Rancor and Reconciliation in Medieval England* (Ithaca, Cornell University Press, 2003).

Hyatte, R., *The Arts of Friendship: The Idealization of Friendship in Medieval and Early Renaissance Literature* (Leiden/New York/Cologne, Brill, 1994).

Illouz, E., *Les Sentiments du capitalisme* (Paris, Seuil, 2006).

Imbach, R., 'Physique ou métaphysique des passions?', *Critique*, 716–17 (2007), pp. 23–35.

— 'Les passions médiévales (perspectives philosophiques)', in I. Boehm, J-F. Ferrary, and S. Franchet 'Espèrey (eds), *L'Homme et ses Passions. Actes du XVII e Congrès international de l'Association Guillaume Budé organisé à Lyon du 26 au 29 août 2013* (Paris, Les Belles Lettres, 2016), pp. 75–96.

— and Atucha, I. (eds), *Amours plurielles. Doctrines médiévales du rapport amoureux de Bernard de Clairvaux à Boccace* (Paris, Seuil, 2006).

Iogna-Prat, D., *Ordonner et exclure. Cluny et la société chrétienne face à l'hérésie, au judaïsme et à l'islam, 1000–1150* (Paris, Aubier, 2000).

— *La Maison Dieu. Une histoire monumentale de l'Église au Moyen Âge (v. 800–v. 1200)* (Paris, Seuil, 2012).

Jacquart, D., 'La maladie et le remède d'amour dans quelques écrits médicaux au Moyen Âge', in D. Buschinger and A. Crépin (eds), *Amour, mariage et transgression au Moyen Âge* (Göppingen, Kümmerle Verlag, 1984), pp. 93–101.

— 'La scolastique médicale', in M. D. Grmek, *Histoire de la pensée médicale en Occident, 1. Antiquité et Moyen Âge* (Paris, Seuil, 1995), pp. 209–10.

— *La Science médicale entre deux renaissances (XIIe–XVe siècle)* (Aldershot, Ashgate, 1997).

— *La Médecine médiévale dans le cadre parisien* (Paris, Fayard, 1998).

— and Thomasset, C., 'L'amour "héroïque" à travers le traité d'Arnaud de Villeneuve', in J. Céard, P. Naurin, and M. Simonin (eds), *La Folie et le Corps* (Paris, PENS, 1985), pp. 143–58.

Jaeger, C. S., 'L'amour des rois: structure sociale d'une forme de sensibilité aristocratique', *Annales ESC*, 3 (1991), pp. 547–71.

— *Ennobling Love: In Search of a Lost Sensibility* (Philadelphia, University of Pennsylvania Press, 1999).

— and Kasten, I. (ed.), *Codierungen von Emotionen im Mittelaleter / Emotions and Sensibilities in the Middle Ages* (Berlin and New York, Walter de Gruyter, 2003).

Javelet, R., 'Intelligence et amour chez les auteurs spirituels du xiie siècle', *Revue d'ascétique et de mystique*, 37 (1961), pp. 273–90 and 429–50.

— *Image et ressemblance au douzième siècle de saint Anselme à Alain de Lille*, 2 vols (Chambéry, Letouzey et Ané, 1967).

Johnson, T. J. (ed.), *Franciscans and Preaching: Every Miracle from the Beginning of the World Came About Through Words* (Leiden and Boston, Brill, 2012).

Jolliffe, J. E. A., *Angevin Kingship* (London, Adam & Charles Black, 1955).

Jong, M. de, 'Sacrum palatium et ecclesia: l'autorité religieuse royale sous les Carolingiens (790–840)', *Annales HSS*, 58/6 (2003), pp. 1243–69.

Jordan, M., *The Invention of Sodomy* (Chicago, University of Chicago Press, 1997).

Joye, S., 'Grégoire de Tours et les femmes: jugements portés sur les couples laïques et ecclésiastiques', in C. La Rocca (ed.), *Agire da donna. Modelli e pratiche di rappresentazione (secoli VI–X)* (Turnhout, Brepols, 2007), pp. 75–94.

Jussen, A., *Patenschaft und Adoption im frühen Mittelalter. Künstliche Verwandtscchaft als soziale Praxis* (Göttingen, Vandenhoeck & Ruprecht, 1991).

Kaster, R., *Emotion, Restraint, and Community in Ancient Rome* (Oxford, Oxford University Press, 2005).

King, P., 'Emotions in Medieval Thought', in P. Goldie (ed.), *Oxford Handbook of Philosophy of Emotion* (Oxford, Oxford University Press, 2010), pp. 167–88.

— 'Aquinas on the Emotions', in B. Davies and E. Stump (ed.), *The Oxford Handbook to Aquinas* (Oxford, Oxford University Press, 2012), pp. 209–26.

Klaniczay, G. (ed.), *Discorsi sulle stimmate dal medioevo all'età contemporanea – Discours sur les stigmates du Moyen Âge à l'époque contemporaine* (Rome, Archivio italiano per la storia della pietà, 2013).

Klibansky, R., Panofsky, E., and Saxl, F., *Saturne et la mélancolie* (Paris, Gallimard, 1989).

Knuuttila, S., *Emotions in Ancient and Medieval Philosophy* (Oxford, Oxford University Press, 2004).

Köhler, E., 'Les troubadours et la jalousie', in *Mélanges de langue et de littérature du Moyen Âge et de la Renaissance offerts à Jean Frappier*, 1 (Geneva, Droz, 1970), pp. 543–59.

Kornbichler, T. and Maaz, W. (eds), *Variationen der Liebe: Historische Psychologie der Geschlechterbeziehung* (Tübingen, Diskord, 1995).

Kriegel, M., 'Mobilisation politique et modernisation organique', *Archives de sciences sociales des religions*, 46 (1978), pp. 5–20.

Krynen, J., *L'Empire du roi. Idées et croyances politiques en France, XIIIe–XVe siècle* (Paris, Gallimard, 1993).

Kuefler, M., 'Male Friendship and the Suspicion of Sodomy in Twelfth-Century France', in S. Farmer and C. Braun Pasternack (eds), *Gender and Difference in the Middle Ages* (Minneapolis, University of Minnesota Press, 2003), pp. 145–81.

La Rocca, C. (ed.), *Agire da donna. Modelli e pratiche di rappresentazione (secoli VI–X)* (Turnhout, Brepols, 2007).

Lachaud, F., *L'Éthique du pouvoir au Moyen Âge. L'office dans la culture politique (Angleterre, v. 1150–v. 1230)* (Paris, Classiques Garnier, 2010).

Lane, C., *Comment la psychiatrie et l'industrie pharmaceutique ont médicalisé nos émotions* (Paris, Flammarion, 2009).

Lansing, C., *Passion and Order: Restraint of Grief in the Medieval Italian Communes* (Ithaca, Cornell University Press, 2008).

Lapidge, M. (ed.), *Columbanus: Studies on the Latin Writings* (Woodbridge, Boydell & Brewer, 1997).

Laursen, J. C. and Nederman, C. J. (eds), *Beyond the Persecuting Society: Religious Toleration Before the Enlightenment* (Philadelphia, University of Pennsylvania Press, 1997).

Lauwers, M. (ed.), *Guerriers et Moines. Conversion et sainteté aristocratiques dans l'Occident médiéval* (Antibes, APDCA, 2002).

— *Naissance du cimetière. Lieux sacrés et terres des morts dans l'Occident médiéval* (Paris, Aubier, 2005).

Lazzerni, L., 'Une jalousie particulière: la "reina de Fransa" dans le Roman de Flamenca', in A. Buckley and D. Billy (ed.), *Études de langue et de littérature médiévales offertes à Peter T. Ricketts à l'occasion de son 70e anniversaire* (Turnhout, Brepols, 2005), pp. 47–57.

Le Deschault de Monredon, T., Elsig, F., Mariaux, P.-A., Roux, B., and Terrier L. (eds), *L'Image en question. Pour Jean Wirth* (Geneva, Droz, 2013).

Le Goff, J., *La Bourse et la vie. Économie et religion au Moyen Âge* (Paris, Gallimard, 1987).

— 'Rire au Moyen Âge', *Cahiers du Centre de recherches historiques*, 3 (1989), http://ccrh.revues.org/2918.

— 'Le rire dans les règles monastiques du haut Moyen Âge', in M. Sot (ed.), *Haut Moyen Âge: culture, éducation et société. Mélanges Pierre Riché* (Nanterre, Publidix; La Garenne-Colombes, Éditions européennes Érasme, 1990), pp. 93–103.

— *Saint Louis* (Paris, Gallimard, 1996).

— 'Le rituel symbolique de la vassalité' (1976), in *Un autre Moyen Âge* (Paris, Gallimard, 1999), pp. 333–99.

— 'Du ciel sur la terre: la mutation des valeurs du xiie siècle au xiiie siècle dans l'Occident chrétien', in *Héros du Moyen Âge. Le saint et le roi au Moyen Âge* (Paris, Gallimard, 2004), pp. 1263–87.

— 'Une musique de jubilation: la musique de l'Occident médiéval', in *Moyen Âge entre ordre et désordre, Catalogue de l'exposition du musée de la Musique, 26 mars–27 juin 2004* (Paris, RMN, 2004), pp. 13–19.

— *Le Moyen Âge et l'Argent* (Paris, Perrin, 2010).

— and Schmitt, J.-C. (ed.), *Le Charivari* (Paris, EHESS/Mouton, 1981).

Le Jan, R., *Famille et pouvoir dans le monde franc (VIIe–Xe siècle). Essai d'anthropologie sociale* (Paris, Publications de la Sorbonne, 1995).

— *La Société du haut Moyen Âge, VIe–IXe siècle* (Paris, Armand Colin, 2003).

— 'Timor, amicitia, odium: les liens politiques à l'époque mérovingienne', in W. Pohl and V. Wieser (eds), *Der frühmittelalterliche Staat. Europäische Perspektiven* (Vienna, Österreichichen Akademie der Wissenschaften, 2009), pp. 217–26.

— 'Entre haine et amour du roi: quelques réflexions sur les émotions politiques à l'époque mérovingienne', in J. Barbier, M. Cottret, and L. Scordia (eds), *Amour et désamour du prince. Du haut Moyen Âge à la Révolution française* (Paris, Kimé, 2011), pp. 15–26.

Le Vot, G., 'Réalités et figures: la plainte, la joie et la colère dans le chant aux xiie–xiiie siècles', *Cahiers de civilisation médiévale*, 46 (2003), pp. 353–80.

Leclercq, J., *Un Maître de la vie spirituelle du XIe siècle, Jean de Fécamp* (Paris, Vrin, 1946).

— *Saint Pierre Damien* (Rome, Storia e Letteratura, 1960).

— *L'Amour vu par les moines au XIIe siècle* (Paris, Cerf, 1983).

— *Le Mariage vu par les moines au XIIe siècle* (Paris, Cerf, 1983).

Lecuppre, G., 'Le scandale: de l'exemple pervers à l'outil politique (xiiie–xve siècle)', *Cahiers de recherches médiévales et humanistes*, 25 (2013), pp. 181–91.

Lecuppre-Desjardin, E. and Van Bruaene, A.-L. (eds), *Emotions in the Heart of the City (14th–16th Century) / Les Émotions au cœur de la ville (XIVe–XVIe siècle)* (Turnhout, Brepols, 2005).

Legros, H., *L'Amitié dans les chansons de geste à l'époque romane* (Aix-en-Provence, Publications de l'Université de Provence, 2001).

Lemoine, M., 'Les ambiguïtés de l'héritage médiéval: Guillaume de Saint Thierry', in B. Besnier, P.-F. Moreau, and L. Renault (eds), *Les Passions antiques et médiévales* (Paris, PUF, 2003), pp. 297–308.

— 'Guillaume de Saint-Thierry et Guillaume de Conches', in N. Boucher (ed.), *Signy l'Abbaye et Guillaume de Saint-Thierry, actes du colloque international d'études cisterciennes, 9–11 septembre 1998* (Signy l'Abbaye, Association des amis de l'Abbaye de Signy, 2000), pp. 527–39.

Lett, D., *L'Enfant des miracles. Enfance et société au Moyen Âge (XIIe–XIIIe siècle)* (Paris, Aubier, 1997).

— *Famille et parenté dans l'Occident médiéval, Ve–XVe siècle* (Paris, Hachette, 2000).

— 'Compte rendu de l'ouvrage de L.-G. Tin, L'Invention de la culture hétérosexuelle', *Clio. Histoire, femmes et sociétés*, 31 (2010), pp. 287–90.

— *Hommes et femmes au Moyen Âge. Histoire du genre, XIIe–XVe siècle* (Paris, A. Colin, 2013).

— 'Familles et relations émotionnelles (xiie–xve siècle)', in A. Corbin, J.-J. Courtine, and G. Vigarello (eds), *Histoire des émotions* (Paris, Seuil, 2016–17, third volume forthcoming), 1: 181–203.

— and Offenstadt, N. (eds), *Haro! Noël! Oyé! Pratiques du cri au Moyen Âge* (Paris, Publications de la Sorbonne, 2003).

Levron, P., 'Naissance de la mélancolie dans la littérature des xiie et xiiie siècles', doctoral thesis, Université de Paris-Sorbonne (Paris IV), 2005, unpublished.

— 'Mélancolie, émotion et vocabulaire. Enquête sur le réseau lexical de l'émotivité atrabilaire dans quelques textes littéraires du xiie et du xiiie siècle', in D. Boquet and P. Nagy (eds), *Le Sujet des émotions au Moyen Âge* (Paris, Beauchesne, 2009), pp. 231–71.

L'Hermite-Leclercq, P., 'La recluse, la femme et l'amour de Dieu chez Aelred de Rievaulx', in C. Duhamel-Amado and G. Lobrichon (ed.), *Georges Duby. L'écriture de l'histoire* (Brussels, De Boeck, 1996), pp. 379–84.

— *L'Église et les Femmes dans l'Occident chrétien des origines à la fin du Moyen Âge* (Turnhout, Brepols, 1997).

Libera, A. de, *La Mystique rhénane d'Albert le Grand à Maître Eckhart* (Paris, Seuil, 1994).

— 'Angèle de Foligno et la mystique "féminine". Éléments pour une typologie', in G. Barone and J. Dalarun (eds), *Angèle de Foligno. Le dossier* (Rome, École française de Rome, 1999), pp. 345–71.

Livet, P., *Émotions et rationalité morale* (Paris, PUF, 2002).

Lohmer, C., 'Multae sunt viae quibus itur ad Deum: Monastic Theology of Peter Damian', in M. Tagliaferri (ed.), *Pier Damiani. L'eremita, il teologo, il riformatore* (Bologna, Edizioni Dehoniane, 2009), pp. 119–28.

Longo, U., 'La conversione di Romualdo di Ravenna come manifesto programmatico della riforma eremitica', in *Ottone III e Romualdo di Ravenna. Imperio, monasteri e santi asceti, Atti del XXIV Convegno del Centro Studi Avellaniti, Fonte Avellana 2002* (Negarine, Il Segno dei Gabrielli editori, 2003), pp. 215–36.

— 'L'attesa della fine: Monaci e eremiti', in E. Pasztor (ed.), *Attese escatologiche dei secoli XII–XIV: dall'età dello spirito al 'pastor angelicus'* (L'Aquila, Colacchi, 2004), vol. I, pp. 43–62.

— 'L'esperienza di riforma avellanita e i rapporti con il mondo monastico', *Reti medievali*, 11/1 (2010), http://www.rmojs.unina.it/index.php/rm/article/view/20.

— 'O *utinam anima mea esset in corpore tuo*! Pier Damiani, l'amicitia monastica e la riforma', *Reti medievali*, 11/1 (2010), http://fermi.univr.it/rm/rivista/saggi/Longo1_10_1.htm.

Lordon, F., *La Société des affects. Pour un structuralisme des passions* (Paris, Seuil, 2013).

Lottin, O., 'Les traités sur l'âme et les vertus de Jean de la Rochelle', *Revue néo-scolastique de philosophie*, 32 (1930), pp. 5–32.

— 'Les mouvements premiers de l'appétit sensitif de Pierre Lombard à saint Thomas d'Aquin', in *Psychologie et morale aux XIIe et XIIIe siècles*, v. II: Problèmes de morale, 1st part (Gembloux, Duculot, 1948), pp. 493–589.

Luce-Dudemaine, D., 'La sanction de la jalousie dans les "novas" du xiiie siècle', *Senefiance*, 16 (1986), pp. 227–36.

Lucken, C., 'Éclats de la voix, langage des affects et séduction du chant. Cris et interjections à travers la philosophie, la grammaire et la littérature médiévales', in D. Lett and N. Offenstadt (eds), *Haro! Noël! Oyé! Pratiques du cri au Moyen Âge* (Paris, Publications de la Sorbonne, 2003), pp. 179–201.

Lutz, C., *Unnatural Emotions: Everyday Sentiments on a Micronesian Atoll and their Challenge to Western Theory* (Chicago, University of Chicago Press, 1988).

Lynch, J., *Godparents and Kinship in Early Medieval Europe* (Princeton, Princeton University Press, 1986).

Macé, L., *Les Comtes de Toulouse et leur entourage, XIIe–XIIIe siècles* (Toulouse, Privat, 2000).

McGinn, B., *Three Treatises on Man: A Cistercian Anthropology* (Kalamazoo, Cistercian Publications, 1977).

— *The Growth of Mysticism: Gregory the Great through the 12th Century* (New York, Crossroad, 1994).

— (ed.), *Meister Eckhart and the Beguine Mystics, Hadewijch of Brabant, Mechthild of Magdeburg, and Marguerite Porete* (New York, Crossroad, 1994).

— *The Flowering of Mysticism: Men and Women in the New Mysticism, 1200–1350* (New York, Crossroad, 1998).

— *The Varieties of Vernacular Mysticism (1350–1500)* (New York, Herder & Herder, 2012).

McGuire, B. P., 'Love, Friendship and Sex in the Eleventh Century: The Experience of Anselm', *Studia Theologica*, 28 (1974), pp. 111–52.

— *Friendship and Community: The Monastic Experience 350–1250* (Kalamazoo, Cistercian Publications, 1988).

— *Brother and Lover: Aelred of Rievaulx* (New York, Crossroad, 1994).

McNamer, S., *Affective Meditation and the Invention of Medieval Compassion* (Philadelphia, University of Pennsylvania Press, 2010).

Madelénat, D., *L'Épopée* (Paris, PUF, 1986).

Maire-Vigueur, J.-C., *Cavaliers et citoyens. Guerre, conflits et société dans l'Italie communale* (Paris, EHESS, 2003).

Mancia, L. E., 'Affective Devotion and Emotional Reform in the Eleventh-Century Monastery of John of Fécamp', PhD, New Haven, Yale University, 2013, unpublished.

Mandressi, R., 'Le temps profond et le temps perdu. Usages des neurosciences et des sciences cognitives en histoire', *Revue d'histoire des sciences humaines*, 25 (2011), pp. 165–202.

Mandrou, R., 'Pour une histoire de la sensibilité', *Annales. Économies, Sociétés, Civilisation*, 14/3 (1959), pp. 581–8.

— *Introduction à la France moderne, 1500–1640. Essai de psychologie historique* (Paris, Albin Michel, 1961).

Manselli, R., 'Il gesto come predicazione per san Francesco d'Assisi', *Collectanea Franciscana*, 51 (1981), pp. 5–16.

Mansfield, M. C., *The Humiliation of Sinners: Public Penance in Thirteenth-Century France* (Ithaca, Cornell University Press, 1995).

Marcus, G. E., *Le Citoyen sentimental. Émotions et politique en démocratie* (Paris, Presses de la Fondation nationale des sciences politiques, 2008).

Marini, E. (ed.), *Agostino d'Ippona. Presenza e pensiero. La scoperta dell'interiorità* (Milan, Franco Angeli, 2004).

Markus, R. A., *Gregory the Great and his World* (Cambridge, Cambridge University Press, 1997).

Marmo, C., '*Hoc autem etse potest tollerari* … Egidio Romano e Tommaso d'Aquino sulle passioni dell'anima', *Documenti e studi sulla tradizione filosofica medievale*, 2 (1991), pp. 281–315.

Martignoni, A., 'Entre textes et images. La performativité proces sionnelle chez les flagellants dans l'Italie de la fin du Moyen Âge', in K. Gvozdeva and H. R. Velten (eds), *Médialité de la procession: performance du mouvement rituel en textes et en images à l'époque prémoderne* (Heidelberg, Winter, 2011), pp. 211–27.

Martin, H., *Le Métier de prédicateur en France septentrionale à la fin du Moyen Âge* (Paris, Cerf, 1988).

Mauriès, P. (ed.), *Les Gays Savoirs* (Paris, Gallimard, 1998).

Mauss, M., 'L'expression obligatoire des sentiments (rituels oraux funéraires australiens)', *Journal de psychologie*, 18 (1921), pp. 425–34.

— 'Les techniques du corps', in *Sociologie et anthropologie* (Paris, PUF, 1966), pp. 362–86.

Mazel, F., *Féodalités (888–1180)* (Paris, Éditions Belin, 2010).

Mazurel, H., 'De la psychologie des profondeurs à l'histoire des sensibilités. Une généalogie intellectuelle', *Vingtième Siècle. Revue d'histoire*, 123/3 (2014), pp. 22–38.

Mélanges de langue et de littérature du Moyen Âge et de la Renaissance offerts à Jean Frappier, 1 (Geneva, 1970).

Melville, G., Schneidmüller, B., and Weinfurter, S. (ed.), *Innovationen durch Deuten und Gestalten. Klöster im Mittelalter zwischen Jenseits und Welt* (Regensburg, Schnell & Steiner, 2014).

Ménard, P., *Le Rire et le Sourire dans le roman courtois en France au Moyen Âge (1150–1250)* (Geneva, Droz, 1969).

Méniel, B., 'La colère dans la poésie épique, du Moyen Âge à la fin du xvie siècle. Un envers de l'héroïsme?', *Cahiers de recherches médiévales*, 11 (special issue, 2004), pp. 37–48.

Mews, C. J., *Abelard and Heloise* (Oxford, Oxford University Press, 2005).

— 'Cicero and the Boundaries of Friendship in the Twelfth Century', *Viator*, 38 (2007), pp. 369–84.

Micha, A., 'Le mari jaloux dans la littérature romanesque des xiie et xiiie siècles', *Studi Medievali*, n.s. 17 (1951), pp. 303–20.

Michaud-Quantin, P., 'Le traité des passions chez Albert le Grand', *Recherches de théologie ancienne et médiévale*, 17 (1950), pp. 90–120.

— *La Psychologie de l'activité chez Albert le Grand* (Paris, Vrin, 1966).

Michelet, J., *Histoire de France. Le Moyen Âge* (Paris, Robert Laffont, 1981).

Miller, W. I., *Bloodtaking and Peacemaking: Feud, Law and Society in Saga Iceland* (Chicago, University of Chicago Press, 1990).

Moeglin, J.-M., *Les Bourgeois de Calais. Essai sur un mythe historique* (Paris, Albin Michel, 2002).

— ' "Performative Turn", "communication politique" et rituels au Moyen Âge. À propos de deux ouvrages récents', *Le Moyen Âge*, 113 (2007), pp. 393–406.

Moore, R. I., *The Formation of a Persecuting Society* (Oxford, Basil Blackwell, 1987).

Morenzoni, F., 'La bonne et la mauvaise honte dans la littérature pénitentielle et la prédication (fin xiie–début xiiie siècle)', in B. Sère and J. Wettlaufer (eds), *Shame Between Punishment and Penance: The Social Usages of Shame in the Middle Ages and Early Modern Times* (Florence, SISMEL/Galluzzo, 2013), pp. 177–93.

— and Tilliette, J.-Y. (eds), *Autour de Guillaume d'Auvergne (1249)* (Turnhout, Brepols, 2005).

Moscovici, S., *L'Âge des foules. Un traité historique de psychologie des masses* (Brussels, Complexe, 1985).

Moulinier, L., 'Magie, médecine et maux de l'âme dans l'œuvre scientifique de Hildegarde', in R. Berndt (ed.), *'Im Angesicht Gottes suche der Mensch sich selbst': Hildegard von Bingen (1098–1179)* (Berlin, Akademie Verlag, 2001), pp. 545–59.

— 'Jean de Salisbury, un réseau d'amitiés continentales', in M. Aurell (ed.), *Culture politique des Plantagenêts (1154–1204)* (Poitiers, CESCM, 2003), pp. 341–61.

Moyen Âge entre ordre et désordre, catalogue de l'exposition du musée de la Musique, 26 mars–27 juin 2004 (Paris, RMN, 2004).

Nagy, P., *Le Don des larmes au Moyen Âge. Un instrument spirituel en quête d'institution, Ve–XIIIe siècle* (Paris, Albin Michel, 2000).

— 'La notion de christianitas et la spatialisation du sacré au xe siècle: un sermon d'Abbon de Saint-Germain', *Médiévales*, 49 (2005), pp. 121–40.

— 'Au-delà du verbe. L'efficacité de la prière individuelle au Moyen Âge entre âme et corps', in J.-F. Cottier (ed.), *La Prière en latin, de l'Antiquité au XVIe siècle. Formes, évolutions, significations* (Turnhout, Brepols, 2006), pp. 441–71.

— 'Les émotions et l'historien: de nouveaux paradigmes', *Émotions médiévales. Critique*, 716–17 (2007), pp. 10–22.

— 'Larmes et Eucharistie. Formes du sacrifice en Occident au Moyen Âge central', in N. Bériou and B. Caseau (eds), *Pratiques de l'Eucharistie dans les Églises d'Orient et d'Occident* (Paris, Études Augustiniennes, 2009), vol. 2, pp. 1073–109.

— 'Faire l'histoire des émotions à l'heure des sciences de l'émotion', *BUCEMA*, hors-série no. 5 (2013), http://cem.revues.org/12539.

Nardini, C., 'Affectio e ratio nell'itinerario mistico del Beniamin Minor di Ricardo di San Vittore', *Annali della Facoltà di Lettere e Filosofia dell'Università degli Studi di Perugia*, 24 (1986–7), pp. 205–28.

Nayt-Dubois, A. and Santinelli-Foltz, E. (ed.), *Femmes de pouvoir et pouvoir des femmes dans l'Occident médiéval et moderne* (Valenciennes, PUV, 2009).

Nelson, J., 'Les reines carolingiennes', in A. Dierkens, S. Lebecq, R. Le Jan, and J.-M. Sansterre (eds), *Femmes et pouvoirs des femmes à Byzance et en Occident (VIe–XIe siècles)* (Villeneuve d'Ascq, Centre de recherches sur l'histoire de l'Europe du Nord-Ouest, Université Lille III, 1999), pp. 121–32.

Neuhausen, K.-A., 'Zu Cassians Traktat De amicitia', in C. Gnilka and W. Schetter (eds), *Studien zur Literatur der Spätantike* (Bonn, Habelt, 1975), pp. 181–218.

Newhauser, R. G. (ed.), *In the Garden of Evil: The Vices and Culture in the Middle Ages* (Toronto, Pontifical Institute of Mediaeval Studies, 2005).

— (ed.), *The Seven Deadly Sins: From Communities to Individuals* (Leiden, Brill, 2007).

Nicoud, M., 'L'adaptation du discours diététique aux pratiques alimentaires: l'exemple de Barnabas de Reggio', *Mélanges de l'École française de Rome, Moyen Âge,* 107/1 (1995), pp. 207–31.

— *Les Régimes de santé au Moyen Âge: naissance et diffusion d'une écriture médicale,* 2 vols (Rome, École française de Rome, 2007).

Nirenberg, D., *Violence et minorités au Moyen Âge* (Paris, PUF, 2001).

Noble, T. and Smith, J. (eds), *The Cambridge History of Christianity,* vol. 3: *Early Medieval Christianities (c. 600–c. 1100)* (Cambridge, Cambridge University Press, 2008).

Nussbaum, M. C., *Upheavals of Thought: The Intelligence of the Emotions* (Cambridge, Cambridge University Press, 2002).

— *Hiding from Humanity: Disgust, Shame, and the Law* (Princeton, Princeton University Press, 2004).

Nygren, A., *Erôs et Agapè,* 3 vols (Paris, Aubier, 1952).

Oberman, H. A. and Van Engen, J. (eds), *Devotio Moderna: Basic Writings* (New York, Crossroad, 1988).

O'Daly, G. and Zumkeller, A., 'Affectus (passio, perturbatio)', in D. Meyer (ed.), *Augustinus-Lexikon* (Basel, Schwabe & Co, 1986), pp. 166–80.

Offenstadt, N., 'Cris et cloches. L'expression sonore dans les rituels de paix à la fin du Moyen Âge', *Hypothèses* 1997 (1998), pp. 51–8.

— 'De la joie et des larmes. Émotions, négociations et paix pendant la guerre de Cent Ans', in *Negociar en la edad media / Négocier au Moyen Âge. Actes du colloque tenu à Barcelone du 14 au 16 octobre 2004* (Barcelona, Barcelona Institución Milá y Fontanals, 2005), pp. 349–68.

— *Faire la paix au Moyen Âge. Discours et gestes de paix pendant la guerre de Cent Ans* (Paris, Odile Jacob, 2007).

Oschema, K., *Freundschaft und Nähe im spätmittelalterlichen Burgund. Studien zum Spannungsfeld von Emotioon und Institution* (Cologne/Weimar/Vienna, Böhlau, 2006).

— 'Toucher et être touché: gestes de conciliation et émotions dans les duels judiciaires', *Médiévales,* 61 (2011), pp. 142–61.

Ottone III e Romualdo di Ravenna. Imperio, monasteri e santi asceti, Atti del XXIV Convegno del Centro Studi Avellaniti, Fonte Avellana 2002 (Negarine, Il Segno dei Gabrielli editori, 2003).

Paez, D. and Rimé, B., 'L'empathie dans le partage social de l'émotion. Processus individuels et processus collectifs', in P. Attigui and A. Cukier (eds), *Les Paradoxes de l'empathie. Entre émotion et cognition sociale* (Paris, CNRS Éditions, 2012), pp. 281–95.

— 'Collective Emotional Gatherings: Their Impact upon Identity Fusion, Shared Beliefs and Social Integration', in M. Salmela and C. von Scheve (eds), *Collective Emotions: Perspectives from Psychology, Philosophy, and Sociology* (Oxford, Oxford University Press, 2014), pp. 204–16.

Palazzo, E., *Les Sacramentaires de Fulda. Études sur l'iconographie et la liturgie à l'époque ottonienne* (Münster, Aschendorff, 1994).

Pancer, N., *Sans peur et sans vergogne. De l'honneur et des femmes aux premiers temps mérovingiens* (Paris, Albin Michel, 2001).

— 'Les hontes mérovingiennes: essai de méthodologie et cas de figure', *Rives nord-méditerranéennes*, 31 (2008), pp. 41–56.

— 'Violence domestique ou conflits politiques? Le cas des Mérovingiennes', in M. Aurell (ed.), *La Parenté déchirée. Les luttes intrafamiliales au moyen âge* (Turnhout, Brepols, 2010), pp. 63–78.

Pasztor, E. (ed.), *Attese escatologiche dei secoli XII–XIV: dall'età dello spirito al 'pastor angelicus'* (L'Aquila, Colacchi, 2004).

Penco, G., 'Eucaristia, ascesi e martirio spirituale', in *Medioevo monastico* (Rome, Pontificio Ateneo S. Anselmo, 1988), pp. 387–98.

Perler, D., *Transformationen der Gefühle. Philosophische Emotionstheorien, 1270–1670* (Frankfurt-am-Main, Fischer, 2011).

Perrin, M., *L'Homme antique et chrétien: l'anthropologie de Lactance (250–325)* (Paris, Beauchesne, 1981).

Pétré, H., *Caritas. Étude sur le vocabulaire latin de la charité chrétienne* (Louvain, Peeters, 1948).

Pezé, W., 'Les émotions et le moi chez quelques théologiens du haut Moyen Âge', *BUCEMA*, hors-série no. 5 (2013), http://cem.revues.org/12538.

Pichery, É., 'Introduction', in Jean Cassien, *Conférences*, ed. M. Petschenig, trans. É. Pichery, 3 vols (Paris, Cerf, 1955–2008), 1: 39.

Pigeaud, J., *Maladie de l'âme. Étude sur la relation de l'âme et du corps dans la tradition médico-philosophique antique* (Paris, Les Belles Lettres, 1981).

— *De la mélancolie. Fragments de poétique et d'histoire* (Paris, Dilecta, 2005).

Piron, S., 'Marguerite, entre les béguines et les maîtres', in S. L. Field, R. E. Lerner, and S. Piron (eds), *Marguerite Porete et le Miroir des simples âmes. Perspectives historiques, philosophiques et littéraires* (Paris, Vrin, 2013), pp. 69–101.

Plamper, J., *Geschichte und Gefühl. Grundlagen der Emotionsgeschichte* (Munich, Siedler, 2012).

— 'L'histoire des émotions', in C. Granger (ed.), *À quoi pensent les historiens? Faire de l'histoire au XXIe siècle* (Paris, Autrement, 2013), pp. 225–40.

Pohl, W. and Wieser, V. (eds), *Der frühmittelalterliche Staat. Europäische Perspektiven* (Vienna, Österreichichen Akademie der Wissenschaften, 2009).

Post, R. R., *The Modern Devotion: Confrontation with Reformation and Humanism* (Leiden, Brill, 1968).

Prochasson, C., *L'Empire des émotions: les historiens dans la mêlée* (Paris, Demopolis, 2008).

Raynaud, C., 'Le courroux et la haine dans les Chroniques de Jean Froissart', *Bulletin du C.R.I.S.I.M.A.*, 2 (2003), pp. 113–234.

Réal, I., *Vies des saints, vie de famille. Représentation et système de la parenté dans le royaume mérovingien (481–751)* (Turnhout, Brepols, 2001).

Réau, L., 'Saint Grégoire', in *Iconographie de l'art chrétien: Iconographie des saints, II* (Paris, PUF, 1958), vol. 3, pp. 609–15.

Reddy, W. M., 'Against Constructionism: The Historical Ethnography of Emotions', *Current Anthropology*, 38/3 (1997), pp. 327–51.

— *The Navigation of Feeling: A Framework for the History of Emotions* (Cambridge, Cambridge University Press, 2001).

— *The Making of Romantic Love: Longing and Sexuality in Europe, South Asia and Japan, 900–1200 CE* (Chicago, University of Chicago Press, 2012).

Régnier-Bohler, D., 'Amour courtois', in *Dictionnaire raisonné de l'Occident médiéval* (Paris, Fayard, 1999), pp. 32–41.

— (ed.), *Voix de femmes au Moyen Âge. Savoir, mystique, poésie, amour, sorcellerie XIIe–XVe siècle* (Paris, Robert Laffont, 2006).

Ribémont, B., 'La "peur épique". Le sentiment de peur en tant qu'objet littéraire dans la chanson de geste', *Le Moyen Âge*, 3–4 (2008), pp. 557–87.

Richez, J.-C., 'Émeutes antisémites et révolution en Alsace', in F. Gambrelle and M. Trebitsch (eds), *Révolte et société. Actes du IVe colloque d'histoire au présent (Paris, mai 1988)*, 2 vols (Paris, Publications de la Sorbonne, 1989), 2: 114–21.

Rieger, A., 'Le motif de la jalousie dans le roman arthurien: l'exemple du roman d'Yder', in *Chanter et dire. Études sur la littérature du Moyen Âge* (Paris, Champion, 1997), pp. 173–89.

Ringbom, S., 'Images de dévotion et dévotions imaginatives. Notes sur le rôle de l'art dans la piété du Moyen Âge', in *Les Images de dévotion, XIIe–XVe siècle* (Paris, Gérard Monfort, 1995), pp. 7–32.

Robinson, I. S., 'The Friendship Network of Gregory VII', *History*, 63 (1978), pp. 1–22.

Rosaldo, M. Z., *Knowledge and Passion: Ilongot Notions of Self and Social Life* (Cambridge, Cambridge University Press, 1980).

Rosenwein, B. H., *To Be Neighbor of Saint Peter: The Social Meaning of Cluny's Property 909–1049* (Ithaca, Cornell University Press, 1989).

— (ed.), *Anger's Past: The Social Uses of an Emotion in the Middle Ages* (Ithaca, Cornell University Press, 1998).

— 'Worrying about Emotions in History', *American Historical Review*, 107 (2002), pp. 821–45.

— 'Eros and Clio: Emotional Paradigms in Medieval Historiography', in H.-W. Goetz and J. Jarnut (eds), *Mediävistik im 21. Jahrhundert, Stand und Perspektiven der internationalen und interdisziplinären Mittelalterforschung* (Munich, Wihelm Fink Verlag, 2003), pp. 427–41.

— *Emotional Communities in the Early Middle Ages* (Ithaca, Cornell University Press, 2006).

— 'Les émotions de la vengeance', in D. Barthélemy, F. Bougard, and R. Le Jan (eds), *La Vengeance, 400–1200* (Rome, École française de Rome, 2006), pp. 237–57.

— 'Emotion Words', in D. Boquet and P. Nagy (eds), *Le Sujet des émotions au Moyen Âge* (Paris, Beauchesne, 2009), pp. 93–106.

— 'Thinking Historically about Medieval Emotions', *History Compass*, 8/8 (2010), pp. 828–42.

— 'The Political Uses of an Emotional Community: Cluny and its Neighbors, 833–965', in D. Boquet and P. Nagy (eds), *Politiques des émotions au Moyen Âge* (Florence, SISMEL/Galluzo, 2010), pp. 205–24.

— *Generations of Feeling: A History of Emotions, 600–1700* (Cambridge, Cambridge University Press, 2016).

Rosier-Catach, I., 'Roger Bacon, Al-Farabi et Augustin. Rhétorique, logique et philosophie morale', in G. Dahan and I. Rosier-Catach (eds), *La Rhétorique d'Aristote: traditions et commentaires de l'Antiquité au XVIIe siècle* (Paris, Vrin, 1998), pp. 87–110.

— 'Discussions médiévales sur l'expression des affects', in D. Boquet and P. Nagy (eds), *Le Sujet des émotions au Moyen Âge* (Paris, Beauchesne, 2009), pp. 201–23.

Rougemont, D. de, *L'Amour et l'Occident* (Paris, Plon, 1972).

Rubin, M., *Corpus Christi: The Eucharist in Late Medieval Culture* (Cambridge, Cambridge University Press, 1991).

Salmela, M. and von Scheve, C. (eds), *Collective Emotions: Perspectives from Psychology, Philosophy, and Sociology* (Oxford, Oxford University Press, 2014).

Sapir Abulafia, A., 'Bodies in the Jewish–Christian Debate', in S. Kay and M. Rubin (eds), *Framing Medieval Bodies* (Manchester, Manchester University Press, 1994), pp. 123–34.

— *Christians and Jews in the Twelfth-Century Renaissance* (London, Routledge, 1995).

— *Christians and Jews in Dispute: Disputational Literature and the Rise of Anti-Judaism in the West (c. 1000–1150)* (Aldershot, Ashgate, 1998).

— *Christian–Jewish Relations, 1000–1300: Jews in the Service of Medieval Christendom* (London, Routledge, 2011).

Sassier, Y., 'Inspirer l'amour, inspirer la crainte? Sources bibliques et patristiques, œuvres parénétiques (vie–xiie siècles)', in J. Barbier, M. Cottret, and L. Scordia (eds), *Amour et désamour du prince du haut Moyen Âge à la Révolution française* (Paris, Kimé, 2011), pp. 27–43.

Scheel, J., *Das altniederländische Stifterbild: Emotionsstrategien des Sehens und der Selbsterkenntnis* (Berlin, Mann, 2014).

Schmitt, J.-C., ' "Façons de sentir et de penser". Un tableau de la civilisation ou une histoire problème?', in H. Atsma and A. Burguière (eds), *Marc Bloch aujourd'hui. Histoire comparée et sciences sociales* (Paris, EHESS, 1990), pp. 407–18.

— *La Raison des gestes dans l'Occident médiéval* (Paris, Gallimard, 1990).

— 'L'imagination efficace', in *Le Corps des images. Essais sur la culture visuelle au Moyen Âge* (Paris, Gallimard, 2002), pp. 345–62.

Scordia, L., 'Concepts et registres de l'amour du roi dans le *De regimine principum* de Gilles de Rome', in J. Barbier, M. Cottret, and L. Scordia (eds), *Amour et désamour du prince du haut Moyen Âge à la Révolution française* (Paris, Kimé, 2011), pp. 45–62.

Sebti, M., *Avicenne. L'âme humaine* (Paris, PUF, 2000).

Sère, B., *Penser l'amitié au Moyen Âge. Étude historique des commentaires sur es livres VIII et IX de l'Éthique à Nicomaque (XIIIe–XVe siècle)* (Turnhout, Brepols, 2007).

— 'Déshonneur, outrage et infamie aux sources de la violence d'après le *Super Rhetoricum* de Gilles de Rome', in F. Foronda, C. Barralis, and B. Sère (eds), *Violences souveraines au Moyen Âge. Travaux d'une école historique* (Paris, PUF, 2010), pp. 103–12.

— 'Le roi peut-il avoir honte? Quelques réflexions à partir des chroniques de France et d'Angleterre (XIIe-XIIIe siècles)', in D. Boquet and P. Nagy, *Politiques des émotions au Moyen Âge* (Florence, SISMEL/Galluzzo, 2010), pp. 49–74.

— 'Penser la honte comme sanction dans la scolastique des xiiie–xive siècles', in B. Sère and J. Wettlaufer (eds), *Shame Between Punishment and Penance: The Social Usages of Shame in the Middle Ages and Early Modern Times* (Florence, SISMEL/Galluzzo, 2013), pp. 123–38.

— and Wettlaufer, J. (eds), *Shame Between Punishment and Penance: The Social Usages of Shame in the Middle Ages and Early Modern Times* (Florence, SISMEL/Galluzzo, 2013).

Sheridan, M., 'The Controversy over Apatheia: Cassian's Sources and his Use of Them', *Studia Monastica*, 39 (1997), pp. 287–310.

Smagghe, L., *Les Émotions du prince. Émotion et discours politique dans l'espace bourguignon* (Paris, Classiques Garnier, 2012).

— 'Sur paine d'encourir nostre indignation. Rhétorique du courroux princier dans les Pays-Bas bourguignons à la fin du Moyen Âge', in D. Boquet and P. Nagy, *Politiques des émotions au Moyen Âge* (Florence, SISMEL/ Galluzzo, 2010), pp. 75–91.

Smail, D. L., 'Hatred as a Social Institution in Late-Medieval Society', *Speculum*, 76 (2001), pp. 90–126.

— *The Consumption of Justice: Emotions, Publicity, and Legal Culture in Marseille, 1264–1423* (Ithaca, Cornell University Press, 2003).

Sodi, M. and Salvarani R. (eds), *La Penitenza tra I e II millennio. Per una comprensione delle origini della Penitenzieria Apostolica* (Vatican City, Libreria Editrice Vaticana, 2012).

Solomon, R. C., *The Passions: Emotions and the Meaning of Life* (Indianapolis, Hackett, 1993).

Somos, R., 'Origen, Evagrius Ponticus and the Ideal of Impassibility', in W. A. Bienert and U. Kühneweg (eds), *Origeniana Septima. Origenes in der Auseinandersetzungen des 4. Jahrhunderts* (Louvain, Peeters, 1999), pp. 367–73.

Sorabji, R., *Emotion and Peace of Mind: From Stoic Agitation to Christian Temptation* (Oxford, Oxford University Press, 2000).

Sot, M. (ed.), *Haut Moyen Âge: culture, éducation et société. Mélanges Pierre Riché* (Nanterre, Publidix; La Garenne-Colombes, Éditions européennes Érasme, 1990).

— 'Héritages et innovations sous les rois francs', in J.-P. Boudet, A. Guerreau-Jalabert, and M. Sot (eds), *Histoire culturelle de la France*, vol. 1: *Le Moyen Âge* (Paris, Seuil, 1997), pp. 17–104.

Sousa, R. de, *The Rationality of Emotions* (Cambridge, MA, MIT Press, 1987).

Soussen-Max, C., 'Violence rituelle ou émotion populaire? Les explosions de violence anti-juive à l'occasion des fêtes de Pâques dans l'espace aragonais', in D. Boquet and P. Nagy (eds), *Politiques des émotions au Moyen Âge* (Florence, SISMEL/Galluzzo, 2010), pp. 149–68.

Southern, R., *Saint Anselm: A Portrait in a Landscape* (Cambridge, Cambridge University Press, 1990).

Spanneut, M., *Le Stoïcisme des Pères de l'Église, de Clément de Rome à Clément d'Alexandrie* (Paris, Seuil, 1957).

— 'L'impact de l'apatheia stoïcienne sur la pensée chrétienne jusqu'à saint Augustin', in A. González Blanco and J.-M. Blázquez Martínez (eds), *Cristianismo y aculturación en tiempos del Imperio Romano* (Murcia, Universidad de Murcia, 1990), pp. 39–52.

— 'Apatheia ancienne, apatheia chrétienne', in W. Haase and H. Temporini (eds), *Aufstieg und Niedergang der römischen Welt*, Teil 2, 36/7 (1994), pp. 4641–717

Spiegel, G. M., 'History, Historicism and the Social Logic of the Text', in *The Past as Text. The Theory and Practice of Medieval Historiography* (Baltimore, Johns Hopkins University Press, 1997), pp. 3–28, 213–20.

Staunton, M., *Thomas Becket and his Biographers* (Woodbridge, Boydell Press, 2006).

Stearns, C. Z. and Stearns, P. N., 'Emotionology: Clarifying the History of Emotions and Emotional Standards', *American Historical Review*, 90 (1985), pp. 813–36.

Stearns, P. N., *American Cool: Constructing a Twentieth-Century Emotional Style* (New York, New York University Press, 1994).

Stella, A., *La Révolte des Ciompi. Les hommes, les lieux, le travail* (Paris, EHESS, 1993).

Straw, C., *Gregory the Great: Perfection in Imperfection* (Berkeley, University of California Press, 1988).

Tabacco, G., 'Romualdo di Ravenna e gli inizi dell'eremitismo camaldolese', in *L'Eremitismo in Occidente nei secoli XI e XII. Atti della seconda settimana internazionale di studio, Mendola, 30 agosto–6 settembre 1962* (Milan, Vita e Pensiero, 1965), pp. 73–121.

— ' "Privilegium amoris": aspetti della spiritualità romualdina', in *Spiritualità e cultura nel Medioevo. Dodici percorsi nei territori del potere e della fede* (Naples, Liguori, 1993), pp. 167–94.

Tagliaferri, M. (ed.), *Pier Damiani. L'eremita, il teologo, il riformatore* (Bologna, Edizioni Dehoniane, 2009).

Théry, J., 'Atrocitas/enormitas. Esquisse pour une histoire de la catégorie de "crime énorme" du Moyen Âge à l'époque moderne', *Clio@Themis. Revue électronique d'histoire du droit*, 4 (2011), http://www.cliothemis.com/Atrocitas-enormitas-Esquisse-pour.

Thomas, J.-F, *Déshonneur et honte en latin: étude sémantique* (Louvain, Peeters, 2007).

Thompson, E. P., 'Rough Music: Le Charivari Anglais', *Annales ESC*, 27 (1972), pp. 285–312.

— 'Rough Music Reconsidered', *Folklore*, 103/1 (1992), pp. 3–26.

Thonnard, F.-J., 'La vie affective de l'âme selon saint Augustin', *Année théologique*, 3 (1953), pp. 33–55.

— 'La psychologie des passions', complementary note no. 42, in Augustine, *La Cité de Dieu, livres XI–XIV*, trans. G. Combès (Paris, 1959), pp. 536–9.

— 'La valeur morale des passions', complementary note no. 40 in Augustine, *La Cité de Dieu, livres XI–XIV*, trans. G. Combès (Paris, 1959), pp. 531–4.

Tin, L.-G., *L'Invention de la culture hétérosexuelle* (Paris, Autrement, 2008).

Tisseron, S., *La Honte. Psychanalyse d'un lien social* (Paris, Dunod, 2007).

Tock, B.-M., 'Les émotions dans le monde régulier au Moyen Âge: quelques pistes de recherche (xiie–xiiie siècle)', *Source(s). Cahiers de l'équipe de recherche Arts, Civilisation et Histoire de l'Europe*, 5 (2014), pp. 15–27.

Treffort, C., *L'Église carolingienne et la Mort* (Lyon, Presses Universitaires de Lyon, 1993).

Valette, J.-R., 'Marguerite Porete et le discours courtois', in S. L. Field, R. E. Lerner, and S. Piron (eds), *Marguerite Porete et le Miroir des simples âmes. Perspectives historiques, philosophiques et littéraires* (Paris, Vrin, 2013), pp. 169–96.

Vallerani, M., 'Mouvements de paix dans une commune de popolo: les flagellants à Pérouse en 1260', in R. M. Dessí (ed.), *Prêcher la paix et discipliner la société. Italie, France, Angleterre (XIIIe–XVe siècle)* (Turnhout, Brepols, 2005), pp. 312–55.

Van Dijk, R. T. M., 'Toward Imageless Contemplation: Gerard Zerbolt of Zutphen as Guide for Lectio Divina', in H. Blommestijn, C. Caspers, and R. Hofman (eds), *Spirituality Renewed: Studies on Significant Representatives of the Modern Devotion* (Louvain/Paris, Peeters, 2003), pp. 3–28.

Van Engen, J., 'Introduction', in H. A. Oberman and J. Van Engen (eds), *Devotio Moderna: Basic Writings* (New York, Crossroad, 1988), pp. 25–35.

— *Sisters and Brothers of the Common Life: The Devotio Moderna and the World of the Later Middle Ages* (Philadelphia, University of Pennsylvania Press, 2008).

— 'Marguerite (Porete) of Hainaut and the Medieval Low Countries', in S. L. Field, R. E. Lerner, and S. Piron (eds), *Marguerite Porete et le Miroir des simples âmes. Perspectives historiques, philosophiques et littéraires* (Paris, Vrin, 2014), pp. 48–9.

Vansteenberghe, E., 'Deux théoriciens de l'amitié au xiie siècle: Pierre de Blois et Aelred de Riéval', *Revue des sciences religieuses*, 12 (1932), pp. 572–88.

Vauchez, A., *La Spiritualité du Moyen Âge occidental, VIIIe–XIIIe siècle* (Paris, Seuil, 1994).

— (ed.), *Histoire du christianisme*, vol. 2: *Naissance d'une chrétienté* (Paris, Desclée, 1995).

— *La Sainteté en Occident aux derniers siècles du Moyen Âge. Recherches sur les mentalités religieuses médiévales* (Rome, École française de Rome, 2014/1981).

Vecchio, S., 'Passio, affectus, virtus: il sistema delle passioni nei trattati morali di Guglielmo d'Alvernia', in F. Morenzoni and J.-Y. Tilliette (eds), *Autour de Guillaume d'Auvergne (1249)* (Turnhout, Brepols, 2005), pp. 173–87.

— 'Il discorso sulle passioni nei commenti all'Etica Nicomachea: da Alberto Magno a Tommaso d'Aquino', *Documenti e studi sulla tradizione filosofica medievale*, 17 (2006), pp. 93–119.

— *Tommaso d'Aquino, Le Passioni dell'anima* (Florence, Le Lettere, 2007)

— 'Passions de l'âme et péchés capitaux: les ambiguïtés de la culture médiévale', in C. Flüeler and M. Rohde (eds), *Laster im Mittelalter* (Berlin and New York, de Gruyter, 2009), pp. 45–64.

— 'Il piacere di Abelardo a Tommaso', in C. Casagrande and S. Vecchio (eds), *Piacere e dolore. Materiali per una storia delle passioni nel Medioevo* (Florence, SISMEL/Galluzzo, 2009), pp. 67–86.

— 'La honte et la faute. La réflexion sur la verecundia dans la littérature théologique des xiie et xiiie siècles', in B. Sère and J. Wettlaufer (eds), *Shame Between Punishment and Penance: The Social Usages of Shame in the Middle Ages and Early Modern Times* (Florence, SISMEL/Galluzzo, 2013), pp. 105–21.

Verdon, L., 'La course des amants adultères. Honte, pudeur et justice dans l'Europe méridionale du xiiie siècle', *Rives nord-méditerranéennes*, 31 (2008), pp. 57–72.

— 'Expressions et usages des comportements affectifs dans le cadre de la seigneurie (Provence, xiiie siècle). L'exemple de l'amour dû au seigneur', in D. Boquet and P. Nagy (eds), *Politiques des émotions au Moyen Âge* (Florence, SISMEL/Galluzzo, 2010), pp. 255–74.

— *La Voix des dominés. Communautés et seigneurie en Provence au bas Moyen Âge* (Rennes, Presses Universitaires de Rennes, 2012).

Veyrard-Cosme, C., 'Littérature latine du haut Moyen Âge et idéologie politique. L'exemple d'Alcuin', *Revue des études latines*, 72 (1994), pp. 192–207.

— 'Introduction', in *L'Œuvre hagiographique en prose d'Alcuin. Vitae Willibrordi, Vedasti, Richarii. Édition, traduction, études narratologiques*, ed. C. Veyrard-Cosme (Florence, SISMEL/Edizioni del Galluzzo, 2003), p. LIX.

de Vial, P., 'Introduction', in Jean of Fécamp, *Confession théologique* (Paris, Cerf, 1992).

Vincent, C., 'Discipline du corps et de l'esprit chez les flagellants au Moyen Âge', *Revue historique*, 302 (2000), pp. 593–614.

Vincent-Cassy, M., 'L'envie au Moyen Âge', *Annales ESC*, 35/2 (1980), pp. 253–71.

Vogel, C., *Le Pécheur et la Pénitence* (Paris, Cerf, 1969).

Vogüé, A. de, *Le Monachisme en Occident avant saint Benoît* (Bégrolles-en-Mauges, Abbaye de Bellefontaine, 1998).

Von Moos, P., 'La retorica medievale come teoria dell'argomentazione ed estetica', in *Entre histoire et littérature. Communication et culture au Moyen Âge* (Florence, SISMEL/Galluzzo, 2005), pp. 293–326.

— (ed.), *Zwischen Babel und Pfingsten. Sprachdifferenzen und Gesprächsverständigung in der Vormoderne (8.–16. Jh.) / Entre Babel et Pentecôte. Différences linguistiques et communication orale avant la modernité (VIIe–XVIe siècle)* (Münster, LIT, 2008).

337

Waaijman, K., 'Image and Imagelessness: A Challenge to [the Modern] Devotion', in H. Blommestijn, C. Caspers, and R. Hofman (eds), *Spirituality Renewed: Studies of Significant Representatives of the Modern Devotion* (Louvain, Peeters, 2003), pp. 29–40.

Wallach, K., '"Amicus amicis, inimicus inimicis"', *Zeitschrift für Kirchengeschichte*, 52 (1933), pp. 614–15.

Wallach, L., *Alcuin and Charlemagne: Studies in Carolingian History and Literature* (Ithaca, Cornell University Press, 1959).

Wéber, E. H., *La Personne humaine au XIIIe siècle* (Paris, Vrin, 1991).

White, C., *Christian Friendship in the Fourth Century* (Cambridge, Cambridge University Press, 1992).

White, S. D., 'Clotild's Revenge: Politics, Kinship, and Ideology in the Merovingian Blood Feud', in S. K. Cohn Jr and S. A. Epstein (eds), *Portraits of Medieval and Renaissance Living: Essays in Memory of David Herlihy* (Ann Arbor, University of Michigan Press, 1996), pp. 107–30.

— 'Politics of Anger', in B. H. Rosenwein, *Anger's Past: The Social Uses of an Emotion in the Middle Ages* (Ithaca, Cornell University Press, 1998), pp. 140–52.

Williams, B., *Shame and Necessity* (Berkeley, University of California Press, 1993).

Wilmart, A., *Auteurs spirituels et textes dévots du Moyen Âge latin. Étude d'histoire littéraire* (Paris, Bloud & Gay, 1932).

— 'Deux préfaces spirituelles de Jean de Fécamp', *Revue d'ascétique et de mystique*, 18 (1937), pp. 5–44.

Woods, R., 'Conclusion: Women and Men in the Development of Late Medieval Mysticism', in B. McGinn (ed.), *Meister Eckhart and the Beguine Mystics, Hadewijch of Brabant, Mechthild of Magdeburg, and Marguerite Porete* (New York, Crossroad, 1994), pp. 159–64.

Wu, T., 'Shame in the Context of Sin: Augustine on the Feeling of Shame in *De civitate Dei*', *Recherches de théologie et philosophie médiévales*, 74/1 (2007), pp. 1–31.

Young, K., *The Drama of the Medieval Church*, 2 vols (Oxford, Clarendon Press, 1933).

Zerbi, P., 'Les différends doctrinaux', in *Bernard de Clairvaux. Histoire, mentalités, spiritualité* (Paris, Cerf, 1992), pp. 429–58.

Ziegler, J., *Medicine and Religion c. 1300: The Case of Arnau de Vilanova* (Oxford, Oxford University Press, 1998).

— '*Ut dicunt medici*: Medical Knowledge and Theological Debates in the Second Half of the Thirteenth Century', *Bulletin of the History of Medicine*, 73/2 (1999), pp. 208–37.

Zimmermann, M., 'Le vocabulaire latin de la malédiction du ixe au xiie siècle. Construction d'un discours eschatologique', *Atalaya*, 5 (1994), pp. 37–55.

FIGURE SOURCES AND CREDITS

1: *Adam and Eve Chased from Paradise*, Masaccio, *c.* 1425, Florence, Santa Maria del Carmine, Brancacci Chapel. Photograph: cote cliché, 07-509578, archive number, CSE-S-000549-9966. © Alinari Archives, Florence, Dist. RMN-Grand Palais/Serge Domingie.

2: Anger powerless before Patience, *Psychomachia*, Paris, Bibliothèque nationale de France, MS. Latin 8085, fol. 59; late ninth century. Photograph: cote cliché, RC-A-52632.

3: John of Salisbury, Letter no. 305, *Ex insperato*, London, British Library, Cotton Claudius B II, fol. 341r; *c.* 1171–80. Photograph: © The British Library Board, Cotton Claudius B. II, f. 341.

4 and 5: *Lancelot-Graal*, with an interpolation of *Perlesvaus*, Paris, Bibliothèque nationale de France, MS. Français 118 and 116, fols. 219 and 667 respectively. Photographs: cotes clichés, NQ-E-001533 and RC-A-11556.

6: *The Manger at Greccio*, Giotto, *c.* 1300, Assisi, Basilica of St Francis, upper church. Photograph: cote cliché, 13-521454, archive number, CAL-F-011082-0000. © Alinari Archives, Florence, Dist. RMN-Grand Palais/Ghigo Roli.

7: *The Descent from the Cross* (detail), Rogier van Weyden, *c.* 1435, Madrid, Museo Nacional del Prado. Photograph: cote cliché, 14-542636, archive number, 534. © BPK, Berlin, Dist. RMN-Grand Palais/Jörg P. Anders.

8: Penitence and Contemplation, *Livres de l'estat de l'ame*, London, British Library, Yates Thompson 11, fol. 29. Photograph: © The British Library Board, Yates Thompson 11, f. 29.

9: *Christ on the Cross* (*Vision des Heiligen Bernhard – sogennantes Blut-kruzifixus*); drawing, Rhineland, fourteenth century. Cologne, Schnütgen Museum, M 340. Photograph: © Rheinisches Bildarchiv, rba_c012422.

10: *Le Roman de Fauvel*, Paris, Bibliothèque nationale de France, MS. français 146, fol. 34; *c.* 1310–20. Photograph: côte cliché, RC-A-11216.

11 and 12: Tomb of Sancho Saiz de Carrillo; tempera on wood, *c.* 1300, Barcelona, Museu Nacional d'Art de Catalunya. Photograph: © Aisa/Leemage.

13: *Sermon* on the *Passion* of Jean Gerson, Valenciennes, Bibliothèque municipal, MS. 230, fol. 57. Photograph: © Bibliothèque municipale de Valenciennes.

INDEX

Note: Page entries prefixed **F** in **bold type** refer to material in Figures

341